re &

Whe

he last date   :h

Kent

& Sussex

Don Taylor, Jeffery Wheatley and Paul James

Fourth edition

First published 1997 by Christopher Helm, London
This edition published 2003 by Christopher Helm, an
imprint of A & C Black Publishers Ltd.,
37 Soho Square, London W1D 3QZ

Copyright © 1997 text by Don Taylor, Jeffery Wheatley & David Burges
Copyright © 2003 text by Don Taylor, Jeffery Wheatley,
David Burges & Paul James

Copyright © 1997, 2003 illustrations by David Beadle, David Boys,
Stephen Message, Dave Nurney, John Reaney & Jan Wilczur

ISBN 0-7136-6420-7

A CIP catalogue record for this book is available from the
British Library.

A & C Black uses paper produced with elemental chlorine-free pulp,
harvested from managed sustainable forests.

www.acblack.com

Typeset and designed by J&L Composition, Filey

Printed and bound in Wales by Creative Print and Design (Wales),
Ebbw Vale

10 9 8 7 6 5 4 3 2 1

CONTENTS

Contents

INTRODUCTION

The aim of this fourth edition of *Where to Watch birds in Kent, Surrey and Sussex* remains the same — to introduce and guide the reader to the best birdwatching sites in the three counties of Kent, Surrey and Sussex. In addition there is a systematic list of all species recorded in the region since 1900, with a brief statement describing their current status and, for some, a few recommended sites where they might be expected.

The first edition was published in 1987. Since then the number of people regularly involved in birdwatching, in the widest sense, has grown dramatically, perhaps more so in the southeast than anywhere else in Britain. The huge, mainly urban population looks to the countryside for much of its recreational needs and despite the increasing pressure of continuous development on the natural environment, these counties boast a wealth of superb birdwatching sites, thus also attracting many birdwatchers from outside the region.

Birdwatching — even twitching — is now an accepted, if still perhaps poorly understood, part of our national culture. The layperson is no longer surprised by the sight of large numbers of people with binoculars and telescopes, sheltering behind seawalls, hurrying down country lanes, or standing around a gravel pit or reservoir. Birdwatchers now have access to more and better equipment, and information exchange so rapid that it would not even have been considered possible ten years ago.

So what is the role for a book such as this? In addition to providing information about sites, the associated birds, habitats, and when to visit, it provides the context in which they sit, within a county and a region. Its aims are two-fold: firstly to provide an efficient tool for those in search of interesting birds, and secondly to fill the gap between the comprehensive county avifaunas, the annual county bird reports, and the vast amount of knowledge in the heads of local birders. We hope it will encourage birdwatchers within and from outside these counties to explore sites that they have not previously visited, submit records to the county bird recorders, and perhaps support their local bird clubs, county wildlife trusts and other conservation groups.

Access for those with disabilities

In the Access sections of this edition, notes have been included, wherever possible, to give some guidance as to the suitability of sites for disabled people. In the main this refers to wheelchairs and access for those with mobility problems. At major sites there are additional comments regarding toilet facilities, etc.

Today, enlightened people try to espouse the 'social model' of disability. In other words instead of disabled people being seen as a problem, more effort is being made to make all aspects of life responsive to everyone and to create 'barrier-free' access to all facilities — what is good design for those with disabilities, is good design for everyone. Since the Disabled Birders Association was founded, advice has been made available to all bodies responsible for reserves. Some facilities have already been improved and there are plans for improvements on a number of other sites managed by the RSPB, Kent Wildlife Trust and others. For those considering reserve design or improvements, remember that a very small percentage of disabled people use wheelchairs and that consideration should also be given to those with mobility problems, for whom distances are the difficulty. By placing simple benches every 100–150 m, a larger number of people can visit, including the elderly and very young, as well as those with mobility problems, as this will greatly increase the distances they can go.

Wide parking bays for wheelchair users are welcome, but creating parking closer to where the birds are is even better. More reserves in the UK could follow overseas designs, where people and vehicles are often taken into the centre of reserves and screened off, rather than being stopped at one end and made to walk.

Websites

In this edition we have also included a selection of website addresses that will provide readers with additional, right up-to-date information about birding in the three counties. Each of the county ornithological societies has produced its own website, as have the observatories at Dungeness and Sandwich Bay. Additional sites of interest include that for the LNR at Rye Harbour, Sussex and, in Surrey, Beddington Sewage Farm has a lively site, while the Barn Elms Wetland Centre, like others, is featured on the WWT site.

The Sites

After careful consideration, a few sensitive breeding species have not been specifically mentioned, as even minimal disturbance can cause them to desert. Some of the habitats too can be destroyed by undue disturbance. Sadly, egg thieves continue to present a major threat to certain, often rare, breeding species.

We have aimed to be as helpful as possible by distilling this information into an easily accessible format. In choosing the sites, we have been fairly selective and those listed fall into one or more of the following categories:

(1) those that hold a high density of breeding, wintering or migratory birds,
(2) those that comprise habitats supporting particular species, which may not occur elsewhere, and
(3) sites representative of a habitat type, e.g. woodland with a good range of birds.

The site accounts have been revised considerably since the third edition, and are the result of the authors' collective knowledge and widespread consultation with local birdwatchers and reserve wardens, who know these sites well. However, new information is always becoming available and we hope that any gaps in these site accounts will encourage others to fill them.

Bird identification and optical equipment are beyond the scope of this book. There are now many good field guides on the market for beginner and expert alike, as well as a number of journals and magazines, which regularly discuss the finer points of identification of particular species or groups. If you are unfamiliar with what is available, it is best to discuss your needs with other birdwatchers, see what they use and decide what is best for you. The same applies to optical equipment, and field trials are essential before purchasing new binoculars or telescopes.

Companies selling binoculars and telescopes regularly visit reserves and bird fairs, where such equipment can be tested.

Bird Clubs and other Birdwatching Groups

Each of the three counties has its own organisation, the Kent Ornithological Society, the Surrey Bird Club and the Sussex Ornithological Society. All produce annual Bird Reports and arrange indoor and field meeting programmes for their members. They also provide a focus for all those interested in birdwatching in the southeast. They also play a crucial role in providing valuable data, which can be used by conservation bodies for protecting important bird sites and habitats.

In addition to these organisations, the RSPB has totals of eight, five and eight Members Groups and five, one and five Wildlife Explorers and Phoenix Groups respectively in Kent, Surrey and Sussex. These groups run very varied programmes of events and are particularly helpful to children and beginners of all ages, who want to become involved with birds, wildlife and conservation issues in general.

The following sections provide a brief introduction to the geography and climate of the southeast, and how these influence its habitats and bird communities.

Geography

The whole of the southeast was once covered by a sea of remarkable purity in which hundreds of feet of white chalk deposits were laid down. The land was later forced up in a broad east–west ridge across the three counties. Over time, erosion eventually removed the chalk from the centre of the dome, exposing the sands and clays of what is now The Weald. The clays were once covered by extensive lowland oak forest, and whilst parts of the area are still among the most heavily wooded in Britain, much of the early woodland has now been cleared for farmland and building development. The sands, especially in the west and at Ashdown Forest, became heathland after early woodland clearances and low-intensity agricultural use, and today represent a significant part of Britain's internationally important heathland resource.

The North and South Downs are all that remains of the overlying chalk. At one time largely used for sheep grazing, the areas not ploughed and converted into arable farmland are, in many places, becoming overgrown with scrub and woodland. The distinctive plant and animal life of the chalk is at risk in the absence of active, traditional management. For example the Downs historically supported Stone Curlews, which depended on a mixture of grazed turf and bare soils provided by spring, rather than autumn-sown, crops. Today they are rare passage migrants. In places, such as at Kingley Vale NNR in West Sussex, the Downs are capped by clay, which produces a very unusual type of vegetation called chalk heath.

Few substantial rivers cut through the South Downs, but in West Sussex the Adur and particularly the Arun have substantial floodplains, providing areas of wet riverside pasture subject to shallow winter flooding, which support large numbers of wildfowl. Like so many wetland sites in the southeast, however, these areas have been subjected to drainage and agricultural improvement. Where the chalk reaches the sea there are spectacular cliff exposures, such as at Dover and Beachy Head. These sites formally supported significant seabird colonies; today, both Fulmars and Kittiwakes breed on the chalk cliffs in significant numbers.

Towards the Thames, the northern slopes of the chalk are overlain by later marine and freshwater deposits. In the west these are mainly the Bagshot series of sands and gravels, comprising the commons at Pirbright and Chobham. Where these have been worked they provide extensive areas of gravel pits, especially on the Greater London/Surrey border. Further east, they give way to London clay and the alluvium of the lower Thames. The broad, muddy estuaries of the Thames, Medway and Swale are internationally important for their wintering and breeding bird populations, but are still under very real threat from damaging developments, largely associated with the ports industry but also from the expanding aviation industry. In addition, if climate trends lead to a significant rise in the sea level, there will be further direct habitat loss, which will prove very difficult to replace.

The Channel coast has large areas where silt and shingle have built up between the higher ground and the sea, notably on the Romney and Walland Marshes, from Dungeness to Pett Level, and at Pagham Harbour. These are all important for breeding, wintering and passage birds, but some are also much degraded because of extensive drainage over the years. At Pagham the sea breached earlier defences leaving a superb intertidal basin. To the west, Chichester Harbour also supports internationally important numbers of wildfowl, waders and breeding terns.

Climate

The southeast has a warmer and drier climate than most other parts of the British Isles, although there are some surprisingly marked differences due to the alignment of the Downs and Weald, relative to the prevailing southwest winds. In Kent the high ground on the North Downs is substantially cooler and wetter. The highest annual rainfall is at Bedgebury, with 825 mm, whilst parts of Sheppey are particularly dry, having less than 533 mm. Much of the north Kent coast and Romney Marshes experience less than 640 mm.

Compared with inland areas, most coastal districts are warmer in winter and cooler in summer. This relative freedom from frost, in coastal areas, is significant in attracting many birds forced from the Continent by severe winter weather. London, too, has a rather milder climate than the more exposed countryside surrounding it, and the really low temperatures in Surrey are usually recorded from the Weald.

Whilst the weather is dominated by the prevailing southwest winds, proximity to the Continent can have dramatic short-term effects on bird populations and movements. Ridges of high pressure across Europe and Asia produce periods of east and northeast winds, which are responsible for many of our more eastern visitors, such as rare warblers in late autumn, or invasions of Smew or Waxwings in hard winters.

FEATURES OF THE REGION'S BIRDLIFE

Kent

For those seeking a genuine wildlife spectacle, the vast numbers of wintering duck, geese and waders on the north Kent marshes have few equals. Much of the grazing marsh had been lost to arable production and 'improved' by drainage, but in recent years has been returned to grassland. Conservation bodies have acquired or manage significant parts of what is left, which provides secure breeding, roosting and feeding sites for many thousands of birds. These sites attract significant numbers of raptors and on a good day in winter the lucky birder could see Hen and Marsh Harriers, Rough-legged Buzzard, Peregrine and Merlin, in rapid succession.

The region's proximity to the Continent contributes directly to the attraction of Kent for the birdwatcher, as some sites have a deserved reputation as watchpoints for visible migration. The unique shingle peninsula at Dungeness provides an excellent opportunity to witness the spring and autumn passage of various seabirds. It is also an arrival and departure point for many passerines, migrating north in spring and south in autumn, when literally thousands of hirundines may be seen arriving or departing over the Channel. In similar fashion, Thanet projects east into the southern North Sea, providing a natural landfall for southbound Scandinavian migrants in autumn. Opportunities for observing visible migration extend to other points along the north coast, into the Swale and Thames, and places like Sandwich Bay, Bockhill and St Margaret's on the east coast. Needless to say, timing is everything, and weather conditions must be just right to produce the birds.

The link with the Continent is further emphasised by the occurrence of more typical European species such as Cetti's Warbler, Serin and even Penduline Tit, while Little Egret has recently colonised southern Britain. All of these have already bred or attempted to breed. Conversely, severe winter weather brings larger numbers of visitors like Red-necked Grebe, Bean and Barnacle Geese, Smew and Goosander from the Netherlands and the Baltic.

Surrey

Unlike the other two counties covered here, Surrey — taken to be the administrative county plus Metropolitan London up to the Surrey Docks — has no coastline and no bird observatories. Many seabirds such as Fulmar, common enough elsewhere, are extremely rare, whilst breeding records for some others, such as Herring Gull, are almost unknown. Two factors go a good way to provide compensating birdwatching opportunities. The first is the large area of inland water. The Thames forms the northern boundary, from the Kent border to Walton-on-Thames. The Thames Valley itself contains large reservoirs and many gravel pits at various stages of exploitation. Some are major moulting and winter refuges for wildfowl. When drained for maintenance, the reservoirs provide a rich habitat for waders and dabbling duck. There are more gravel pits in the Blackwater Valley and in a belt across the centre of the county from Send to Godstone.

A number of sewage farms, especially that at Beddington, have proved of continuing interest at all times of year and between them, these various wetland sites provide breeding, stopover and wintering sites for many species of waterbirds, migrants and breeding passerines.

A second factor arises from the heavily built-up character of the south London suburbs. The northern part of the county is heavily watched because so many observers live there. This has produced an excellent network, using the grapevine, pagers, telephones, birdlines and Internet newsgroups. London's many parks and gardens, although heavily used for more general recreation, have plenty of interest for the urban birder. Some have stretches of water which hold enough wintering wildfowl to merit inclusion in the national wildfowl counts. Richmond Park is the biggest. Battersea Park, the Surrey Docks and Wimbledon Parks are all well worth visiting.

Surrey's best-known feature, and the one which adds most to the conservation value of its birdlife, is the heathland that covers much of the western part of the county. Some of it is used for training by the MoD, which affords a degree of protection. Much of the rest is managed as public or NT open space. There are lowland heath NNRs at Chobham and Thursley. The commons there and elsewhere support important populations of Nightjar, Woodlark and Dartford Warbler, and other typical heathland species such as Hobby, Tree Pipit and Stonechat. There are also one or two pairs of breeding Curlew. Great Grey Shrikes and several raptor species are often seen in winter.

The countryside is extremely varied. A small area may contain copse, hill, common, pond and field, with a corresponding diversity of birdlife. Surrey is one of the most heavily wooded counties in England. Birds in the woodland along the North Downs and the Greensand Hills (which extend into Kent) include owls, raptors, Firecrest and Crossbill.

Sussex

With its long, south-facing coastline, birdwatchers in Sussex, like those in Kent, are well placed to observe the spectacular migration of birds in both spring and autumn. Many birders migrate to the coastal fringe, where the headlands at Beachy Head, Seaford Head and Selsey Bill concentrate the visible migration of seabirds and passerines. These sites, and the coastal wetlands of Chichester, Pagham and Rye Harbours, host tens, if not hundreds of thousands of the more common migrants and winter visitors, whilst rarities occur annually.

A particular feature of Sussex is its river valley systems, which cut south through the South Downs to the coast. The Arun, Adur, Ouse and Cuckmere each provide some excellent birdwatching areas, even if agricultural improvements have reduced their attractiveness, in particular, to breeding birds. The same applies to the wide lowlands of the Pevensey Levels and Walland Marsh to the east, but their size does make them more attractive to wintering geese. Inland, several reservoirs, mainly in the eastern half of Sussex, and the gravel pits at Chichester provide further opportunities for observing wildfowl.

The rest of the county comprises three main habitats. These are the chalk of the South Downs, which plunge into the sea at Beachy Head, The Weald with its clay and sandstone outcrops, and the Greensand heaths of the north and west. These are part of the same heathland complex that is found in southwest Surrey and eastern Hampshire.

Chalk downland is still an important refuge for many of the once-widespread farmland birds, such as Grey Partridge and Corn Bunting that have undergone such dramatic declines in the last 30 years. Stone Curlew used to breed here and it is hoped that it may yet return.

The Weald is heavily wooded and supports typical woodland bird communities. Where there are outcrops of sandy soils, such as at Ashdown Forest, a more diverse and partly heathland bird community is found. The western heathlands running up to the Surrey and Hampshire borders support important, though smaller, numbers of the typical heathland species found on Surrey heaths. As in Surrey and Kent, great efforts are being made to restore this important habitat.

ACKNOWLEDGEMENTS

We wish to express our gratitude to the wardens of the bird observatories and some of the RSPB, EN and county wildlife reserves mentioned in this book, for their considerable advice and assistance. Local observers have also kindly checked and improved site texts. We apologise to those we may have inadvertently omitted, and especially thank the following for their contributions to this fourth edition: Chris Abrams, Bo Beolens, Geoff Burton, Phil Chantler, Martin Coath, John Davies, David Hale, Tim Hodge, Ian Hodgson, Norman McCanch, Murray Orchard, Chris Reynolds, Ian Roberts, Jerry Warne, Brian Watmough and Barry Wright, for Kent; Martin Baxter, Frank Cannings, John Clark, Ian Davis, David Dicker, Simon Elson, the late Rupert Hastings, Roger Hawkins, Barry Marsh, Mick Pankhurst, Shaun Peters, John Steer and Roger Suckling, for Surrey; and Phil Bance, Chris Corrigan, Jon Curson, Richard Fairbank, Owen Mitchell, John Newnham, Sarah Patton, Alan Perry, Barrie Watson and Barry Yates, for Sussex.

We are especially grateful to the artists: Dave Beadle, David Boys, Stephen Message, David Nurney, John Reaney and Jan Wilczur, whose drawings so enhance the presentation.

The maps were drawn by Brian Southern.

The authors will be pleased to receive any information and ideas which might usefully be incorporated into future editions of this guide, and hence benefit readers. Correspondence (please enclose a SAE if a reply is required) should be addressed c/o A & C Black (Publishers) Limited, marked for the attention of Don Taylor (Kent), Jeffery Wheatley (Surrey) or Paul James (Sussex).

HOW TO USE THIS BOOK

Field guides are essential for critical bird identification but can only give general information on distribution and migration patterns. Although birds are very much conditioned in their behaviour by instinct, and the nature of their perception is remote from our own, their habits and movements will be better understood with more experience and local knowledge. We have attempted to elucidate some of the phenomena that affect bird behaviour, especially the influence of the weather, tides and seasons.

THE REGION

The region under discussion comprises the counties of Kent, Surrey and Sussex. Each county is treated separately and each site within the county is numbered, located on a map and described under subheadings, which are explained below.

Also included are a number of additional sites for each county. They may be good sites for specific species, but at only one season; they may be examples of a specialised habitat; they may be included for their general interest; or simply as an alternative to the more popular areas. A lettered map shows the location of each.

Habitat

This section describes the extent of the area covered and the main bird habitats. Where relevant, comments on the plants and other aspects of natural history are included.

Species

The aim is to give a sample of the main species of interest, and what they are likely to be doing — whether resident, breeding, on passage or wintering. Some indication as to the frequency of occurrence and the numbers involved is also attempted, to give the visitor an idea of what to expect — single birds, small parties or large flocks. This section cannot list every species found in an area. For reasons of space, commoner birds are usually excluded.

In order to keep pace with rapid changes in the birding world, we have made a few changes. Scientific studies, using DNA, are providing greater understanding of avian relationships, for example, whether a subspecies should be recognised as a species or not. In this edition we occasionally make mention of distinct forms, such as Yellow-legged and Caspian Gulls, which are increasingly considered to be species. The British Ornithologists' Union makes such decisions for all species on the British List and the English and scientific names that are used can be checked in the Systematic List of Species section.

At the start of this section, some reference is usually made regarding the ornithological importance of the area. The text, therefore, is written in broadly chronological order, to help the reader follow the pattern of bird events through the year. In some instances, main birdwatching sites have been described, in greater detail, where we feel more explanation is needed for a particular area within the general locality.

Timing

This is a particularly important section, which should help the reader to avoid wasted visits. It includes such details as appropriate weather conditions. Visible bird migration is largely dependent on weather and large numbers of birds seen one day may be followed by none the next, if the wind direction or cloud cover has changed. Time of day may also be significant — get there before the birds are disturbed by other humans and try not to disturb them yourself! At coastal sites the state of the tide is most important, particularly if you want to see waders well — they roost at different localities at high tide, sometimes a long way from where they feed.

Note: Any information about opening times refers to that which was in operation in 2003, as does that given for details regarding entry to reserves, parks and gardens and for tolls.

Access

This section tells you (a) how to get to the site from main towns and A-class roads, often directing you along minor roads, (b) where to park and (c) what paths to take when you arrive. Maps will often show a maze of roads leading to a birdwatching site; we have usually described one practicable route. Also, the distance you need to walk is often included.

Certain areas, such as military firing ranges or wardened reserves, may have special access restrictions. A number of the more interesting sites in Surrey, for example, are used for military training, and there are prohibitions concerning entry, at least at certain times. Visits to such places therefore require careful advance planning. Check this section for possible problems in good time. The Thames Valley reservoirs, with some useful exceptions, require permits from Thames Water and, sometimes, prior notification of visits. Public footpaths and roads often permit access to riversides, marshes and lakes, but do not give the right to trespass on private land through which they may pass. If you wish to stray from public footpaths, seek permission from the owner first.

Calendar

This is a quick-reference summary section, so the information is of necessity selective. For convenience, the calendar year has been split into periods, which generally relate to the ornithological seasons, although some species obviously do not fit this pattern. December–February is winter for a large proportion of winter visitors to the region; March–May is spring, covering the migration period, when the majority of summer visitors arrive; summer, in respect of maximum breeding activity and relatively little migration, includes June–July, although return migration for some species, that breed within the Arctic Circle, commences during this period; and autumn migration is protracted, with movement throughout August–November.

Within this section we have included peak periods for certain species. If no further qualifying comment is made, the bird concerned is likely to be present during the relevant 2–4 month period, given correct conditions, as often explained in the text. The order in which species are listed follows *The Birds of the Western Palearctic*, the order most often used in field guides. This should facilitate quick reference to identification points.

Measurements

Throughout this book we have used measurements in those units that we feel are most readily understood. Distances are normally stated in miles and yards, while surface areas are given in hectares and heights in metres.

The Maps

The maps have been drawn specifically for this book. Each is numbered to cross reference with the sites and access to the sites described, e.g. 1. Sites within the main area also have a map and this is given a letter reference, e.g. 1a.

Ordnance Survey map numbers are also given. These refer to the Explorer 1:25,000 Series, e.g. OS Explorer 148.

The use of Ordnance Survey maps is recommended, as they provide a good general appreciation of the nature of many sites, and access to them via main roads. In the text, we have occasionally quoted a map reference, e.g. TQ 826685, for Motney Hill, Kent. For anyone unsure of how to read these references, the National Grid Reference System is clearly explained on the OS Maps.

The following are invaluable additional guides: for Kent the A–Z Kent Street Maps, covering 254 towns and villages, published by Geographers' A–Z Map Company Ltd; for Surrey the Ordnance Survey Street Atlas of Surrey, which is scaled at 2.5 inches to 1 mile, shows footpaths, names farms, ponds, hills and other features, and indexes over 20,000 roads. A London A–Z street guide may also be helpful; for East Sussex and West Sussex there are useful Ordnance Survey County Street Atlases, published by George Philip, at 3.5 inches to 1 mile.

Key to Maps

▬	Sea/inland water
▭	Area of interest, eg. reserve
★	Viewpoint
ⓅP	Car parking
Ⓗ	Birdwatching hide
㏗	Public house
■	Building
⁰⁰⁰⁰	Sewage farm
– · – ·	County boundary
– – – –	Footpath

KENT

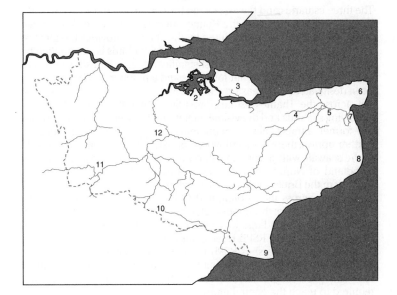

1 Hoo Peninsula
2 Medway Estuary
3 The Swale and Isle of Sheppey
4 Canterbury Ring Woods
5 Stour Valley
6 Thanet

7 Sandwich and Pegwell Bay
8 St. Margaret's Bay and Bockhill Farm
9 Dungeness
10 Bedgebury Forest
11 Bough Beech Reservoir
12 Abbey Meads and Leybourne Lakes
Country Park

Habitat

The three estuaries and the associated lowlands that comprise the North Kent Marshes complex are the Thames, Medway and Swale. Of the three areas, the Hoo Peninsula, bordered by the Thames, provides the greatest variety of habitats. The importance of the area for birds is exemplified by the various protection orders. Most significantly, as a Ramsar site, it is of international importance, but four SPAs and a number of SSSIs have also been designated. At the eastern end, the Isle of Grain and Allhallows look out across the Thames estuary, providing a good site in autumn for observing seabirds and the visible migration of passerine migrants, whilst the former attracts falls of Scandinavian night migrants in autumn. Further upriver, there are sand workings; extensive mudflats on one side of the seawall, with grazing marsh on the other; the predominantly oak woodland of Northward Hill, now a NNR, which contains the largest heronry in the British Isles, as well as extensive flooded areas; wide, reed-lined fleets, across the Cooling and Cliffe Marshes, which include Rye Street RSPB reserve; the flooded clay pools and North Quarry at Cliffe, the former area now largely owned by the RSPB; more extensive mud-flats in Higham Bight RSPB reserve; further grazing land and reed-lined ditches at Shorne Marshes RSPB reserve, and finally Great Chattenden Wood. There is limited parking but the seawall, minor roads and public footpaths provide good access for much of the area. Long walks are required to reach the central marshes.

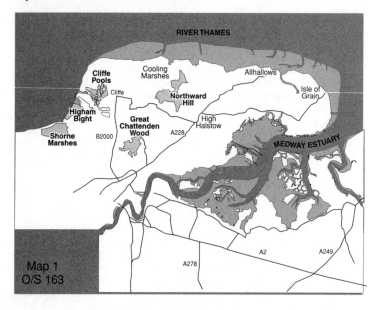

Species

On this stretch of the Thames Marshes, with careful planning, close to 100 species can be seen on a single day in winter, with perhaps 120 in May, such is the diversity of habitat. Divers, grebes, wildfowl, raptors and waders, plus some typical woodland species, all occur. The pools on Cliffe reserve are particularly attractive to grebes and a variety of dabbling and diving duck, whilst good numbers of waders roost there. Small numbers of Bewick's Swans and White-fronted Geese, along with Marsh and Hen Harriers, Common Buzzard, Peregrine and Merlin, regularly winter on Cooling and St Mary's Marshes, where flocks of Golden Plover also feed. The mudflats attract wintering waders, with particularly large numbers of Dunlin and Knot. A few Long-eared Owls are resident, but immigrants join them to form small roosts in winter, when Short-eared Owls also hunt the marshes. Rock Pipit is a regular winter visitor, while Snow Bunting and an occasional Shore Lark may be anticipated. However, Lapland Bunting has become scarce.

The tendency we have to associate spring with nesting means that spring comes early on the Thames Marshes, as by February the Grey Herons return to repair their nests in the Northward Hill heronry, where Little Egret also breeds, having recently colonised several counties along the south coast. The departure of the grey geese often coincides with the arrival of the first Chiffchaff, Wheatear and possibly an early Garganey. By late April, the song of Nightingales echoes from Northward Hill, Great Chattenden Wood and the hawthorn scrub on Cliffe Pools reserve. Early May often sees a strong passage of migrant waders, which are particularly attracted to the wetland areas at Northward Hill and Cliffe. A wide variety of species breeds, including duck and waders on the marshes, migrant warblers on all of the reserves and woodland birds in Great Chattenden Wood and at Northward Hill.

From midsummer Yellow-legged Gulls gather in Higham Bight, often flying across the river to feed on rubbish dumps in Essex, so you need to be there early in the morning to see them. Up to 100 or more of this bird can be seen here site in autumn. The return of migrant waders is a feature of early autumn. When water levels are appropriate, Cliffe Pools reserve often attracts 20 or so different wader species on any one day. The wetland at Northward Hill also attracts a variety of waders. As autumn progresses, if winds veer northeast, migrant passerines can be expected, whilst seabird passage may be observed from Grain, Allhallows, Lower Hope Point and Shornmead Fort. The flocking of Little Terns is another regular feature of autumn, but by mid-October the majority of summer

Grey Herons & Little Egrets nesting

migrants have flown south and the winter visitors have replaced them. Stormy weather in November often brings seabirds into the estuary and along the Thames. Large numbers of Kittiwakes may be involved, often with skuas or auks, and even occasional petrels.

Main Birdwatching Zones

Many of the marshland and estuarine species can be expected along the length of seawall between Shorne Marshes and Yantlet Creek, and on the Isle of Grain, but there are several quite distinct areas, each with its own attractions, that are described in detail. Working downriver they are: Shorne Marshes and Higham Bight RSPB reserves; Cliffe Pools RSPB reserve and the North Quarry; Cooling, Halstow and St Mary's Marshes; Northward Hill RSPB reserve; Coombe Bay, Allhallows, Yantlet Creek and Stoke Lagoon; and the Isle of Grain. In addition, particularly for woodland birds, Great Chattenden Wood is included, as it too is part of the extensive Hoo Peninsula.

SHORNE MARSHES and HIGHAM BIGHT RSPB RESERVES
(Map 1a)

Habitat

Part of this largely marshland area is still used by the Metropolitan Police as a firing range, which may restrict visiting. The western end has pools

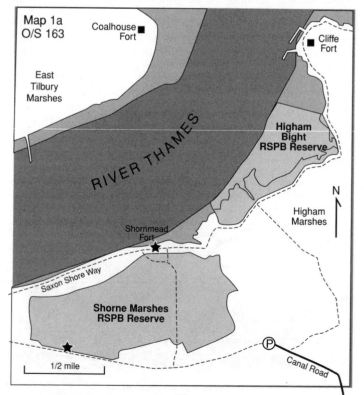

Map 1a
O/S 163

Coalhouse Fort

Cliffe Fort

East Tilbury Marshes

RIVER THAMES

Higham Bight RSPB Reserve

N

Higham Marshes

Shornmead Fort

Saxon Shore Way

Shorne Marshes RSPB Reserve

P

Canal Road

1/2 mile

attractive to both migrant and breeding waders, as well as the Scarce Emerald Damselfly. The extensive mudflats in Higham Bight provide good feeding for ducks, waders and gulls. The river wall forms the northern boundary of the reserve and though it is some way from the mouth of the Thames Estuary seabirds can still be anticipated.

Species

It is winter when the largest numbers of feeding birds occur in Higham Bight, but as the tide comes in, sometimes racing across the mudflats, the waders in particular can be seen at closer range, before they fly to roost, often within Cliffe Pools reserve. Migrant freshwater waders occur on Shorne Marshes in spring and autumn, while good numbers of Lapwing and Redshank breed. In autumn, when winds swing into the northerly quarter, seabirds may well fly upriver as far as Shornmead Fort. Some may continue even further, while others return to the estuary. One advantage of watching here is that the river is comparatively narrow and the species mentioned for other seawatching sites, like petrels, may be seen at closer range.

CLIFFE POOLS RSPB RESERVE and NORTH QUARRY (Map 1b)

Habitat

Between the village of Cliffe and the river there is an extensive area of fairly unique habitat, covering some 700 ha from Higham Marsh to Lower Hope Point. It comprises about 200 ha of water-filled clay pits, another 100 or so are pits filled with river dredgings, some of which are now over-grown with sea aster, whilst others contain shallow, flooded areas. The RSPB reserve at Cliffe covers about 230 ha, including some 27 ha of 'fresh' pools and 111 of saline lagoons. This represents 10% of the English total, a scarce EU-notified Biodiversity Action Plan habitat. The Alpha pool adds another 60 ha of this habitat to the total. The water level in the flooded areas, that attract many waders in autumn, has been at the mercy of the elements. RSPB management will seek to control this and to create a variety of feeding and roosting opportunities for wintering and migratory waders and wildfowl. Muddy fringes ensure that a good variety of waders can rest and feed during their autumn migration. The rare annual beard grass, more often associated with the eastern end of the Hoo Peninsula, can be seen around the Coastguard Pool. Along the river, even at low tide, there is only a narrow foreshore, but there are extensive mudflats in Higham Bight, as mentioned above. Hawthorn scrub and bramble, quite widespread around the pools and along the bank below the radar tower, attract Nightingales, warblers and finches. Long-eared Owls occasionally roost in the denser hawthorn. Northeast of Cliffe a footpath forms the northwest border of Ryestreet Common, an area of grazing marsh owned by the RSPB. Finally, there are two flooded chalk quarries; the North Quarry is now well vegetated and though a limited amount of quarrying still occurs along the northern edge, it attracts many species. It can be viewed quite well from the road during the winter. A fishery is being created in the South Quarry and there are plans, too, for a nature reserve, with hides for public viewing.

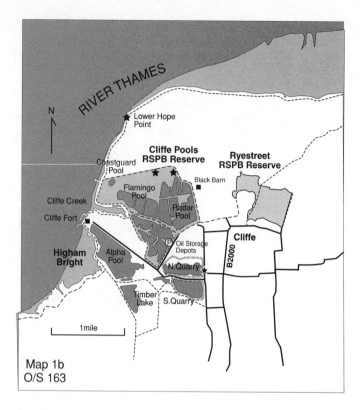

Map 1b
O/S 163

Species

The flooded pools on Cliffe reserve attract a variety of waterfowl in winter. Few winters pass without visits from one of the diver species or the rarer grebes, all three divers and both Red-necked and Slavonian Grebes have made prolonged stays. Up to 100 Cormorants often roost on the Alpha Pool and a few Bewick's Swans can occasionally be seen, although they usually prefer to graze on the marshes. Diving duck, such as Tufted and Pochard, frequently outnumber the dabbling ducks on the pools, where Goldeneye is a regular winter visitor, but Scaup somewhat scarcer. Smew and Long-tailed Duck occur infrequently, the former more often when the weather is severe on the Continent. Larger numbers of dabbling duck, particularly Shoveler and Gadwall, favour the North Quarry; Greylag and Canada Geese often feed there too, while Little Egrets regularly roost there and feed on the reserve.

Although the wader roost sites vary, the Alpha Pool frequently attracts several hundred Redshanks, whilst the coastguard pool, close to the river wall, is often favoured by Ringed Plover. A Kentish Plover has wintered here and Avocet is now regularly wintering in some numbers. They feed in Higham Bight when the tide drops, where they can sometimes be difficult to find among all the Shelduck, and either roost at Timber Lake or on one of the Black Barn pools, where they can be seen from the Hope Ramp. Common and Green Sandpipers are occasionally seen in winter. Hen Harrier and Short-eared Owl often hunt the vegetation surrounding the pools, amongst which small flocks of Linnets regularly feed, but the once-familiar Twite is now extremely scarce. At this season, Ryestreet Common attracts a variety of raptors.

By late March the wintering duck are departing and the local birds are dispersing onto the marshes to breed. An attractive drake Goldeneye can sometimes be observed displaying, prior to departure. Garganey may appear by the end of the month, along with other early migrants, like Little Ringed Plover, Sand Martin, Wheatear and Chiffchaff. The scene changes more dramatically during April, with the arrival of Common Terns and summering passerines, like Yellow Wagtail, Sedge and Reed Warblers, while migrant waders, such as Whimbrel and Greenshank, can also be anticipated. Broad-billed and Marsh Sandpipers, both extreme rarities, have occurred in May. About 20 pairs of Common Terns usually breed at Cliffe, along with a few pairs of Pochard, Gadwall and Ruddy Duck, whilst later in the season crèches of up to 50 young Shelduck occur. Increasing numbers of Avocets breed most years.

The muddy fringes of the Black Barn pools attract a good selection of migrant waders in autumn, commencing with Little Ringed Plover, and adult Little Stint and Curlew Sandpiper from early July. Greenshank, too, feature at this time, whilst small numbers of Ruff, a few Spotted Redshanks and Wood Sandpipers are also regular, with Temminck's Stint an almost annual visitor. Over the years American vagrants like White-rumped, Pectoral, Stilt and Buff-breasted Sandpipers have all been seen here. With the increase in Little Egret numbers in the UK, gatherings of up to 50 may occur.

Although Cliffe reserve is some way from the mouth of the Thames, the autumn passage of seabirds — auks, skuas, Kittiwakes and terns — can sometimes be quite evident. The bend in the river at Lower Hope Point makes a good watchpoint. Some birds continue up the Thames, whilst others often circle over the river, before returning east. Storm-driven birds are often seen here and occasionally on the pools in late autumn, including Manx Shearwater and occasionally Leach's Petrel, Grey Phalarope and Little Auk. Another feature of late autumn is the flocking of Little Grebes, with up to 180 on the pools from late October.

COOLING, HALSTOW and ST MARY'S MARSHES (Map 1c)

Habitat

This area was once prime grazing marsh, dissected by reed-lined ditches and more open fleets, with small beds of common reed. Access is limited to the few public rights of way, but much of the area, which has largely reverted to grassland, having been substantially converted to arable during the 1960s and 70s, can be viewed from the seawall. The fleets and ditches support valuable duck food plants such as common spike-rush, fennel pondweed, soft hornwort and spiked water milfoil. Water Voles find this habitat to their liking. Dragonflies and damselflies are also quite common, as is the introduced Marsh Frog. Along the drier seawall, a mix of common and unusual plants can be seen. Here the meadow barley of the grazing marsh is replaced by the sea barley, which develops a characteristically spiky head as it dries. The small pink flowers of the rare sea clover are difficult to find, but do occur among the bright yellow masses of common and narrow-leaved bird's-foot trefoil. The slender hare's ear can also be found, with some searching. The ungrazed tall grasses and

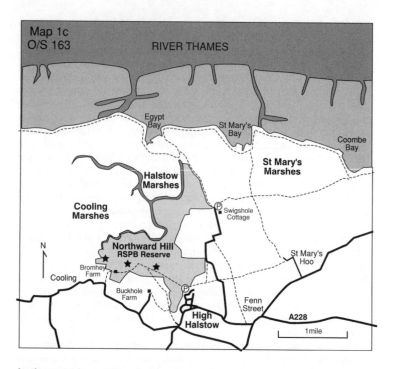

herbs provide excellent habitat for moths and butterflies. Common Blue and Meadow Brown are abundant, while migrant Painted Ladies frequently settle on thistles and Marbled White has recently spread to this area. Grasshoppers, too, are numerous and among their relations the Roesel's bush cricket is a Thames estuary speciality. There is relatively little saltmarsh along this stretch of the river, but the mudflats are extensive, supporting vast numbers of laver spire shells, which are the main food of Shelduck.

Species

While interesting species can be seen year-round, it is the numbers of wintering wildfowl, raptors and waders that often attract the greatest interest. A few Bewick's Swans are often present, and up to 100 or more White-fronted Geese regularly graze the marshes. Well over 1,000 Shelduck may be seen feeding on the mudflats at low tide, or swimming on the river when the mud is covered. At least 5,000 Wigeon and over 3,000 Teal regularly winter here, usually with at least 500 Pintail, about 200 Shoveler and a similar number of Gadwall. Sometimes they can be seen feeding or swimming along the river, sometimes over the marshes. Dunlin is by far the commonest wader, with 15,000 regularly wintering on the Thames Marshes, feeding on the exposed mud, from which many fly to roost on the Essex marshes. Over 4,000 Knot, nearly 1,000 Redshank, and similar numbers of Curlew and Grey Plover also winter. Flocks of Golden Plover regularly feed on the grazing marshes, providing attractive flight patterns against the sky when disturbed, possibly by Hen or Marsh Harriers hunting along the ditches. In the reeds a few Bearded Tits can usually be seen, or heard, most often in late autumn. Small flocks of Snow Buntings sometimes feed along the seawall, but Lapland Buntings are scarce and more difficult to locate, as they may feed on the grazing marsh, attracted by the hay put out for the cattle, which also attracts flocks of wintering Corn Buntings.

Among the flocks of over 500 Golden Plover present in winter, many assume their most attractive breeding plumage before departing in spring. Little Grebe breeds along the edges of the ditches, where a variety of ducks also nest, including a few pairs of Pochard and, occasionally, Garganey, whilst Redshank favours the damper pastures. Over the meadows, Skylark, Meadow Pipit and Yellow Wagtail are all quite numerous breeders, with Sedge and Reed Warblers favouring the waterside vegetation.

NORTHWARD HILL RSPB RESERVE (Map 1c)

Habitat

The wood is some 55 ha in extent, lying on a ridge of London clay that rises to about 60 m, giving it a commanding view over the marshes towards the river. Oak woodland is the most obvious, with extensive dense hawthorn, some ash coppice, sycamore scrub and clearings surrounded by a dense understorey of bramble and fern. Under the oaks the ground cover is deep leaf litter, but elsewhere dog's mercury, yellow archangel and bluebells proliferate. A pond on the northern fringes adds variety. With this mix of new growth and old and decaying timber, it is a bird-rich habitat, and a good site for butterflies, notably White-letter Hairstreak, which flies from mid-June. In addition, Small Red Damselfly was discovered in 2002. A 250-ha extension to the north, bordered on the east by Decoy Fleet, now includes flooded pasture and reedbeds, which can be observed from three hilltop viewpoints.

Species

Dawn and dusk visits in winter often provide a very different view of the bird species using the wood. The shelter of the dense hawthorn thicket not only provides a winter home for hard-to-see Long-eared Owls, but also provides them with a food source in the form of roosting passerines. Several hundred thrushes and finches roost; on occasion even larger numbers of Stock Doves and Woodpigeons seek shelter here, whilst probably in excess of 3,000 corvids, a large percentage of which are Jackdaws, fly in to roost. During the day, these birds feed on the grazing marsh or in the surrounding fields, hedgerows and orchards. The wood will be comparatively quiet, apart from the thin calls of a roving tit flock, possibly with attendant Goldcrests, and the gentle tapping of resident Great Spotted Woodpeckers. A few Woodcock winter and may be seen probing the deep leaf litter with their long bills, if you are very lucky. When the marshes are flooded, good numbers of Wigeon, Teal and Pintail can be seen. Common Buzzard is a traditional winter visitor and Peregrine, as well as Merlin, feed over the marshes by day, the latter roosting in scattered trees on the marsh below the hill. Passerines like Tree Sparrow and Corn Bunting are essentially winter visitors to the reserve, and are an added attraction at this time.

Activity in the heronry commences early in the year, when returning birds carry branches in to effect repairs to their nests. They can be observed distantly from the road to the northeast, which avoids any disturbance. A closer approach can be arranged in advance with the wardens. By mid-March, when the first Chiffchaffs arrive, many of the 150+ pairs of Grey Herons will be on eggs, and resident woodland species will be singing. By late April or early May, the wood is alive with the songs of Nightingales and woodland warblers, and Little Egrets are active in the heronry. Very occasionally, rarer species like Golden Oriole may add to the variety of song. Other excitements can be anticipated on the marshes, where migrant, freshwater waders steal the limelight, though a drake Garganey is always a delight to see. Flocks of Black-tailed Godwit, attractive in their orange summer plumage, visit the flooded pools, along with others like Ruff — often in their breeding finery — Spotted Redshank, Wood Sandpiper and perhaps a rarity like a Black-winged Stilt. Mediterranean Gulls, often in full breeding plumage, may be seen among the feeding flocks of Black-headed Gulls, and Hobby replaces Merlin.

About 70 species usually breed on the reserve, with 250–300 pairs of Rooks in the wood, where several pairs of Shelduck, a few pairs of Turtle Dove and up to 15 pairs of Nightingale breed fairly regularly. About 40 pairs of Avocet nest on the wetland islands and can be seen from the viewpoints. A few pairs of Water Rail and numbers of Lapwing and Redshank also breed, along with several species of duck and passerines like Yellow Wagtail, Meadow Pipit, Sedge and Reed Warblers, Reed Bunting and possibly Bearded Tit.

In late summer, as in spring, the wetland pools again attract a variety of freshwater waders, but the wood is quiet again, as the summer migrants disperse. By October, the marshes play host to Hen Harrier, Merlin and wintering duck, whilst small influxes of Goldcrests can be anticipated in the woods. Although the delights of the subtle seasonal changes are only really appreciated by frequent visitors, there is much for the occasional visitor too. One guaranteed attraction at Northward Hill is the heronry, and it can be most impressive during the early spring, before the trees are in full leaf.

COOMBE BAY, ALLHALLOWS, YANTLET CREEK and STOKE LAGOON (Map 1d)

Habitat

This relatively small site contains all the diverse habitats associated with the general area. North and east of the seawall there are small patches of saltmarsh and shingle bays, with an expanse of mudflats at low tide. On the landward side there are freshwater grazing marshes, dissected by ditches, with small reed-lined lagoons. The seawall below the caravan park faces northeast across the mouth of the estuary, providing a good vantage point for seawatching. Further west, beyond the yachting enclosure, lies Coombe Bay, with more extensive saltmarsh, which occasionally attracts Jack Snipe in early spring, and shingle banks on which waders roost at high tide. South from the mouth of Yantlet Creek is Stoke Lagoon, an attractive wetland site, essentially formed by a freshwater drainage system and enclosed on all sides by bunds. The meadows are too heavily grazed for much flora to stabilise, although there is one well-established salsify community along the Yantlet seawall, which flowers in May–June.

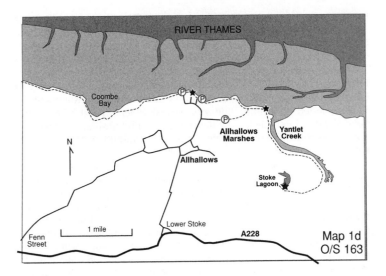

Species

A similar range of species to those upriver can be expected on the mud-flats, with numerous gulls and significant numbers of Brent Geese, Shelduck, Grey Plover, Dunlin and Redshank, while Oystercatcher and Turnstone are more plentiful here. At high tide a wader roost forms on the shingle bank at the mouth of Yantlet Creek. The sand and shingle bays, with the adjacent short grass on the seawall, frequently attract a small wintering flock of Snow Buntings. Another, more occasional, speciality of the same habitat is Shore Lark. Lapland Bunting is now scarce and prefers the longer grass of the grazing marshes. Throughout the year, Stoke Lagoon adds variety. In winter, good numbers of dabbling duck — Wigeon, Gadwall, Teal and Pintail — feed there, whilst freshwater waders like Greenshank and Spotted Redshank occasionally overwinter. Hen Harrier, Merlin, Peregrine and Short-eared Owl may be seen hunting throughout the area.

Wheatear can be expected before the end of March and the lagoon is a fairly reliable site for an early Garganey. During April and May, a variety of migrant waders can also be expected though the water level may be

Grey Plover, Knot, Dunlin

too high for the shorter-legged sandpipers. The former arable areas reverted to grazing marsh now host some numbers of breeding Oystercatcher, Lapwing and Redshank.

By autumn, the water level in the lagoon is usually lower and the area is consequently more attractive for a wider variety of migrant waders. Freshwater species like Wood Sandpiper, Ruff and Spotted Redshank can be expected, along with Little Stint and Curlew Sandpiper. Rarer species have included Spoonbill, Blue-winged Teal, Black-winged Stilt, Greater Yellowlegs and Red-necked Phalarope. Another interesting feature of the autumn is the build-up of Little Terns in the mouth of Yantlet Creek, where 50–100 or more may roost by early August.

From August to November, when the wind blows from a northerly direction, some seabird passage can be anticipated. Another feature of the autumn here is the visible migration of passerine migrants as they coast westward, with hirundines and pipits replaced by thrushes and finches as the season progresses. Seabird passage is more easily observed at high tide, as the birds fly closer inshore. In August and September species like Arctic and Great Skuas and various terns are regular, while a few Mediterranean Gulls occur among the numerous gulls off Allhallows. By October a wider range of seabirds can be expected, including Gannet, Pomarine Skua, possibly a Sabine's Gull, Kittiwake and the larger auks, whilst Puffin and even Storm Petrel occur from time to time. Later in the month, flocks of wintering geese, ducks and waders also arrive. In November northerly storms sometimes produce large numbers of Kittiwakes, while rarer species like Leach's Petrel, Glaucous Gull and Little Auk are always possible.

ISLE OF GRAIN (Map 1e)

Habitat

Much of the northern area, between Yantlet Creek and Grain Village, is grazing marsh, surrounded on three sides by the seawall. To the northeast is Roas Bank, an extensive area of mudflats, about 1 mile (1.6 km) wide. Rich in invertebrates, it attracts large numbers of feeding waders and gulls, particularly in winter. The northeast-facing coastline makes a good vantage for observing autumn seabird movements and the visible migration of passerines. Of particular interest is the recently created Grain Foreshore Country Park, administered by Medway Unitary Authority, which operates from the beach car park, by the church on the Thames, to Smithfield Fort by the Medway. The area is being managed for wildlife and, although much of the old sycamore scrub has been removed to benefit the flora, there is still enough to hold migrants. Eventually, the park will have facilities such as toilets, etc. An area of particular significance, between the village and the seawall, adjacent to the school playing fields, is the moat — the remains of the old Grain fort — which forms a natural landfall for autumn passerine migrants. This area of scrub covers undulating ground, where sycamore, hawthorn and bramble are dominant. The area south to Smithfield Fort, on the landward side of the seawall, is essentially pasture, with bramble, more hawthorn scrub, reed-lined ditches and pools — another attractive area for passerine migrants.

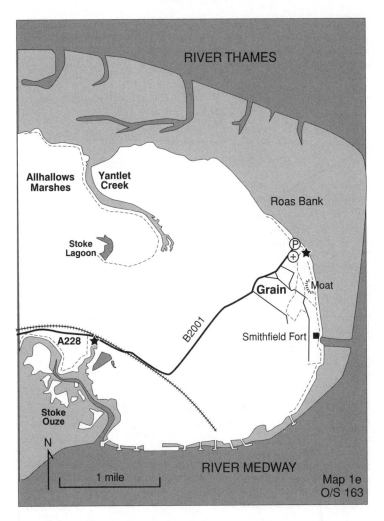

RIVER THAMES

Allhallows
Marshes

Yantlet
Creek

Roas Bank

Stoke
Lagoon

Moat

Grain

B2001

Smithfield Fort

A228

Stoke
Ouze

N

1 mile

RIVER MEDWAY

Map 1e
O/S 163

Species

In winter, the narrow stretch of mudflats at the mouth of the Medway estuary is a good area for close views of waders, as the tide ebbs. Grey Plover, Knot and Bar-tailed Godwit can be expected amongst the numerous Dunlin, while flocks of Brent Geese can often be seen 'commuting' between Essex and the Medway. On the grazing marshes, large numbers of Curlew sometimes flock, whilst Hen Harrier, Peregrine and Merlin regularly hunt.

This site generally is of greater interest in autumn, particularly when the wind swings north and seabird passage can be anticipated, as described for the previous site. When the wind is from the northeast, migrant passerines can be expected in the moat and scrub to the south, including pipits, wagtails, chats, common warblers and flycatchers, with the possibility of a rarer species like a Red-backed Shrike. By October

Goldcrests and a few Firecrests can be expected, and with an influx of these species there is always the anticipation of finding a Yellow-browed Warbler, or even a rarer eastern warbler like Pallas's or Dusky. In north-west winds, particularly in late autumn, species such as Grey Phalarope and Sabine's Gull have occurred. Cormorants perch on the buoys and old towers in the estuary mouth and, as the autumn progresses, wintering waders return to feed on the exposed mud.

GREAT CHATTENDEN WOOD (Map 1f)

Habitat

A deciduous woodland containing sizeable areas of hornbeam and hazel — formerly coppiced — with oak standards. Past coppicing cycles mean that there is no genuinely old timber. Bluebells form an attractive carpet of blue in the spring, when early purple orchids can also be seen. There is limited access, as much of the southern section is MoD land. The main footpath runs along the ridge between Lodge Hill and Cliffe Woods estate. Lodge Hill is an open area with hawthorn and gorse scrub and good views of the surrounding area.

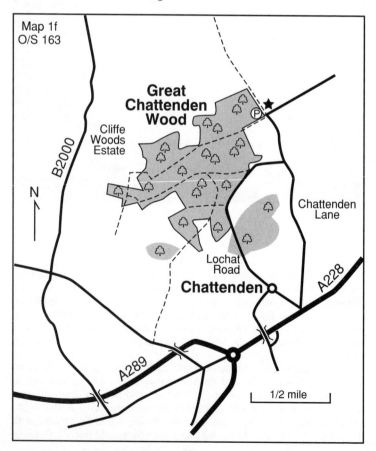

Species

Sparrowhawk, Little and Tawny Owls are resident and the last named may be heard hooting early in the year, when winter visitors like Woodcock and possibly Common Buzzard occur. Both Green and Great Spotted Woodpeckers are present, along with Treecreeper and possibly Nuthatch, although the latter is scarce. Lesser Spotted Woodpecker, Willow Tit, Hawfinch and Lesser Redpoll have all declined and now only the last named may occur from time to time. The song of summer migrants like Nightingale and the six common warblers dominates spring, but the 'purring' of Turtle Doves is now less common. Other residents include Jay and Bullfinch, while rarer species like Golden Oriole may make occasional brief visits.

In autumn other passerine migrants like Redstart and Spotted and Pied Flycatchers may visit briefly, but by early September the woods will be quiet again, apart from the calls of roving tit flocks. By October winter thrushes and finches will be arriving and a visit to Lodge Hill should provide a good opportunity to witness visible migration. Of significance during late autumn and winter are the enormous roosts of several hundred Carrion Crows and Magpies.

Timing

As at all coastal localities, the state of the tide is important in determining where many of the bird species can be best seen. At low tide all those species that feed on the mudflats will generally be very distant, but as the tide rises, they feed closer to the seawall. The waders fly to roost as the mud becomes covered, whilst species like Shelduck may simply swim on the river. High tide is also the best time for seawatching in the Thames, particularly if the wind veers northwest in autumn. Visible migration of passerines tends to be heaviest in the morning though it can continue throughout the day in light northwest winds, especially when a vigorous depression has lasted for 2–3 days, as this causes a build-up of migrants in northern Europe. Early-morning visits are best to hear woodland birdsong and migrant passerines are usually easier to see at the same time, when they are feeding most actively. It is also worth being out during the period before dusk for species like Barn Owl. Flocks of corvids gather before going to roost, and Woodcock may be seen flying from their daytime woodland roosts to feed in adjacent fields.

Access

For Shorne Marshes (Map 1a) follow Canal Road from Lower Higham. There is usually room to park at TQ 703740. Follow the cycle track west and view the freshwater pools from TQ 684738. The footpath north from TQ 695737 crosses the reserve to Shornmead Fort, where seawatching is best towards high tide. Further east, Higham Bight can be viewed from the Saxon Shore Way.

For Cliffe Pools reserve (Map 1b) take the B2000 from Rochester or, from the Rochester by-pass, the A289, off the A2. As you reach the outskirts of the village, turn left towards the North Quarry. Turn left again and park to view the quarry, in winter, from TQ 732757, or wherever there is a gap in the shrubs. Turn right between the quarries and continue to the end of the tarmac road, turn right towards the oil storage depots, near which you can park. Until the Cliffe RSPB reserve is opened and new directions are available, you should stick to the public rights of way, as shown on Map 1b and the OS map. The car park for the reserve will be at

TQ 726764. To reach Lower Hope Point, follow the footpath to the seawall, which you follow in a northerly direction until you reach the stone obelisk that marks the point — just over a mile-and-a-quarter from Cliffe Creek. To visit the Alpha pool, follow the footpath round the south side of Cliffe Creek past Cliffe Fort. From here look south over Higham Bight, then walk back round the southern side of the Alpha Pool along the seawall, following the path across the north end of Timber Lake, which often attracts good birds, as it less disturbed. This circuit is about 3 miles long. In autumn, the wader pools are best viewed from the new RSPB ramps beside the Black Barn road at approximately TQ 727776 and TQ 722778. There is room to park cars near here, having followed Pickles Way from the village.

It is possible to walk the length of the Thames Marshes from Cliffe to Allhallows, along the seawall, a distance of over 12 miles. From Cliffe village it is also possible to walk alongside Ryestreet RSPB reserve and beyond to overlook part of Cooling Marshes. There are also public rights of way across Halstow and St Mary's Marshes (Map 1c). To reach Halstow Marshes, continue along the narrow lane through Cooling and High Halstow towards Fenn Street. After just less than 3 miles from Cooling, turn left along an unmarked road, via Clinchstreet Farm towards Swigshole Cottage, a mile-and-a-half or so, but car-parking bays are extremely limited along this narrow lane. There are several possible circuits following the tracks and public footpaths. A track to the north reaches Egypt Bay. There you can follow the seawall east to St Mary's Bay, then back south across the marsh and west to Swigshole Cottage — a 4 mile walk. Alternatively, a 5 mile walk takes you east across St Mary's Marsh to Coombe Bay, then west around the seawall to St Mary's Bay, and south and west across the marsh again. Several other public rights of way, from St Mary's Hoo across the marshes, are shown on the OS Explorer series map 163.

Northward Hill RSPB reserve (Map 1c) is approached through High Halstow village. Follow the brown RSPB road signs from the main street to the RSPB car park. Trails start here: the long one leads to the Saxon Shore Way, which you follow west, through and along the edge of the wood, to reach the three viewpoints overlooking the wetland. For details of parking for larger groups (coaches are inadvisable) and arrangements to visit the heronry, contact the wardens at the RSPB Office (see Useful Addresses, p. 306).

To reach Allhallows (Map 1d), follow the minor road off the A228 at Fenn Street for 4 miles, turning right along Avery Way to the British Pilot inn. There is usually room to park here. For seawatching, in particular, instead of turning right along Avery Way, continue straight ahead into the caravan park (there is usually a charge for entry) then turn right to park at the seafront. From here you can also walk east along the seawall to Yantlet Creek, or west to Coombe Bay. From the British Pilot a track continues east, across the marsh to the seawall, close to the mouth of Yantlet Creek. Follow the seawall south and eventually west, along the creek for about 2 miles to Stoke Lagoon on the right. Keep behind the seawall as you approach the lagoon to avoid disturbing the duck and waders.

To reach the Isle of Grain (Map 1e), follow the A228 from Rochester. About a mile-and-a-half beyond Lower Stoke, it is possible to park and look over Stoke Ooze to the south, where a variety of waders can be seen in the saltmarsh and muddy creeks. Immediately adjacent, to the east, is a flooded lagoon that attracts duck and occasionally Bewick's Swans in winter. Follow the B2001 to Grain village, turn right into the High Street and park in the Beach car park just beyond the church. This is the start of the Country Park, and the coastline here provides vantage points for viewing the estuaries of both the Medway and Thames.

Great Chattenden Wood (Map 1f) is best approached from the A289 then A228. Turn left and follow Chattenden Lane north along the eastern edge of the residential area for about 1.25 miles (2 km). The road narrows and then makes a sharp turn to the east, at the top of the hill, where there is just room to park a car at TQ 754738. A footpath straight ahead, to the northwest, takes you downhill along the edge of the wood and the open scrubby hillside, or you can take the main footpath through the wood along the ridge towards Cliffe Woods estate. There are other footpaths off Lochat Road.

Calendar

Resident: Little Grebe, Great Crested Grebe, Little Egret, Grey Heron, Greylag Goose, Shelduck, Gadwall, Shoveler, Pochard, Tufted Duck, Red-legged and Grey Partridges, Water Rail, Oystercatcher, Ringed Plover, Snipe, Barn, Little, Tawny and Long-eared Owls, Green and Great Spotted Woodpeckers, Bearded Tit, possibly Nuthatch, Reed and Corn Buntings.

December–February: Probably divers and rare grebes, Bewick's Swan, White-fronted and Brent Geese, Wigeon, Scaup, Goldeneye, Marsh and Hen Harriers, Sparrowhawk, Common Buzzard, Peregrine, Merlin, Avocet, Golden and Grey Plovers, Knot, Ruff, Jack Snipe, Woodcock, Short-eared Owl, Rock Pipit, Stonechat, and possibly Snow Lapland Buntings.

March–May: Little Egret and Grey Heron (Northward Hill heronry), Garganey, Hobby, migrant waders including Whimbrel and Greenshank, Wheatear, Whinchat, woodland summer visitors including Nightingale and *Sylvia* warblers.

June–July: Breeding residents, duck and waders including Garganey and Avocet, Common Tern (breeding colony), Yellow Wagtail, Nightingale, Sedge and Reed Warblers, woodland warblers, Bearded Tit. In July, return wader passage, Yellow-legged Gull.

August–November: Little Grebe (November peak), Manx Shearwater, possible Storm and Leach's Petrels, Brent Goose (from October), Marsh and Hen Harriers, Common Buzzard, Sparrowhawk, Peregrine and Merlin (all six from October), migrant waders — Little Ringed and Ringed Plovers (August peak), Little and Temminck's Stints, Curlew Sandpiper, Ruff, Black-tailed Godwit, Whimbrel, Spotted Redshank, Greenshank, Wood Sandpiper, returning winter waders (from October), Pomarine, Arctic and Great Skuas, gulls possibly including Mediterranean and Glaucous, Sandwich and Little Terns, auks, Whinchat, Wheatear, winter thrushes, migrant warblers, Goldcrest, finch passage, possibly Lapland Bunting.

Habitat

The huge tidal basin is characterised by large and small saltmarsh islands, a maze of creeks, extensive mud and the brackish grazing marshes of the Chetney Peninsula. The estuary attracts a wealth of wintering waterfowl and waders, while the islands and grazing marshes support a diverse population of breeding birds. Man's intervention has had a significant impact, but despite many threats, a reasonable balance has been maintained to date. The main changes have occurred along the north shore, much of which is privately owned and inaccessible to the general public. The construction of the Kingsnorth power station is an example of an industrial development that has benefited certain bird species. The jetty joining the tanker terminal off Oakham Ness has been connected to the mainland, forming a sheltered bay, which now attracts huge numbers of duck at high tide, while the undisturbed saltmarshes are used by many waders at high tide. Neither of these sites is open to the public, although arrangements can be made for organised groups to visit the Nature Study Centre within the power station grounds.

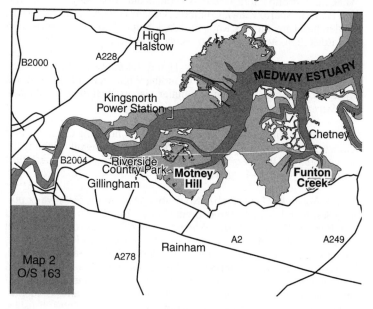

Species

Winter on the Medway estuary can provide spectacular sights, as geese, duck and waders flight across the industrial skyline. It is such a valuable area for thousands of wintering birds that it is not only ranked as internationally important for the total numbers of wildfowl that use it, but also for two individual species — Shelduck and Pintail, with 3,600 and 1,000 respectively wintering here. The attraction of nearby Elmley, as a safe and relatively undisturbed haven for wintering duck, has probably been partially responsible for the reduction in the numbers of dabbling duck now wintering in the Medway, compared to the early 1970s. Even so, nationally important numbers of up to 2,500 Brent Geese, 3,600 Wigeon, 1,500 Teal and 150 Shoveler can still be seen at Barksore Marshes. Internationally important numbers of some 2,800 Grey Plover, 5,500 Knot, 20,000 Dunlin and 2,900 Redshank also winter here, whilst of national importance are 4,400 Oystercatchers, 500 Avocets, 700 Black-tailed Godwits and 1,400 Curlew.

Great Crested Grebe and Goldeneye favour some of the deeper channels and can be seen well at high tide from the south shore. Rarer grebes sometimes occur here too, and it is one of the more reliable sites for the attractive Red-breasted Merganser. Hen Harrier, Merlin, Peregrine and Short-eared Owl hunt over the saltmarsh and grazing marshes, whilst Rock Pipits are frequently seen foraging along the creeks and edges of the saltmarsh.

As winter progresses, numbers of duck and waders decline, but many species are still present in small numbers into early April. By this time, there is usually a peak count of some 1,500 Black-tailed Godwits, while migrant waders like Whimbrel can be expected, along with early passerine migrants such as Wheatear and Yellow Wagtail.

The Medway islands attract an interesting variety of 35 breeding species, but needless to say they should be left undisturbed while the birds are nesting. Some islands attract large colonies of Black-headed Gulls and smaller numbers of terns, including 300 pairs of Sandwich, up to 200 pairs of Common and a small colony of 15 pairs of Little Terns, although their numbers tend to fluctuate more. Among the Black-headed Gull colonies a few pairs of Mediterranean Gull breed.

Return wader passage is a feature of the autumn and for some species the annual peaks occur at this time, with up to 1,000 Ringed Plover, 1,700 Black-tailed Godwit and 600 Avocet. Roost counts of 100 Whimbrel, 100 Spotted Redshanks and 100–150 Greenshank are fairly regular, but they often favour the inaccessible saltmarshes at Kingsnorth. Little Egret is now virtually resident and flocks of up to 250 have been seen at Oakham Ness. Of other less common species, the Osprey is a regular autumn visitor. During October, winter visitors like Brent Goose, Hen Harrier and Merlin return, while the numbers of wildfowl start to increase again.

Main Birdwatching Zones

Although its size makes the Medway estuary a daunting area to watch, there is ample opportunity to see many of the bird species. Access is limited, but there are stretches where roads provide good vantage points and there are public footpaths or rights of way along parts of the extensive seawall system. A boat would certainly make more sites accessible and is well worth considering, although it can be dangerous and knowledge of the estuary and its tides are essential.

The attraction for many visitors to the area are the wintering wildfowl and waders. To avoid unnecessary repetition, as many birds occur at all sites, the information under the named sites concentrates more on those species that seem particularly to favour each. Three sites are included along the south shore: the Riverside Country Park at Horrid Hill; Motney Hill and Otterham Creek; and Funton Creek, Bedlams Bottom and Chetney.

RIVERSIDE COUNTRY PARK (Map 2a)

Habitat

The Horrid Hill Peninsula provides an excellent vantage point for observing the landscape of muddy creeks and saltmarsh islands that is the southern Medway. Nor Marsh, leased by the RSPB, is the nearby large island. By following the Saxon Shore Way, along the seawall to the west, you can view the saltmarsh of Copperhouse Marshes, with the main channel and Hoo Salt Marsh beyond. The hawthorn and bramble scrub of Riverside Country Park provide an attractive habitat, particularly for both whitethroats in summer, while the small brackish pond is rich in amphibians and insects. The Saxon Shore Way along the edge of the estuary to the southeast, which takes you towards Motney Hill, also provides good views over the saltmarsh and estuary.

Species

During winter, good numbers of waders, including hundreds of Grey and Ringed Plovers, Turnstone, Redshank and Dunlin are visible from Horrid Hill, as they fly by to and from their roosts on the islands, an hour or two either side of high tide. The roosting flocks of waders and wildfowl can be seen well on Copperhouse Marsh. When the tide is full, it is a good spot from which to observe Great Crested Grebes at close range and occasionally a Slavonian Grebe. Red-breasted Merganser is also easy to see at this time, with a few Goldeneye and possibly a Scaup or two. Looking across to Nor Marsh, you may be fortunate to see a Hen Harrier

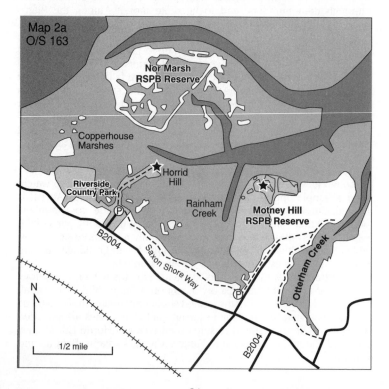

34

hunting and one or two Little Egrets are usually in this area. Other raptors may include Sparrowhawk and Peregrine. Water Rails winter in the area and the pond in the Country Park may provide a better opportunity for good views than the reedbed at Motney Hill. As the mud becomes exposed again, waders start feeding. Amongst the numerous Dunlin and Redshank, you may find 50 or more Black-tailed Godwits; 100–200 will probably be wintering somewhere in the southern Medway and this is one of their favoured haunts. In March, around 700 may be present, while even larger numbers occur in autumn, but they then tend to feed and roost further east in the estuary. The gulls are also worth studying, Mediterranean occurs regularly and Glaucous Gull has also been seen here. In summer, noisy colonies of Black-headed Gulls can be observed on the islands.

Brent Geese on mud

Of the smaller birds, Rock Pipit is common along the shore in winter and the scrub may attract feeding flocks of tits and finches, while warblers like Lesser Whitethroat and Whitethroat may be present in late spring and summer. In autumn the whole area, including the scrub on Horrid Hill, attracts migrant passerines and falls of Goldcrests have been observed. Little Egrets have markedly increased and up to 30 or more may be seen in this area in late summer. Another interesting feature of this stretch of the estuary concerns the autumn migration of skuas and waders, some of which fly overland. In northwest winds, Arctic, Great and occasionally Pomarine Skuas have been seen heading southwest over Gillingham, often flying over the Riverside Country Park as they leave the estuary.

MOTNEY HILL and OTTERHAM CREEK (Map 2a)

Habitat
The RSPB manages a small reserve at Motney Hill. Looking west from the Motney Hill Peninsula there are extensive creeks and mudflats at low tide. The sewage works at the northern tip is not open to the public, but there is quite an extensive reedbed alongside Otterham Creek.

Species

In winter, the estuary mudflats and high water attract a similar range of species to those at Horrid Hill, including Brent Goose and the rarer grebes on occasion. Otterham Creek is also favoured by the rarer grebes and Black-tailed Godwit. The reedbed regularly holds Water Rail, Snipe, Kingfisher and Reed Bunting, though the first-named species will require some patience before it is seen, except in severe conditions, when it is far more confiding. It is more likely to be located by hearing its pig-like squeal. Short-eared Owl often occurs in winter, when Stonechat can also be anticipated, perched on the low scrub or fence posts surrounding the sewage works. Flocks of Skylarks tend to winter here as well. The reedbed occasionally attracts Bearded Tit and it holds a good population of breeding Sedge and Reed Warblers, the latter often hosting Cuckoos.

FUNTON CREEK, BEDLAMS BOTTOM and CHETNEY (Map 2b)

Habitat

The road between Lower Halstow and Kingsferry Bridge runs alongside Funton Creek and Bedlams Bottom, with Barksore Marshes and Chetney to the north. Against the distant industrial backdrop of Grain, the estuary here is a truly impressive sight, particularly when flocks of duck and waders flight across.

Chetney Peninsula consists of brackish grazing land, divided by fleets and ditches. The vegetation of the surrounding saltmarsh is typical, with common cord-grass, sea purslane and marsh samphire the dominant species. The pasture behind the seawall has a number of grass species, including common saltmarsh grass, sea barley and marsh foxtail, with patches of sea club-rush, common reed and common spike-rush along the fleets and ditches.

Species

Winter, again, probably provides the most impressive viewing. Barksore Marsh is inaccessible to the general public, but it does hold a large wader roost. Some of the birds flying to and from the roost can be seen from Chetney Hill. Up to 2,000 Grey Plover occur, as well as 1,000 Oystercatchers. Using the car as a hide, Funton Creek and Bedlams Bottom is one of the best places to see Brent Geese and up to 700 Pintail at very close range. As the tide rises, the birds are pushed closer to the road. Good views can also be expected of Grey Plover, Dunlin and Redshank, whilst up to 30 Red-breasted Mergansers occur at the mouth of Funton Creek and over 200 Avocets now winter here, with peak numbers closer to 600 in autumn. It is also much favoured by a flock of roosting Little Egrets. Rock Pipits feed in the saltmarsh.

A public footpath across Chetney provides opportunities for good views over the area, where Hen Harrier, Merlin, Peregrine and Short-eared Owl regularly hunt during winter. Also, there may be a small flock of Bewick's Swans and some grey geese, usually Greylags, but sometimes White-fronts as well.

During summer, several duck and wader species breed, including Shelduck, Shoveler and Redshank, while large populations of Skylark, Meadow Pipit and Yellow Wagtail successfully breed on the Chetney Peninsula.

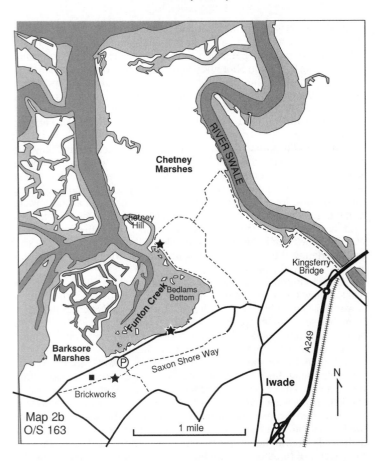

In autumn, Greenshank and Spotted Redshank make use of the Barksore roost and can be seen feeding on the mud along Funton Creek and Bedlams Bottom when the tide is low, whilst Avocets and Black-tailed Godwits also frequent this stretch of mud.

Timing

Timing your visit is quite critical, as it is important to coincide with the period either side of high tide for the best views of most of the wildfowl and waders. Stormy weather may well bring seabirds into the estuary, while in autumn winds from the north encourage seabird movements across the mouth of the estuary, and initiate some overland passage. Passerine migrants are most easily seen and heard early in the morning. Much of the area is shot over by wildfowlers, in season, and they too take advantage of the high tide's influence on the movement of duck.

Access

The western end of the southern Medway is adjacent to the B2004, which can now be reached from the Hoo Peninsula through the Medway tunnel. This avoids the congested Medway towns. Coming from the east, in Rainham, turn north off the A2, along the B2004 for just short of a mile. Turn left at the road junction. Motney Hill Road, the turning for Motney

Hill, is about 500 yards on the right, and for the Riverside Country Park, at Sharp's Green, just over 1 mile (1.6 km), again on the right (Map 2a). Park in the country park car park, then walk out along Horrid Hill Peninsula or west along the Saxon Shore Way. In the reception centre there are toilet and catering facilities. An information board provides an update on birds in the area, as well as information about birdwatching cruises on the Medway. Gates may present a barrier for some wheelchair users, but ask for assistance at the centre. There are a good number of benches along the shore.

At Motney Hill, park in the small car park, on the left, about 200 yards along Motney Hill Road. Follow the road and seawall towards the sewage works, looking out over the estuary and Rainham Creek to the left, and at the reedbed on the right. It is possible to walk round the shore of Motney Hill to the west, for a closer view of Rainham Creek, as far as the sewage works' perimeter fence. To view Otterham Creek, follow the road almost as far as the no entry signs to the sewage works, where the Saxon Shore Way continues round the edge of the field on the right across to the seawall bordering the creek. Access is limited for wheelchair users and those with mobility problems.

To reach Funton Creek and Bedlams Bottom (Map 2b), return to the B2004, follow the road east onto the minor road through Upchurch and Lower Halstow for just over 4 miles to Funton Brick Works, on the right. From there the estuary opens up before you on the left. In winter, the field opposite the brick works often attracts Golden Plover and other waders at high tide. On the right, just beyond the brickworks, there is usually room to park by the start of a footpath south. Follow it a short way and turn right along the Saxon Shore Way. There is an excellent panoramic view over the eastern end of the Medway Estuary. Further along Funton Creek there are a few narrow places where you can pull off the road. This area can also be reached from the A249, from Kingsferry Bridge or Iwade. Turn into Old Ferry Road, then along the Lower Halstow road to Bedlams Bottom. If there is room, park beside the road. This can provide close views of birds on a rising tide. A public footpath leads along the western edge of the Chetney Peninsula, cutting across the grazing marsh from Chetney Hill to the Swale, and then along the Swale to Kingsferry Bridge — a distance of about 4 miles. It is another mile-and-a-half back along the road to the start. Alternatively, park close to Kingsferry Bridge by the Ridham Dock road and walk northwest along the Swale, then across Chetney. The recommended walks are not suitable for wheelchair users or those with mobility problems.

Calendar

Resident: Cormorant (non-breeders), Greylag Goose (feral) Shelduck, Oystercatcher, Ringed Plover, Redshank, Reed Bunting.

December–February: Red-throated and Great Northern Divers (boat trips), Great Crested Grebe, possibly Red-necked or Slavonian Grebes, Little Egret, Bewick's Swan, Brent Goose, Wigeon, Pintail, possibly Scaup and Eider, Goldeneye, Red-breasted Merganser, Hen Harrier, Merlin, Peregrine, wintering waders including Avocet, Grey Plover, Black-tailed Godwit and Curlew, Short-eared Owl, Kingfisher, Rock Pipit, possibly Brambling (adjacent orchards).

March–May: Departing winter wildfowl and waders, Whimbrel, Yellow Wagtail, Wheatear, Sedge and Reed Warblers.

June–July: Breeding duck and waders, including Shelduck, Oystercatcher and Ringed Plover, Black-headed Gull colonies, Yellow Wagtail, Sedge and Reed Warblers.

August–November: Black-necked Grebe (August–September), Brent Goose (from October), possibly Osprey, Hen Harrier and Merlin (from October), Peregrine, returning winter waders, Avocet, Black-tailed Godwit (early-autumn peak), Whimbrel, Spotted Redshank, Greenshank, Arctic Skua, migrant passerines including common warblers and flycatchers (August–September), Goldcrest and Firecrest (October).

3 THE SWALE AND ISLE OF SHEPPEY
OS Explorer 149

Habitat

The Isle of Sheppey, in the mouth of the Thames, comprises a variety of habitats attractive to birds and includes the Elmley NNR, the integral RSPB Elmley Marshes reserve and the English Nature Swale NNR.

The scrub-covered cliffs between Warden Point and Leysdown, and the coastal strip to Shellness facing northeast, form a natural landfall for regular autumn passerine migrants and occasional rare vagrants. Other parts of the north-facing coast, from Warden Point to Sheerness, include farmland, more scrub-covered cliffs and built-up areas, where migrants also occur. Over the years, rarities like Rock Thrush and Pied Wheatear have been seen. The mudflats along this shore and the Swale, attract feeding waders, whilst the saltmarsh and shell spit at Shellness provide natural high-tide wader roosts. The path along the seawall by the Swale provides good views over the saltmarsh and nature reserve.

During the 1960s, much of the traditional pasture was drained and turned over to arable. However, since 2000, several changes more beneficial to wildlife, have occurred. Whilst remaining mainly arable, a large triangle of the marshes, from the Harty road east to the Leysdown holiday camps and south towards Shellness hamlet, has been returned to sheep and cattle grazing, with summer hay cutting. When these fields become wet in winter, they attract many thousands of plovers and wildfowl, especially when tides are high.

On higher ground, farmers have planted many thousands of saplings to create small thickets and shelterbelts for gamebirds. This has created weedy areas between the bushes, producing a dramatic increase in the numbers of finches, buntings and voles using the area.

Capel Fleet is quite wide in places and parts of it can be seen well from the Harty road. The level of water and season determine the species

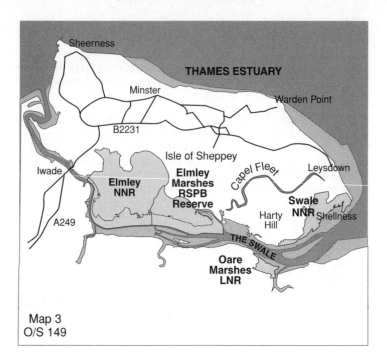

Map 3
O/S 149

present. The saltings east of Ferry Inn are part of the Swale NNR and form a much-favoured high-tide wader roost. There is no public access, but it is possible to view it from the pub car park. From the footpath near Mocketts Cottages, on Harty Hill, there is a good view west over the marshes towards Bells Creek. The public footpath provides the only access to this area. There are few trees and hedgerows in this open landscape and it can be cold and bleak in winter, but the rewards are there for those who persevere.

Opposite Ferry Inn, on the south side of the Swale, is Oare Marshes nature reserve, where the Kent Wildlife Trust has returned part of the area to traditional grazing marsh and has also created flooded areas, which are particularly attractive to breeding and migrant waders.

Species

The numbers of wildfowl, waders and raptors present in winter are one of the great attractions at that time of year. The variety can also be quite impressive. Offshore, rafts of divers and grebes occur from time to time, seals too, are regularly seen, not only off the point but along the Swale as far as Elmley. Also in the Swale, Brent Geese and Red-breasted Merganser are regular, with occasionally rarer grebes and Eider. In recent years, the Harty road has become quite a mecca for the raptor watcher. On any one day in winter, it is quite possible to see Marsh and Hen Harriers, Peregrine, Merlin, Kestrel, possibly Sparrowhawk and Common Buzzard, and in some winters Rough-legged Buzzard, as well as Little, Barn and Short-eared Owls.

Although the flocks of White-fronted Geese are often distant, there are opportunities to study them at closer range. Their evening flights, particularly across the setting sun, provide a memorable picture. In severe con-

Short-eared Owl

ditions, small flocks of other geese can be expected, like Bean, Pink-feet, or more rarely, Barnacle Geese. Grey geese species are often present in early January. Brent Geese frequently feed on the arable and, while flocks of Golden Plover favour the pasture.

Wheatear and an early Garganey may be seen before the end of March, when the flock of White-fronted Geese usually departs. One of the highlights of spring is the presence of a large flock of Black-tailed Godwits, while the bubbling call of Whimbrel is another typical sound, as they pause to feed en route north. The concentration of over 3,500 pairs of Black-headed Gulls in the mouth of Windmill Creek is another impressive sight. A few pairs of Common Terns breed on the saltmarsh between Windmill Creek and Harty. Summer is quieter, though Avocets and quite a few ducks now breed successfully, particularly within both the Elmley and Swale NNRs, and at Oare. The Avocet young are always a joy to watch, as are the crèches of downy young Shelduck.

Autumn commences early with the appearance of returning migrant waders, like the freshwater sandpipers and stints. By mid-August, the numbers and variety of passerine migrants increase, with species like Whinchat quite widely scattered and warblers and flycatchers seemingly more concentrated along the coastal strip. If the wind veers northwest, it is a good time to seawatch. Movements of both Arctic and Great Skuas are regular. By October, Pomarine Skua can also be anticipated. Gannets, auks, terns and flocks of waders returning for the winter all add to the interest, along with the visible migration of Skylarks, corvids and finches. Migrant raptors also feature at this time.

Main Birdwatching Zones

The principal areas of interest are largely determined by available access. There is no public right of way over Eastchurch Marshes, between Capel Fleet and Windmill Creek, an area that frequently attracts wintering White-fronted Geese, Mute and Bewick's Swans. Several footpaths over Harty and Leysdown Marshes provide better access to the eastern end of the island.

Elmley NNR, including Elmley Marshes RSPB reserve, is dealt with specifically, while the eastern block is described in four parts: the coastal strip between Warden Point and Shellness; the Swale NNR; Capel Fleet and Leysdown Marshes and, on the south side of the Swale, Oare Marshes LNR.

ELMLEY NATIONAL NATURE RESERVE (Map 3a)

Elmley forms a major part of the Swale marshes, which are of international importance for wildlife. This reserve is unique in that it is the first NNR to be both wholly owned and managed by an organisation with farming roots, approved by EN to manage an NNR. The 930 ha of the reserve make Elmley the largest farmland NNR in the English lowlands.

Habitat

The main area of the reserve consists of grazing marsh divided by a network of ditches and fleets, some of which are reed-lined. Outside the seawall boundary, the reserve is fringed by saltmarsh and intertidal mud. The grassland is managed by carefully managed cattle and sheep grazing to produce a variety of subtly different habitats. Water levels in the fleets and ditches are controlled, which is essential for sustaining wildlife. Feeding birds, rare plants and numerous insect species depend on the brackish conditions. Among the many rare insects is the rare rove beetle *Emus hirtus*, which also occurs on the neighbouring RSPB reserve. Saltmarsh provides a natural defence against the erosive power of the sea, as well as high-tide roosting opportunities for ducks and waders. In summer, plants like golden samphire and sea lavender add patches of yellow and mauve respectively to this attractive landscape.

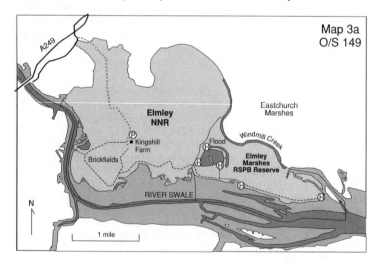

Species

In winter, Marsh and Hen Harriers, as well as Short-eared Owl, hunt over the long grass, while flooded areas attract large numbers of Wigeon and other duck and wader species. Golden Plover feed on the pasture and flocks of several hundred are often present. In summer, the short-grazed grassland, with ditches full of water, encourages high densities of

Redshank and Lapwing to breed. Yellow Wagtail also breeds successfully. It is often during autumn when rare vagrants appear. In recent years these have included Greater Yellowlegs and Kent's first Pallid Harrier.

ELMLEY MARSHES RSPB RESERVE (Map 3a)

Habitat

As part of the NNR, the reserve also includes pasture, dissected by reed-lined fleets, with no hedgerows and few trees. The area managed by the RSPB, which is bordered by the Swale to the south and Windmill Creek to the north, includes the 'flood', which is essentially flooded grazing land. Water depth is controlled by pumping to provide optimal feeding and roosting conditions for wildfowl and waders. On the remaining fields, numerous pools and seasonal floods have been created, which are allowed to dry out during the course of the spring to reveal lots of muddy edges. These wet margins provide important habitats for insects and feeding sites for birds, especially ducklings and wader chicks. Here, and elsewhere on the reserve, grazing by cattle and sheep is carefully controlled by the wardens to provide the right conditions for birds and other wildlife. The livestock are moved and restricted to certain areas at different periods, to create either nest-hiding tussocks, particularly for Redshank and wildfowl, or short swards of grass for grazing Wigeon and nesting Lapwing.

As a result of the flooding, the reserve now holds not only a variety of wintering and breeding bird populations, but also provides a sheltered haven for huge numbers of roosting waders during high tide.

The five hides are strategically sited, not only to overlook the flood, but also for viewing the estuary. The tidal range is significant in the Swale and the vast area of mud attracts feeding waders and dabbling duck at low tide. At high tide, there may well be grebes and diving duck to be seen, depending on the season.

The orchard and surrounding trees at Kingshill Farm provide welcome cover for passerines in this almost treeless landscape and have attracted numerous migrants, including Golden Oriole, Red-backed Shrike, and Barred and Yellow-browed Warblers. Long-eared Owl has become a more frequent visitor to the orchard in recent years. Water Voles are common on the marshes and numerous rare invertebrates are associated with the brackish water dykes. Notable recent colonists include the Scarce Emerald and Small Red-eyed Damselflies.

Species

Winter probably provides some of the most spectacular sights, certainly in terms of sheer numbers. A stooping Peregrine over the flood may disturb thousands of duck and waders. At times there may be up to ten duck species, with average peak counts in recent years of 15,000 Wigeon, 2,900 Teal, 900 Pintail and 425 Shoveler. Such large numbers of Pintail usually occur during high spring tides, especially during strong winds, when they seek refuge from the rough weather on the estuary where they normally feed. Waders use the flood for roosting at high tide and impressive numbers of species like Dunlin, Grey Plover and Bar-tailed Godwit are often present. Migrant freshwater waders like Spotted Redshank and Greenshank sometimes overwinter. In recent years,

Avocets have wintered on the Swale, with numbers increasing to 400 in February, as passage birds returning to their breeding sites stopover on the estuary. Curlew often feed in the grass north and east of the flood.

As you scan over Windmill Creek, it would be surprising if either a Marsh or Hen Harrier, or a Short-eared Owl did not appear, while in some winters a Rough-legged Buzzard may hunt there. From the Swale or Spitend hides, species such as Red-breasted Merganser, Goldeneye and occasionally Eider, or a rarer grebe may be seen, when the tide is high. As the water level drops, waders leave the safety of the flood to feed on the mud. Rock Pipist feed along the rocky edges. Sadly, Lapland Buntings, which used to be regular winter visitors are now scarce.

During March the numbers of wintering duck decrease quite rapidly, though Shoveler numbers may increase for a while, when migrants drop in. Other winter visitors also disperse. By the end of the month, early migrants like Wheatear and Garganey may have arrived, while the build-up of Black-tailed Godwits will have commenced, over 1,000 may be present in March. Other migrant waders on their way north pause briefly to feed, and by late April and early May passerine migrants, like Whinchat, may be perched on the fence posts or wire, while Reed Warblers sing from the reed-lined ditches.

During May many waders are in their splendid summer plumages. Ruff, in particular, are quite spectacular, while the aptly named 'Dusky' (Spotted) Redshank is another most attractive wader worth looking for. It is a good time for rarities, with occasional sightings of species like Marsh Sandpiper and almost annual visits by Temminck's Stint, while a trip of Dotterel may be present on the pasture for a few days. A Spoonbill or two may also appear and join the now regular Little Egrets.

June, also, produces the occasional unexpected rarity, like Great Reed Warbler, while on a more regular basis it is a time when ducklings and newly fledged waders are evident. Passerine species too, like Yellow Wagtail, will be busy feeding their short-tailed youngsters. The Black-headed Gull colony, which can be viewed from the Spitend hide, is a particularly noisy hive of activity at this time.

As far as waders are concerned, spring moves imperceptibly into autumn, as returning migrants reappear. By mid-June the first Spotted Redshanks and Green Sandpipers are back, followed early in July by Little Stint and Curlew Sandpiper, in varying numbers. The adults appear first, followed by the fresh-plumaged youngsters a month or so later. It is not unusual to identify 20 or more wader species during August and September. Careful scrutiny may occasionally reveal rarer visitors like Pectoral Sandpiper and Red-necked Phalarope, or vagrants from both east and west, such as Oriental Pratincole and Wilson's Phalarope.

As autumn progresses, Marsh and possibly Montagu's Harriers may be seen 'sailing' over the marshes with barely a flap, while delicately attractive Little Gulls and Black Terns also visit the flood. The eclipse plumages of the various dabbling duck provide identification puzzles, but careful observation may reveal a Garganey resting in the grass or feeding in the shallows. The roost of Spotted Redshanks may number 100 or more birds, while the calls of Whimbrel and Greenshank are frequently heard.

By late September and early October, wintering waders slowly replace the migrants, and other winter visitors, like Hen Harrier, Merlin, Peregrine and Short-eared Owl start to reappear.

WARDEN POINT and SHELLNESS (Map 3b)

Habitat

The 4 mile stretch of coast, either side of Leysdown, comprises an interesting variety of habitats. It rises from the shell spit at Shellness to about 30 m at Warden Point, where the London clay forms unstable, crumbling cliffs, rich in fossils. The cliff top is grassed, with scrub and bramble, while a few trees and shrubs grow in the mature gardens, all providing shelter and food for migrant passerines, particularly in autumn. Hens Brook and the sycamore-lined Second Avenue, west of Warden Point, are much favoured by warblers and crests.

Between Leysdown and Muswell Manor, there is a pitch-and-putt golf course, further grassland, with hawthorn scrub and a few plantations of trees. Towards Shellness, beyond the chalets, is a small sandy beach, backed by marram grass. Beyond the hamlet, which is strictly private, lies the shell spit. Falls of autumn passerine migrants often concentrate in the vegetation planted in the chalet gardens and the trees surrounding Muswell Manor.

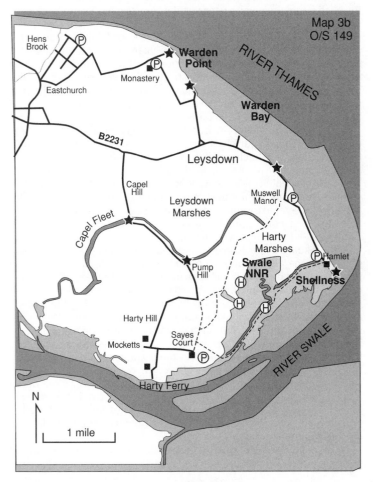

Species

Offshore, between Leysdown and the point, flocks of Great Crested Grebes often gather to feed in winter, whilst up to 300 Red-throated Divers are occasionally seen. Small flocks of dabbling duck often rest on the sea, drifting into the Swale as the tide rises.

While the mudflats are exposed, large numbers of waders and Brent Geese feed. As the mud becomes covered, many of these birds can be seen well, close to the shore, before they fly towards Shellness and into the Swale. If a Purple Sandpiper is present, it can usually be seen feeding with the Turnstone. Good numbers of waders roost on the shell spit at the point or further up the Swale at Harty Ferry. Others fly farther, to Elmley, while some roost on the field close to the rough road, behind the coastal chalets; a spot to which Merlin is also attracted. Around 1,000 Brent Geese winter, but the feeding flocks may be well scattered. At high tide, however, they often gather on the arable land, where they continue to feed. Careful observation of this flock may produce examples of the pale-bellied race or the even rarer Black Brant, whilst the rare and extremely attractive Red-breasted Goose has occurred.

The sandy beach and small area of marram grass, between the last of the chalets and the hamlet, occasionally attracts a few Snow Buntings, as does the shingle spit, but Shore Lark is a rare visitor. A Stonechat or two can be expected along the coastal strip and Rock Pipits feed along the ditches in the saltmarsh. In March, particularly late in the month, it is sometimes possible to witness the departure of wader flocks, as they set off for northern Europe. It is now that the first Wheatear of spring can also be anticipated. Migrant Whimbrel may well be heard calling; they some-times stop and feed on the mussel beds exposed at low tide just off Shellness. Common and Little Terns arrive from late April.

Spring visible migration can be well observed from above Warden Bay during fine weather and light southwest winds, when movements of wag-tails, hirundines and finches may occasionally produce a rarity like Serin. Similar winds may produce falls of warblers, including the occasional Wood Warbler, which the sycamores in Second Avenue may attract.

In autumn, there are frequent opportunities to observe migration. This may involve seabirds, waders arriving from northern Europe or westerly movements of corvids, finches and other passerines, many of which coast west — following the shoreline.

Arctic Skua can be expected from late July, and by mid-August a strong passage may involve up to 100 or more birds in a day. Seabird movements are dependent on the wind veering into the northerly quar-ter and even a light wind in August will initiate some movement. The best viewing is probably from Shellness, where you can sit below the seawall, as the skuas often follow the coast from Herne Bay into the Swale. Some continue west and probably migrate overland. It is often possible to observe them thermalling high over the mouth of the estuary. Others fly back out of the Swale, often close to the point, sometimes alighting on the sea, where small flocks form. Manx Shearwaters can also be seen well, particularly when the tide is high, and they too may fly out of the Swale. Small groups of migrant waders, like Curlew Sandpiper, can some-times be seen feeding on the mud, while flocks of Knot and Bar-tailed Godwits may occasionally be seen arriving from the northeast, often fly-ing into southwest winds.

In September, peaks of up to 100 Great Skuas may occur and there is always the possibility of the rare Long-tailed Skua. Sandwich, Common and Little Terns are regular, as are a few Arctic, but normally later in the month, while Black Terns occasionally form large flocks, sometimes roosting on the shell spit. In strong northerly winds and inclement conditions Sooty Shearwater is a possibility. With a northeasterly influence, particularly in such conditions, falls of migrant passerines are also anticipated. Common warblers, flycatchers and chats often occur. Any small patch of vegetation, including the trees around Muswell Manor, may attract rarer species like Red-backed Shrike or possibly Bluethroat, whilst October has produced Red-breasted Flycatcher, Pallas's Warbler and Rustic Bunting. On a more regular basis, the low vegetation close to the point blockhouse, may be alive with Goldcrests after a good fall. Another good area to find passerine migrants, such as Pied Flycatchers, crests and warblers, is where the land rises at Warden Point. The Monastery gardens and the trees around the caravan park are all worth checking, as are Hens Brook and the Second Avenue sycamores. Wood Warbler is regular in August and Yellow-browed Warbler virtually annual here in late September–early October.

Passage in October tends to produce a wider range of seabirds. Pomarine Skua is regular in small numbers and, like the other skuas, occasionally rests on the sea at the mouth of the Swale. Strong winds may initiate large movements of Gannets and Kittiwakes, and occasionally produce rarer species, like Sabine's Gull and possibly Storm Petrel. In northeast winds, watching from Warden Point can be more profitable, as birds seem to fly more readily into the Thames. Movements of the large auks — Guillemot and Razorbill — are often more obvious from here, given the extra height. In inclement conditions, seawatching from your car may be a practical solution and parking it on the seawall, between Leysdown and Muswell Manor, is often a good alternative. Flocks of Brent Geese can be seen arriving, often with Wigeon and other dabbling ducks. Raptors like Hen Harrier, Peregrine, Merlin and occasionally Rough-legged Buzzard, along with Short-eared Owl, follow the coastline west and are best seen from Shellness. Seaduck like Common Scoter and Eider often occur, while Velvet Scoter and Long-tailed Duck are occasionally seen. Movements of the commoner diurnal migrants may involve daily totals of several thousand Starlings and Chaffinches, and hundreds of Lapwings, Skylarks, thrushes and corvids. It is in northwest winds, again, that the most concentrated movements occur. Northerly storms in late October and November may produce rarer seabirds, like Leach's Petrel, Little Auk and possibly Grey Phalarope.

SWALE NATIONAL NATURE RESERVE (Map 3b)

Habitat

The Swale NNR includes an extensive strip of some 220 ha of the old grazing marsh, once typical of the North Kent Marshes, adjacent to the seawall between Shellness Hamlet and Harty Ferry. Three hides are open to the public, providing views over areas of flooded marshland that are particularly attractive to freshwater waders and other waterbirds. Bunds have been created and the water levels in some of the main wet areas can be controlled by the use of permanent pumps. Limited access to the reserve is signed from the seawall and in winter it is generally necessary to wear wellingtons to negotiate the wetter areas. One noticeable feature is the scattering of raised humps around the reserve, which are the result of ancient salt workings. These used to be a common feature throughout the marshes of Sheppey.

The grazing marsh is intersected by freshwater or brackish ditches and attracts varied and interesting populations of plants and animals. Grass Snakes and Slow-worms are common, although rarely seen, whilst the brackish ditches and, in particular, the fleet alongside the seawall, contain Smooth Newts, dragonflies, Rudd and Water Voles. Marsh Frog is abundant throughout the reserve and extremely vocal in summer, whilst the seawall is a good area in most summers for butterflies, including Gatekeeper, Small Heath, Meadow Brown and skippers, often in very high numbers.

Swale NNR incorporates saltmarsh, protected by a 800 yard-long spit, composed of cockleshells, which is still extending southwest. The shell spit produces a distinctive flora and fauna, including the rare Ray's knott-grass, and breeding Ringed Plovers and Little Terns. The broad stretch of tidal sand and mudflats is rich with invertebrate life. In winter, the bivalves, marine worms and snails form the principal food of many hundreds of waders, while the eelgrasses above the low-water mark provide an important food source for Brent Geese. The saltings are particularly rich in plant life. Common cord-grass is dominant, with saltmarsh grasses and glassworts well represented. Other abundant species include sea aster, sea lavender, sea purslane and golden samphire, which all take their turn to flower and in turn attract a myriad of butterflies, moths and other insects, including the scarce Ground Lackey Moth.

Species

As elsewhere on lowland Sheppey, winter is of particular interest, but the improved habitat within the reserve now offers greater attraction for migrant and breeding birds as well. A walk along the seawall adjacent to the reserve is invariably a pleasant experience at any season, and affords good views across the saltings into the Swale and to the mainland of Faversham and Oare beyond. In wet winters, bird numbers build up quickly and often peak at 5,000 Wigeon, 800 Teal, 300 Mallard, 100 Shoveler, 80 Gadwall, 5,000 Golden Plover and 3,000 Lapwing, with lower numbers of other wetland birds.

As well as providing feeding and resting places for thousands of wintering ducks and waders, the saltings support a winter roost for as many as 20 Hen Harriers. Twite used to feed in the saltmarsh and around the car park, but they have become very scarce, while in the grass on the other side of the seawall, Lapland Buntings occasionally winter, but they too are now scarce. Hearing their distinctive *tuc-a-tuc teu* call is often the easiest way to locate the species. If you enjoy being alone with the sea, sky and wildlife, this is an ideal place to visit at any time of the year.

CAPEL FLEET and LEYSDOWN MARSHES (Map 3b)

Habitat

This area, now a mixture of grazing marsh and arable, is dominated by Harty Hill, some 25 m high and the fairly broad, reed-lined Capel Fleet, which stretches from Leysdown Marshes to Bells Creek. Much of the area can be scanned from Capel Hill to the north, Harty Hill in the south or

Pump Hill towards the east. A few hedgerows and groups of trees remain and others are being created, to provide shelter for birds and other forms of animal life, but many of the elms that once dominated the landscape have gone.

Species

Although a good variety of species can be seen throughout the year, it is probably winter that offers the greatest interest. Between January and late March, up to 500 White-fronted Geese usually graze the fields. If they choose the Eastchurch Marshes they will be distant, but on Leysdown Marshes they are more approachable along the public footpaths. Scanning from Capel Hill is one way of locating the flocks. In severe conditions, small numbers of the rarer geese may also be present, plus a few Whooper Swans to supplement the regular small flock of Bewick's. Golden Plover and Lapwing feed on the arable fields and pasture either side of the Harty road, often numbering several thousand. A few Ruff occasionally winter along Capel Fleet, where Redshank and Snipe are regularly seen from the Harty road. Marsh and Hen Harriers, Merlin, Peregrine and Short-eared Owl often hunt along the fleet, while one or two Stonechats regularly winter and Corn Buntings gather in flocks to feed, sometimes perching on the powerlines. Towards dusk a Barn Owl will often appear.

Marsh Harrier

Whilst there are berries in the few roadside hedgerows, Redwings and Fieldfares will remain to feed. A Little Owl is often perched in the dead elms close to Sayes Court. From here it is possible to walk to the seawall and along the Swale, or inland across Harty Marshes to Muswell Manor. Within this area, one or two Merlins, several Marsh and Hen Harriers and Short-eared Owls regularly hunt and it is not unusual to see a Merlin associating with a Hen Harrier on a hunting foray, hoping that maybe a Meadow Pipit will take flight. On occasions a few Hen and 10–15 Marsh Harriers roost near the eastern end of Capel Fleet, when they can be viewed from the elevated parking area by the Harty road at Pump Hill.

At other times of year, that part of Capel Fleet visible from the Harty road has attracted a variety of interesting species, including rare waders like Black-winged Stilt and Pectoral Sandpiper in midsummer, and on one occasion a Black-headed Bunting. In early autumn the rarer Montagu's Harrier is occasionally seen.

OARE MARSHES LOCAL NATURE RESERVE (Map 3c)

Habitat

Oare Marshes LNR, managed by the Kent Wildlife Trust, supports a wide variety of plants, birds and other wildlife. It comprises nearly 70 ha of traditional grazing marsh, reedbed and saltmarsh, dissected by freshwater and brackish dykes. The Swale flows along the northern boundary and is joined by Faversham Creek to the east, and at low tide the extensive mudflats attract many feeding ducks, waders and gulls. Careful management, which includes controlling the water levels and varying the amounts of livestock grazing, not only produces a variety of vegetation heights, but also creates suitable grazing marsh habitat for breeding

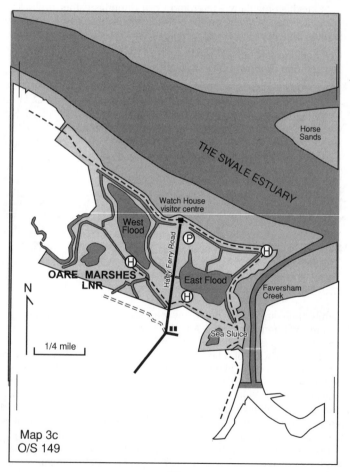

Map 3c
O/S 149

waders like Redshank and Lapwing. The floods, man-made pools and islands attract a wide variety of wintering and migrant wader and duck species, a number of which also nest. Among the wild flowers growing on the marsh is the scarce slender hare's-ear.

Species

The pattern of birdlife on Oare is similar to that on different parts of the Isle of Sheppey. However, there is the added advantage of having easy access to a comparatively small area in which birds are concentrated. In winter, the floods hold good numbers of Teal, Wigeon and a few elegant Pintail, with increased numbers of waders flying in to roost during high tide, including Redshank, Dunlin and Grey Plover. A few Little Egrets are often present. Raptors that can be anticipated include Marsh and Hen Harriers, Merlin and Peregrine, which hunt in the area, sometimes visiting from across the Swale. The occasional Common Buzzard is seen, whilst both Short-eared and Barn Owls can be seen hunting, silently, low over the ground. Bittern and Water Rail may winter in the reedbeds, from which the 'pinging' calls of Bearded Tits can be heard. Rock Pipits frequent the rocky foreshore and a few Water Pipits winter on the marsh, often attaining their attractive breeding plumage before they depart in late March or early April. By then the first spring migrants — Sand Martin, Wheatear and perhaps a Garganey — can be anticipated, while Little Ringed Plover, Whimbrel and Greenshank will be among the first migrant waders. A few scarcer waders like Wood and Curlew Sandpiper and possibly Temminck's Stint may make brief visits in May. By this time the resident waders, Oystercatcher, Ringed Plover, Lapwing and Redshank, will be nesting or have young, along with at least six species of duck and Little Grebe, the diminutive young of which are always a delight to see. Water Rail is resident in the reedbeds, which also attract breeding Sedge and Reed Warblers, and Yellow Wagtails nest on the grazing marsh.

The prolonged autumn passage of waders provides plenty of opportunities to test your identification skills, with the adults arriving a few weeks before the fresh-plumaged juveniles. Numbers and variety, as always, depend on the prevailing weather systems, but by mid-July a few

Black-tailed Godwits

Little Stints, Wood and Curlew Sandpipers should be present, along with the commoner Greenshank, Whimbrel and Common Sandpiper. Through August and into September, in excess of 20 wader species will be present, particularly during high tide. Numbers of Black-tailed Godwits may peak at around 800 and in recent years rarer visitors have included White-rumped Sandpiper and Red-necked Phalarope.

At this time an Osprey may sometimes fish along the Swale and situated as it is, close to the mouth of the estuary, passage seabirds like skuas, gulls and terns frequently fly upriver, some occasionally visiting the reserve. In northerly winds, seawatching from the seawall by Faversham Creek can be rewarding. The movement of waders and a few Little Egrets to and from their high-tide roosts along the Swale, can also be impressive. In late autumn species like Sabine's Gull and Grey Phalarope have visited the reserve.

Timing

The state of the tide has a considerable influence on the behaviour of the birds that feed in the estuary, so timing is particularly crucial. As the mud becomes covered with water, shortly before high tide, the waders in particular fly to their respective roosts, returning again as the mud becomes exposed. High tide is also the best time to see those species that swim on the sea or in the Swale, as they are then much closer to shore.

In autumn, passerine migrants are best located in the early morning, whilst seawatching is generally most productive shortly after the wind veers northwest. Afternoon movements can be quite impressive, if the wind veers around noon. Some passage continues next day, provided the wind remains from the north, but it is likely to be less marked thereafter. Visible migration of passerines tends to be heaviest in the morning, although it can continue throughout the day, if a northwest wind keeps blowing. Late-afternoon visits are necessary to see the Hen Harriers coming to roost, and also to observe a Barn Owl hunting or perched on a fence post.

Access

From the M2 or A2 take the new A249, by-passing Iwade and over Kingsferry Bridge onto the Isle of Sheppey. About 1 mile beyond the bridge take the rough road to the right, signposted Elmley Marshes RSPB reserve (Map 3a). Follow the road for 2 miles to Kingshill Farm. The extensive landscape either side of the road is part of Elmley NNR. To prevent disturbance to wildlife, visitors are requested to view from their vehicles. There is a toilet block and information board at the car park. The reserve is open daily, except Tuesdays, 9am–9pm or sunset when earlier. It is a further mile or so to the flood, with its three hides. Those with mobility problems may request permission to drive this stretch and the nearest hide is relatively close, although a gate limits wheelchair access. The Swale and Spitend hides are a further 800 yards, and another mile respectively.

To reach the eastern end of the island, continue along the A249, beyond the Elmley turning, for just over 800 yards. Turn right at the roundabout and follow the B2231 towards Eastchurch and Leysdown.

For Warden Point (Map 3b), take the Eastchurch road rather than the bypass, turn left in the village, then first right after less than 800 yards. About 2 miles along the road, just 400 yards from the cliff edge, there is ample room to park on the right, where the buses turn. For Second Avenue and Hens Brook drive back towards Eastchurch for about 1 mile.

As you negotiate the second sharp bend, turn right into Third Avenue. Second Avenue — lined with sycamore trees — is on the left. Hens Brook is at the northwest end of First Avenue. A rough track, south from the Warden Point parking area, leads back to the B2231 close to Leysdown.

For Capel Fleet and Shellness (Map 3b) take the Eastchurch bypass for Leysdown. The Harty Ferry road, leading to Capel Fleet and Sayes Court, is reached via turning to the right off the B2231, just over a mile east of Eastchurch. It is about 4 miles (6 km) to the Ferry Inn at Harty. After just under a mile, park and scan Capel Fleet to the right. Passing bays, along the next mile or so of narrow road, provide useful scanning points to survey the marshes, but don't park in them if the road is busy. There is a good, slightly raised parking area at the end of this stretch, at Pump Hill, near to which Marsh and Hen Harriers sometimes roost. Continue along the winding road, but instead of turning right to the Ferry Inn, carry straight on and park by the old church at Sayes Court. Follow the footpath north, then southeast to the seawall, or further north then northeast across Harty Marshes to Muswell Manor.

To reach Shellness (Map 3b), follow the B2231 through Leysdown to the sea, where you can view the mudflats. The road runs along the seawall for nearly 600 yards, turns inland to Muswell Manor, then left back to the seawall, where it is possible to park. There is a further car park another three-quarters-of-a-mile along the rough road, behind the coastal chalets, before it enters the private Shellness Hamlet. Please respect the privacy of the hamlet by not trespassing. From here you can walk east to the shore, then south to the point, or directly south to the point alongside the saltmarsh of Swale NNR. Alternatively, to visit the hides in Swale NNR, walk west along the seawall public footpath towards Sayes Court for about three-quarters-of-a-mile. You can also continue to Sayes Court, where another right of way leads back across Harty Marsh to Muswell Manor, a circuit of over 6 miles.

For visible migration in spring, turn left along Warden Bay road just before you reach Leysdown. Continue along Jetty Road where you can park on the low slope, as the land rises towards Warden Point, and overlook Warden Bay.

Oare Marshes LNR (Map 3c) is on the south side of the Swale at Harty Ferry. From the A2, at the west end of Faversham, take the B2045 for just over a mile and turn left into Oare. After 200 yards turn right and follow the narrow winding road out of Oare for about a mile to the Kent Wildlife Trust car park below the river wall. Two new hides, with access for those with mobility problems, provide good views across the estuary and over the East flood. A footpath circuits the entire eastern half of the reserve and there are seats at intervals on the trail. Another footpath leads to a hide looking north over the West flood. Both sides can also be viewed from the seawall and parking bays provide good views over much of the reserve for observers with disabilities. The Watch House visitor centre, which has displays on the history and natural history of the site, is open at weekends and during bank holidays.

Calendar

Resident: Little Grebe, Little Egret, Cormorant (non-breeders), Greylag Goose, Shelduck, Gadwall, Teal, Shoveler, possibly Eider (non-breeders), Water Rail, Oystercatcher, Ringed Plover, Snipe, Redshank, Barn Owl, Meadow Pipit, Corn Bunting.

December–February: Red-throated Diver, Great Crested Grebe, possibly Bittern, Bewick's Swan, White-fronted and Brent Geese, winter duck including peak numbers of Wigeon and Pintail, Red-breasted Merganser, Marsh and Hen Harriers, Sparrowhawk, possibly Common and Rough-legged Buzzards, Merlin, Peregrine, Golden and Grey Plovers, Knot, Sanderling, possibly Purple Sandpiper, Bar-tailed Godwit, Turnstone, Short-eared Owl, possibly Shore Lark, Rock Pipit, Stonechat, Bearded Tit, possibly Twite and Lapland Bunting, Snow and Corn Buntings.

March–May: Brent Goose, Garganey, Marsh Harrier, Avocet, Temminck's Stint, Ruff, Black-tailed Godwit (peak March–April), Whimbrel, Spotted Redshank, Yellow Wagtail, Wheatear.

June–July: Breeding duck, including Garganey, possibly non-breeding Wigeon and Pintail, Marsh Harrier, breeding waders including Avocet, breeding Common and Little Terns, Yellow Wagtail, Sedge and Reed Warblers.

August–November: Manx and possibly Sooty Shearwaters, possibly Storm and Leach's Petrels, Gannet, possibly Rough-legged Buzzard, Marsh and possibly Montagu's Harriers, Hen Harrier and Merlin (from October), Little and Temminck's Stints, Curlew Sandpiper, Bar-tailed Godwit, Whimbrel, Spotted Redshank, Greenshank, Wood Sandpiper, Turnstone, Pomarine (October), Arctic and Great Skuas, Little and possibly Sabine's Gulls, Kittiwake, Sandwich, Common, Arctic, Little and Black Terns, large auks, possibly Puffin and Little Auk, Short-eared Owl, Whinchat, Wheatear, migrant warblers, including possibly Yellow-browed, Pied and possibly Red-breasted Flycatchers, and from October possibly Twite and Lapland Bunting, and Snow Bunting.

4 CANTERBURY RING WOODS

OS Explorer 150

Habitat

The Blean woodlands form a broad arc, on the London clay, north and northwest of Canterbury. A considerable amount of the once vast Forest of Blean remains, and though there are few stands of really mature oaks, there is much 100–180-year-old high forest. Oak and sweet chestnut predominate, with smaller areas of other broad-leaved trees, like hornbeam — favoured by Hawfinches — alongside a number of well-established, as well as young, conifer plantations.

It is the variety and extent of woodland here that is important. Many woodland birds depend on a range of different-aged trees, with mature stands as well as dead wood. Plantations, sometimes dominated by sweet chestnut, usually consist of mixed blocks of coppice, or coppice

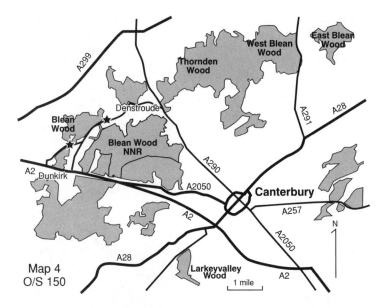

Map 4
O/S 150

with standards, separated by broad rides. The blocks are coppiced in rotation, creating open, heath-like clearings; a habitat, in Kent, that is favoured by Nightjar. To the east of the city there is somewhat similar woodland, on Thanet sands, but now much disturbed by replanting and sand excavation.

To the south are scattered woods on the slopes and plateaux of the North Downs. Their mainly calcareous nature contrasts greatly with the more acidic Blean. The variety of plant species is typically greater and it is here you can find the best displays of spring woodland flowers, with at best a profusion of orchids among the more common primroses, blue-bells, wood anemones and dog's mercury. The lady orchid is probably the star attraction for botanists. In Britain this species is only found in Kent, with the best colonies in the woods south of Canterbury.

Species

The downland woods probably hold higher densities of birds throughout the year, but the vastness of Blean is an attraction in itself. Woodland in winter is comparatively quiet. All of the resident species are present, but they are less vocal and more difficult to locate. Mixed flocks of tits move quite extensively as they forage for food. Finches and thrushes, includ-ing wintering Fieldfares and Redwings, may roost in denser, more sheltered woods, whilst Crossbill and Siskin are especially attracted to conifers like the larch. In some winters, the rare Red Kite is recorded, but Sparrowhawk is much more likely to be seen, with infrequent visits by a Hen Harrier or Merlin from the marshes to the east or northwest. Another species that may be disturbed from the edges of the woodland rides is the Woodcock; the local breeding population is supplemented by wintering birds from the Continent.

The birdlife used to be particularly rich in summer, with good breed-ing populations of all three woodpeckers, including the scarcer Lesser Spotted Woodpecker, Tree Pipit, Nightingale and Nuthatch. However, the populations of some of these appear to fluctuate from year to year, whilst others have shown marked, almost inexplicable, declines in recent years. For instance, it is interesting to compare Nuthatch numbers. In a 310-ha area, there was a decline from the mid-1990s population of c.20 pairs to just one in 2001, eight the next year and four in 2003. Tree Pipit is no longer common, Redstart no longer breeds and Wood Warbler is a scarce visitor. Kent has over 25% of the British breeding population of Nightingale. The Blean Wood block alone holds over one per cent, with over 40 singing males, though density is patchy, the species being absent from extensive areas. The common woodland warblers and tits are well represented, Sparrowhawk continues to increase and Kestrel is another successful breeding raptor.

Nightingale

Fungi are one of the autumn attractions; the damp woods of the Blean area probably support a richer variety than the drier, chalk woods. Among the more conspicuous species are the colourful russulas and the aptly named stinkhorn.

Of the butterflies, Purple Hairstreak may be seen flying high among oaks, but sadly the Pearl-bordered Fritillary is now extinct here.

Main Birdwatching Zones

There are several different approaches to woodland birdwatching, depending on the time of year and the species you wish to see. Raptors often soar and are best seen from high vantage points; much of Blean Wood can be overlooked from the road between Dunkirk and Denstroude. Feeding flocks of passerines, particularly in winter, can often be seen quite easily by finding a site where the woodland narrows along a valley and a road crosses it. For example, try just south of Holly Hill in Blean Wood.

There are many attractive walks along the public footpaths in these woods, but in summer, when the foliage is dense, it is often a matter of hearing the birds first. It can be beneficial to sit quietly on the edge of a clearing, where there is a better chance of seeing birds as they sing or collect food. When water is in short supply, find where they drink, then sit and wait.

The following two areas combined should produce most of the woodland species to be expected in the Canterbury 'ring' woods: Blean Woods NNR and Larkeyvalley Wood.

BLEAN WOODS NNR (Map 4a)

This NNR of 509 ha comprises three reserves run respectively by the RSPB, the Woodland Trust and EN. They are managed by the RSPB in partnership with the other two bodies.

Habitat

About one-fifth of the reserve is sweet chestnut coppice, often with large amounts of silver birch, and occasionally a few beech. There are also extensive areas of tall oak forest, with an understorey of hazel, hornbeam, chestnut and other species. Management is aimed at establishing greater variety, including heathland. Some 9 ha, in two discrete blocks, has already been created. Other management includes the cutting of small coppice compartments, conversion of some coppice to oak forest, creation of glades and ponds, and widening of the rides, many of which are already fairly broad and grassy; while non-management entails allowing many of the oaks to die naturally of old age.

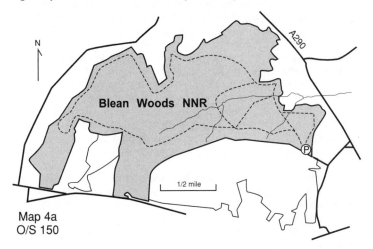

Map 4a
O/S 150

Bracken is generally abundant and heather is locally quite common. In recently coppiced areas, there is often a good display of common cow-wheat. This attractive plant is the food of caterpillars of the Heath Fritillary, one of Britain's rarest butterflies, which has scattered colonies throughout Blean forest, including Blean Woods NNR. On the edges of the forest rides, the flora is quite attractive in some places, with a good show of violets in spring. As the coppice regenerates, bramble, honeysuckle and other climbers develop into a tangled undergrowth favoured as nest sites by Garden and Willow Warblers, and Nightingales.

Several streams and drains flow through the wood. Most dry out in summer, but a man-made pond within the reserve remains flooded and attracts a variety of birds, including an occasional Kingfisher as the young disperse from their breeding areas.

Species

The quiet winter months are enlivened by parties of tits, as they search busily for food in their quest for survival. Blue and Great Tits are usually most numerous, with fewer Long-tailed, whilst Marsh Tit is now much less frequently seen. These mixed flocks often attract a few Goldcrests and Treecreepers. The drumming of the Great Spotted and the echoing 'yaffle' of the Green Woodpecker are common sounds, more frequent in taller forest. In fact, very few of the typical woodland species occur in the sweet chestnut at any time of year.

The first Chiffchaff is usually heard in the second half of March and heralds the appearance of the other warblers throughout April and May. The various species prefer different woodland types: Whitethroats are found in dense young coppice regrowth, with plenty of bramble; Garden and Willow Warblers typically select medium-age coppice; whilst Blackcap and Chiffchaff more often occur in high forest. Lesser Whitethroat is very scarce in Blean Wood and Grasshopper Warbler, which was formerly almost numerous, has disappeared from here, as elsewhere in Kent. Wood Warbler, is a scarce, sporadic visitor.

Nightingales are best seen in late April and early May, shortly after they arrive, but before leaf emergence conceals them. They are most easily located in young coppice or other dense undergrowth by their song, which can be heard throughout the day or night. Tree Pipit, another typical woodland summer visitor, is no longer common, but once found they are fascinating to watch, as they perform their parachuting song flights in recently coppiced clearings with standards.

In May, the last of the summer visitors arrive. Turtle Dove here is mainly found in coppice and conifer plantations in the middle years of their growth. Nightjar, however, is present only during the earliest years of the woodland management cycle, but some are attracted to the newly created heathland. A warm June evening is the ideal time to search for this species. The birds are sensitive to disturbance, so it is essential to keep to the rides, from where the churring, wing-clapping and *goo-ik* calls are easily heard. Such an evening is also a good time to look and listen for roding Woodcock.

From midsummer, as the adults become increasingly occupied with feeding their young and the leaves are full, it becomes much more difficult to observe woodland birds. Song also tails off rapidly. If a Crossbill invasion occurs, this is the period when they start to appear in the conifers. By late August, most of the visitors have departed and the long quiet autumn begins.

LARKEYVALLEY WOOD (Map 4b)

Habitat

Located on the slopes of a dry chalk valley, Larkeyvalley Wood has a rich and interesting flora. Mature beech forest is present, as is coppice of hazel, ash, hornbeam and other species, mostly under oak standards.

The thin chalk soils, in particular, support a diverse ground flora with several scarce plants. Where there is heavy shade, this may be sparse, but elsewhere there is a well-developed calcareous flora, including sanicle and woodruff. Fly and bird's-nest orchids are two of several orchid species present. The most abundant species of the woodland floor are probably dog's mercury, wood anemone and bluebell, while bramble is very apparent in recent clearings.

The wood is owned and managed, as a public open space, by the enlightened Canterbury City Council. Management has re-established a

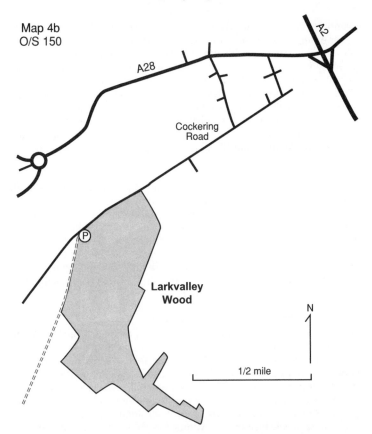

Map 4b
O/S 150

A28

Cockering
Road

A2

P

**Larkvalley
Wood**

N

1/2 mile

coppice regime in what had become rather neglected woodland, and has developed a system of widened rides through the wood. Vegetation has responded well to the cutting, with luxuriant growth of coppice and ground flora. Particularly noticeable in recently cut areas have been wood spurge and the rarer caper spurge, the latter normally regarded as an introduction to Britain, but quite possibly native here. The great storm of October 1987 affected this wood more than most around Canterbury, especially the areas of beech on thin chalk soils. Along with the coppicing, replanting and natural regeneration, a more varied younger plant structure now exists.

Species
Larkeyvalley Wood in winter can be alive with birds, far more so than many Kent woodlands. The stands of mature beech represent one of the most interesting areas; especially when there has been a heavy beech mast crop, these areas can hold well over 100 birds of several species. Blue, Great, Marsh and Coal Tits are generally all present, while Nuthatch is less common than formerly, but can sometimes be seen well as they move up and down the smooth boles of the beeches. Chaffinches and Bramblings add to the lively scene; on occasions 100 of the latter species alone have been seen feeding here.

A circuit of the wood reveals more species. This is one of the better woods in which to see the now scarce Hawfinch, although it is almost essential to know the calls, especially the loud *tic*, to locate them. All three woodpeckers are present, with Great Spotted the most numerous. Parties of Long-tailed Tits, often with attendant Goldcrests or Treecreepers, are frequently encountered. Jays seem quite common here and winter is probably the easiest time of year to see this colourful species well.

Spring sees the appearance of the common woodland warblers. Chiffchaff and Willow Warbler, Blackcap and Garden Warbler are the most frequent species here. Their relative abundance is likely to change as the coppicing programme progresses. Tree Pipits have rapidly become established in the clearings and Nightingales have recolonised the wood.

Timing

In wooded areas, early mornings are generally more productive at all times of year, as birds tend to sing and feed more actively then, and it is often less windy. The dawn chorus in May can be dominated by Nightingales, so much so that other species may be difficult to hear. Dusk visits are also recommended: in winter to locate roosts and hear Tawny Owls hooting, whilst Woodcock circle overhead and call from February onwards; and in late May to early June to hear Nightjars churring and see Woodcock roding — at this time of year it is usually 9pm before you can expect to hear either.

Access

To access Blean Woods NNR from Canterbury, take the A290 Whitstable road. After a mile-and-a-half turn left into Rough Common and follow the road for around 400 yards, where a track leads off to the right into the wood, marked by a brown tourist sign 'Blean Woods Nature Reserve'. The reserve car park is another 400 yards along this track. Five trails of varying lengths, including a dog-walkers' route, are way-marked by black, red, green, white and brown arrows on posts beside the paths. All are fairly level and relatively firm, even in winter. The green trail is usually suitable for wheelchair access. Reserve leaflets are on sale at the car park.

For Holly Hill follow the road north from Dunkirk for three-quarters of a mile, turn sharp left and drive southwest for another 400 yads to TR 078601.

For Larkeyvalley Wood (Map 4b) take the A28 Ashford road out of Canterbury. After crossing the bridge over the A2 dual carriageway, take the first left, St Nicholas Road, through a housing estate. At the T-junction 400 yards along this road, turn right and follow Cockering Road for about 1 mile, where the car park is visible on the left, at the edge of the wood. The many paths allow good access, but the steepness of the slopes makes the area unsuitable for those with mobility problems. A leaflet describing the site and the footpaths should be available at the car park.

Calendar

Resident: Sparrowhawk, Kestrel, Tawny Owl, all three woodpeckers, common woodland passerines, including Treecreeper, but relatively few Marsh Tits and Nuthatches, possibly Hawfinch.

December–February: Woodcock, feeding parties of tits, Treecreeper and Goldcrest, possibly Siskin and Crossbill.

March–May: possibly Hobby, Turtle Dove, Tree Pipit, Nightingale, common woodland warblers, possibly Wood Warbler.

June–July: Breeding residents and summer visitors, including Woodcock, Nightjar (Blean Woods), Lesser Spotted Woodpecker, Tree Pipit, Nightingale, occasionally Crossbill.

August–November: most breeding summer visitors depart by late August. Irruptive species such as Crossbill may be present and winter visitors like Woodcock and Siskin return.

5 STOUR VALLEY   OS Explorer 150

Habitat

The stretch of the Stour Valley that extends east from Sturry to Grove Ferry comprises one of the few remaining freshwater wetland areas in Kent, characterised by extensive reedbeds, shallow lagoons, well-established gravel pits, wet woodlands of willow and alders, marsh and grazing meadows.

On the north side of the river there is a footpath from Fordwich to Hersden Lake. The gravel pit at Westbere, used for sailing, is surrounded by reedbeds and mature willows and alders. Between there and the lake at Hersden the reedbeds are extensive, with grazing marsh south of the river and the wooded slopes of Trenleypark Wood beyond. In spring, this diverse habitat supports an almost unique dawn chorus of marsh and woodland species in close proximity. There is an equally diverse range of breeding species. Further east the Stodmarsh NNR, between Stodmarsh and Grove Ferry, is within a broad, open valley, with more extensive reedbeds, shallow lakes and grazing marsh.

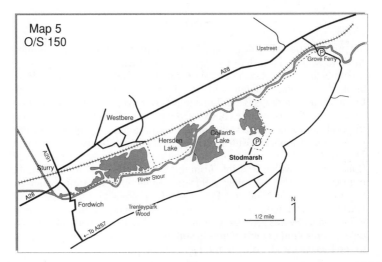

Species

With its proximity to the coast, this variety of wetland habitat attracts many different species. In winter it is not unusual for a diver, and occasionally a rarer grebe, to visit one of the lakes. In severe conditions any wintering Bitterns and Water Rails are often easier to see, while small flocks of Bewick's Swans, White-fronted Geese, and possibly Bean or Pink-footed Geese, may graze on the more open pastures or fly in to roost on the lakes at dusk. The cold-weather sawbills, Smew and Goosander, occasionally visit the lakes, which often hold some numbers of wintering Wigeon, Teal, Shoveler and Gadwall. Hen and Marsh Harriers regularly glide over the reedbeds, whilst Sparrowhawk, Merlin and possibly Short-eared Owl hunt along the valley. Water Rail is present but not easy to see, while a Kingfisher might be glimpsed as it flashes along the river. In the reedbeds, Bearded Tits proclaim their presence from time to time, with their distinctive 'pinging' calls, whilst bursts of song from the more secretive Cetti's Warbler can also be anticipated. Wintering Chiffchaffs are not uncommon.

Bearded Tit

Spring in the valley is announced by the arrival of an early Garganey or Sand Martin. From late March, the variety will increase, as passage migrants drop in and summer visitors arrive. Freshwater waders like Ruff, Spotted Redshank, Green and Wood Sandpipers can be expected. Common and perhaps Black Terns may hover over the lakes, while song from the reedbeds includes both Sedge and Reed Warblers, which breed in good numbers in the valley. Marsh Harriers flap and glide over the reeds, while a migrant Osprey or a few Hobbies can be expected. In late May and early June up to 40 Hobbies may hunt together, often over Collard's Lake, which is visible from the Stodmarsh Road, while a southern rarity may visit the valley at this time. In recent years rarities such as Red-footed Falcon, Collared Pratincole, Caspian Tern and Great Reed Warbler have all been seen, while Purple Heron and Spoonbill are scarce visitors. Mute Swans form large non-breeding flocks and with the remarkable colonisation of Little Egrets in southern Britain it is now quite usual to see this species feeding in the reed-fringed pools.

The volume of song diminishes as the breeding species busily feed their young. All too quickly the marshland waders return on their journey south. Many of the spring migrants can be expected again, some lingering for longer periods, as the autumn journey does not have quite the same urgency. Young Hobbies may be seen with the adults, as they learn the art of catching prey, while large numbers of hirundines and wagtails may gather to feed and roost in the reedbeds for a few days, before continuing their long journeys south. As autumn progresses, the winter visitors return.

Main Birdwatching Zones

Much of the Stour Valley can be visited via public rights of way, but human disturbance is one of the principal threats to some of the more sensitive breeding species. Access to Stodmarsh NNR is carefully controlled and more detailed information is given for that site, from both the Stodmarsh and Grove Ferry ends, with a few notes concerning Fordwich and Westbere under Additional Sites.

STODMARSH NNR (Map 5a)

Habitat

Stodmarsh NNR includes approximately 240 ha of alluvial marshland south of the Great Stour and the reedbeds are the largest in southeast England. The significance of the reserve is reflected in one of its

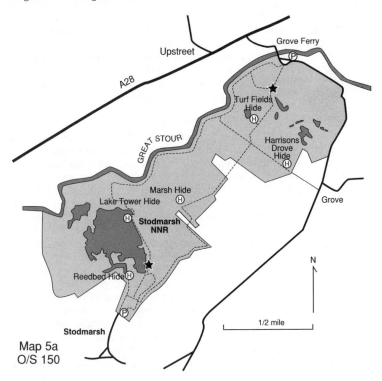

European designations as a Wetland Area of International Importance under the Ramsar Convention. The western end, near Stodmarsh, has three hides — Lake Tower, Marsh and Reedbed — that all provide good viewpoints. At the Grove Ferry end, EN has been responsible for significant improvements, not only for the wildlife, but also for observers. More freshwater lakes and reedbeds have been created, an excellent viewing ramp has been constructed and two more hides — the Turf Fields and Harrison Drove hides — erected. The latter overlooks a shallow lagoon, where waders and dabbling duck can be seen well as they feed.

EN owns the freehold of the reserve, at the south end of which there is a fine copse of alders. There is good public access along the flood protection barrier, known as the Lampen Wall, and along the river wall east to Grove Ferry. West of the Lampen Wall, where shallow, open water is surrounded by dense reeds and willows, the colliery tip forms a backdrop. Shingle-covered rafts attract Common Terns to breed. Recent bund-construction work has made it possible to control water levels and EN's management programme also includes reed harvesting and grazing the meadows with cattle. In addition, a small herd of Konik ponies is used to manage areas of willow scrub and other vegetation in the wetter areas. The Reedbed hide overlooks lagoons surrounded by reeds, in which you may be fortunate enough to have good views of a Water Rail and possibly a Bittern. An area of flooded meadow, which can be viewed from the Marsh hide, attracts dabbling duck and freshwater waders.

The wide range of aquatic plants include species like greater bladderwort, frogbit and flowering rush, which occur in some of the pools; greater spearwort and great water dock grow in the reed swamp, which is dominated by common reed. Another eye-catching species is the amphibious bistort, the pink flowers of which form an attractive spectacle in summer.

Other interesting aspects of wildlife include large numbers of bats, mainly Noctule, which feed over the lagoons in summer. The reserve is also rich with invertebrates, notably moths, flies, spiders and dragonflies, including relatively scarce species such as Hairy Dragonfly and Red-eyed Damselfly. Of the mammals the Water Vole is most frequently seen, often noisily crunching reed stems beside the Lampen Wall.

Species

Two of the principal winter attractions are the possibilities of seeing Bittern, as well as roosting Hen and Marsh Harriers. Up to ten or so of both these raptors have been seen flying low over the reeds before they drop in to roost at dusk, but Marsh Harrier has been commoner in recent years. The sites vary between years, often close to the colliery tip, but occasionally near the southern edge of the reedbed, east of the Lampen Wall, where the birds are relatively close, providing excellent viewing. Other winter specialities are White-fronted Goose and Bewick's Swan, although the latter has become relatively scarce. Water Pipit, which may often be seen from the Marsh and Harrison Drove hides, is regular, as is Siskin, which is usually found feeding in the alders, while the distinctive 'pinging' note of the resident Bearded Tits often emanates from the reedbeds. Bursts of Cetti's Warbler song may be heard from the willows amongst the reeds. In severe winters the opportunity to have good views of Bittern and also Water Rail increases, as larger numbers occur and they tend to become more confiding as they seek food.

In spring, an early Garganey may be attracted to the flooded meadow in front of the Marsh hide, or seen from the ramp feeding on the fringes of the lakes. Sand Martins can be expected by late March, when Chiffchaffs, which often overwinter, should be singing from the alders, or the dense sallow scrub at the other end of the Lampen Wall. By late April, a wide variety of summer visitors and passage migrants is normally present. Yellow Wagtails will be feeding in rough pasture and the song of Sedge and Reed Warblers echoes from the reeds. One of the most abundant breeding passerines is the Reed Bunting, a species which is present throughout the year, although the local breeders tend to disperse and numbers may be low for a short time, until autumn migrants and winter visitors replace them.

Several raptors can be anticipated in May, including Marsh Harrier, Hobby and possibly a migrant Osprey, while rarer species like Golden Oriole occasionally occur, and the wader pools at Grove Ferry are likely to attract scarcer species such as Temminck's Stint and Wood Sandpiper, or perhaps even a Marsh Sandpiper. Exceptionally, a Slender-billed Gull made a brief visit in 1999. Dawn and dusk visits can be profitable in late spring and early summer, when there is the possibility of hearing rarer species like Spotted Crake and the 'booming' of a Bittern, as well as Nightingale, although this species also sings in daylight. Bittern formerly bred but has been strictly a winter visitor for some years, although careful management may well encourage this wonderful species to breed here again. The intriguing, trilling song of the Water Rail and the fascinating drumming of the Snipe, when displaying, are also more commonly heard at dawn and dusk. June invariably produces a rare visitor or two, the Baillon's Crake in 1998 was the first live bird of this species to be identified in Kent.

As summer progresses, steadily more broods of young hatch and the adults become increasingly active, searching for food. A colony of Cormorants has increased to over 50 pairs in recent years and feeding birds fly constantly to the coast and back to collect food for their young. Common Terns should also be feeding young, but Little Terns are now scarce visitors from their coastal breeding colonies. Sitting on the Lampen Wall can be a delight as Bearded Tits zip by continuously, whilst numerous broods of ducklings paddle in the shallows of the lakes, which can be viewed from the ramp. By late August numbers of Yellow Wagtails and hirundines roosting in the reedbeds increase to hundreds and thousands respectively. In September, following a good breeding season, flocks in excess of 300 Bearded Tits may gather, occasionally erupting high into the air, and some move southwest to winter elsewhere in the country. When an easterly airstream brings rarer late-autumn passerines to the coast, a few may penetrate further inland, as Isabelline Shrike and Pallas's Warbler have done, but by mid-November there is usually greater anticipation for the return of the winter visitors.

Timing

Dusk visits are of particular interest in winter, while dawn and dusk visits in spring may well produce a few extra species. In spring and summer, early mornings are best for songbirds, but migrant waders feed all day. Visits towards dusk in early autumn are a must to see the large numbers of roosting hirundines, a much-favoured source of food for Hobbies that may be observed hunting them. Strong winds can be troublesome, fewer birds sing and wildfowl tend to shelter in the reeds.

Access

To reach the Stodmarsh end from Canterbury, take the A257 Sandwich road (Map 5). After about one-and-three-quarers of a mile turn left and follow Stodmarsh Road for just over 3 miles to the village of Stodmarsh. Turn left immediately after the Red Lion pub. There is a large car park for the reserve at TR 221609 (Map 5a), just over 400 yards along the track, which has a good tarmac surface. Please do not park in the village. There is also a log at the toilet block and a chalkboard, worth checking for recent sightings — enter your own observations as you leave. A short nature trail, designed for wheelchair users, takes you through willows and alders to the Lampen Wall then back to the car park. An alternative is to continue along the track on foot, which provides two options. Either continue straight on to the Reedbed hide, which is suitable for wheel-chair users or turn right onto the Lampen Wall, which provides excellent vantage points for viewing the reserve, including the Lake Tower hide. Walk the length of the Lampen Wall and a similar distance along the river wall to the east, before turning southeast across the grazing marsh, then southwest by the Marsh hide to complete a circuit of about 3 miles. There is also access to the reserve from Grove Ferry Inn, where there is a large car park, as well as toilet facilities, which operate on the RADAR key scheme. The viewing ramp is about 350 yards along the footpath and the Turf Fields hide is a similar distance further, both are accessible for wheelchair users. The Harrison Drove hide is another 400 yards along grass paths, which can be wet at times. This hide will also be wheelchair accessible once the access path has been improved.

Calendar

Resident: Little and Great Crested Grebes, Cormorant, Greylag and Canada Geese, Shelduck, Gadwall, Teal, Shoveler, Pochard, Tufted Duck, Water Rail, Snipe, Redshank (relatively few in winter), Kingfisher, Cetti's Warbler, Bearded Tit, Reed Bunting.

December–February: Little Egret, Bittern, White-fronted Goose, Wigeon, Hen and Marsh Harriers (regular roosts), Water Pipit, Siskin.

March–May: Little Egret, possibly Bittern or Spoonbill, Garganey, Marsh Harrier, possibly Osprey, Hobby, migrant freshwater waders (late April–May), Black Tern, Sand Martin, Yellow Wagtail, Sedge and Reed Warblers, possibly Golden Oriole (May).

June–July: Breeding wildfowl, waders and Common Tern, plus resident and summering passerines.

August–November: Little Egret, Marsh Harrier, Hobby, migrant freshwater waders (August–September), possibly Black Tern (August), roosting Sand Martins, Swallows and Yellow Wagtails (August–September), Bearded Tit (eruptive flocks September).

Habitat

Though heavily built-up, the Isle of Thanet (as it is sometimes referred to) has not only considerable interest for local birdwatchers, but also much to attract visitors. A glance at a map of northwest Europe will immediately show the reason for this interest. Situated at the southern end of the North Sea, it is an obvious point for observing the migration of a wide variety of species, from divers over the sea, through visible migration of passerines like finches, to warblers and flycatchers in the coastal scrub.

The coastline, from Ramsgate in the south to Margate in the north, is essentially chalk cliff, with a rocky foreshore and sandy bays. Between Foreness Point and North Foreland, much of the clifftop is grassy, while lines of trees fringe North Foreland golf course. These open areas provide an obvious landfall for southbound migrants in autumn, particularly in inclement weather. A mile or so inland of Foreness Point is Northdown Park, effectively a sheltered haven for passerine migrants, despite the human disturbance. The large, mature, private gardens of the houses close to the cliff edge inevitably attract a good variety of migrants too. However, the numerous narrow roads and public footpaths make much of the area accessible for human visitors too.

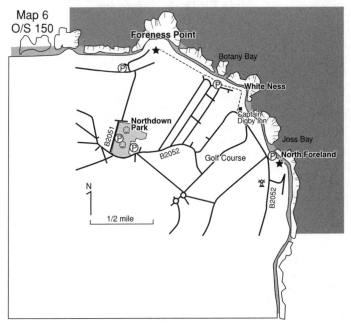

Species

Autumn migration can be a most exciting period, producing a wide variety of interesting species in certain weather conditions, but Thanet is also one of the most reliable localities in Kent to see both Fulmar and Purple Sandpiper well. One might also include Ring-necked Parakeet, which was added to the British List in 1983, although feral birds have been breeding on Thanet since 1972. Fulmar only bred for the first time on Thanet as recently as 1973, but since then up to a dozen or so pairs usually breed.

In winter, it is often the most inclement weather conditions, particularly northerly gales, which produce the greatest excitement for hardened seawatchers. Large numbers of Red-throated Divers and auks can be expected. Fulmar, Purple Sandpiper and Ring-necked Parakeet can all be seen during the first quarter, while spring brings an increase in the variety of birds at sea, as well as a good variety of passerine migrants. The latter half of June and July tends to be relatively quiet, although the passage of Common Scoters often commences at this time.

Probably the most rewarding period is late autumn, again when the wind is from the north. Such scarce seabirds as Pomarine Skua and Little Auk are virtually annual, particularly in stormy weather, and there is always the possibility of a Leach's or Storm Petrel. Storm-driven birds sometimes find refuge in sheltered spots like Ramsgate harbour, which in recent years has held Shag, Grey Phalarope and Sabine's Gull. Raptors and a variety of passerine migrants also occur and few autumns pass without the occurrence of rarer species like Richard's Pipit and Yellow-browed or Pallas's Warblers.

As at all migration points, regular watching is likely to bring the greatest rewards, though a good understanding of the weather conditions may enable casual visitors to be there at the right time, when movements of seabirds or falls of passerine migrants occur.

Main Birdwatching Zones

The whole area is relatively small, but the time of year, prevailing weather conditions and particular interests of the observer will often dictate where effort should be concentrated. Two areas are described in greater detail: the coastal stretch from Foreness Point to North Foreland, and Northdown Park. However, passerine migrants, in particular, are likely to turn up in any patch of vegetation; both Ramsgate (TR 383661) and Margate cemeteries (TR 351693), for example, as well as King George VI Memorial Park (TR 393661 or TR 393657) have produced some extremely exciting species over the years. Both Red-legged and Grey Partridges thrive in the abundant cauliflower fields. Further west, at Minnis Bay, there is the added attraction of coastal marshes, as well as good seawatching possibilities from Reculver Towers (see Additional Sites, p. 108).

FORENESS POINT and NORTH FORELAND (Map 6)

Habitat

The chalk cliffs are approximately 15 m high on this stretch of the Thanet coast, providing excellent vantage points for seawatching. Much of the clifftop is grassed, with some arable land, particularly close to the cliff edge at North Foreland. At Foreness Point, the open grassland is now backed by a housing development, the gardens of which can already boast rare vagrants — the first Booted Warbler for Kent in 1984 to name just one. The short grass of the pitch-and-putt golf course may attract Mediterranean Gulls, as well as migrant pipits and wagtails, as the North Foreland golf course can, but there is no public access onto it. The rough grass between Foreness Point and the clifftop towards White Ness may conceal tired migrants and autumn visitors like Lapland Bunting. The arable field at North Foreland often attracts passerine migrants as well as roosting gulls — always worth checking for scarcer species. The hedgerows and trees lining the roads that border North Foreland golf course are also most attractive for migrant passerines.

At low tide, the mussel-encrusted rocky platforms provide abundant food for waders such as Turnstone and Purple Sandpiper. At high tide, these rocks are covered and any remaining sandy strips below the cliff form natural roost sites for waders, provided that they are undisturbed. Some of the bays are cut off at high tide, effectively preventing human disturbance, when these birds are more easily seen from the clifftop. On occasions the car park at Joss Bay is used as a roost by Turnstone, Ringed Plover and even Curlew.

Species

Foreness Point is undoubtedly one of the most reliable sites in the south-east to see Purple Sandpiper. In winter, although they spread out over the mussel-covered rocks to feed, they often form into a single flock at each high tide, and a flock of up to 50 usually roosts in one of the sheltered bays. If disturbed, they may fly west to roost on the harbour walls at Margate.

Small flocks of Eider occasionally feed offshore, while several other waders, such as Oystercatcher, Turnstone and Curlew, and the ever-hungry Rock Pipit, feed around the rock pools. Black Redstarts regularly winter, often feeding at the base of the cliffs. Winter gales, particularly from the north, can produce several hundred Red-throated Divers and larger numbers of Kittiwakes and auks, mainly Guillemots and Razorbills, but occasionally the rarer Puffin. To seawatch for these species you may find some shelter in the lea of the coastguard station at Foreness Point, or in your own car, which you can park quite close to the cliff edge at Joss Bay, or by the sewage works at North Foreland. Cold-weather movements may occasionally involve geese and duck from the Continent, as well as Lapwings and Skylarks. It is worth checking the gull flocks as they roost in the fields; look for the 'white-winged' species. Mediterranean Gull is fairly regular, but both the huge Glaucous Gull and the more elegant Iceland Gull are scarce. Yellow-legged Gull is more regular in autumn.

The up-Channel seabird passage in spring is best viewed from Dungeness, as the birds are normally too distant to be seen from Thanet. However, some passage can be expected, with species like Whimbrel and Little Tern flying west into the Thames estuary. The former can be anticipated from mid-April, while the latter generally peaks in early May, when a few of the wintering Purple Sandpipers may still be present. Throughout this period the majestic flight of the Fulmar can be studied at close range, often at eye level within a few feet, as the bird glides along the edge of the cliff.

Purple Sandpipers

Earlier in spring, passerine migrants such as chats and wagtails can be anticipated, feeding amongst the clifftop grass, or in the fields of cauli-flowers. It is worth checking the hedgerows and trees that fringe North Foreland golf course for species like warblers, crests and flycatchers. From mid-March Black Redstarts may sit prominently on fences, dropping onto the ground to feed, while White Wagtails (the pale, grey-mantled Continental race) are easy to see, as they feed in the short grass. Firecrest is another early migrant, favouring the denser foliage of evergreen trees — listen for its call, which is lower and more powerful than that of the Goldcrest. By the end of the month Wheatears will be feeding in the open, while Chiffchaffs call and sing from the trees. In light westerly winds some raptor passage may be observed from White Ness or the Joss Bay car park, where Hen Harriers, Common Buzzards, Sparrowhawks and Merlins that have probably wintered in southern Britain can be seen moving north-east. Migrant raptors from further south might include Marsh Harrier, Osprey and possibly a Red Kite.

From mid-April, Yellow Wagtail can be expected on the short grass of the golf courses, where a migrant Ring Ouzel might also feed, and both whitethroats and possibly a Pied Flycatcher may forage in the hedgerows and trees. A glimpse of a red tail indicates the presence of a Redstart. In early May, Whinchats perch on the low bushes, fence wires or posts. Overhead a Hobby may occasionally be seen, more often than not on passage, while the visible migration of species like Turtle Dove can occa-sionally be quite marked, as they coast westwards.

Autumn invariably provides the greatest opportunity to see a good mix of seabirds, migrant raptors and passerines. One species that is notice-ably absent from the autumn seabird movements is Fulmar. Once the young have left the breeding cliffs, few will be seen until the adults return in November.

Some seabird passage can be expected in August, with small flocks of Common Scoter flying east off Foreness Point, or south off North Foreland. In periods of northerly winds, the first Arctic and Great Skuas of the autumn can be anticipated. Small numbers of Black Tern can also be expected in late August and early September, when numbers of Pied Flycatchers generally peak, and the rarer Icterine Warbler is almost annual. Increased numbers of up to 30 Great and 50 Arctic Skuas can be expected on good days in September, when Sandwich Tern passage also peaks, with perhaps 300 flying east in a day. Gannet numbers may increase to 100 or more per day, with as many as 1,000 Kittiwakes, and small numbers of Manx and occasionally Sooty Shearwaters also possi-ble, the latter generally coming closer to shore in inclement conditions. It is a good time too to look for Shags, much slighter looking than the Cormorant and comparatively scarce.

October sees a further change in the composition of passage, with numbers of migrant finches coasting west. At sea, flocks of Brent Geese flying west into the Thames estuary may exceed 1,000 per day late in the month, while small flocks of Velvet Scoter and a few Pomarine Skuas also occur. Sparrowhawk, Merlin and also Short-eared Owl can be seen flying in off the sea or coasting westwards. Hen Harrier too is fairly regular in October, when rarer species like Rough-legged Buzzard feature as rewards for long periods of observation. Newly arrived Woodcock may be disturbed from patches of cover around the clifftops in the early morning, while Woodlark and Richard's Pipit are almost annual visitors. Lapland Buntings may be flushed from the longer grass by the clifftop path. Other passerines, like Goldcrest and Firecrest, are generally most numerous in the woodland fringes in October, when Yellow-browed or Pallas's Warblers may also appear.

Northerly storms in late October and early November may produce movements of auks, including the rare Little Auk, which is almost annual at this time. Leach's Petrels too are occasionally driven close inshore during strong winds.

NORTHDOWN PARK (Map 6)

Habitat
A relatively small town park, much of which consists of short-grassed playing fields. However, small parts are wooded and there are areas of cultivated gardens. The northeast corner borders some rough wasteland, which is generally less disturbed and attracts migrant passerines.

Species
The park is one of the most reliable sites for resident Ring-necked Parakeets. They frequently perch in the rows of sycamores that line the footpaths, but are more often located by their raucous calls. Most bird-watchers probably prefer to see and hear them in their native haunts, but if you can accept them, they are attractive and fun to watch. Another species that winters here is Firecrest, most likely to be found in the denser, more sheltered evergreens, in which the Siberian race of Chiffchaff, *P. c. tristis*, is occasionally seen. By late March, an early Wheatear may be feeding on the playing fields, or a Chiffchaff singing in the trees, but it is likely to be late April before many spring visitors return, and May is *the* month when rarer migrants are likely to occur. The arrival of a Collared Flycatcher in May 1984 focused attention on the site, which produced all four flycatcher species that spring. Pied Flycatcher and Firecrest are regular spring migrants, as are most of the common warblers, while the open fields may also attract an occasional Ring Ouzel.

The passage of migrants returning south during autumn can make visits then most rewarding. In August, species like Lesser Whitethroat, Wood Warbler and Pied Flycatcher are fairly regular among the commoner migrants, but beware of the confusion that can be caused when migrant Reed Warblers occur away from their natural, reedbed habitat. With a northeasterly influence, Scandinavian migrants like Wryneck or Icterine Warbler may appear. By late September and early October Chiffchaffs have generally replaced Willow Warblers, while an easterly wind may produce a Red-breasted Flycatcher. Goldcrest and Firecrest numbers peak in October and, when there has been an influx of these species, it is worth checking the trees and bushes carefully to see if you can find a Yellow-browed or Pallas's Warbler. Listen too for the distinctive call of the Serin, which is almost annual on Thanet. By early November numbers of Fieldfares and Redwings are present, but only remain as long as food is readily available for them.

Timing
The clifftop footpath and park are popular with locals walking their dogs, so early-morning visits are important, particularly during the migration periods, when falls of night migrants can be anticipated. Other

passerine migrants disperse inland quite quickly, after feeding along the hedgerows and narrow lines of trees close to the coast.

Passerine migration is closely linked with prevailing weather conditions. An easterly wind tends to drift migrants over the Continent westwards, and rain often forces them to make landfall. In optimum conditions, after dawn, it is possible to witness migrants actually dropping from the clouds. If a belt of rain passes through just before dawn, there may be an obvious fall of migrants as dawn breaks. Northeast winds early in autumn, linked with troughs of low pressure, may well bring Scandinavian night migrants to Thanet. Later in the season, ridges of high pressure across the Continent and further east are necessary to bring rarer Siberian warblers to Kent's shores.

Visible seabird passage is also dependent on the vagaries of the weather. Thousands of seabirds gather in the North Sea in autumn and many move south through the English Channel. When the wind is northwest, the movement may be more southerly and watching from Joss Bay or North Foreland should be more productive. When the wind is from the north or northeast the birds can be seen well from Foreness Point. Although strong northerly winds often bring birds closer to shore, light winds may have the same effect if the birds become disoriented in fog. A marked passage may also be precipitated when the wind suddenly veers northwest, and in these conditions it may commence at any time of day. While the wind is from the north, early-morning watches tend to be more productive and the movement may cease as the wind drops.

Access

The coastal areas and Northdown Park (Map 6) are bordered on the landward side by the B2052. To visit North Foreland, follow the B2052 north from Broadstairs. Immediately beyond the lighthouse, turn right into Crescent Road. The sewage works is on top of the cliff to the left. Seawatching can be good from here. Back on the B2052 and about 400 yards further on, there is a car park on the right, opposite Elmwood Avenue, which overlooks Joss Bay. From here you can see gulls either feeding offshore or roosting in the arable field on the clifftop to the south. Check the hedgerows and bushes for migrants.

Further along the B2052, near the Captain Digby Inn, where the road turns southwest, there is a footpath along the clifftop to White Ness; from there it leads northwest to Foreness Point. The wader roost sometimes forms in Botany Bay and the birds can be seen well from the top of the cliff. Access to this stretch of the coast is also possible by car. Follow the B2052 for about 800 yards beyond the Captain Digby Inn, turn right into George Hill Road and second right along Kingsgate Avenue.

Northdown Park is bordered by the B2052 to the south and the B2051, Queen Elizabeth Avenue, to the west, in which you can park. There is also a small car park at TR 380702, in the southeast corner of the park, where Ring-necked Parakeets can often be heard calling from the holm oaks. To drive to Foreness Point, follow Queen Elizabeth Avenue north, turn sharp right and left at the corner of the park into Princess Margaret Avenue, which brings you to the pitch-and-putt golf course. Park in the spaces provided. Walk along the tarmac road, which leads round the golf course fence, along the clifftop, to the coastguard station. This is a good seawatch point, from which you can also see gulls and other species feeding on the rocky shoreline. At the appropriate season, check the pitch-and-putt course and the clifftop grass and arable for migrants. For the disabled virtually all these sites are easily accessible, with viewing possible from vehicles, but the walk to Foreness Point and back is the longest at nearly 1 mile and there are no seats or benches en route.

Calendar

Resident: Fulmar (usually absent September–November), Red-legged and Grey Partridges, Ring-necked Parakeet, Rock Pipit.

December–February: Red-throated Diver, Great Crested Grebe, possibly Eider, Oystercatcher, Ringed and Grey Plovers, Turnstone, Sanderling, Purple Sandpiper, Curlew, possibly Glaucous or Iceland Gulls, Kittiwake, auks, Rock Pipit, Black Redstart, Firecrest, Snow Bunting.

March–May: Hobby (April–May), Purple Sandpiper, Whimbrel (passage), Little Tern (peak passage April–May), Black Redstart, Ring Ouzel, Firecrest, Serin (almost annual April–May).

June–July: Breeding Fulmar, Common Scoter (passage), Mediterranean Gull (July peak).

August–November: Manx and possibly Sooty Shearwaters, Gannet, Shag, Brent Goose (October), Common Scoter, Velvet Scoter (October–November), Sparrowhawk and Merlin (October), Woodcock (October–November), Great and Arctic Skuas (September peak), Pomarine Skua (October), Little Gull (November peak), Mediterranean Gull, Kittiwake, Sandwich Tern, Little Tern, Black Tern (August–September peak), auks possibly including Puffin (November peak) and Little Auk (almost annual late October–November), Short-eared Owl (passage October–November), Woodlark (almost annual October), Richard's Pipit (almost annual late September–early October), Icterine Warbler (almost annual August–September), Yellow-browed and Pallas's Warblers (almost annual October), Firecrest and Goldcrest (October peaks), Pied Flycatcher (August–early September peak), finch passage (October peak), Serin (almost annual October–November), possibly Lapland Bunting (October–November).

7 SANDWICH and PEGWELL BAY

OS Explorer 150

Habitat

Much of Pegwell Bay is now a nature reserve, managed by the Kent Wildlife Trust and EN, and the Kent Council County Country Park is part of the reserve. It includes Shellness Point, dune pasture, saltmarsh, beach and tidal mudflats to the north and south of the River Stour estuary, and

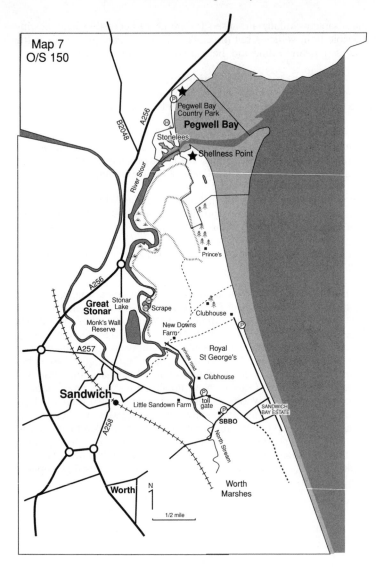

Stonelees, a mixture of wildlife habitats supporting a range of unusual and sensitive plants and animals. The areas of saltmarsh and sand dunes are continually being formed from the accretion of silt, sand and shingle. It is the last remaining complex in Kent containing all these habitats.

The lime-rich soils, formed from the sand and shells, provide favourable conditions for several particularly interesting plants. The dune flora includes sea holly, with its associated broomrape, and sea sandwort, while on the saltings the sharp rush, not found elsewhere in Kent, is abundant. Adjacent to the coastal strip south of the reserve are the Prince's and Royal St George's golf courses and to the west, bordered by the river, an area of arable and grazing land dissected by ditches. At the south end lies the Sandwich Bay Estate and the Bird Observatory, which also includes in its census area part of the Worth Marshes.

North of the town of Sandwich is Pfizer's Monk's Wall Reserve, just southwest of the plant, which can be viewed from the A256 bypass. On the opposite side of the road is Stonar Lake, between the road and the river, which attracts wintering wildfowl. Further north just beyond the Ebbsfleet turning is Pegwell Bay Country Park, which is a good spot from which to view the saltings and mudflats of Pegwell Bay, looking southeast across the estuary to Shellness Point.

Species

The list of winter specialities is considerably increased if the weather is severe on the Continent. The rarer grebes, swans, geese and ducks can then be expected, plus larger numbers of many of the commoner species. In a normal winter, wildfowl feed in the bay, the mudflats attract a variety of waders, the saltmarsh, dune pasture and shingle beach hold a few Twite, a small Snow Bunting flock, maybe a Lapland Bunting or two and possibly a Shore Lark. Raptors like Hen Harrier, Merlin and possibly Peregrine, as well as Short-eared Owl, hunt over the grazing marsh. Much of the up-Channel spring passage is too distant to be observed from the beach, apart from those birds that sometimes follow the coast, like Brent Goose and possibly Avocet, but numbers of several waders increase during April, when they pause to feed in the estuary. Sandwich Tern, which does occasionally winter, is one of the earliest spring migrants, followed by a wide variety of non-passerines and passerines, whilst rarer species like Kentish Plover are almost annual in Pegwell Bay.

Kentish and Ringed Plover

Little Terns still breed, due largely to the constant attention of wardens, which is minimising the disturbance that has limited their success in recent years.

In autumn, as at other east coast sites, weather is a major factor in determining the numbers and variety of birds. At some stage, Scandinavian migrants like Wryneck, Icterine Warbler and Red-backed Shrike inevitably appear and at the same time there should be larger numbers of commoner migrants like Pied Flycatcher. On the mudflats there will be a greater variety of waders, including Little Stint, Curlew Sandpiper, Whimbrel and Greenshank that normally favour freshwater marshes. Offshore, the numbers of terns increases, and they can be seen feeding in the estuary, roosting at the point, or migrating south. Later in autumn, flocks of Common Scoter occur at sea, sometimes with Velvet Scoter, Eider and Red-breasted Merganser, whilst stormy weather may also bring divers and auks into the bay.

Main Birdwatching Zones

Most of the region is dealt with in two parts, the area north of the River Stour, known as Pegwell Bay Country Park including Stonelees, and the area south of the estuary and east of the river, which is described under the general heading of Sandwich Bay Bird Observatory. Two other areas are worth visiting: Pfizer's Monk's Wall Reserve, which requires a permit for access, attracts wintering and migrant ducks and waders when the fields are sufficiently flooded, and Stonar Lake, which often holds rarer grebes and ducks in winter.

PEGWELL BAY COUNTRY PARK (Map 7)

Habitat

Essentially an area of saltmarsh and mudflats, but there is an open space of grasses and thistles to the south, which attracts finches and buntings in autumn and winter. The hide, which overlooks the estuary, provides excellent viewing across the mudflats, as well as shelter during inclement weather. A little further south is Stonelees, with scrub vegetation ranging from the low-growing dewberry and young blackthorn bushes to mature hawthorn and trees such as sycamore, ash and a variety of willows. A good variety of migrants can be seen during the appropriate seasons.

The saltmarsh reflects a stage in the natural colonisation of the mudflats by vegetation. Plant species include common cord-grass, sea blite, sea lavender, sea purslane and sea aster, the seeds of which attract various finches.

Species

The mudflats are rich in invertebrate life and support a large number of waders in winter, with over 1,500 Dunlin, about 1,100 Oystercatchers, over 300 Grey Plover and Curlew, between 200–300 each of Ringed Plover, Knot, Bar-tailed Godwit and Redshank, and up to 200 each of Sanderling and Turnstone. These roost either at Shellness Point, on the fields behind the point, or on the old hovercraft launching pad. They can usually be seen well feeding close to the saltmarsh both before and after high water.

Snipe and the rarer Jack Snipe can sometimes be seen feeding along the saltmarsh ditches on the edge of the estuary. Usually about 150 Shelduck winter, with smaller numbers of Brent Geese and dabbling duck. In the bay Eider and Common Scoter may be seen, with the occasional Velvet Scoter or Red-throated Diver, but of the more distant species Cormorant is likely to be the easiest to identify.

Amongst the Linnets and Goldfinches feeding on seeding plants, not only on the saltmarsh, but also in the open area, there may be a few Lesser Redpolls and Twite, although both have become scarce. Stonechats, too, favour this stretch of open ground. If the finches, or even the waders, suddenly take flight, look quickly for the cause, it may be a Merlin hunting or possibly a Hen Harrier gliding over the saltmarsh.

Spring is typified by sudden increases in the numbers of Brent Geese in late March and Bar-tailed Godwits a month later, when they pause to feed in the estuary, before continuing their long flights north. Other migrant waders can be expected including, appropriately, Kentish Plover, so-named because the first specimen was taken here. By May, many waders are in their more attractive summer plumage, when the brilliant red of the Knot is a pleasure to see. Rarer species like Curlew Sandpiper or Temminck's Stint occasionally occur and in recent years careful scrutiny of the migrant flocks of Ringed Plover, mostly of the northern, tundra race, *C. h. tundrae*, has produced the rare Broad-billed Sandpiper.

An easterly wind in May might produce a few Scandinavian passerine migrants in the hawthorn scrub at Stonelees, like a Bluethroat or a Wryneck, and Icterine Warbler has been heard singing there.

Sandwich and Little Terns are usually present throughout the summer and can be seen feeding in the estuary, while crèches of Shelduck duck-lings are fascinating to watch as they dive one after the other. A careful study of the gulls might reveal the presence of a few non-breeding Mediterranean Gulls, usually in first-summer dress. Several *Sylvia* warbler species breed at Stonelees.

Autumn passage commences with returning waders from early July. When the tide is low, species like Common and Green Sandpiper can be seen along the ditches in the saltmarsh. Whimbrel and Greenshank also favour this area. The numbers of terns slowly increase at Shellness Point and they are best seen on an incoming tide in the evening, when the light is good and there is a possibility of finding a rare Roseate Tern. If the flock is suddenly disturbed, it may indicate the presence of an Arctic Skua. From late August it is worth checking the Stonelees scrub for migrants, particularly after a northeast wind and rain, as these conditions might bring rarer Scandinavian migrants like Red-backed Shrike and Wryneck. In August–September there is also a significant passage of Redshank and Curlew, but of the shore waders only Ringed Plover is seen in numbers markedly higher than those remaining to winter, with up to 500 occasionally present. Northerly gales in late autumn may cause rare species like Grey Phalarope or Sabine's Gull to shelter in the bay, along with large numbers of Brent Geese and other wildfowl.

SANDWICH BAY BIRD OBSERVATORY (Map 7)

Habitat

The uniqueness of the reserve area around Shellness Point has already been described. South of the point, the golf courses provide extensive tracts of suitable habitat for a variety of ground-nesting birds, such as Skylark and Meadow Pipit, but access is limited to the public footpaths. Some of the dune slacks are reed-lined and have developed as oases of self-sown willows, which attract many species of migrants. Others, close to the observatory, have been specifically planted with willows and alders, and are used very successfully as mist-netting sites. The Sandwich Bay Bird Observatory Trust was responsible for the construction of a wader scrape with islands, close to the river. Visiting is restricted to mem-bers, who are finding the hides, including the specially designed photo-graphic hide, quite excellent, particularly for viewing waders. The first autumn attracted both Pectoral and White-rumped Sandpipers. A second flood is being developed close to the Field Centre, and will be open to all visitors.

The maturing gardens of the Sandwich Bay Estate attract migrant passerines, as do the small plantations of trees on its southern edge. The SBBO census area includes that part of Worth Marshes east of the North Stream. Covering some 1,300 ha of privately owned dunes and marshland, it is a complex and fascinating area, greatly attractive to a wide variety of bird species. Its uniqueness also makes it particularly attractive to botanists. Nine native orchids occur, including the rare and fascinating lizard orchid, whilst the equally rare bedstraw broomrape is another local speciality. The migration of butterflies, like Painted Lady and Clouded Yellow, can be witnessed as they cross the coast, while several uncommon species of migrant moths are caught each summer in the observatory moth trap.

Species

A walk along the shore towards the point in winter may be cold and bleak, but it can be most rewarding. To see the roosting waders well you should plan to be near the point an hour or two before high tide. Offshore there may be a flock of Common Scoter, possibly with a Velvet Scoter or two, and small groups of Great Crested Grebes. Sanderling scurry along the water's edge. A wintering flock of up to 50 Snow Buntings sometimes leaves the shore to feed on the short grass of the golf course. Shore Larks are generally scarce, but may be found along the sandy beach, while a few Twite might be present in the saltmarsh near the point, but they too are scarce now. Looking inland over the arable and pasture you will be unlucky not to see a Short-eared Owl or two and a Hen Harrier, whilst a Merlin or a Peregrine might disturb the waders at the point. The wader flocks are worth checking carefully, as species like Little Stint and Avocet have been known to winter.

Back on Worth Marshes, small flocks of Lapland Buntings occasionally winter, though less frequently in recent years, and as many as 3,000 Golden Plover may be seen. In colder conditions, it is here that you might find some grey geese and a few Bewick's Swans. One or two Green Sandpipers and an occasional Water Pipit can also be anticipated. Cold-weather movements involve Lapwings and Skylarks overland, whilst offshore a variety of duck and possibly geese may occur.

March generally sees considerable change, sometimes on a daily basis. Numbers of wintering birds decrease, there are influxes of returning winter visitors like Redwing and Fieldfare, while Brent Geese move north and the first spring visitors arrive. Wheatear and Black Redstart can often be found around the Estate, with Chiffchaff and Firecrest in the scattered clusters of trees. Throughout April and May there are almost daily arrivals of summer migrants passing through, but any 'falls' are usually small compared with those of autumn. Visits after mid-April will almost certainly guarantee an interesting variety of species, even more so if there is an easterly wind. The visible migration of hirundines, Goldfinches and Linnets coasting north can be quite marked, particularly in light west to northwest winds. Most of the common warblers and chats, e.g. Sedge Warbler, Lesser Whitethroat and Whinchat can be expected, but relatively few Redstarts and Pied Flycatchers occur in spring, unless there are sufficient easterly winds. Raptor passage sometimes involves a variety of species, including possible Red Kite, Marsh Harrier, Common Buzzard and Sparrowhawk, with Hobby and possibly

Snow Bunting

Montagu's Harrier or Honey Buzzard in May. Dotterel is almost annual in early May, usually resting or feeding on arable. Blue-headed Wagtail, a striking Continental race of the Yellow Wagtail, can be quite numerous and some may stay to breed. Golden Orioles are virtually annual, but usually stay only briefly and can be difficult to see, despite the brilliant yellow plumage of the male. Another striking species, the Hoopoe, occurs occasionally, as does the attractive Bluethroat.

Although the main migration is complete before the end of May, and one expects June to be a time for studying breeding birds, a number of quite unexpected southern rarities have appeared, like Red-footed Falcon and Sardinian Warbler. July has also had its highlights. Careful scrutiny of the tern flocks, which can be studied at close range from the point, has produced such extreme rarities as Caspian and Royal Terns. Another interesting aspect of July is the early-autumn wader passage. From early in the month, on the scrape, along the river and on the marshes, the numbers of Common Sandpipers increase quite rapidly to around 50 or more by the start of August.

Throughout August and September, although the sea and shore continue to attract an interesting variety of seabirds and waders, including a few Black Terns, Little Gulls and more distant Gannets, the observatory staff normally concentrate their activity on the trapping area. There is a steady flow of passerine migrants, featuring chats, warblers and flycatchers, with the expected, but not always predictable arrival of rarer species like Wryneck, Red-backed Shrike and Icterine Warbler from Scandinavia. Subsequently, rarer warblers from farther east, such as Yellow-browed and Pallas's, are eagerly anticipated. Visible migration is another impressive feature of October, with hirundines during the first week, followed by finches and thrushes later in the month. Raptor passage in late autumn may produce a Common or a Rough-legged Buzzard, in addition to the regular Hen Harriers, Sparrowhawks and Merlins. Late October and early November can produce excellent seawatching, particularly in east to southeast, and sometimes northeast winds, when numbers of geese, duck and Little Gulls may occur, with the occasional rare grebe or Little Auk. Seabird enthusiasts may be tempted to move a little further south and watch from the end of Deal pier.

Timing

The best time to view waders, gulls and terns in Pegwell Bay, from the Country Park, is when an incoming tide coincides with late afternoon or early evening. The light then is usually excellent. Early mornings are recommended for finding passerine migrants, in the observatory area and elsewhere.

Access

From Thanet take the A256 south past the Viking ship in Pegwell Bay (Map 7). Just under a mile from the Viking Ship, the Pegwell Bay Country Park gates can be seen on the left. Drive in, park (for which there is a small charge) and follow the shore path north and south to view the estuary. The hide is particularly welcome in inclement weather. It is about 300 yards from the car park and there are no resting places en route for those with mobility problems. At the appropriate time of year, check the open grassland and the scrub to the south of the hide and the mixed habitat at Stonelees.

Continue south, then keep left at the roundabout. Stonar Lake is less than a mile or so further south, to the left of the road. Park where there is room on the right. The lake can be viewed by looking over the fence. Access to the Monk's Wall Reserve is by permit, available free from Sandwich Tourist Information Centre, at the Guildhall, which is sign-posted in the town centre: open every day, 10am–4pm, or from Pfizer's West Site visitor's centre, on the Sandwich to Ramsgate Road, open Monday–Saturday, 7.30am–7pm. The entrance is signposted opposite Sandwich Industrial Estate. Viewing from the grass verge is possible, though distant. However, be aware that the traffic can be heavy.

To proceed to Sandwich Bay Bird Observatory, drive a short way south, cross over the bridge and turn left into Upper Strand Street. Turn right at the road junction, then follow the road, turning sharp left, for 1.25 miles (2 km) to the Toll gate. It is possible to park in a small lay-by, on the left just before reaching the gate. A toll, normally more expensive in summer, is payable. Reduced rates are available for SBBO members. However, if you inform the gatekeepers you are visiting the Field Centre you may obtain entry at a much-reduced rate. Follow the road for just over 300 m, turn right and the new Field Centre and Observatory building is on the right, with a large car park. There are a number of interesting walks along the public rights of way, but it is recommended that you check with the staff regarding access and what can be expected. It is best to book in advance if you wish to stay in the newly built Field Centre and Observatory accommodation. The facilities are first class, including not only the expected dormitory style accommodation, but also a self-contained flat, which is available for hire. Both the flat and dormitory accommodation are suitable for those with disability problems.

One route to the point that involves less walking is to drive south from the observatory turning, although you must pay the full toll to do so. Turn left through the Sandwich Bay Estate, left again along the shore, where you can park among the dunes on the right, close to the old Prince's golf clubhouse. It is about 2 miles to Shellness Point, along the shore.

Calendar

Resident: Cormorant (non-breeders), Shelduck, Kestrel, Oystercatcher, Ringed Plover, Redshank, Meadow Pipit.

December–February: Red-throated Diver, Teal, Pochard and Goldeneye (Stonar), Eider, Common Scoter, Hen Harrier, Peregrine, Merlin, Water Rail, Golden Plover, Jack Snipe, Green Sandpiper, possibly Glaucous Gull, Short-eared Owl, Stonechat, possibly Twite, Snow and perhaps Lapland Buntings.

March–May: Brent Goose and Shoveler (March passage), possibly Red Kite, Marsh and possibly Montagu's Harriers, Common Buzzard, Sparrowhawk, Hobby, Avocet, Kentish (almost annual) and Little Ringed Plovers, Dotterel (almost annual), Woodcock (March passage), Bar-tailed Godwit (peak late April), Whimbrel, Greenshank, Green Sandpiper, Sandwich and Little Terns, Black Redstart and common chats on passage, Ring Ouzel, common warblers on passage, Firecrest, Golden Oriole (almost annual).

June–July: Breeding Shelduck, occasional Quail, Mediterranean Gull and Sandwich Tern (non-breeders), Little Tern (small colony), breeding Cuckoo, Turtle Dove, Yellow Wagtail, possibly Stonechat, common warblers.

August–November: Common Scoter, Red-breasted Merganser, Hen Harrier (October–November), Sparrowhawk (peak passage October), Merlin, Little Stint, Curlew Sandpiper, Woodcock (from October), Whimbrel, Spotted Redshank, Greenshank, Green and Wood Sandpipers, Common Sandpiper (peak July–August), Arctic Skua, Little Gull, Sandwich, possibly a Roseate, Common and Black Terns, Wryneck, common chats on passage, Ring Ouzel, wintering thrushes (from October), common warblers on passage, Yellow-browed Warbler (almost annual), possibly Pallas's Warbler (first week November), Firecrest, Pied Flycatcher, Red backed Shrike, returning Snow and possibly Lapland Buntings.

8 ST MARGARET'S BAY and BOCKHILL FARM OS Explorer 138

Habitat

The coast either side of St Margaret's Bay faces southeast, while the valley south of the bay runs northeast to southwest, providing a natural funnel for passerine migrants in particular. The high point of the cliff, close to the war memorial, provides another point from which to view visible migration. Below the chalk cliffs, which reach nearly 90 metres above Fan Bay, there is a rocky shoreline. On top, the grassy slopes interspersed with scrub, sycamore copses and a small boggy area in a narrow valley, provide a variety of attractive habitats, not only for birds, but also a variety of butterflies. Twenty-nine species are annual, which is high for one site, including Small, Chalkhill and Adonis Blues, as well as Dingy Skipper. Additionally, in the last decade, there have been sightings of a Swallowtail and two Monarchs. The open, arable fields above Fan Bay and the Cut provide another habitat, while the coastal path, which is very popular with holidaymakers during the summer, provides easy access. The Bockhill side is generally more open, with arable fields close to the clifftop path, narrow hedgerows and scattered bushes, all of which attract migrants from time to time.

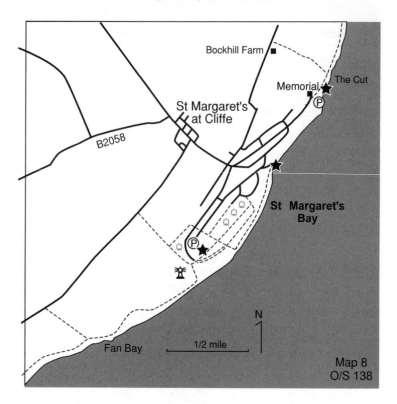

Species

Breeding Fulmars return by late November to inspect their nest sites, but the clifftop area is relatively bleak at this season. Common residents seek shelter in the wooded valley, whilst the rocky shoreline is home for Rock Pipits and might produce wintering Black Redstarts, which often feed at the base of chalk cliffs. Purple Sandpiper is scarce here, but can be seen a little way along the coast in Dover Harbour or on the concrete apron at Folkestone Warren. Severe conditions may produce cold-weather movements involving wildfowl offshore and flocks of Skylarks, pipits and thrushes coasting along the cliffs, or arriving off the sea — over 2,000 Skylarks arrived in an hour on 4 January 1985.

Although it is not an ideal spot for seawatching, as the birds are generally distant, some of the annual up-Channel spring passage can be observed, with flocks of Brent Geese and Common Scoter in March–April and terns and skuas in April–May. When there is a good movement of Pomarine Skuas off Dungeness, some are seen here. In late summer or early autumn it is a good site for Balearic Shearwater.

The northeasterly passage of finches can be quite marked in early spring and Sparrowhawks regularly move out in April. Occasionally there are obvious increases in the numbers and in the volume of song, from species like Willow Warbler, but unlike more prominent coastal sites, spring falls are rare. However, although their stays are invariably brief, Serins are seen occasionally in May.

Regular observation has shown that raptor migration is annual, with migrants often appearing over the dips in the coastal cliffs and either

Firecrest

continuing inland or coasting north. Early in the season Marsh Harrier and Common Buzzard are annual, as are Red Kite, Osprey, Honey Buzzard and Hobby, the last two more frequently in May. Montagu's Harrier occurs occasionally and rarities like Black Kite and Red-footed Falcon have also been seen. This is an extremely good concentration for what is essentially a single site, where the birds can on occasion be seen arriving low over the sea.

The breeding colonies of Kittiwakes are not easily viewed, although there are one or two good vantage points, but their onomatopoeic calls announce their presence along the white cliffs. The summer, however, will produce relatively few species, as the area becomes increasingly disturbed by the volume of human holiday traffic. Nevertheless the pleasure gained from watching Fulmars gliding by at eye level and the occasional glimpse of a Peregrine make visits well worthwhile.

It is autumn that frequently attracts a greater variety of species, with regular marked falls of passerine migrants. Two or three falls of 500+ warblers are annual and occasionally 1,000 may be present, usually when Chiffchaffs and Blackcaps are at their peak in mid-September.

The visible migration of hirundines, thrushes and finches can also be quite spectacular. An unprecedented arrival of 1,200 Ring Ouzels along this stretch of coast in October 1998 is just one example of what can happen in optimum conditions. Exceptionally, there were 93 Firecrests at Bockhill and 62 at St Margaret's on 21 September 1996, whilst on 10 October 1998 there was an interesting variety, including 14 Common Buzzards, a Honey Buzzard, seven Short-eared Owls, a Tawny Pipit, a Shore Lark and 35 Redstarts.

As autumn progresses, the pattern of species changes. The peak numbers of Yellow Wagtails, Tree Pipits, Whinchats, Wheatears, Reed Warblers, Whitethroats, Lesser Whitethroats, Willow Warblers and Pied Flycatchers occur in August and early September, followed by Swallows, Redstarts and Chiffchaffs in September, with House Martins and Blackcaps in late September and early October. It is October that is often the most exciting in terms of variety and numbers: the highest counts of finches are recorded, as they fly southwest, or arrive off the sea, depending on the wind direction, as hirundines in particular favour flying into the wind. Movements often include Chaffinches, Bramblings, Goldfinches, Lesser Redpolls and Siskins. Ring Ouzels and the winter thrushes, Fieldfare and Redwing, often occur in good numbers, while the passage of Goldcrests and Firecrests can be fascinating to watch as they search hungrily for insects, slowly moving up the valley, darting between bushes, or from shrub to shrub on the clifftop.

One of the pleasures of watching migrant passerines in the valley at St Margaret's is that they can usually be seen well. Although they are often feeding in the treetops, the tops of the trees in the valley can be at eye level for the observer. Other alternatives are to spend some time near the lighthouse at the top of the valley, or on the clifftop near the war memorial at Bockhill, as birds frequently fly southwest.

Other arrivals from the Continent in October may include the greyer mantled Coal Tit *Pa. ater*, with Blue and Great Tits, while different species may dominate from year to year. In 1983, for example, over 2,000 Jays flew southwest during October. Of the rarer species, Woodlark and Lapland Bunting are annual, as are Yellow-browed and Pallas's Warblers. Other autumn rarities may include Icterine Warbler and Red-breasted Flycatcher, or possibly Tawny Pipit on the open fields. Exceptionally, vagrants such as Red-flanked Bluetail, Booted and Dusky Warblers, as well as Nutcracker have occurred, while there have been six records of Radde's Warbler.

It is not only passerines that are a feature of autumn, several raptors may also occur: Hobby is now annual, up to six have been seen in a day, whilst Sparrowhawk is perhaps most regular in October. When autumn migration is late, early November can be interesting, with large numbers of winter thrushes, and scarcer finches like Brambling, Siskin and Crossbill. During 1–3 November 1993, for example, there were over 30,000 Redwings and Fieldfares, with nearly 150 Crossbills between 1–8 November. In stormy conditions, Little Auks sometimes appear close inshore in St Margaret's Bay.

Like elsewhere, it is those that watch one site regularly who can anticipate the excitement of discovering an unexpected rarity. Great Snipe and Penduline Tit might seem extraordinary species for such a locality, but both occurred in October 1983, whilst an Alpine Accentor was seen in May 2000. It is not a typical wader site but Dotterel is an annual autumn visitor, often attracted to cropped pea fields and other arable land before ploughing commences.

Timing

For much of the year, early-morning visits are recommended, particularly in late summer, to avoid the holidaymakers. It is also the period when newly arrived night migrants are likely to be more active, while the visible migration of passerines is most marked during the hour after dawn.

An understanding of the weather conditions that influence migration is of great value during spring and autumn passage. The optimum conditions for a fall of passerine night migrants of Scandinavian origin involve a northeast airflow, with a clear sky at dusk, followed by cloud cover and rain towards dawn. Visible migration is most spectacular in northwest winds.

Access

From Dover take the A258 towards Deal and turn right to St Margaret's at Cliffe along the B2058 (Map 8). Continue through the village towards St Margaret's Bay for about half-a-mile, then turn right along St Margaret's Road for about half-a-mile, where there is ample parking space on the grass on the left — just before the road turns sharply left. This area is not suitable for those with disabilities, as the paths are often narrow and steep. However, visible migration can be observed from the parking area. The short stretch of rough road to the left cuts across the top of the valley, with a small sycamore copse on the right, which is worth checking for passerine migrants. Follow the footpath northeast, along the edge of the valley, looking carefully for migrants on the bushy slopes. If there has been an obvious fall, it is worth finding a good vantage point, looking northwest across the valley, and settling down to watch the migrants as they move slowly up the valley. Visible migration is best observed close to the top of the valley. Some migrants tend to coast along the cliff edge, while others will fly up the valley. A footpath passes by the lighthouse to the cliff edge and southwest to Fan Bay, where the arable fields attract wagtails, pipits and chats. Seawatching is best from the beach, near the Coastguard pub, in St Margaret's Bay.

The clifftop area near Bockhill Farm can be reached by following Granville Road, opposite St Margaret's Road, towards the war memorial where there is a car park. The Saxon Shore Way follows the clifftop and there are footpaths inland, as well as the narrow road by Bockhill Farm, which provide some access to the hedgerows and small copses that attract migrants. Kissing gates by the car park restrict movement for wheelchair users but for those with mobility problems there are a few benches along the Saxon Shore Way.

Calendar

Resident: Kestrel, Rock Pipit, Corn Bunting.

December–February: Fulmar (breeders return), Black Redstart, Stonechat.

March–May: Brent Goose (up-Channel passage), Sparrowhawk and finch passage (April), arrival of passerine migrants such as warblers and possibly Golden Oriole (May), raptor passage (May).

June–July: Fulmar, Kittiwake, breeding warblers.

August–November: Sparrowhawk (October), wildfowl movements offshore (late October–November); passage of a wide variety of passerine migrants, including Woodlark (October), Whinchat, Ring Ouzel, winter thrushes and warblers, including Wood, Yellow-browed and Pallas's, Firecrest, Pied Flycatcher, finches and Lapland Bunting.

9 DUNGENESS   OS Explorer 125

Habitat

The huge shingle spit at Dungeness forms a unique habitat. With its aridity and relatively sparse vegetation it is akin to a desert and one of the few places in Kent where Wheatears regularly breed. Projecting into the English Channel and with its close proximity to the Continent, it is an important site for studying migration and seabird passage. In that respect

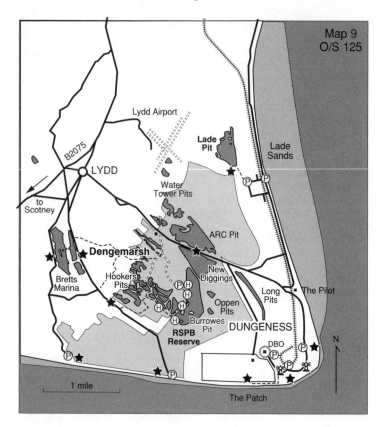

Map 9
O/S 125

it was a natural choice for the establishment of the first Kent Bird Observatory in 1952.

Shingle extraction in the area has produced a number of flooded pits, which form an important winter refuge for duck and other wildfowl. These pits, particularly those under the auspices of the RSPB, regularly attract Smew and Goosander, while the scattered islands provide nesting sites for a variety of gulls and terns.

The nuclear power stations at Dungeness, strangely, have added to the area's interest for some bird species. These man-made cliffs have attracted Black Redstarts to breed and have even been prospected by Fulmars, while the warm-water outflows — known locally as 'the Patch' — attract numerous feeding gulls and terns, including Mediterranean Gull and Roseate Tern. Being close to shore, it offers an excellent opportunity to study the confusing range of plumages displayed by both gulls and terns.

Species

As at all sites that attract passage birds, timing is crucial to witness major falls of passerines, peak seabird movements, or the often all-too-brief visits of rarities. Even if you can anticipate the optimum weather conditions, how often do they occur when you are free to make a visit? Not often enough, certainly, but at Dungeness, with its interesting variety of habitats, it is usually possible to find something to make a visit worthwhile.

The main seasonal attractions tend to be as follows, in winter: divers, gulls and auks on or by the sea, rarer grebes, a Bittern or two and duck on the pits, and geese, wild swans and raptors on Dengemarsh. In spring, highlights include falls of regular passerine migrants and the up-Channel seabird passage, highlighted by the now eagerly awaited passage of Pomarine Skuas in late April and early May. Migrant waders also occur and there is a possibility of southern rarities in late May and early June, such as a Red-footed Falcon or Woodchat Shrike. In summer, there are breeding terns and waterfowl, and Mediterranean Gulls and possibly a Roseate Tern on the RSPB Reserve or the Patch. In autumn, falls of Scandinavian night migrants, occasionally accompanied by rarer species like Wryneck, Barred Warbler or Red-backed Shrike, are the main attraction, while in late October or early November there is a possibility of rarer warblers from farther east, like Yellow-browed or Pallas's and perhaps a Penduline Tit.

Pomarine Skua

Main Birdwatching Zones

The Dungeness area is conveniently subdivided into a number of different sites, all of which have their own particular attractions. On any one day, depending on the circumstances and your own interests, it is quite possible to visit all of the sites described. However, if you are particularly interested in the ringing activities at the observatory, or seabird passage from the point, then the daylight hours will all too quickly disappear.

The following sites are described in detail: the observatory area, including the sea; the RSPB reserve, including Hooker's Pits, the New Diggings and the ARC Pit; the outlying areas of Lade Sands and Lade Pits; Dengemarsh Road, which cuts through the extensive RSPB reserve; and Scotney Pit on the coast road towards Rye.

DUNGENESS BIRD OBSERVATORY (Map 9)

Habitat

There has been a marked increase in vegetation during the lifetime of the observatory. Close to the shore, sea kale provides flocks of Greenfinches with ample seeds in autumn, attracting over 500 birds on occasions. The disturbed stretches of shingle, in particular, now have a rich and varied flora, while in the more sheltered trapping area the sallows have multiplied rapidly. At the northern end of the observatory area are two ancient gravel diggings — the Long Pits. These have developed into a rich habitat for birds, with a small reedbed often attracting migrants. Large areas of gorse and broom towards the point are also attractive to freshly arrived passerines. It is not only migrant birds that attract attention but also moths, butterflies — a migrant Monarch was seen in October 2001 — and dragonflies. Information on these groups, as well as the flora, is published in the annual Dungeness Bird Observatory Report.

A private road, running round behind the old lighthouse, leads to the bird observatory, which is housed in the end of a row of cottages, surrounded by a dry moat and partially sheltered from the strong winds by a high earth and shingle bank. The thick bramble and other vegetation in the moat attract passerine migrants, which may be trapped in the Heligoland traps by the observatory staff.

Species

In winter, the trapping area attracts relatively few birds, although a small flock of Blue and Great Tits may also include a few Goldcrests, with possibly a Firecrest and one or two Chiffchaffs. Woodcock can be found amongst the sallows during cold weather, while Stonechats perch atop the gorse, in which a Dartford Warbler may skulk — these two species are often closely associated in their favoured habitat.

The strip of shore by the fishing boats invariably attracts large numbers of gulls and it is here that the huge Glaucous and possibly the scarce Iceland Gull may be found, sometimes following the fishing boats. Close scrutiny might also reveal the presence of a Caspian Gull. On the sea, large numbers of Great Crested Grebes and Red-throated Divers are usually present, while Guillemot is often the commonest auk and Gannets sometimes fish close to the shore. Offshore movements of the latter three species may be witnessed in certain weather conditions.

The observatory enjoys particularly long and varied periods of migration, partially due to its southerly location. The earliest spring migrants are usually Wheatear, Black Redstart and Chiffchaff, with the peak numbers often before the end of March, when Ring Ouzel and Firecrest can also be expected. However, it is often late April before the bulk of the summer migrants arrive and large falls of Willow Warblers — the commonest migrant — can be anticipated. Early May can be particularly exciting, especially if southerly winds predominate, although clear nights often mean that the birds fly directly inland. A strategically placed belt of rain is an almost essential ingredient for the best falls of migrants.

Witnessing the up-Channel passage of seabirds, duck and waders is also much dependent on certain weather conditions. A change from persistent northerly winds to a southwest or, even better, a southeast air flow often precipitates a marked passage, with birds coming quite close to the point. Recording is usually analysed on a numbers per day basis, so figures mentioned usually refer to peak day totals.

On peak days several hundred divers can be expected, the vast majority being Red-throated. The spring peak of this species is usually in late March, while Black-throated and Great Northern tend to occur slightly later, with peaks of just single figures on average. Brent Goose numbers sometimes peak in late February, but more usually in March, when up to 7,000 have been counted and peaks of 1,000 or more in a day are now annual. Common Scoter movements can be most impressive from late March, throughout April and into early May, when several thousands can be seen passing up-Channel in flocks of up to several hundred — however, a total of 27,000, on 8 April 1978, was exceptional. Smaller numbers of the larger Velvet Scoter are annual, with exceptional peaks of up to 230 in early May. Other seaducks, like Eider and Red-breasted Merganser, and dabbling ducks such as Shoveler, Teal and Garganey also migrate up-Channel at this time.

The passage of Bar-tailed Godwits can be highly concentrated and quite spectacular, with peaks of up to 4,000 or more in late April. Whimbrel, too, regularly fly up-Channel, with occasional peaks of up to 700 in early May. A possibly more attractive sight, if you are lucky, might be a flock of Avocets. The spring passage of Pomarine Skuas has been well documented and many of the flocks that pass Dungeness have been seen some 90 minutes earlier off the Sussex coast, from Beachy Head. The widespread use of mobile phones and pagers now means that birdwatchers at Dungeness can learn in advance when to expect them. Early May is the peak time for these splendid birds, frequently in light southerly winds. The maximum day total is 151, which included a flock of 40, but peaks of 20 or more are almost annual. The passage of Arctic and Great Skuas is more prolonged and less dramatic, with just ones and twos flying past, totalling 40 or more in the case of Arctic, but usually fewer than 20 Great Skuas per day. An added bonus for a lucky few could be an adult Long-tailed Skua.

Little Gull is another species that has been recorded with increased regularity in recent years, with totals very occasionally reaching 200 or more in April or early May. Kittiwakes, too, fly up-Channel in spring, with totals of up to 200, but it is the terns that seem to move almost continuously throughout April and much of May. Usually peak counts of Sandwich Tern exceed 200, with over 1,000 exceptional, while Common Terns frequently exceed 1,000 and exceptionally 3,000. Much smaller numbers of Arctic Terns also occur, usually in late April and early May. The first Little Terns invariably occur in the second week of April and passage continues into May, with peaks of up to 100, while Black Tern totals occasionally exceed a similar figure.

With all this activity offshore, there are times when the trapping area is deserted, but on occasions falls of migrants coincide with peak passage movements, presenting the visiting birdwatcher with quite a dilemma. When he, or she, leaves the coast to search for a Golden Oriole, that will inevitably be the time the long-awaited Pomarine Skua flock appears!

As May turns to June, there is always the possibility of a rarity. Serin and Golden Oriole are near-annual visitors, but other vagrants may include species like Black Kite, Honey Buzzard, Hoopoe, Tawny Pipit, Red-breasted Flycatcher or Ortolan Bunting. On the sea Manx and occasionally Balearic Shearwaters occur in June and July, when there are also peak numbers of returning adult Cuckoos. By late July post-breeding dispersal brings the first autumn passerine migrants to Dungeness, and the numbers and variety steadily increase during August. Once again weather has an important influence on the species present. Early-morning rain may well grounds

British migrants leaving the country, such as Lesser Whitethroats, Wheatears and Willow Warblers, while an easterly wind is likely to produce Continental migrants, like Pied Flycatcher, Redstart and Whinchat. It is in these conditions, particularly during September, that the falls may include rarer species like Wryneck, Icterine Warbler, Tawny Pipit, Bluethroat or Red-backed Shrike.

By early October the pattern changes considerably. The numbers and variety of summer visitors decline, while winter visitors and late-autumn migrants like Robin, Goldcrest and Firecrest increase. Diurnal movements of finches are a regular feature; hirundines, also, move through in large numbers. Dartford Warbler and Woodlark are regular migrants at Dungeness in October, whilst rarer species that have been recorded include Rustic Bunting and eastern warblers like Dusky, Radde's and Pallas's.

On the sea, the Patch is a great attraction from early autumn. A number of the locally bred terns and gulls can be seen begging food from the adults — an ideal opportunity to study plumages. Among all the Common Terns it might be possible to locate the scarce Roseate Tern, and as autumn progresses, migrant Arctic Terns can also be expected. Late August is the peak time for Black Terns, on occasions numbering over 100, and there is always a possibility of the rare White-winged Black Tern — usually in juvenile plumage — while an Arctic Skua may occasionally cause havoc among birds over the Patch. A check of the gulls is also worthwhile; Yellow-legged Gull is a regular visitor in autumn, when peaks of up to 20 or more are recorded, while a Caspian Gull might also test your identification skills.

The down-Channel passage in the autumn is not so marked or reliable as the spring movement, although a few species can be expected in good numbers. Gannets may total 500 or more in a day, with a peak usually in October, Brent Goose numbers vary considerably but may occasionally reach 3,000 in late October or early November, but Common Scoter tends to migrate closer to the French coast and relatively few are seen. Totals of 100 or more Sandwich Terns are fairly regular, with the peak in September, while similar numbers of Little Gulls pass west, with the highest counts usually in late September, but in some years later. Autumn numbers are sometimes higher than those recorded in spring. Rarer species include Sabine's Gull and Sooty Shearwater, and in stormy conditions later in the year possibly Little Auk or Leach's Petrel.

DUNGENESS RSPB RESERVE (Map 9)

Habitat

Through careful management, Burrowes Pit — another flooded gravel pit — has become a site of great importance to wintering wildfowl, breeding gulls and terns, and migrant waders. The vegetation on the islands is controlled to provide suitable conditions not only for the breeding gulls and terns, but also for grebes and duck. The scrapes prepared for migrant waders are attracting an increasing variety.

Visible from the Lydd–Dungeness road are the ARC Pit to the north and the New Diggings to the south — adjacent to Burrowes Pit. From the visitor centre there is a carefully marked track, which takes you over the shingle through well-vegetated areas of bramble and gorse, much favoured by passerine migrants. The trail passes the Hooker's Pits, some of which have dense beds of common reed. The reserve has recently been extended and more wader pools have been created, some over-looked by new hides.

Species

The visitor centre and the four hides that overlook Burrowes Pit provide very welcome shelter in winter, while you study the wildfowl without disturbing them. Few winters pass without a visit from a diver or two, while Red-necked Grebe seems to be the most regular of the three rarer grebes. In some winters, Bewick's Swans occasionally come in to roost, but it is the duck that provide the greatest spectacle. Smew now occur annually, increasing in numbers with the severity of the weather. Ruddy Duck has increased so dramatically that peak numbers now exceed 100, whilst Goosander and Goldeneye seem to favour the ARC Pit. Some of the shore waders roost on the low shingle banks or sandy foreshore close to the hides, while the larger gulls, including Glaucous on occasions, favour the low islands or the shingle for roosting. A large percentage of the wintering Lesser Black-backed Gulls are of the dark, Scandinavian race *L. f. intermedius*. Hen Harrier, Merlin and Sparrowhawk often hunt over the area. Merlin in particular likes to hunt the Starlings as they arrive to roost at the Oppen Pits — east of Burrowes. A Peregrine may also be seen at this time of year.

Smew

One of the early signs of spring is the raucous cry from a returning Sandwich Tern. In 1978 this species recolonised Kent, here at the RSPB reserve. The increase was quite dramatic, reaching 350 pairs in 1985, but they sometimes desert the area completely and the colony has been known to move to Rye Harbour in East Sussex. Some 50 pairs of Common Terns also breed on Burrowes pit, with about 150 pairs of Black-headed Gull. Formerly, the colonies of both species were much larger, but they are now dispersed over several sites, rather than just on the RSPB reserve. Amongst them one or two of the larger white-winged Mediterranean Gulls can occasionally be seen. There is quite a cacophony of sound in late summer, when the young are begging for food.

From July, a wide variety of waders visit the reserve, some, all too often, making only the briefest of stays, though occasionally one or two of the rarer visitors deign to pause for a few days. The list of rare visitors in recent years is quite mouth-watering, not only waders, such as Least and Buff-breasted Sandpipers and Long-billed Dowitcher, but rare terns too, including Caspian and Sooty. Sadly, they do not all arrive at the weekend! Yellow-legged Gull is most frequently seen in autumn. Caspian Gull too, can be occasionally picked out in the roost by the avid gull watcher.

Many of the regular and rarer autumn passerine migrants can also be expected. A walk around the shingle track will often produce Whinchats and occasionally a Wryneck or Red-backed Shrike.

LADE SANDS and LADE PITS (Map 9)

Habitat

At low tide a large expanse of sandy mudflats is exposed, providing an attractive food source for thousands of shore waders and gulls. At high tide many of these roost just inland of the coastal cottages, on the fields by Lydd airport or at Lade Pits. This is another flooded gravel pit, with islands and shallow edges that have attracted natural vegetation such as osiers, sallows and reeds, which provide a sheltered haven not only for wintering duck, but a wide variety of migrants and breeding species, like Great Crested Grebe.

Species

In winter, when the sandy mud is exposed, up to 1,300 Oystercatchers regularly feed, busily probing the mud. About 300 Sanderling usually feed here, frequently running along the ebbing tideline. Maybe 1,000 Dunlin, up to 70 Grey Plover and a few Bar-tailed Godwits and Curlew help give the impression that much of the sandy surface is alive. Check carefully through the gulls, you might discover a Glaucous or an even rarer Ring-billed Gull among them. At sea, as the tide brings them closer to the shore, you can expect up to 1,000 Great Crested Grebes and possibly Eider and Common Scoter, while day totals of over 100 Red-throated Divers are counted flying by, and smaller numbers are usually visible on the sea.

Lade Pit at this time frequently attracts one of the rarer grebes, sometimes a Bittern, certainly a variety of ducks, including Gadwall, Goldeneye and Ruddy Duck, and for one brief period an extremely rare Canvasback. In severe conditions numbers of Scaup may also be seen. Over the fields near the airport, a few Curlew and flocks of Golden Plover feed, often disturbed by a Hen Harrier, as it hunts low over the ground. Chiffchaffs and occasionally Black Redstarts winter here, and they can certainly be seen in early spring, when terns and rarer gulls can also be expected. Little, Mediterranean and the exceptionally rare Laughing Gull have all been recorded. In autumn, depending on the water level, it may also be an attractive to freshwater waders, like Green and Common Sandpipers.

DENGEMARSH (Map 9)

Habitat

This area includes a mix of habitats, with arable and grazing land, gravel pits, shingle scrub and gorse. The Dengemarsh Road runs from Lydd roundabout to the shore, with farmland to the east and Brett's Marina to the west — several flooded pits now used by windsurfers and water-skiers. Further south, the RSPB lease part of their reserve to the MoD, while east of the road are a few more flooded gravel workings, with small reedbeds of *Phragmites* and the Hooker's Pits beyond. In recent years some freshwater marsh has been created on this part of the RSPB reserve, attracting breeding Lapwing and Redshank. It is also proving attractive to passage waders. The Dengemarsh gully, which also falls within the RSPB reserve, is a deeper ditch running parallel to the road, towards the sea, containing more common reed, a few gorse bushes and bramble. It frequently provides shelter from the prevailing winds for tired passerine migrants, including on occasion such extreme rarities as Dark-throated Thrush and Subalpine Warbler.

Species

The arable fields attract a number of geese and swans, particularly in winter when, in addition to the resident Greylag and Canada Geese, a few Bean Geese and both Bewick's and a few Whooper Swans may be seen. In severe conditions flocks of White-fronts, Pink-feet and Barnacle Geese have also occurred. The flooded pits occasionally attract divers and rare grebes, while about 1,500 Wigeon now graze there in winter, along with other dabbling duck. Common diving duck are also regular visitors and Long-tailed Duck occurs occasionally. Hen Harrier, Merlin and Peregrine hunt over the fields and an occasional Short-eared Owl can be expected. Ruff sometimes feed on the close-cropped pasture by the main road. The reeds attract Bearded Tits and Bittern is an almost annual winter visitor.

During spring, migrant passerines can often be discovered feeding in the fields or scrub. In recent years such rarities as Hoopoe, Black-eared Wheatear and Black-headed Bunting have been found. Shore waders like Grey Plover and Bar-tailed Godwit — in their attractive summer plumage — along with Whimbrel, often rest and feed on the fields and freshwater marsh between the road and Hooker's Pits. Freshwater waders, like Common and Green Sandpipers, the occasional Greenshank and Spotted Redshank are attracted to the newly created marsh, as well as the muddy fringes of these shallow pits, on both spring and autumn passage.

The protracted autumn passage commences as early as mid-June and during the next three to four months a variety of waders can be anticipated. Of the extreme rarities, a Collared Pratincole was present in June 1986, a Terek Sandpiper in August 1982 and a Long-billed Dowitcher in December/January 1990/91, while Pectoral Sandpiper has been seen several times in recent years. In early September it may be possible to study Black Terns at close range on Brett's Marina, in more sheltered conditions than the coast often offers, while the rare White-winged Black Tern has been known to favour this area.

SCOTNEY PIT

Habitat

A large, maturing gravel pit, with islands for breeding gulls and a few wildfowl, that straddles the Kent/Sussex border alongside the Lydd–Rye road. The surrounding areas are largely pasture, with some flooded pools adjacent to the road at the eastern, Kent end.

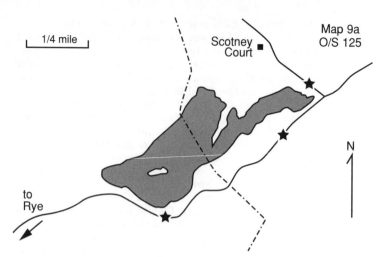

Species

As with other pits in the area, Scotney attracts a variety of wildfowl in winter, often including a few Scaup, as well as the occasional diver and rarer grebe. The pasture, often on the distant Sussex edge, has attracted a wintering flock of White-fronted Geese in recent years and in some winters scarcer grey geese, like Bean and Pink-feet, may be present. At the eastern end, the pasture near the road is often flooded and may hold a variety of waders, particularly at high tide. Some numbers of Golden Plover can be expected, along with scarcer species like Ruff and possibly a Little Stint. As spring approaches wintering birds disperse, an early Garganey may appear and migrant waders like Greenshank and Whimbrel can also be anticipated. Breeding species include Herring and Lesser Black-backed Gulls on the islands, a few Lapwings and one or two pairs of Oystercatchers and Ringed Plovers. During autumn the general pattern will be similar to that described for the other pits in the area.

Timing

Several different aspects need to be considered when planning trips to Dungeness. Seawatching can be difficult, due to the southerly aspect, and the angle of light is generally better early morning and late afternoon — times that quite a number of seabirds tend to favour too. Onshore winds usually bring birds closer inshore, particularly in dull, misty conditions, while the bay east and north of the point provides shelter from southwest gales for a number of seabirds.

The state of the tide controls the distribution of many of the waders and gulls feeding on Lade Sands. As the tide rises, they come closer to the shingle bank before flying to roost on the various pits and areas of undisturbed shingle. A rising tide is also a good time to watch for gulls at the fishing boats.

Predicting falls of passerine migrants is difficult. Given clear skies they tend to fly straight over. Rain towards dawn may produce falls, if other conditions are suitable — southerly winds in spring and more easterly winds in autumn are best.

Access

Take the Dungeness road from the Lydd roundabout. After just over 1 mile you will see Boulderwall Farm signposted on the right and a gravel track leading to the RSPB reserve visitor centre and car park (Map 9). The reserve is open daily, 9am–9pm, or sunset, whichever is earlier. The visitor centre is open 10am–5pm: the charge is £3 for non-members, £2.00 concessionary, £1.00 children or £6.00 family groups. Disabled birdwatchers can drive to four of the hides (ask at the visitor centre or phone beforehand). Seats are provided at strategic points around the visitor trail.

Another quarter-of-a-mile along the Dungeness road you will see the ARC Pit on your left, with the New Diggings on the right. Park beside the road to view these two pits, but take care, the traffic tends to be fast-moving. An additional RSPB car park, viewing points and visitor trail are planned for this part of the reserve and will provide access to the ARC pit, thus avoiding the necessity to park on the busy road.

A further mile-and-a-half and the road bends to the left, leading to The Pilot pub and the coast road to the north, whilst a right turn leads to Dungeness. After less than a mile the fishing boats are visible on the left, with a convenient pull-in for cars on the right. A short walk accesses the shore by the fishing boats, in the lee of which you can often find shelter from the prevailing southwesterlies.

The Dungeness road continues south, then turns west by the new lighthouse. To reach the observatory, turn left immediately before the old lighthouse (there is a cafe and parking on the right) and follow the tarmac surface northwest by the power station fence and on over the moat to the observatory building, where there is further space for parking. Check with the warden as to what birds are present in the trapping area, which is not easily accessible for wheelchair users.

'The Patch' may be reached by following the power station fence back to the gate, where there is room to park. Walk to the shore and about 400 yards west. Seawatching is best undertaken closer to the point in most conditions, and the coastguard signal station building provides some shelter in inclement weather. This is reached by walking along the shore, or by parking near the cafe and walking south from the old lighthouse. A 'Friend of Dungeness' membership permits access to the two seawatching hides on the shingle bank. The steepness of this bank may restrict access for wheelchair users.

Lade Sands extend at least 4 miles north from the Pilot pub to Littlestone. Lade Pit is between the coast road and Lydd airport and can be approached by following the coast road for a mile-and-a-half from the Pilot. Turn left into Taylor Road and park near the corner of Williamson and Taylor Road. From here, walk across the shingle to view the pit from its southern shore. The nature of the terrain makes the walk to Lade Pit unsuitable for wheelchair users.

Dengemarsh Road also leads from the Lydd roundabout and reaches the coast about 3 miles south. Scan the pasture, arable fields and flooded areas from various points. Two footpaths to Hooker's Pits leave this road at approximately 1-mile intervals from the roundabout. The second footpath links the Dengemarsh and Dungeness roads at Boulderwall Farm, via the southern edge of the flooded fields and Hooker's Pits. A turning to the right about a mile-and-a-half from the roundabout, opposite Manor Farm, leads west then north, following the range fence, and provides good vantage points to view the largest pool of Brett's Marina. When there is no firing on the range, it is possible to drive to the coast, to scan for wintering scoter flocks, from the right-angle bend at TRD39184. Much of this area and the next are suitable for those with mobility disabilities, as they can be viewed from the roads.

Scotney Pit (Map 9a) straddles the Kent/Surrey border at TR 013190, about a mile-and-a-half from Lydd, on the road to Rye. There are various pull-ins from which it can be viewed. The Kent end can be seen well from the minor road to Scotney Court at TR 019196.

Calendar

Resident: Great Crested Grebe, Greylag and Canada Geese, Gadwall, Red-legged and Grey Partridges, Water Rail, Oystercatcher, Meadow Pipit.

December–February: Red-throated Diver, Great Crested Grebe (wintering flocks on sea from the point north), Red-necked and possibly Slavonian or Black-necked Grebes, Bittern, Bewick's and possibly Whooper Swans, Teal, Shoveler, Pochard, Eider and Common Scoter (on the sea), Goldeneye, Smew, Goosander, Ruddy Duck, Hen Harrier, Peregrine, Merlin, Grey Plover and Sanderling (Lade Sands), possibly Ruff, Woodcock, Mediterranean and Glaucous Gulls, Stonechat, possibly Dartford Warbler, Chiffchaff, Firecrest.

March–May: up-Channel passage of divers (Red-throated peak in March, with most Black-throated and Great Northern in late April); Fulmar, Garganey, Shoveler (spring peak in March); up-Channel passage of Eider, Common and Velvet Scoters, and Red-breasted Merganser; Hobby, Avocet (up-Channel passage), possibly Kentish Plover, up-Channel passage of Bar-tailed Godwit and Whimbrel (early-May peak), Pomarine, Arctic and Great Skuas; Mediterranean and Little Gulls (up-Channel peak May); up-Channel passage of Sandwich, Common, Arctic, Little and Black Terns; down-Channel passage of Guillemot and Razorbill; Hoopoe (almost annual), Black Redstart, Wheatear, Ring Ouzel, Sedge and Reed Warblers, Whitethroat, Chiffchaff and Willow Warbler, Firecrest, Golden Oriole (annual in recent years).

June–July: Little Egret, Manx Shearwater, Ringed Plover, Mediterranean and Little Gulls (non-breeders summer), Black-headed Gull (breeding colonies), Common Gull (a few pairs breed), Kittiwake (post-breeding flock on shore), Sandwich Tern, possibly Roseate Tern, Common Tern (breeding colonies), Cuckoo (peak numbers of returning adults), Yellow Wagtail, Black Redstart, Wheatear, Whitethroat.

August–November: Little Egret, Sooty and Manx Shearwaters (September peak), Leach's Petrel, Gannet (October peak), Garganey, Sparrowhawk (from October), Little Stint, Woodcock (from October), Greenshank, Green and Wood Sandpipers, Arctic and Great Skuas, Mediterranean and Little Gulls, Arctic Tern, Black Tern (peak numbers late August–September), White-winged Black Tern (almost annual on 'the Patch' or the pits), up-Channel passage of Guillemot and Razorbill, Wryneck, Woodlark, large diurnal passage of hirundines, Black Redstart (October peak), Wheatear, Whinchat, Stonechat, Ring Ouzel (October peak), Dartford Warbler (annual in October), Lesser Whitethroat, Yellow-browed and Pallas's Warblers, Goldcrest (October peak), Firecrest (late October– November peak), Pied Flycatcher, Red-backed Shrike, diurnal passage of finches, especially Goldfinch (up to 1,000 daily in October).

Habitat

Just south of Goudhurst, Bedgebury Forest is situated on higher undulating terrain, in sharp contrast to the lowland Weald to the north. Although much of the plantation is coniferous, there is still some sweet chestnut coppice. One of the attractions of this area is the Pinetum, with its wonderful and varied collection of conifers set on grassy slopes rising from Marshall's Lake. The Pinetum has recently been extended and a new lake has been created at the top of Dallimore Valley, where the new education and visitor centre is proposed and which the Forestry Commission plans to open in 2006. Much of the management will benefit a wide variety of wildlife, including a number of bird species. The extension includes areas of grassland, heathland, acid bog and small ponds along the stream in the Dallimore Valley. This increase in the range of habitats is most welcome and will make visits even more rewarding at certain times of the year — there are over 900 species of fungi for any visiting mycologists to enjoy.

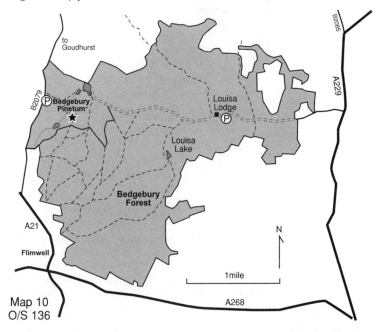

Species

In winter, the dense foliage of the cypress trees, within the Pinetum, is much favoured by finches for roosting. This has always been one of the most reliable localities for seeing the handsome Hawfinch well; sadly, numbers have declined markedly, but single-figure totals are still possible. Other finches such as Chaffinch and Brambling also roost here. How far these birds disperse during the day is unknown, but from high vantage points overlooking the Pinetum small groups may be counted as they arrive from outlying areas. The loud 'ticking' of the Hawfinch is a characteristic sound of the late afternoon, less obvious than in the past, but still one of the best ways of locating one. The numbers of Bramblings fluctuate considerably from year to year, but counts of up to 300 have occasionally been recorded.

There is little obvious birdlife in the forestry conifer plantations, but perseverance will produce its rewards. Woodcock may be disturbed from areas of bracken and there is always a slender chance of seeing the resident Sparrowhawks. Coal Tit and Goldcrest are among the commonest passerines in the conifers, but roving flocks of tits may contain 4–5 species, possibly including Marsh Tit. The larch plantations are favoured by Siskin and Lesser Redpoll, and Louisa Lake occasionally attracts Little Grebe and Kingfisher, which add to the variety. These species may also be seen at the new lake. The lily-covered Marshall's Lake, in the Pinetum, occasionally attracts a pair of Mandarin and Grey Wagtail can also be anticipated there.

Hawfinch

The great storm of October 1987 wreaked havoc with several conifer plantations. Though some were replanted, the FC took the opportunity to permit some natural regeneration. They created broader rides, which are much favoured by Nightjar, a species that is also attracted by the open, more heath-like habitat, which Stonechat and Tree Pipit have found to their liking.

During spring, the residents become more vocal and some of the winter visitors, like Redwing and Brambling, may sing before migrating north. All three woodpeckers will be busy excavating new nest holes, while Nuthatch lines the entrance of its chosen nest hole with mud. This is the time to familiarise oneself with the song of the Goldcrest, and to listen carefully for the subtly different, more strident, less variable and shorter song of the most attractive Firecrest. By early May, a variety of common woodland warblers are establishing breeding territories. The soft 'purring' of the Turtle Dove is inevitably a late addition to the woodland chorus. From late May to early June is the best period for hearing and seeing both Woodcock 'roding' and Nightjar displaying, though both continue into early July.

Irruptions of Crossbills tend to occur every 3–4 years, often followed by breeding, which commences early the next year. Most irruptions consist of two waves, with the first in late June–July, followed by a second, which normally peaks in October. The distinctive, hard *chup-chup* flight calls are often the first evidence of the species' presence, but look carefully at all the larches anyway, the seeds of this conifer are much favoured. Siskins may sometimes be found in the summer and breeding has occasionally been confirmed.

Seeing any raptors, apart from the resident Kestrels, normally requires a great deal of patience. By selecting a high vantage point overlooking the forest and scanning diligently over the treetops, you may be fortunate to see the occasional Sparrowhawk and, during summer, a Hobby. The former is often accompanied by a flock of Starlings, while the latter may seek its prey amongst a flock of feeding House Martins or Swallows, although in spring they are more partial to dragonflies. An interest in these insects is not confined to Hobbies and many birders now seek to identify them during the summer months. The variety in Bedgebury is excellent and 20 species have been identified, including Golden-ringed Dragonfly, as well as Downy and Brilliant Emeralds. Louisa Lake is a favourite site for many of them.

The dense plantation areas become very quiet as the migrants disperse, but mixed flocks of tits and warblers occur during August. Although migration is rarely obvious at such a wooded inland locality, species like Pied Flycatcher and Wood Warbler do occur from late August into September. By October the winter thrushes replace the summer migrants and the finches will again be flying in to roost. If there has been an irruption of Crossbills, look carefully at all of them, the first Two-barred Crossbill for Kent was discovered here in October 1990.

Timing

Most woodland species are more active and vocal early in the day, whilst roosting birds are best seen from mid-afternoon until dusk. For Woodcock and Nightjar visit some of the young conifer plantations between 9pm and 10pm from late May. Fine weather with little wind makes it much easier to hear bird calls and song. The Pinetum is popular with the general public, causing considerable disturbance and making listening difficult during the middle of the day, particularly at weekends. In winter, a morning visit to nearby Bewl Water (see p. 203) and an afternoon visit to Bedgebury makes a worthwhile day's outing.

Access

From Goudhurst take the B2079 south towards Flimwell. About 3 miles on the left is a public car park (Map 10). From Flimwell follow the A21. Turn right along the B2079 for about 1 mile to the car park on the right. To visit the Pinetum an entrance fee is payable at the shop in the car park, where there are also toilets. Admission £3.50, senior citizens £3.00, children £1.50 and family £9.00. Normal opening times are 10am–6pm. The new entrance for the education and visitor centre will be at TQ 712330, less than half-a-mile south of the present car park.

Follow the hedge-lined footpath towards the Pinetum, the cypress trees, usually favoured by roosting finches, are about 400 yards southeast of the gate, just over a sharp rise.

There are numerous rides and public footpaths through the forestry plantation, and losing your sense of direction is surprisingly easy. You might find a compass worthwhile! The forest can also be approached from the A229 between Cranbrook and Hawkhurst. Driving south from Cranbrook, just over half-a-mile south of the B2085 to Goudhurst junction, turn right into Park Lane and follow the narrow road for about 1 mile, as far as the 'Road closed to unauthorised vehicles' barrier, and park. The track ahead, past Louisa Lodge, accesses the Pinetum. For Louisa Lake, take the track to the left, about 400 yards beyond Louisa Lodge, for about 600 yards. Other reasonable vantage points over the forest can be found along Park Lane, some overlooking clearings within the forest. Returning to the A229 junction, be aware that fast traffic can appear from a blind bend. As some of the paths are steep, particularly in the Pinetum, there is limited access for wheelchair users and benches there and in the forest are infrequent. However, the circumstances should be much improved once the new centre is opened in 2006.

Calendar

Resident: possibly Mandarin, Sparrowhawk, Woodcock, Barn and Tawny Owls, all three woodpeckers, possibly Grey Wagtail, Goldcrest, Marsh and Coal Tits, Nuthatch, Treecreeper and commoner woodland passerines.

December–February: Fieldfare, Redwing, Brambling, Siskin, Hawfinch, residents and other finches.

March–May: Hobby (May), Tree Pipit, Stonechat, common woodland warblers, Firecrest (occasionally in winter) and Spotted Flycatcher (early May).

June–July: Residents, including Woodcock roding; breeding summer visitors as above, plus Nightjar and Turtle Dove, possibly Firecrest, Siskin and Crossbill (following irruptions).

August–November: Summer migrants leave by mid-September. From October wintering Woodcock and thrushes, winter finches return to roost.

11 BOUGH BEECH RESERVOIR

OS Explorer 147

Habitat

This man-made reservoir of some 115 ha, first flooded in 1969–70, is the largest stretch of fresh water in Kent. Its irregular, natural shoreline is surrounded by woodland, fields and hedgerows. A road, which runs across the northern end of the reservoir, provides excellent views of the nature reserve, about 26 ha in extent, which is managed by the Kent Wildlife Trust.

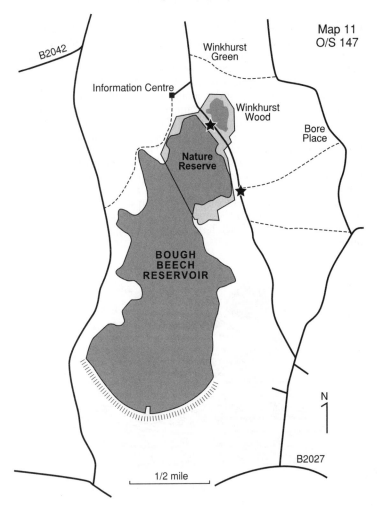

When the water level falls sufficiently to expose large areas of mud, migrant waders are attracted. Footpaths provide access to some of the surrounding, mainly deciduous, woodland. With this wide range of habitats and given almost daily coverage, throughout its 30-year history, it is unsurprising that a total of 246 species had been recorded by the end of 2002.

Species
The numbers and variety of wildfowl present on the reservoir in winter will depend on the severity of the weather. Great Crested Grebes will be present, with large numbers of noisy Greylag and Canada Geese, which commute between the reservoir and the surrounding fields. Of the dabbling duck, Wigeon, Teal and Mallard are often quite numerous, with smaller numbers of Shoveler and Gadwall, and occasionally Pintail. Pochard and Tufted Duck are often present in good numbers, a few Goosander are regular in winter, but Goldeneye has become a less-common passage migrant. During a prolonged cold spell, the variety may be augmented by a Red-throated Diver or one of the rarer grebes. Smew and

101

Bewick's Swans most often visit in these conditions. With luck, the resident Sparrowhawks may show over the surrounding woodland. Careful observation should produce views of Snipe, often well camouflaged amongst the vegetation on the water's edge.

A few spring migrants, including Little Ringed Plover, may appear before the end of March but, depending on the weather, it may be several weeks before the main arrival of summer migrants. Many of these may be seen from the footpaths through some of the surrounding woodland. This is the best time to witness the extraordinary courtship display of the Great Crested Grebe. Migrant raptors, such as Osprey, Marsh Harrier and Common Buzzard, are regular and there are occasional sightings of rarer migrants like Honey Buzzard. Common Sandpiper is a regular spring migrant, but other waders seldom stay long, if at all, influenced by the urgency to reach their breeding grounds. Even so rarities do occur at this time — all four records of Kentish Plover have been in spring. Terns, including the attractive Black Tern, occur regularly, but again tend not to linger.

Goosander

In summer, Hobbies, present in the general area, can usually be seen. It is fascinating to watch the young Great Crested Grebes being fed, or riding on the backs of their parents, or to see the young Shelduck diving and following their parents. A duck Mandarin may appear with her brood, as this species occasionally breeds here successfully.

By July, there is often evidence of early-autumn migration, as the returning waders pause to feed at a more leisurely pace than in spring. They often stay several days and there is a good opportunity to see Green, as well as Common Sandpipers and the elegant Greenshank at close quarters. Ringed Plover and Dunlin are also regular, whilst other species such as Little Stint, Spotted Redshank and Black-tailed Godwit are virtually annual. Any rarer waders are most likely to occur in August–September and over the years these have included five American species, Temminck's Stint and Red-necked Phalarope. As numbers of Little Egrets continue to increase there is a possibility of seeing one here during this period. Ospreys are virtually annual autumn visitors. Garganey should also be looked for, although their identification is more difficult in autumn. In addition, many passerine migrants can be expected, such as Wheatear, Whinchat and Yellow Wagtail. The occurrence of a Radde's Warbler here in October 1984 demonstrates that extreme rarities can turn up anywhere.

Timing

Viewing from the road, you look southwest over the reservoir, thus morning visits enjoy the best light. Early morning is also preferable for small passerines, as they are most active then. Evening visits are recommended for roosting birds and possibly roding Woodcock in the breeding season.

Access

The reservoir and the entire nature reserve can be viewed well from the public road just south of Winkhurst Green (Map 11), along which there is ample room to park. From the south, this road can be reached from the B2027, turning north about a mile-and-a-half west of Chiddingstone Causeway, following the road to Winkhurst Green and Bough Beech nature reserve. From the north, the B2042 runs southwest from Riverhead to Ide Hill. The Winkhurst Green turning is to the east just 1 mile south of Ide Hill. The height of the hedge between the pavement and the reserve limits viewing, over much of the area, for wheelchair users, but short lengths on both sides of the road are cut lower for viewing.

The Kent Wildlife Trust information centre, just northwest of the reserve, is sited in an old oasthouse, with car parking and toilet facilities. It is open to the public, free of charge, 11am–4.30pm at weekends and on Wednesdays in April–October. For woodland birds, one footpath heads south from here, while others lead from the viewpoint, at the south end of the causeway, to Bore Place, where you can follow the narrow road north, before taking another footpath back towards the information centre.

Calendar

Resident: Great Crested Grebe, Cormorant, Grey Heron, Mandarin, Greylag and Canada Geese, Sparrowhawk, Kingfisher, Grey Wagtail, and a good variety of typical woodland species, including the three woodpeckers, Marsh Tit, Nuthatch and Treecreeper.

December–February: Wildfowl including Wigeon, Teal, Shoveler, Pochard, Tufted Duck, Goosander and possibly Ruddy Duck, Water Rail, Snipe and a roost of at least 10,000 gulls, mostly Black-headed, but on occasions rarer species.

March–May: Migrant waders and terns, possibly Osprey, passerine migrants and returning summer visitors.

June–July: Breeding Grey Heron, Shelduck, Mandarin, Cuckoo, resident woodland birds, common warblers, including Reed, and Reed Bunting.

August–November: possibly Little Egret, overland migration of Brent Geese (late October–November), possibly Garganey, Osprey, Hobby, Snipe, return passage of migrant waders and terns, with Greenshank, Green and Common Sandpipers quite common, passerine migrants, including Yellow Wagtail and Whinchat.

12 ABBEY MEADS and LEYBOURNE LAKES COUNTRY PARK

Habitat

This is an extensive area essentially of old gravel and sand workings. Abbey Meads comprises a large pit and an area of scrub and marsh between the River Medway and the railway line. It is part of the Holborough–Burham SSSI. Much of the area between the railway line, the A228 and Leybourne Way to the south is being managed as a new country park by Tonbridge and Malling Borough Council. This will include a few wildlife areas. The northern section of Burham SSSI is situated on the other side of the river, to the northeast, over which there is a panoramic view of the North Downs. The southern section, opposite Abbey Meads pit, contains a heronry. The pit is fringed with some mature reedbeds, willows and sallows. A small area north of Abbey Meads also has stretches of marsh, common reed and mature hawthorn scrub. The Brookland windsurfing lake has some mature willows and small reedbeds. The new Leybourne Lakes Country Park is being designed to cater for wide-ranging local interests, including windsurfing, scuba diving and fishing, as well as areas managed for wildlife. Either side of the

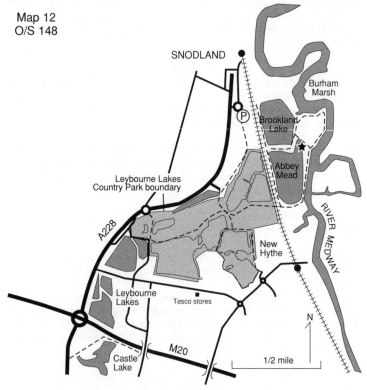

Map 12
O/S 148

SNODLAND

Burham Marsh

Brookland Lake

Abbey Mead

Leybourne Lakes Country Park boundary

A228

RIVER MEDWAY

New Hythe

Leybourne Lakes

Tesco stores

N

M20

1/2 mile

Castle Lake

104

M20, the Castle and Leybourne Lakes are surrounded by mature alders and some woodland. These sites increase the diversity of species that can be seen in the area as a whole.

Species

As with many sites it is regular watching that produces a good variety of species and this area is no exception. An occasional diver may occur during winter and Slavonian Grebe is fairly regular. The vagaries of the weather have a strong influence, not only on the presence of divers and grebes but particularly on the wintering duck population. Normally, there are good numbers of Gadwall, Teal, Shoveler, Tufted Duck and Pochard, along with a few Shelduck, a small number of Smew and 1–2 Goldeneye. In severe conditions the numbers of Smew increase and Goosander may occur. In most winters a Little Egret is seen, a Bittern or two find refuge amongst small beds of common reed, usually around Abbey Meads pit, while from the same areas Water Rails squeal, Cetti's Warblers may call, occasionally bursting into song, and Bearded Tits 'ping'. Snipe can be seen feeding in the marshy areas adjacent to the river, or on the river mud when the tide is low. The river also attracts numbers of Teal and in particularly hard weather Water Rails can be seen feeding on the mud at the edge of the reeds. A small roost of Long-eared Owls is occasionally located, but this species is prone to undue disturbance, so avoid getting too close. A Short-eared Owl and wintering raptors like Hen Harrier and Merlin are occasionally seen.

Early Sand Martins are usually the first sign of spring, followed by Chiffchaffs in song — small numbers regularly overwinter in the area. Other passerine migrants like Redstart and Wheatear are occasionally seen, and by mid-April Sedge and Reed Warblers will be singing, the latter species playing host to Cuckoos. Numbers of hirundines can be quite impressive and a Red-rumped Swallow has been seen here. If you stand between Abbey Meads and the river before dawn, you are likely to be deafened by the volume of Nightingale song — it is magnificent — which continues during the day. Several *Sylvia* warblers, such as both whitethroats and Blackcap, also sing during daylight hours, and Grasshopper Warbler is still fairly regular, thus up to ten warbler species may be seen in a day. Other woodland species, like Lesser Spotted Woodpecker and Coal Tit, are occasional around the Leybourne and Castle Lakes, either side of the M20. Kingfisher and sometimes Grey Wagtail are seen at these lakes too. Displaying Great Crested Grebes are another attraction in early spring. Few of the lakes or pits have shallow edges, so migrant waders are difficult to find and early-morning visits are essential to see any, before they are disturbed.

Summer is relatively quiet, but young Great Crested Grebes are always a delight to observe. Flocks of both Greylag and Canada Geese gather to moult, often favouring the larger lakes, a Hobby may be seen feeding on dragonflies, 1–2 pairs of Kingfishers will be breeding and the Sedge and Reed Warblers are actively feeding their broods.

In autumn, large numbers of hirundines feed over the lakes, which again attract a few migrant waders and possibly terns. A wintering Stonechat usually appears during October. In late October and early November the well-established overland passage of Brent Geese can sometimes be witnessed. The panoramic view of the North Downs to the northeast, from which direction they fly, provides a good opportunity to see a flock. Waders like Redshank and sometimes Dunlin feed on the exposed river mud and both Green and Common Sandpipers are known to winter in the same habitat.

Timing

For an essentially inland site, being aware of the state of the tide may seem strange, but at low tide species like Redshank and Shelduck move upriver to feed on the exposed mud. Windsurfing on Brookland lake is most popular at weekends, as is fishing on a number of the pools west of the railway. For least disturbance early mornings are best, but late-afternoon and dusk visits can also be rewarding.

Access

There are several access points and the choice will be determined partly by how long you wish to stay and by what you wish to see. The car park by Brookland Lake near Snodland, at TQ 707615, can be reached from the A228 (Map 12). If driving from the M20, turn left, immediately right and drive over the A228, then turn right and filter left, over a narrow bridge into the car park. From the north, turn left by the Royal Mail buildings, left at the roundabout, then sharp right over the narrow bridge. Walk under the railway bridge and follow the footpath by Brookland Lake. This path takes you around Abbey Meads, along the river wall and eventually back to the car park. If you have more time you can cross the railway at the south end of Abbey Meads into the Leybourne Lakes Country Park, where there are several well-marked footpaths. You can follow one that runs north beside the canal back to Brookland Lake car park. A car park for the Leybourne Lakes Country Park will be opened in June 2004 at TQ 697603, with access from the roundabout on the A228. There are several footpaths around Leybourne and Castle Lakes and in the woodland by the M20. Parking is limited in the residential estates, but it may be possible at TQ 695595, in Springfield Road, for Leybourne Lake and at TQ 695592, in Willow Road, for Castle Lake. The Abbey Meads area is not suitable for wheelchair users or those with mobility difficulties, but the Leybourne Lakes Country Park will have good access.

Calendar

Resident: Great Crested Grebe, Grey Heron, Kingfisher, possibly Lesser Spotted Woodpecker, Grey Wagtail, Cetti's Warbler, Reed Bunting.

December–February: possibly divers or rare grebes, Cormorant, possibly Little Egret, Bittern, Gadwall, Teal (along the river), Shoveler and good numbers of Tufted Duck and Pochard, 1–2 Goldeneye, small numbers of Smew, possibly Goosander, Water Rail, Snipe, Redshank, possibly Green and Common Sandpipers, possibly Long-eared Owl and Bearded Tit, Chiffchaff.

March–May: migrant waders and terns, Cuckoo, Nightingale, Sedge and Reed Warblers, *Sylvia* warblers.

June–July: Greylag and Canada Geese (moulting flocks), breeding residents and Sedge, Reed and *Sylvia* warblers.

August–November: migrant waders and terns, a few migrant passerines like Whinchat and Wheatear, returning winter visitors, including Stonechat.

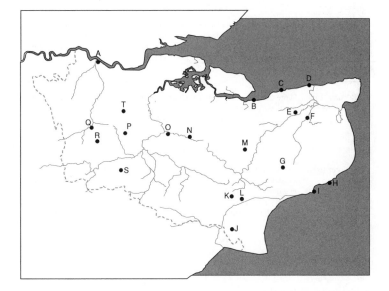

Key & Site	Habitat	Birds of Interest	Peak Season	Nearest Town
A Dartford Marshes	Mudflats, salt and grazing marsh	Sparrowhawk, shore waders, Yellow-legged Gull, with Arctic and Black Terns also possible in autumn, Stonechat, plus usual migrants	All year	Dartford
OS Explorer 162 TQ 544757	*Park safely in one of the lay-bys just north of the roundabout on the A206 or on the marsh track that veers left just before a crash barrier and continues to the disused fireworks factory. Follow the main track past the gun club to the River Thames and take the footpath east towards Littlebrook to view the area. Not suitable for those with mobility problems.*			
B South Swale LNR	Tidal mudflats, shingle/shell beach, saltmarsh, grassland	Brent Goose, shore waders, Hen Harrier, Eider, Short-eared Owl, Bearded Tit, Snow Bunting	Winter	Faversham
OS Explorer 149 TR 045655	*A LNR managed by the Kent Wildlife Trust. Limited parking. Access west along the Saxon Shore Way from the Sportsman pub (TR 062647) or north along footpath from Nagden (TR033631). Best for geese and waders two hours before high tide. Not suitable for wheelchair access or for those with mobility problems.*			

Key & Site	Habitat	Birds of Interest	Peak Season	Nearest Town
C Swalecliffe	Shingle beach, Marsh, brook and scrub	Divers, Brent Goose, seaduck, waders (winter), waders, terns and passerine migrants (spring and autumn)	All year	Whitstable
OS Explorer 150 TR 130674 TR 137675	*Limited parking at end of Whitstable Promenade or at end of Swalecliffe Court Drive, between which there is a concrete pathway, but limited access for those with mobility problems. Explore the trees and scrub around the sewage works and trees in the churchyard for additional passerine species, particularly migrants.*			
D Reculver to Minnis Bay	Shore, coastal marshes	Seabirds, including divers, possibly shearwaters and petrels, Gannet, scoters, skuas and auks; migrant passerines, Snow Bunting, possibly Shore Lark	Autumn and winter	Herne Bay
OS Explorer 150 TR 226693	*Follow the Thanet Coastal Path east from the car park. In the autumn take footpaths inland to Chambers Wall, or west towards Bishopstone for passerine migrants. Seawatch from Reculver Towers in northerly winds. For those with mobility problems there is a short uphill walk, but the Thanet Coastal Way can be negotiated by wheelchair users, provided you have sufficient muscle power.*			
E Fordwich and Westbere	River, mature gravel pits, reedbeds, wet woodland	Usual reedbed species, Gadwall, Kingfisher, possibly Lesser Spotted Woodpecker	All year	Canterbury
OS Explorer 150 TR 179598/ TR 197610	*Parking is restricted at both ends. From Westbere cross the railway line and follow the footpath in both directions in turn. Railway crossing and narrow paths make this unsuitable for wheelchair users. No resting places either.*			
F Seaton Pits and Preston Marshes	Mature gravel pits, reedbeds permanent pasture	Usual waterfowl and reedbed species; resident Kingfisher, woodpeckers and Grey Wagtail; Bittern, Smew, harriers and Firecrest in winter; migrant duck and terns in spring and autumn; Hobby, Yellow Wagtail and Nightingale in summer.	All year	Canterbury
OS Explorer 150 TR224588	*Limited parking space, but also available in Wickhambreux near the Rose pub. Follow public footpath from map reference to Deadmill Bridge and back to view main pit and thus add variety. Alternatively, under the Countryside Stewardship Scheme, follow a circular walk from the bridge along the east bank of the Little Stour, then cross Preston Marshes to Preston church, before returning to Deadmill Bridge. Check the woodland edge for Firecrest and other woodland species. Not suitable for those with mobility problems.*			
G Lyminge Forest–West Wood	Mainly conifer woodlands	Sparrowhawk, Tree Pipit, Nightingale, Firecrest, Goldcrest, Marsh Tit, possibly both Siskin and Crossbill	Spring and summer	Folkestone
OS Explorer 138 TR 142440	*Turn off the B2068 at Sixmile. Drive east for just under half-a-mile to the car park on the right. Early morning is preferable to hear calls and song in order to locate these specialised woodland species. Suitable for wheelchair access, with good habitat adjacent to car park.*			

Key & Site	Habitat	Birds of Interest	Peak Season	Nearest Town
H Samphire Hoe	Cliffs, wildflower grassland created from tunnel spoil	Divers, possibly Shag, Fulmar, seaduck, Peregrine, possibly Purple Sandpiper, auks, Rock Pipit, Black Redstart, Stonechat	Winter	Dover
OS Explorer 138 TR 294391	*Owned by Eurotunnel and managed in partnership with the White Cliffs Countryside Project. Access is via a tunnel off the A20 at TR 299395. Entrance fee for car park. Good disabled access with frequent benches.*			
I Folkestone Warren	Chalk cliff, scrub, rocky coast	Fulmar, possibly Shag, Purple Sandpiper, Mediterranean Gull, Rock Pipit, passerine migrants, possibly raptors	Winter, spring and autumn	Folkestone
OS Explorer 138 TR 247377	*Turn off Wear Bay Road by the Martello Tower (TR 240373) and follow the rough road to the car park almost by the concrete apron, where a few Purple Sandpipers winter. Scan the cliff and sea for Fulmar and other seabirds. Locked gate and stile make it unsuitable for wheelchair access.*			
TR 256385	*The footpaths in the Warren are more accessible from the 'Cliff-top Cafe' and visible migration can be observed from on top of the cliff in spring and autumn. Try in clear weather with northerly or easterly winds for passerine migrants, or on a warm, clear spring day for a chance of a raptor. The trees around and below the cafe are worth checking for warblers and flycatchers. The Warren is unsuitable for disabled access.*			
Copt Point TR 240364	*Park close to Copt Point, walk up to the high point. Depending on the tide, check the gulls on the rocky foreshore or over the sewage outflow—over 200 Mediterranean Gulls may be present in autumn. Seawatching can be worthwhile in southerly winds. Steep climb for wheelchairs.*			
J Walland Marsh	Reedbed, grazing marsh and arable	Mute and Bewick's Swan flocks, Hen and possibly Marsh Harriers, possibly Peregrine, Golden Plover, Barn and possibly Short-eared Owls	Winter	Lydd
OS Explorer 125 TQ 978244	*Follow the footpath from the bend in the road near the Woolpack Inn to overlook the reedbed, where Hen Harriers roost (TQ 981241). Water Rail and Bearded Tit may also be heard there. The favoured site for the Bewick's Swan flock may vary from year to year. Check with the RSPB on Dungeness reserve. Difficult for wheelchair access, as best viewing is from on top of steep bank and grass approach can be rutted..*			
K Fagg's Wood	Mixed woodland	Sparrowhawk, Hobby, Woodcock, possibly Nightjar, Tawny Owl, Nightingale, woodland warblers, Goldcrest, Nuthatch, Hawfinch, possibly Crossbill	Spring and summer	Ashford
OS Explorer 125 TQ 987347	*From the car park, follow the various rides. More song and greater activity early morning. Dusk or dawn visits for Woodcock roding, Nightjar and calls of Tawny Owl. Access on some rides suitable for wheelchairs, but they can be rutted.*			

Key & Site	Habitat	Birds of Interest	Peak Season	Nearest Town
L Ham Street Woods NNR	Mixed woodland	Sparrowhawk, Hobby, Tawny Owl, all three woodpeckers, Nightingale, Marsh Tit	Spring and summer	Tenterden

OS Explorer 125
TR 004337

Comprises Bourne, Barrow and Carters Woods. From the car park there are numerous paths from which to view the range of different trees and understorey, with an opportunity to see Purple Emperor butterflies. Pre-dawn you might just hear hooting of Tawny Owl above the volume of Nightingale song. Rough paths make this unsuitable for wheelchair access.

Key & Site	Habitat	Birds of Interest	Peak Season	Nearest Town
M Challock Forest	Conifer and chestnut coppice	Woodcock, Nightjar, Tawny Owl, Nightingale, woodland warblers, possibly Crossbill	Spring and summer	Ashford

OS Explorer 137
TR 023499

From the car park, follow the various rides in Kings Wood. Coppiced areas with 3–4 years' growth usually preferred by Nightjars. Dusk visits around 9.30pm in early June for Nightjar and roding Woodcock. Limited access for wheelchairs, as rides can be deeply rutted.

Key & Site	Habitat	Birds of Interest	Peak Season	Nearest Town
N Leeds Castle	Mixed woodland, lakes	Ornamental waterfowl, Mandarin, possibly Hobby in summer, Kingfisher, Grey Wagtail	All year	Maidstone

OS Explorer 137
TQ 837538

Fee for entrance to castle grounds and car park, limited room outside, but public footpaths provide reasonable access through to Broomfield (TQ 840527). Mandarin favours the narrow River Len. Get to know your duck in beautiful surroundings. Good access for wheelchair users from main car park. Seats at reasonable intervals.

Key & Site	Habitat	Birds of Interest	Peak Season	Nearest Town
O Mote Park	Parkland, lake and reedbed	Great Crested Grebe, Mandarin, Water Rail (winter) possibly Mediterranean Gull, migrant terns and passerines, all three woodpeckers, Kingfisher, Grey Wagtail, Nuthatch, Siskin (winter)	All year	Maidstone

OS Explorer 148
TQ 773553

From the car park complete a circuit of the lake and stream; look over wall to small lake. Visit early morning to see migrants, before disturbance by dogs and their owners. Popular with the general public. Some access suitable for wheelchair users and frequent seats for those with mobility problems.

Key & Site	Habitat	Birds of Interest	Peak Season	Nearest Town
P Mereworth Woods	Conifer and chestnut coppice	Woodcock, Nightjar, Tawny Owl, all three woodpeckers, Tree Pipit, Nightingale, possibly Stonechat, woodland warblers, Marsh Tit, possibly Crossbill	Spring and summer	Tonbridge

OS Explorer 148
TQ 635550

One option: park at TQ 625560, follow track east through coppice to find a good vantage point at around 9.30pm for roding Woodcock and displaying Nightjar, in late May early June. Preferred sites will depend on finding suitably coppiced areas with 3–4 years' growth. Unsuitable for those with mobility problems.

Key & Site	Habitat	Birds of Interest	Peak Season	Nearest Town
Q Sevenoaks Wildfowl Reserve	Managed gravel pits	Wildfowl, passage waders and terns, Kingfisher, Grey Wagtail, Siskin (winter)	Winter, spring and autumn	Sevenoaks
OS Explorer 147 TQ 522564	*Private reserve open weekends and Wednesdays (10am–5pm). Visitor hall with Exhibition Centre. Admission fee. Membership enables daily visits, except Mondays, with access to a wider area. Special 'disabled friendly' features create good access for all.*			
R Knole Park	Wooded deer park	Sparrowhawk, Stock Dove, all three woodpeckers, Tree Pipit, Redstart, Stonechat, warblers	Spring and summer	Sevenoaks
OS Explorer 147 TQ 541524	*One option: park at River Hill. Extensive walks possible in attractive deer park, with Fallow, Sika and Red Deer. Old timber much favoured by Stock Doves, woodpeckers and Redstarts. Stonechats were attracted to more heath-like areas created by October 1987 storm. There are no benches and swing gates may restrict disabled access, though main paths are suitable for wheelchair users.*			
S Tudeley Woods RSPB reserve	Woodland, heath and pasture	Hobby, Nightjar, all three woodpeckers, Tree Pipit, Stonechat, woodland warblers, Spotted Flycatcher, numerous Marsh Tits, possibly Willow Tit, Nuthatch, possibly Crossbill	Spring and summer	Tonbridge
OS Explorer 136 TQ618434	*A long and a short trail lead from the car park through Tudeley Woods. A new trail will lead to Pembury Heath for a different range of species. Not suitable for those with mobility problems.*			
T Trosley Country Park	Wooded, chalk downland	Sparrowhawk, Green and Great Spotted Woodpeckers, woodland warblers, Marsh Tit, Hawfinch (winter)	All year	Sevenoaks
OS Explorer 148 TQ635613	*From the car park—fee payable—there are two marked trails, the longer one leads to the grassland area down steep slopes. The shorter, more level one through woodland, might just be manageable in dry weather by wheelchair users, for whom the toilets have facilities. In winter Hawfinch may be present around the car park.*			

SURREY

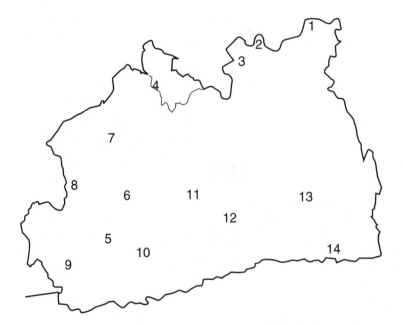

1 The Thames through London
2 Barnes
3 Richmond Park and environs
4 The Upper Thames Valley
5 The Wey Valley, Eashing to
  Guildford
6 Papercourt Gravel Pits, Send and
  Wisley
7 The Northwest Surrey Commons

8 Farnham and the Blackwater
  Valley
9 Southwest Surrey Commons
10 Albury and District
11 Central Surrey Commons
12 Dorking Hills and Lakes
13 Reigate to Godstone
14 Hedgecourt, Wire Mill and
   District

1 THE THAMES
THROUGH LONDON

The area described runs along the southern banks of the Thames from its entry into Surrey at the Surrey Docks, west for about 11 miles to Putney (Map 1a). Sites are dealt with from east to west.

Habitat

The Thames is tidal for the whole of the area described here and long stretches of mud and stones are exposed at low tide. Old industrial and commercial buildings, including the Bankside and Battersea power stations rise among more modern constructions along the waterfront. The river is crossed by 18 bridges which, with the numerous buoys, pilings, wharves and moored river craft, provide perches and breeding sites for the district's birds. There are several parks and open spaces with riverside frontages, the largest being at Battersea. River and air pollution levels are much reduced and still improving.

After their closure in the 1970s, the Surrey Docks became a wasteland and the site was quickly exploited by land- and waterbirds. The docks have been redeveloped with a watersports centre, parkland, industrial buildings and housing (Map 1a). The area is well worth watching because of the nature of the new habitat, which is unusual, so close to central London. Panoramic views of the river can be had from generous lengths of broad footpath. Some of the old docks have been filled in and most of the dockside buildings have been cleared, although a few have been left to give a flavour of the area as it once was. Greenland Dock is now used for watersports and is effectively a rectangular lake. Canada Dock is full and has an outlet to the Thames. The Ecological Parks Trust has taken over Lavender pond, part of the old Lavender Dock, and created reedbeds, a small wood and some marsh with sluices, which permit water to wash over a simulated flood meadow. The surrounding area has been landscaped with small mounds, rough grass, copses and patches of scrub. Russia Dock has been converted to woodland. An artificial mound (Stave Hill) gives views over the entire site.

Southwark Park runs for half-a-mile along the west side of the docks. It has mature trees and shrubberies and is heavily used. A pond with an island provides nest sites for waterfowl.

The William Curtis Ecological Park, 1 mile upriver, is a small green area along the waterfront to the west of Tower Bridge. It has produced no records of very unusual species, but has a Thames frontage.

From Southwark Cathedral through Tooley Street to Bankside the streets are noisy and river access is poor but the old commercial buildings provide useful habitat of a kind that is becoming scarcer. The decommissioned Bankside Power Station, now converted to the Tate Modern, has a tall brick tower and many ledges. There is a small area of grass and bushes open to the public between its entrance and the Thames. Blackfriars Bridge has piers with broad ledges.

At Southbank, tall buildings to the east and west of Waterloo Bridge have attracted various breeding species. Jubilee Gardens provides a green space with spots private enough for Song Thrushes. There are good

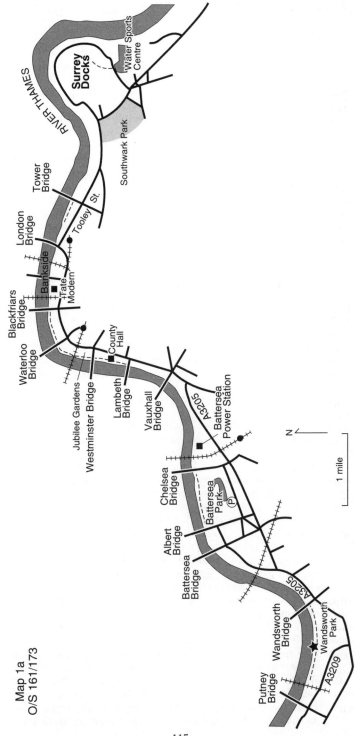

Map 1a
O/S 161/173

RIVER THAMES

Surrey Docks

Water Sports Centre

Southwark Park

Tower Bridge

London Bridge

Tooley St.

Blackfriars Bridge

Bankside

Tate Modern

Waterloo Bridge

County Hall

Jubilee Gardens

Westminster Bridge

Lambeth Bridge

Vauxhall Bridge

A3205

Battersea Power Station

N

1 mile

Chelsea Bridge

Battersea Park

P

Albert Bridge

Battersea Bridge

A3205

Wandsworth Bridge

Wandsworth Park

A3209

Putney Bridge

views of the Thames. Archbishop's Park at Lambeth is a public open space with grass, trees and shrubberies next to the more bird-rich but private grounds of the Archbishop's Palace.

Further upriver, at Battersea, there is a park with a large lake and islands for breeding wildfowl. Its northern boundary is the three-quarter-mile stretch of the Thames embankment between the Chelsea and Albert bridges. The Peace Pagoda, sports track and recreational activities of the many users of the park give it a busy, cosmopolitan atmosphere. A 0.5-ha area of an old Battersea Power Station cinder dump at the northeast corner of the Park has been converted to woodland by the London Wildlife Trust and has trees mature enough for woodpeckers and warblers. The power station itself, a well-known London landmark with its four chimneys, one at each corner, is no longer in use and is likely to be preserved as an exhibition and leisure centre.

The River Wandle passes through King George's Park and joins the Thames at Wandsworth Creek, where there are wooden pilings in the river. Just to the west is Wandsworth Park, mostly playing fields but with a long river frontage overlooking extensive shallows that are exposed at low tide and continue further upriver to Putney Bridge.

Species

The Thames Valley is a flyway for seabirds. Bridges are among the more likely places to provide sightings of a few species that are relatively scarce in Surrey, such as Fulmar, Shag, Kittiwake, Glaucous Gull and Sandwich Tern. Cormorant, Grey Heron, duck and the commoner gulls may be seen at any time of the year. Good places to look for Shag and Cormorant are on the piers of the bridges, on buoys in the vicinity of the Festival Hall at Southbank, on the pilings by Battersea Power Station and at the mouth of Wandsworth Creek.

The London parks have had their stock enriched by escaped and introduced wildfowl of many other indigenous and exotic species — a fact which may please the eye but makes recording difficult. Hybrids of the genus *Aythya* are sometimes found. These are usually of Tufted or Pochard origin and can closely resemble scarcer members of the genus such as Lesser Scaup. Scaup and Ferruginous-type hybrids, too, are occasionally found. Bill characters are important for distinguishing the species, especially the amount and distribution of black on the nail. Battersea Park has a heronry. Mute Swan, Tufted Duck, Black Swan and, occasionally, Pochard have bred there. Tufted Duck also breeds in small numbers at Surrey Docks, Southwark Park and King George's Park.

Wintering waterfowl downriver at Surrey Docks have included one or two Ferruginous Duck, which unlike their cousins in the parks and inner reservoirs appeared to be genuine immigrants and not escapes or hybrids. Migrant duck such as Common Scoter are sometimes found on the river and other species may be forced onto it in hard weather including Shoveler and Goosander, and occasionally a Smew or Red-breasted Merganser. Pintail on the foreshore at Wandsworth and elsewhere are possibly of feral origin.

Kestrel is the commonest raptor but Sparrowhawks are increasing. They have bred at Battersea Park and can be seen carrying prey at Surrey Docks, Wandsworth and probably elsewhere. Migrant Hobbies appear occasionally. Peregrines are one of the marvels of today's London. They bred at Battersea Power Station in 2001 and are now regularly seen on the tower at the Tate Modern. Moorhens and Coot breed on most of

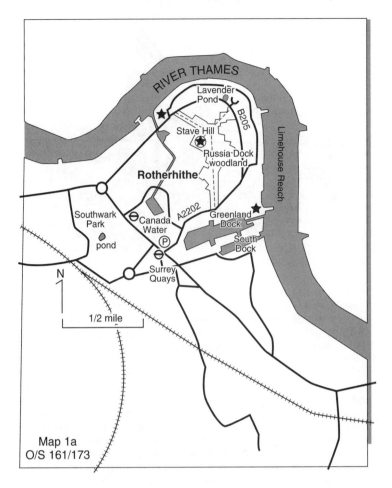

Map 1a
O/S 161/173

the ponds. Migrant crakes and waders are fewer, but a Spotted Crake found in a car park at Waterloo shows that they pass through. A Purple Sandpiper has appeared as a foreshore bird at Battersea.

The commoner gulls and terns appear along the Thames in appropriate season. A few summering gulls are sometimes found from Chelsea Reach, at Battersea, down to the Surrey Docks and may help the mid-May birder to that elusive Surrey 100 species in a day. Herring Gull, a common enough breeder in coastal counties, has bred once in Surrey, on the roof of the County Hall building at Lambeth. Lesser Black-backed and Herring Gulls breed on buildings on the north side of the Thames and further Surrey colonisation is possible. Yellow-legged Gulls are now being fairly regularly seen along the river.

Auks have appeared at Westminster and other places as part of a storm-driven wreck, and very occasionally odd birds have spent weeks moving up- and downriver with the tides. Stock, Collared and migrant Turtle Doves are sometimes seen in the parks, as well as the ubiquitous feral Rock Doves. Woodpigeons and Swifts are appearing in central London in increasing numbers as air pollution declines.

Black Redstart

Swallows are rarely seen except as migrants, although their breeding sites are getting closer to the centre of the area. House Martins nest on buildings at the Surrey Docks and has attempted to do so on County Hall. Waste ground at Surrey Docks and on other cleared sites has offered at least a transient site for Yellow Wagtail, which is otherwise an extremely scarce breeder in the more rural parts of Surrey. The species is currently absent but Grey Wagtails have begun to breed in creeks along the waterfront.

Black Redstart has bred at Bankside and Battersea power stations. They are still seen or heard in the streets between Tower Bridge and Waterloo, but breeding has become erratic. Tooley Street, old buildings between Blackfriars Bridge and Waterloo Bridge and the riverside area up to Vauxhall Bridge can also produce one for the persistent observer. The song, which includes a phrase like the rattling of ball bearings, may be the first evidence of the species' presence, and carries well even above the roar of traffic.

Wren, Dunnock, Blackbird, Song Thrush, Blue Tit and Magpie can all be found in the breeding season in the parks and in tiny green areas like the Bankside frontage, provided there are a few bushes and trees. Reed Warblers breed at Lavender Pond and Whitethroat can be found at Surrey Docks in May, where a Firecrest has been found in November, and Sedge and Wood Warblers occur on passage. Goldfinch breeds on waste ground.

Timing

Low tide is best for watching the Thames foreshore. Some of the parks and open spaces are less busy during the week than they are at weekends. Stormy conditions, especially North Sea gales, can bring interesting vagrants to the river.

Access

Public transport within the area is good but may not be convenient if travelling from some distance. When parking, remember that congestion charges may apply, currently on weekdays only and for the area between Tower Bridge and Vauxhall. Check when planning your journey.

The Jubilee Line goes from Waterloo to Canada Water. From north of the Thames, the most convenient Underground station is Surrey Quays. Greenland Dock is a quarter-of-a-mile from Surrey Quays, along the south side of the A2202 (Redriff Road). Southwark Park has an entrance close to Surrey Quays station. If you have a car, park in Rotherhithe or at the Surrey Quays shopping centre. Some of this area has good wheelchair access providing views over the Thames and the various parklands and waters.

Steps lead down from the west side of Tower Bridge to a waterside area, which includes the William Curtis Ecological Park. Bankside can be approached from Blackfriars Bridge or Southwark Street. Entrance to the Tate Modern (via the north entrance for wheelchairs) is free except for special exhibitions and accessible toilets are provided on each floor. Good views of the Thames can be had from Bankside and from the public promenades at the Festival Hall and the National Theatre, both by Waterloo Bridge, at Southbank. A disabled toilet is available in the old County Hall. For Battersea Park take the train (mainline service from Waterloo) to Queenstown and walk a quarter-of-a-mile along Queenstown Road. The nearest Underground station is Vauxhall (Victoria Line) and there are also buses. Local parking is possible but expensive. A parking bay for the disabled is in Albert Bridge Road. There is good wheelchair access in the park.

A promenade runs along the embankment west of Wandsworth Bridge but there is rather limited space for roadside parking. Adjacent streets offer parking space for King George's Park. There is roadside parking on the east side of Wandsworth Park.

Calendar

Resident: Great Crested Grebe, Greylag and Canada Geese, Mallard, Tufted Duck, Kestrel, Sparrowhawk, Peregrine, Moorhen, Coot, Pied and Grey Wagtails, Blackbird, Jay, Magpie, Goldfinch, Greenfinch, House Sparrow.

December–February: Cormorant and occasionally Shag in hard winters, duck on the Thames, chance of Ferruginous Duck, peak gull numbers, occasional auks (usually Guillemot or Razorbill).

March–May: Most likely time for Shag. Common Gull passage in March, terns from about 10 April, and most gulls leave by early May. Black Redstart on territory, most easily found in May and June, when the males are singing. Migrant warblers, especially at Surrey Docks and Battersea Park.

June–July: Breeding wildfowl in the parks and at Surrey Docks, Peregrine, small numbers of feeding Swifts by the river at Vauxhall, House Martins nesting at Surrey Docks.

August–November: Return of gulls, with Lesser Black-backed Gull passage. Look for Yellow-legged Gulls on the Thames barges. Migrant terns and passerines.

Habitat

Barnes has been an important site for birds ever since reservoirs were built there in the 1890s. The 'S' bends of the River Thames, which provides the course for the annual Oxford and Cambridge Boat Race, wind round the Barnes peninsula opposite Hammersmith Bridge (Map 2).

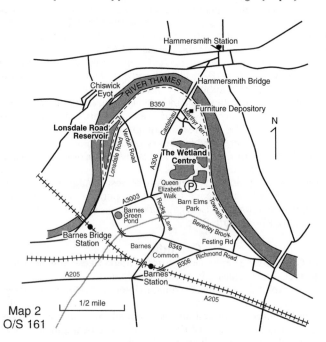

Map 2
O/S 161

Lonsdale Road Reservoirs formerly stretched all along the south side of the river west of Hammersmith Bridge. Only the most westerly basin, shaped like a bulging boomerang, survives, lying north–south against the river. This basin, also known as Leg o' Mutton on account of its shape, is no longer in commercial use and has been converted to a nature reserve. Its banks have become overgrown with thick vegetation. The dam at the north end has a good growth of reeds below it. Elms along the riverbank have now gone but there are some magnificent black poplars with a varied understorey of trees and bushes. Rafts have been moored in the reservoir to encourage nesting birds. There is a footpath around the whole site. The charm of Lonsdale Road Reservoir is that the birds may be seen, without hides, at much closer quarters than is usual, and residents and long stayers often become quite tame. New or irregular observers are not guaranteed scarce or rare birds, but the regulars consider themselves sufficiently well rewarded to keep going back. Spring and autumn migrants tend to stop off for short periods of a day or so and this is where the regular watcher scores.

Barn Elms Reservoirs, a group of four rectangular basins, had a limited variety of habitats but over 190 species were recorded there, many of which were uncommon. It was particularly strong on waterfowl and maritime wanderers. The Wildfowl and Wetlands Trust has now converted most of the site, officially known as The Wetland Centre but often referred to as Barn Elms or Barn Elms WWT, into an outstanding wetland reserve. A wildfowl collection on the west side is well displayed and fenced off from the much larger area maintained for wild birds. Reedbeds, wet meadows, dykes, pools of various sizes and depths, thickets and islands have been created, providing a much greater variety of habitat than previously existed. The old reservoirs froze over quite easily so that they tended to miss the hard-weather influxes of waterbirds, which at such times would move to the nearby Thames. Time will tell if this happens to the new waters when there is another hard winter.

Outside the western boundary of the centre there are large Victorian villas and mature gardens. At the north end there is a pond, the Harrods Furniture Depository and a new housing estate. To the east willows and acacias mark the riverbank and to the south are the mature playing fields of Barn Elms Park, with Barnes Common beyond. The common suffers from traffic noise but has rough grass, scrub and trees. There is a pond at Barnes Green. A towpath runs round the river frontage from Putney to Barnes Bridge.

Essex Skipper butterflies are quite abundant in the rough grass beside the river at Barn Elms and in the northeast corner at Lonsdale Road. Large and Small Skippers also occur, as do Common and Holly Blues and Meadow Browns. Purple Hairstreaks occur on Barnes Common and may turn up in the few oaks at the northwest end.

Species

Over 150 species have been recorded at The Wetland Centre since it was opened in 2000 and the number is climbing fast. The creation of new reedbeds has already been rewarded with wintering Bitterns. Little Egrets and a Cattle Egret have also appeared. Pintail, possibly of feral stock, have bred for the first time anywhere in the London area. Pochard and Little Ringed Plovers have also bred. A Marsh Harrier has been seen in spring and Redshank have been displaying. Waders on passage include godwits, Spotted Redshank, sandpipers and Turnstone. The seabird list includes Arctic Skua, Caspian and Yellow-legged Gulls and Kittiwake. Black Redstart (sometimes seen on the Furniture Depository), Ring

Bittern

Ouzel, Firecrest and Twite are among passerine migrants. Sedge, Marsh and Reed Warblers have bred or held territory. Reed Buntings breed. Listen for Cetti's Warbler and look for overwintering Chiffchaffs, including the Siberian race *P.c. tristis*. Ring-necked Parakeets may be heard from the front of The Wetland Centre and found in Barn Elms Park.

Little and Great Crested Grebes are breeding residents at Lonsdale Road Reservoir. Up to 80 Cormorants roost and feed and Mute Swans breed. Red-crested Pochards are annual, mostly in autumn, but thought to be of feral origin from the London parks, although some autumn or winter records might involve genuine vagrants. Pochard, a rare breeding bird in Britain, has successfully bred at the site, and Mallard and Tufted Duck breed annually. Duck numbers rise in October, reach a peak in the New Year and are usually well down by March. The reservoir is a regular loafing area for ducks, and Shoveler can often be very close. In winter there are usually a handful of Wigeon, Teal and Gadwall and up to 50 Mallards. Shoveler numbers peak at up to 200, Tufted Duck rather more. Pintail and Scaup are occasional. Scarcer duck include both Ferruginous and Ring-necked. Hard weather brings the largest numbers, provided the water remains unfrozen. Ruddy Duck is now seen regularly. Sparrowhawks are seen from time to time and breed nearby. Hobbies are becoming more frequent. Water Rails occur on passage as do a few waders, mainly Common Sandpipers. Gulls of all the commoner species can be seen on the foreshore east of Hammersmith Bridge; Yellow-legged Gulls often occur there. Common Terns breed on a raft and Reed Warblers in the reeds. Scarcer passerine migrants included a Subalpine Warbler in 2003.

Barnes Common has produced a Common Nighthawk. Great Spotted Woodpecker occurs in the big trees by the river, as has Monk Parakeet. Winter thrushes are found in Barn Elms Park. Blackcaps are present in the breeding season. Long-tailed Tits and Bullfinches are more likely in the winter. Reed Buntings sing along the riverbank and at Barn Elms pond. The pond at Barnes Green is crowded with wild and feral water-fowl including Mandarin and Shelduck, many of them breeding.

Timing

As birds on Lonsdale Road Reservoir can be viewed from all points of the compass, light is generally not a problem. The large parties of Swifts in May and August disperse well before dusk. The Wetland Centre is worth a visit at any time during its opening hours.

Access

Most of Lonsdale Road Reservoir can be well seen from the towpath and footpath at any time. Park in Verdun Road, opposite the north entrance. The nearest Underground station for the reservoir and The Wetland Centre is Hammersmith (Piccadilly, District and Hammersmith & City lines) but the closure of Hammersmith Bridge to traffic has complicated access. The nearest railway station is Barnes, a ten-minute walk away.

The entrance to The Wetland Centre is in Queen Elizabeth's Walk. There is a car park of moderate size, for which there is a charge. Free parking spaces are provided for the disabled. The visitor centre is excellent, if a shade expensive. Special care has been taken to provide good wheelchair access to the visitor centre and the mostly concrete paths round the site. There are six hides. The Peacock Tower hide has lifts to its three stories for wheelchair users. The centre is open 9.30am–6pm in summer and 9.30am–5pm in winter. It is closed on Christmas Day.

Calendar

Resident: Little and Great Crested Grebes, Canada Goose, Mallard, Tufted Duck, Kestrel, Pied Wagtail, Reed Bunting.

December–February: Chance of divers and the scarcer grebes, peak Great Crested Grebe numbers, Bittern, Grey Heron, peak wildfowl counts including large flocks of Shoveler, good numbers of Teal and a sprinkling of Goldeneye, sawbills, etc. Peak counts for most gulls with a chance of rarities, winter thrushes. Cetti's Warbler, overwintering Chiffchaff.

March–May: Look for Marsh Harrier at The Wetland Centre. Peak spring passage of waders and terns (Common, Arctic, Black) from the second week of April. Most waders are only infrequently seen and may fly over without stopping. Arctic Tern is scarce, but more likely at this season than in autumn.

June–July: Breeding wildfowl, Little Ringed Plover, Sedge and Reed Warblers, Reed Bunting, possible Redshank and Marsh Warbler. Flocks of feeding Swifts. Yellow-legged Gull numbers build up. Scarce migrants or vagrants such as Cattle Egret.

August–November: Yellow-legged Gulls on the foreshore. Chance of Little Egret at The Wetland Centre. Wader passage (stronger than in spring) mainly involves Common Sandpipers, with a few Oystercatchers, godwits, etc. Wintering ducks and gulls start to return. Little Gull is scarce, but more likely at this season. Common and Black Terns also tend to be more frequent in autumn. Pipits, warblers, Siberian Chiffchaff.

3 RICHMOND PARK AND ENVIRONS
OS Explorer 161

Habitat

Richmond Park and the adjacent gardens and commons extend for about 5 miles southeast from Kew to Wimbledon (Map 3). The Thames towpath, which has something to offer at most times of the year, marks the western boundary of Kew Gardens. The Gardens cover 120 ha and provide the chance of some relaxing birding. They include a lake with ornamental waterfowl and good stands of mature trees. There is a palm house and an 18th-century pagoda.

Three wooded islands (Brentford and Long Aits) in the Thames can be seen from the towpath at the north end of Kew Gardens. The towpath continues past the gardens to the west end of Old Deer Park, where there is a small nature reserve with willows, water and sedges. Isleworth Ait can be seen from here. The towpath then continues south through Richmond, passing Corporation Island (Richmond Ait) and on to

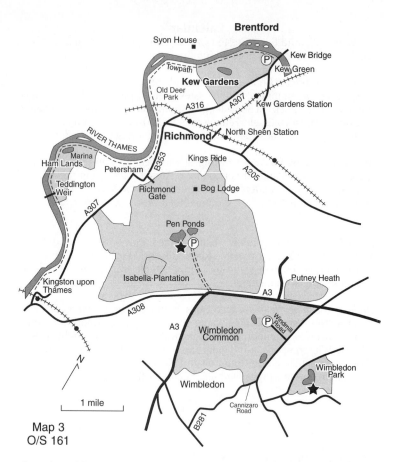

Map 3
O/S 161

Petersham Meadows, Eel Pie Island, Ham Lands, a secluded marina and Teddington Weir.

Petersham Meadows are not much visited by birdwatchers but Ham Lands, with approximately 80 ha of rough grass partially invaded by scrub, has produced a number of interesting records. A marina with wooded surrounds and a raft for birds can be seen from the towpath. Mammals include Fox and Badger. Teddington Weir has ledges for perching and plenty of visitors to feed the birds.

Richmond Park has NNR status and covers c.950 ha and is 8 miles (12 km) round. The bulk of it is rough grass with plantations of mature mixed woodland. Pollarded oaks are dotted about the open areas. Damp flushes here and there lead down to Pen Ponds, two connected waters in the middle of the park. This area tends to be the most interesting part of the site. The upper pond has a reedbed at one end and is partially surrounded by trees and fenced off. The abundant cover and good grazing supports a famous population of Red and Fallow Deer, which permit close approach but should, as park notices will remind you, be treated with caution especially in the rutting season (autumn).

Wimbledon Common, with Putney Heath to the north, covers some 461 ha and is an area of grass, scrub and mixed woodland on gravelly subsoil. It has SSSI status. There are ten ponds. The adjacent Wimbledon

Park is a rather dull, municipal affair, but it has a good-sized lake with bankside cover and is attractive to wintering and breeding wildfowl.

Species

Little and Great Crested Grebes breed in the parks across the area. Hobbies can be seen in summer. The commoner birds are often very tame: in heavily used areas, Robins and tits will follow you from bush to bush hoping for crumbs, and Nuthatches will feed from the hand.

Great Spotted Woodpecker

There are heronries on Brentford Ait and Corporation Island; also check Isleworth Ait. At Kew, looking across the river to Syon House, many Grey Herons may be feeding in marshy areas on the other bank, the birds coming from one of the Brentford and other heronries, and possibly a few Snipe.

Black Swans and Egyptian Geese have raised young at Kew from time to time. The rather tame Red-crested Pochards often seen at Kew and in Richmond Park are escapes or possibly feral birds.

Yellow-legged and Caspian Gulls have been seen among the gulls feeding and loafing at Eel Pie Island. There have been rare winter occurrences of Guillemots on the river at Kew, as elsewhere on the Thames and adjacent reservoirs.

Ring-necked Parakeets, part of the feral population in northern and central Surrey, are quite often seen. Parties of up to 20 are not uncommon along the Thames Valley from Kew to Walton and Egham and are best looked for by Pen Ponds in Richmond Park. The birds appear to be able to survive hard winters. They nest in holes in trees, sometimes visiting gardens for apples and other fruit. Ring-necked Parakeets have been known to cause confusion with inexperienced birdwatchers, but now appear in most field guides.

Green Woodpecker is frequent in Kew Gardens, which is a good place for the commoner breeding water and woodland birds. Migrants at Kew have included Red Kite, Firecrest and Pied Flycatcher.

About 45 bird species breed in Richmond Park. Pen Ponds have the commoner breeding waterfowl including Great Crested Grebes. Grey Herons are regular at the upper pond, as are large numbers of Gadwall in winter and Pochard, a very scarce breeder in Surrey, has raised young more than once. Mandarin has colonised. Little and Tawny Owls are present. Stock Doves are common round the oaks. This is a good place for woodpeckers, though Lesser Spotted Woodpecker can be elusive. Great Spotted is the commonest. There is a good variety of warblers and other woodland passerines. Meadow Pipit breeds in rough grass. Watch the pollarded oaks west of Pen Ponds for Tree Sparrow. Reed Bunting, which is present all year, can be absurdly tame and will approach to within a few feet in well-used areas such as the shore of Pen Ponds or the small pond in Isabella Plantation. Large raptors, including Honey Buzzard and Red Kite, are seen occasionally. Watch for a Hobby or two in summer. Spring overshoots have included Golden Oriole and Ortolan Bunting. The ponds receive wintering flocks of Tufted and other duck. Very occasionally Bearded Tit (a scarce species in Surrey at any time) has been found in the reedbed. Scrub at Bog Lodge can attract migrants including Whinchat and Wheatear and once a Barred Warbler. Stonechat and the odd Dartford Warbler have wintered. Overall, about 100 species are recorded in the park in an average year.

The bushes on Ham Lands support a good variety of warblers in summer. Winter visitors to the river and meadows at Ham include Goosander, occasionally a Short-eared Owl, Fieldfares and Redwings. Common Terns have attempted to breed at the marina on Ham Lands towpath. There are many Ring-necked Parakeets.

Wimbledon Common and Putney Heath hold a variety of woodland and open-country birds including breeding Tree Pipit. Ornamental rowans with large, persistent berries lining one of the adjacent streets have sustained wintering Waxwings. Wimbledon Park Lake attracts wintering Shoveler and Goosander. Great Crested Grebe and Canada Goose breed. Migrants in summer include Garden Warbler in the lakeside scrub.

Timing

The towpath is most comfortably walked in the downstream direction to keep the sun as far as possible behind you. Kew Gardens and Richmond Park have opening and closing hours which vary seasonally. It is best to try Richmond Park early in the day, when there are fewer people about, especially for the chance of a migrant wader at Pen Ponds. The park can become very crowded, particularly on summer weekends. Evenings may be best for Tawny Owls, if the park is open.

Wimbledon Common is best early in the day and is likely to be unrewarding for birdwatching on summer afternoons. Wimbledon Park Lake can only be well seen from the southeast, so mornings are best here too.

Access

Kew Gardens is on the A307 (Kew Road). Park at the main entrance in Kew Green, at the north end or at the riverside car park reached from Kew Green via Ferry Lane. There is an admission charge. Opening hours are currently from 9.30am daily except Christmas Day and New Years Day. Closing time varies from 3.30pm to 6.30pm. Wheelchair access is possible to many areas, and there are wheelchairs for hire, parking spaces for the disabled, a cafeteria, visitor centre and fully accessible toilets. There is a bus route around the grounds. The towpath can be reached from a number of points at the Kew end, including the riverside car park at Kew Gardens. There is a long stretch from just south of Kew to near Twickenham Bridge where no access is possible. Kew Gardens Underground station is on the District Line.

Richmond Park can be reached from the A307 or the A3. There are several car parks on the perimeter road in the park and one on higher ground in the middle, overlooking Pen Ponds. Designated disabled parking is available at the Isabella Plantation car park, access via Ham Cross. Many of the paths are suitable for wheelchairs. The nearest railway station is North Sheen, a three-quarter-mile walk south along the B353 (Manor Road), then right into Sheen Road to the Kings Ride entrance. Alternatively go to Richmond (train or Underground) and take the 371 bus to Richmond Park Gate.

Putney Heath and Wimbledon Common are readily accessed from the A3 by taking the Putney Heath exit just north of the entrance to Richmond Park. Wimbledon Common can also be approached from Parkside or, from the south, along Cannizaro Road and West Side Common. There is a car park at the windmill. The Windmill Nature Trail has been designed to be accessible to wheelchair users. The entrance to Wimbledon Park is in Wimbledon Park Road, SW19.

Calendar

Resident: Great Crested Grebe, Canada Goose, exotic waterfowl of various origins, Sparrowhawk, Kestrel, Little and Tawny Owls, Stock Dove, Ring-necked Parakeet, woodpeckers, Meadow Pipit, Nuthatch, Reed Bunting, Grey Partridge has been introduced into Richmond Park.

December–February: Wintering Gadwall, Tufted Duck, Pochard, Shoveler, Goldeneye, Goosander. Smew is becoming regular on Pen Ponds. Short-eared Owl has wintered in Richmond Park, as has Dartford Warbler.

March–May: Heronries. Southern migrants in Richmond Park. Wintering duck leave but watch for Mandarin and lingering Pochard. Stock Doves active, warblers and Tree Pipit arrive.

June–July: Breeding waterfowl, Hobby, pipits, Blackcap, Garden Warbler.

August–November: Wintering duck and Stonechats begin to return. Migrant terns and chats. Fieldfare (small numbers) and Redwing (flocks) from the end of September.

4 THE UPPER THAMES VALLEY

Habitat

The upper part of the Thames Valley from Weybridge west to the Surrey border at Staines broadens into an extensive plain of low-lying soils and gravels. It has been exploited for various commercial purposes, the most important of which, for the birdwatcher, is the supply of water to the metropolis. The system of reservoirs that now exists has been constructed in stages since the turn of the 19th century and has had a major impact on the birdlife of the area. The reservoirs are of a distinctive bunded design, being excavated from the gravel floor and built up above ground level with surrounding embankments, which have sloping, grass-covered sides up to about 9 m high which are sometimes grazed by sheep or cattle. Occasionally individual reservoir basins are drained, exposing a large expanse of gravelly mud that converts the larger ones into a kind of tideless estuary. The gravels have been heavily worked for building materials and there are many pits, some being excavated, others water-filled or at intermediate stages of maturity.

Because of the size of the larger waters, a telescope is advisable for reservoir observation, especially in winter when there may be difficult identification problems with divers, grebes or duck. A telescope is best for good views at the reservoirs generally, since binoculars on their own will often not have enough range.

The eastern edge of Windsor Great Park runs down the Surrey border at Egham. It includes Virginia Water, one of the county's larger lakes.

Species

Gulls were scarce in the London area in the 19th century but now roost on the western reservoirs in huge numbers. Divers, grebes and many seabirds, wildfowl, waders and passerines use them on passage or for wintering. Drained reservoirs quickly attract breeding and migrant waders, sometimes including rarities, and they may stay long periods. The grassy slopes on the sides of reservoirs provide suitable habitat for pipits and other migrants. The gravel pits offer a more stable habitat for breeders and species nesting at least sporadically in suitable places include Shelduck, Pochard, Little Ringed Plover, Ringed Plover, Redshank and Sand Martin, as well as commoner waterbirds such as Little and Great Crested Grebes, Moorhens, Coot and Canada Geese. Airborne feeders and hunters include Hobby, Peregrine, House Martin and Swift.

Main Birdwatching Zones

The reservoirs and gravel pits at Walton are a compact group mostly within sight of one another. The Staines area, a little higher up the Thames, is covered next. It contains some of the biggest reservoirs in the London area and enough gravel pits to make it almost more water than land. It straddles the river and includes the Spelthorne district, which is part of the old county of Middlesex but now in the administrative county of Surrey. Virginia Water, set in old parkland, is 3 miles southwest of Staines town centre.

WALTON RESERVOIRS and PITS (Map 4a, OS Explorer 161)

Habitat

The main reservoirs at Walton-on-Thames are the Knight and Bessborough group, Queen Elizabeth II and Island Barn. Island Barn Reservoir is on an island in the River Ember. Chelsea and Lambeth have been decommissioned and are being excavated for gravel. There are plans to construct a nature reserve when extraction is complete. Since they have, in the recent past, held Squacco Heron, breeding Ruddy Duck, Avocet, breeding Little Ringed Plover, Temminck's Stint, White-rumped Sandpiper, Cetti's Warbler, Marsh Warbler and numerous breeding Reed Warblers, the long-term prospects appear good. Knight and Bessborough Reservoirs are deep, and among the last of the local reservoirs to freeze in hard weather. Occasionally they are drained, attracting numerous waders.

Molesey Heath and Hersham Gravel Pit lie between Island Barn and Queen Elizabeth II Reservoirs. Molesey Heath is an area of rough ground and scrub. Hersham Gravel Pit has been partially filled, leaving an area of badly drained, made-up ground.

Hersham Sewage Farm, at the south end of the site and running alongside the railway to Hersham station, is disused and overgrown. It is worth a scan at any time of the year, but will be most interesting if not dry.

Esher Rugby Club (TQ 122659) is fringed on two sides by poplars. Elmbridge Leisure Centre, on the Thames a short distance to the west of Walton Reservoirs, has an avenue of poplars by the approach road and a substantial area of scrubland behind the car park. Hurst Park has riverside frontage at the east end and areas of damp meadow and scrub.

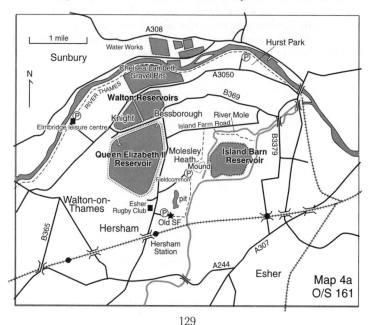

Species

Great Northern and other divers can remain at Walton for long periods, sometimes moving from one reservoir to another or visiting those in the Staines group. The whole group may be profitably scanned for the scarcer grebes and for Eider, Long-tailed Duck, Ruddy Duck and other wildfowl. The basins are attractive to various waders that feed on the shelving concrete edges. Hobbies are often seen in summer. There are few breeding species on the reservoirs but Shelduck occasionally breed and Common Terns regularly do so on rafts at Queen Elizabeth II.

Goldeneye are mainly found on Knight and Bessborough, peaking at over 40 in March or April. Goosander, occasional divers and a large flock of wintering Coot are found there, and small numbers of Smew are occasionally present in winter. Recent vagrants at Knight and Bessborough have included Pied-billed Grebe, Manx Shearwater and Leach's Petrel.

Queen Elizabeth II Reservoir is important as a winter wildfowl haven, especially for Shoveler, and the reservoir also attracts unusually large numbers of wintering Cormorant, currently over 600. The winter gull roost is extremely large and sometimes includes Mediterranean, Yellow-legged, Iceland and Glaucous Gulls. There is a strong passage of waders, Little Gulls and terns. Recent vagrants have included Fulmar, Leach's Petrel, Storm Petrel and Ortolan.

Island Barn Reservoir often holds a large flock of wintering Teal as well as other duck, the scarcer grebes and sometimes divers.

Molesey Heath has Sedge Warblers and Lesser Whitethroats. Rough ground around Hersham Gravel Pit is worth checking for Mandarin, Egyptian Geese and Shelduck. The Mandarin feed mainly on land rather than water and may be flushed from the rough grass, where there may also be a Short-eared Owl in winter. Large flocks of Lapwings have been seen at the same season. Numbers of other waders depend on the amount of surface water. There may be Jack Snipe, Water Pipit and roving flocks of finches (including Twite on rare occasions) in winter. Ring-necked Parakeets breed locally and may be seen flying over. Hersham Sewage Farm has breeding Reed Warbler and Reed Bunting.

Poplars at Elmbridge Leisure Centre were the original site of the Ring-necked Parakeet roost, but this has now moved to poplars at Esher Rugby

Ring-necked Parakeets

Club, where peak numbers have exceeded 6,000. Scrub behind the leisure centre holds many warblers in summer.

There is a large autumn and winter Mute Swan flock on the Thames at Hurst Park, typically peaking at over 100. Various waders and pipits have bred or attempted to breed on rough ground but are subject to considerable disturbance.

Timing

Walton reservoirs are open from 7.30am to 4.30pm, Monday–Thursday, but close at 1.30pm on Friday. There is no entry on Bank Holidays. Some of the reservoirs and all the gravel pits can freeze over in long spells of severe weather, driving wildfowl onto the Thames or to more distant unfrozen localities. Deeper reservoirs, which do not normally freeze, include Knight and Bessborough. Yachting can disturb waterfowl at Island Barn, so visit early. Avoid misty mornings, when the reservoir can be fogged out even if the surrounding area is clear. Ring-necked Parakeets arrive at the Rugby Club roost in a 45-minute period starting at dusk, about 4.30pm in December and January, when numbers normally peak.

Access

The entrance to Knight and Bessborough Reservoirs is on the A3050 (Hurst Road), but note that a Thames Water birdwatching pass is needed for access, which is via a steep flight of steps.

Island Barn Reservoir can be approached from Island Farm Road, turning down Ray Road to the entrance. There is room to park a car in adjacent roads. The water can be viewed from the top of the steps by the sailing club. A special permit from Thames Water (normally only granted to wildfowl counters) is needed. To avoid this, park in Approach Road at the entrance to Molesey Heath and walk across the heath to a mound, from the top of which partial views over Island Barn can be obtained. This is also the best area for warblers.

For Hersham Sewage Farm and Gravel Pit, park in the lane on the edge of the estate 500 yards north of the railway bridge over Molesey Road and to the east of it. A footpath connects the two sites, affording views of both. It then turns left along the River Mole, where large numbers of duck may be seen in winter. Park in the same lane for Esher Rugby Club and walk back to cross over Molesey Road. A footpath leads round the north side of the poplars.

Access to Queen Elizabeth II Reservoir is by special arrangement with Thames Water. There is a steep bank. Elmbridge Leisure Centre and Hurst Park have car parks. Paths in this area afford views of the Thames.

Wheelchair users can see the Esher Rugby Club parakeets from Molesey Road. No other part of the Walton Reservoirs and Pits site is accessible by wheelchair.

STAINES and DISTRICT (Map 4b, OS Explorer 160)

Habitat

Heathrow Airport, northeast of Staines, provides a noisy backdrop to the district. There are gravel pits either side of the Thames out to Wraysbury and beyond. Some of the older ones are used for watersports.

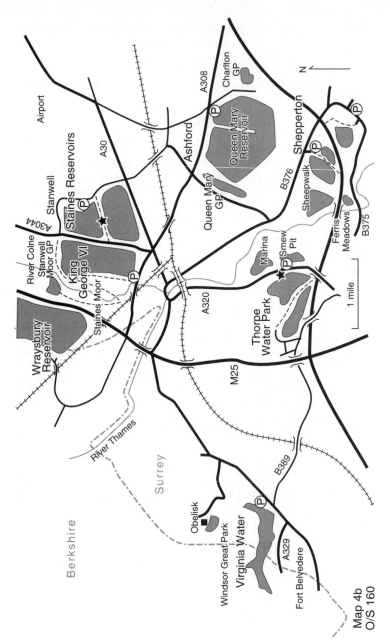

Wraysbury, King George VI, Staines and Queen Mary reservoirs are all within a short distance. Wraysbury has nature reserve status on account of its wildfowl and a Peregrine nest box has been placed there. Staines Reservoirs comprises two basins divided by a causeway with a public footpath along it. The water depth, about 3 m, is very suitable for diving duck. From time to time, one or other of the Staines basins is drained for maintenance, an operation that leaves a rich habitat of shallow pools, shingle bars and mud with deeper channels between. This can be especially fruitful if it is the north basin, because of the direction of the light. (The general effect, from the causeway, has been likened to looking across the Channel.) In such circumstances patience is called for, to wait until the feeding waders move to the closer expanses of mud and sand.

Staines Moor is a flat valley of the River Colne between Wraysbury and King George VI reservoirs. Parts of the meadow are waterlogged and there is a small gravel pit and a shallow pool at the north end. The main part of the moor has an interesting flora and is a designated SSSI, largely on that account. The northern part, including the pit at Stanwell Moor, is not within the SSSI. The M25 runs along the western edge of the site.

Queen Mary Reservoir, to the east, is over 1 mile wide. A long causeway running north–south almost divides it into two but does not reach the southern side. The causeway separates the west end of the reservoir, which is used for sailing, from the east end, which is a wildfowl reserve. It is a roosting place and is usually off-limits to birdwatchers and yachtsmen. The causeway has attracted many scarce migrants. Disturbance from sailing has tended to reduce the reservoir's attractiveness to birds, but it is still a very important site. Queen Mary tends not to freeze over completely in hard weather because of the turbulent water at the intake. Queen Mary Gravel Pits are on the western side of Queen Mary. Charlton Gravel Pits and a waterworks lie to the east.

There is a large and complicated group of pits at Shepperton, half-a-mile (1 km) south of Queen Mary Reservoir. Two of them, Sheepwalk Lake and adjacent Poole End Lake, are Surrey Wildlife Trust reserves. The pits are in various stages of their lifecycle and new ones are still being opened. Some of the older ones are used for watersports, angling and other recreational purposes.

Lying a little to the south of the Thames, Thorpe Water Park is part of a series of old pits that have been landscaped and used for pleasure craft, watersports and passive recreation. It has a small reserve and an interesting pit across the A320 from Thorpe Water Park. One of the pits at nearby Penton Hook is used as a marina. Others at Penton Hook and behind Thorpe are water-filled and disused, attractive to both wintering and summering species. All are relatively easy of access and can provide productive birdwatching.

Species

Staines Reservoirs are of national significance for Shoveler, Tufted Duck and Ruddy Duck. Knight and Bessborough Reservoirs are nationally important for Shoveler and Ruddy Duck, and Thorpe Water Park is for Smew.

Black-headed Gulls and Common Terns breed on rafts in the north and south basins of Staines Reservoirs. If the floors of any of the reservoirs are exposed in spring and early summer there will be breeding waders, especially Lapwing and Little Ringed Plover. Ringed Plover breeds very sparingly in the Thames Valley and might also choose such a site. Hobbies appear in spring and late summer, feeding on hirundines. Little Gull and Black Terns sometimes occur in large numbers during spring or autumn passage. A flock of Black-necked Grebes can be seen at close range in autumn. Peak numbers are lower than formerly, possibly because of the frequent draining and refilling operations, but this is still the best Surrey site for the species. Rare waders which have occurred on the drained basins include American vagrants such as Baird's Sandpiper, Long-billed Dowitcher, Lesser Yellowlegs and Wilson's Phalarope. Red-necked Phalarope appears occasionally in autumn. Yellow Wagtails appear regularly along the causeway at Staines in spring and autumn.

Wildfowl numbers build up in winter, with good numbers of Smew in some years. Winter duck include over 500 Tufted. Sparrowhawks regular. A Merlin may occasionally attack any small seed-eating birds feeding on vegetation that has grown up after drainage. Look for Peregrine perched on the pylons.

Staines Moor is a significant wintering site for Golden Plover and sometimes also attracts some of the rarer geese, such as Bean, which has occurred in severe winter weather. Jack Snipe and Short-eared Owl may also occur in winter. The bank of King George VI Reservoir bordering the moor is worth examining for chats, Ring Ouzel and other migrants. The pits and pools at Stanwell Moor attract various waterbirds, including Spoonbill and Red-necked Phalarope at least once.

Queen Mary has a major winter gull roost and smaller numbers roost on Staines and Wraysbury Reservoirs. The gulls fan out in all directions for 30 miles or more each day to feed in the surrounding countryside, and their regular morning and late-afternoon movements are a common sight across much of Surrey. Queen Mary Reservoir has a good record for divers and the scarcer grebes and is a major wildfowl site, especially for Great Crested Grebe and Shoveler. Large numbers of Goosander are often present in cold spells. Other wintering duck include smaller numbers of Gadwall, Teal, Pochard and Goldeneye. Skuas and White-winged Black Tern have been recorded on passage, as have storm-driven Sabine's Gulls. The adjacent gravel pits can be seen well from the embankment, giving views, at suitable times, of spring overshoots such as Spoonbill, and migrant or breeding waders. Migrants at Charlton Gravel Pit have included Little Egret and Scaup.

Shepperton Gravel Pits have large numbers of wintering Coot and Tufted Duck and smaller numbers of other wildfowl. Excavations and infilling disturb breeding activities and the water levels are in some places unstable, so that Great Crested Grebe and Coot may be seen nesting high and dry on sandbanks. Egyptian Geese have recently bred at Ferris Meadows Gravel Pit (TQ 077662). The tree-lined causeways across some of the pits hold migrant passerines in spring and autumn. Little Ringed Plover and Sand Martins exploit suitable sites. Common Terns can be seen here, as elsewhere in the Staines area, in summer and have bred in the general area in appropriate conditions. Corn Buntings formerly bred in fields around the pits but are now absent.

Thorpe Water Park and the adjacent pits are worth scanning for migrant terns, which do not seem to mind the boats and water-skiers. Grebes and Canada Geese breed there and are present all year. The site is best in winter when there are occasional divers, Red-necked and Slavonian Grebes, a flock of Smew that may number over 20 and many Goosander, as well as other wildfowl and a good mix of gulls. The pit across the A320 from Thorpe Water Park is often the best one for Smew.

Timing

The basins at Staines are very large, but on a day with good light the north side can be seen excellently from the causeway. The southern basin is more difficult to view in strong light, and better watched on a duller day or in the morning or evening. Staines is especially good in autumn, when Black-necked Grebe numbers peak and there is the chance of seeing a variety of terns and other migrants. There will not be a large number of waders at Staines unless one of the basins is drained. This seems to happen quite often for maintenance or other reasons, but there is no regular cycle.

Many people use the drier parts of Staines Moor for dog walking and exercise, and there is some fishing. Early morning is best.

Early morning will also be best at Thorpe on the busier spring and winter days, though for most of the pits disturbance is not a serious problem and a visit at any time of day will do.

Access

The reservoirs at Staines are best approached from the A30, turning north into Town Lane, which runs along the east side. The public footpath between the basins gives good views. It is reached by ramps from Town Lane or Stanwell Moor Road. Staines Moor lies to the west of King George VI Reservoir and can be accessed from a lay-by on the A30 at the southern end, or from the north at Stanwell Moor, parking in Hithermoor Road and following a concrete footpath to the moors. Paths across the moors are uneven and often muddy. There is a railway station at Staines. Buses run from Staines to Stanwell Moor.

Visits to Wraysbury and King George VI require special permission from Thames Water, which are not covered by the normal permit.

A Thames Water birdwatching pass is needed to access Queen Mary Reservoir. The pass also covers access to Kempton and Walton. The entrance is at the northeast corner, adjacent to the junction of Ashford Road and Staines Road West. The reservoir is open 7.30am–4.30pm, Wednesday–Sunday, for permit holders. King George VI and Wraysbury Reservoirs are not open to public access.

Shepperton Gravel Pits can be seen quite well from surrounding roads but are most conveniently explored from the public footpath that crosses the main part of the site. This can be accessed from Fairview Drive, a turning south off the B376 (Laleham Road) half-a-mile west of the bridge over the M3. There is room to park a car at the end of Fairview Drive. A path leads out between the Littleton Lane East and Sheepwalk pits. Access to Poole End Lake is from Sheepwalk. Another approach to the site is from the B375 in Shepperton. Leave the car in the public car park in Church Road, close to the cricket ground. Walk a quarter-of-a-mile back to Cemetery Lane, on the other side of the road. The cemetery itself is at the end of the lane. Walk through the cemetery and take the public footpath that runs by the Sheepwalk pits and lake.

Thorpe Water Park is on the A320 between Chertsey and Staines. Alder Valley buses stop outside. There is a car park inside the main entrance, for use by patrons. Alternatively cars can be pulled off the road onto the grass. A five-bar gate beside the A320 affords good views over much of the water and more can be seen from a public footpath that runs across the park from St Mary's Church, on Coldharbour Lane, to the A320. Parking at the church is possible but congested. Try, obviously, to avoid parking there on Sunday mornings. The best Smew pit, on the opposite side of the A320, can be viewed from the footpath. Park in the adjacent lay-by. Other nearby pits can be seen well from surrounding roads, where there are a number of small lay-bys such as those on the west side of the A320 south of the bridge over the M25.

The concrete path to Staines Moor is suitable for wheelchairs but most, if not all, of the rest of the site as described is not.

VIRGINIA WATER (Map 4b, OS EXPLORER 160)

Habitat

Windsor Great Park is mature old parkland. The main lake, Virginia Water, is surrounded by gently rising ground, on which are stands of oak, sweet chestnut, beech, ash and pine, dense with rhododendrons in parts. There are patches of heathland grasses and broad lawns of the kind that occasionally attracts an overshooting Hoopoe in spring. It is possible to walk around the lake and also, on the north side, to a smaller water, Obelisk Pond.

Species

There is a heronry on private land at Fort Belvedere to the south. It has up to 40 nests in good years. Records go back to 1607 and show that the site of the heronry has moved several times. Although it is currently in mixed woodland, virtually all of the nests are in Scots pine.

Windsor Great Park is strikingly like the native Oriental haunts of its colony of Mandarin. Being a tree-nesting species, the Mandarin may not always be obvious in summer, although there are always a few to be seen. They will sometimes rest on the grass by the lake if undisturbed. Numbers rise after the breeding season and up to 100 are possible in December. Wood Ducks are occasionally seen. For some reason, this close relative of the Mandarin has been much less successful in adapting from its native North America to Britain. The males, which have boldly striped and crested heads and lack the Mandarin's orange 'sails' on the wing, are easily separated in breeding plumage. Females, birds in moult and immatures require more care and are best distinguished by different head markings on the females and traces of a greenish head gloss on the males.

A few Reed Warbler breed in the small stands of reeds established along the water's edge, among the more extensive sweet flag. They should be easy to hear in May or June, although they may be harder to see because their song posts are usually well below the top of the reeds.

There are many species of woodland birds, including the three woodpeckers, Nuthatch and Marsh Tit. Hawfinches have been reported but are hard to find and the best chance may be in the Berkshire part of the park. Winter brings Siskin and Redpoll to alders around the lake and other finch flocks may contain Brambling.

Timing

The Fort Belvedere heronry is very active in May and June. Mandarin is best seen in December and January. Early-morning visits in May give the best chance of finding migrants and warblers. Avoid afternoons, especially in summer, when the park can get rather full.

Access

Approach Virginia Water from the A30. There is very limited parking in lay-bys in Wick Lane and Wick Road, otherwise use the official car parks, the most convenient of which is on the west side of the road just north of the junction with the B389.

Access to Fort Belvedere is usually restricted to those carrying out census or research work and is controlled by the Crown Commissioners, Windsor Great Park, to whom application should be made if required. The entrance is in the A329 (Blacknest Road), off the A30 south of Virginia Water. A key from the Commissioners is needed.

Calendar

Resident: Great Crested Grebe, Canada Goose, Mandarin (Virginia Water), Tufted Duck, Ruddy Duck, Sparrowhawk, Ring-necked Parakeet.

December–February: Black-necked Grebe (Staines), divers (Staines), grey geese, Mandarin flock (Virginia Water), Gadwall, Teal, Shoveler, Pochard, Tufted Duck, Long-tailed Duck (Staines), Goldeneye, Goosander, Red-breasted Merganser, Smew (Thorpe), A Peregrine may be seen at Staines. Golden Plover (Staines Moor). Peak time for gull roosts, including a few Mediterranean and Glaucous Gulls. There is sometimes a Black Redstart in the vicinity of the towers at the west end of Staines Reservoirs causeway. Fieldfare, Redwing, Brambling. Severe winter weather may bring Snow Buntings to exposed parts of the margin of the reservoirs — check the causeway at Staines. Peak time for Ring-necked Parakeet, 4,000+ have been recorded roosting at Esher Rugby Club.

March–May: Spring wader passage. Parties of Avocets are now being seen more often in spring. Common, Arctic, Sandwich, Little and Black Terns, White and Yellow Wagtails.

June–July: Overshoots such as Spoonbill and Hoopoe. Hobbies feeding over the reservoirs and pits. Black-headed Gull and Common Tern breed. Possibility of Little Ringed Plover.

August–November: Black-necked Grebe and terns at Staines (peak August). Best chance of White-winged Black Tern in August/September. Return wader passage peaks in August. Goldeneye return from mid-November.

5 THE WEY VALLEY, EASHING TO GUILDFORD OS Explorer 145

Habitat

From Eashing, above Godalming, through to Guildford (Map 5) the River Wey has been spared most of the river improvements commonly applied by water authorities and it winds through a floodplain of water meadows, willow and alder copses. A shallow canal, the River Wey Navigation, runs parallel with part of it and is used by a small number of pleasure craft, mainly in the summer. In midsummer the river and canal margins

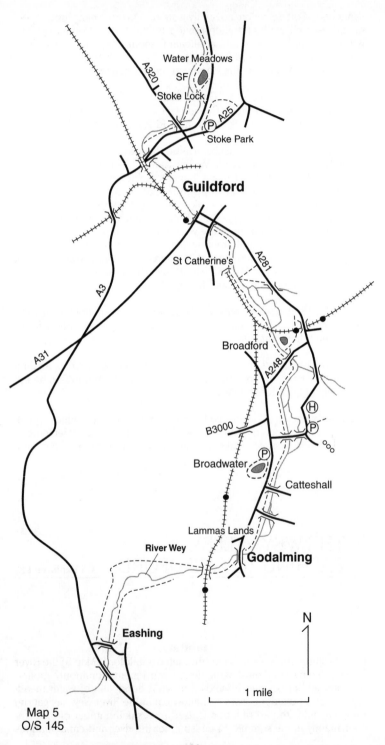

Water Meadows
SF
Stoke Lock
A320
P
A25
Stoke Park

Guildford

St Catherine's
A281
A3
A31
Broadford
A248
B3000
H
P
○○○
Broadwater
P
Catteshall
Lammas Lands
River Wey
Godalming
N
Eashing

1 mile

Map 5
O/S 145

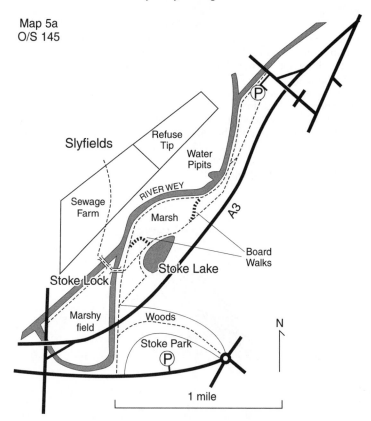

Map 5a
O/S 145

have stands of alder, purple loosestrife, agrimony, balsams, thistles and sedges and there are many species of dragonfly. Wey Valley Marshes are the largest Surrey remnant of the water meadow and marshland habitat now threatened in so many parts of England.

At Unstead there is a modernised sewage farm (Godalming Sewage Farm), much of which can be seen from a public footpath across it. Thames Water has cooperated in converting the old sludge lagoons into an excellent nature reserve. There is a platform for terns.

At Guildford the valley passes through a narrow gap in the North Downs and then broadens out to the best-developed section of water meadow and marsh, at Stoke, which is now managed as a nature park.

The Stoke area (map 5a) has gravel deposits overlaying London clay. Excavation of gravel for road works has left a landscaped pool with a small island. Higher levels of clay support fine fringing woodland in Stoke Park. The A3 runs through the valley but the road is quite well screened by high earth banks. There are examples of five habitats: river, water meadows and marsh, a lake and island, a meadow with mature hedgerows, and mature woodland with some very old chestnut trees. The remaining lagoons on the older part of Guildford Sewage Farm, on the north side of the river, are in poor condition and inaccessible, but most its old bird specialities can be seen in more agreeable circumstances round and near the lake. There is a wet meadow on the north side of the River Wey at TQ 008525. It has a scrape and is viewable from the towpath on the opposite bank.

Species

Water Rails, Lapwings, Snipe, Sedge Warblers, Reed Warblers and Reed Buntings breed on marshes and wet meadows in the Wey Valley.

At Eashing, approaching from the A3 end, there may be a Grey Wagtail on the river by Eashing Bridge. The riverside path downstream passes a small marsh and an alder copse. The riverbanks at this point are quite high. Species to look for at appropriate times include Water Rail, Snipe, Kingfisher, Lesser Redpoll, Sedge Warbler and Siskin. Steep hillside woods then lead into Godalming. The Lammas Lands in Godalming have many Mute Swans, Canada Geese and Mallard, and occasionally an Egyptian Goose. In winter there are Lapwings, Snipe, Fieldfares and Redwings. Barnacle and other feral geese are often present.

Sedge Warbler

Broadwater Lake, at Farncombe, is popular with anglers, notably for its carp. It has an island with breeding waterbirds including grebes. Grey Herons and Kingfishers may be seen. Wintering species include Coot, Mallard, Shoveler, Pochard and Tufted Duck, and occasionally others, such as Pintail.

From Catteshall, on the edge of Godalming, follow the towpath along the River Wey Navigation to Guildford. Unstead Sewage Farm is a good place to see breeding Water Rails. Common Terns have begun to breed there. The site has a few Jack Snipe and Water Pipit among its wintering birds. Regular migrant waders include Green, Wood and Common Sandpipers. Vagrants include Black-necked Grebe, Little Egret, Bittern, Spoonbill, Red Kite, Goshawk, Spotted Crake and Black Redstart. The water meadows between Unstead and Guildford flood in most winters and have attracted Bewick's and Whooper Swans.

At Broadford there is another small marsh tucked against the railway line. This is not easy to view, but at the right time the open mud, reeds and rushes will hold a few migrant waders and warblers. Reed Buntings are conspicuous here and along the next stretch of locks into Guildford. Passing under the hill at St Catherine's you are suddenly in a narrow outcrop of

Greensand with a railway tunnel through it. Meadows on the opposite side of the river sometimes flood in winter, attracting gulls and wildfowl.

Another excellent area is at Stoke, with a large variety of waterside and woodland birds. Breeding species on the lake and in the marsh include Great Crested Grebe, Tufted Duck, Water Rail and, since the provision of a raft, Common Tern. The site has been visited by many of the scorcer Surrey migrants, including Red-throated and Great Northern Divers, Purple Heron, Brent Goose, Eider, Osprey, Peregrine, Avocet, Kentish Plover, Red-rumped Swallow and Yellow-browed Warbler. There may be an impressive number of birds on winter mornings, with Pochard, Tufted and other duck on the lake, a flock of gulls, up to 200 Canada Geese feeding on the grass and a large party of Stock Doves and Woodpigeons working the field. Look for Red Kite, Common Buzzard, Hobby or other raptors that may be passing through.

Old hedges provide a varied food supply for thrushes and, in summer, are ideal for Lesser Whitethroats. The marsh by the river supports Reed and Sedge Warblers. Riverside alders and thistles provide food for many Goldfinches, Redpolls and Siskins at appropriate times. Tree Sparrows used to like the many woodpecker holes but have now been lost. Old pollarded willows provide nest sites for Treecreeper and occasionally a Little Owl.

The wet meadow on the north side of the Wey is a major British wintering site for Water Pipits, with occasional Scandinavian Rock Pipits among them. The woods in Stoke Park usually hold all three species of woodpecker and, in summer, a significant population of warblers. Migrant Wood Warblers come through in May.

Timing
Stoke Water Meadows are best in the early morning because birds on the shore of Stoke Lake are then less likely to have been disturbed.

Access
The Eashing stretch can be entered by turning east at the Eashing exit of the A3, 1 mile north of Milford. Footpaths enable you to follow the river from Eashing to Guildford. A public footpath runs across Guildford Sewage Farm and a new path has been made across the west end of the site, leading to a hide that may be locked. For permission to explore further, apply to Thames Water, to whom the site is known as Godalming Sewage Farm.

The Stoke area can be approached from a car park in Burpham, at TQ 011527. This is the easiest way to get to the Water Pipit area, which can be viewed from the towpath. The woods and the lake can be explored on foot from the car park of the Spectrum sports centre on the north side of Stoke Park. Walk to the junction of the A25 and the A320, at TQ 010510, and proceed through the crescent-shaped wood on the north side of the A25, along a gravel path that leads to the river. Another approach is along the towpath, from the Woking road. There is also a footpath from Slyfields across Guildford Sewage Farm to Stoke Lock, where there are bridges. The unmodernised part of the sewage farm is difficult to view from adjacent footpaths. Permits to enter should be sought from Thames Water, but may not be worth the trouble.

Broadwater Lake has a car park and a good path with a bench or two starting from it. None of the remaining area described is suitable for wheelchairs, although limited views can be obtained from the parking areas at Stoke and Unstead.

Calendar

Resident: Canada Goose, Mandarin, Tufted Duck, Sparrowhawk, Kestrel, Little and Tawny Owls, Kingfisher, Green, Great and Lesser Spotted Woodpeckers, Grey Wagtail.

December–February:Teal,Shoveler,Goldeneye,up to 40 Wigeon,Water Rail, Lapwing, Snipe, Jack Snipe, gulls and Water Pipit at Stoke. Redwing, Fieldfare,Siskin,Redpoll,Brambling and Reed Bunting throughout.

March–May: Green and Common Sandpipers, Redshank, Greenshank, Yellow Wagtail, Water Pipits coming into summer plumage prior to departure.

June–July: Hobby, check for breeding Common Terns at Stoke and Unstead, hirundines, Sedge and Reed Warblers, Lesser Whitethroat, Whitethroat, Garden Warbler, Blackcap.

August–November: Hobby, Lesser Black-backed Gull passage, Common Tern, waders including Ruff.

6 PAPERCOURT GRAVEL PITS, SEND AND WISLEY   OS Explorer 145

Habitat

There are old gravel pits in the Wey Valley around Send and extensive commons at Wisley (Map 6). None of the pits are currently being worked and some of the exhausted pits have been filled in. Land around an old pit in Potter's Lane (TQ 025552) has been landscaped. Send village has two mature pits, but the most interesting pits are a group of four extending south and west from Papercourt Farm, of which the sailing club uses the largest and deepest. There is a smaller, undisturbed pit near the sailing club building. Two others west of Tannery Lane have been declared the Papercourt Marshes nature reserve by the Surrey Wildlife Trust. One is shallow, with muddy banks and currently partly overgrown with willow scrub. The other is smaller and has sandy margins. Restoration work is planned. Ripley Sewage Farm is adjacent. The River Wey and the Wey Navigation run to the north and east through a network of channels and water meadows, controlled by locks and weirs. There are wet meadows at Papercourt Lock and Broad Mead. Newark Priory is an overgrown ruin by the river and adjacent to a meadow that is flooded in winter. There is a second sewage farm at Old Woking, partially modernised. The Royal Horticultural Society (RHS) gardens are a mile or so downriver, at Wisley. Wisley Common, east of the gardens, has marshy areas, extensive conifer woods and a small lake (Boldermere).

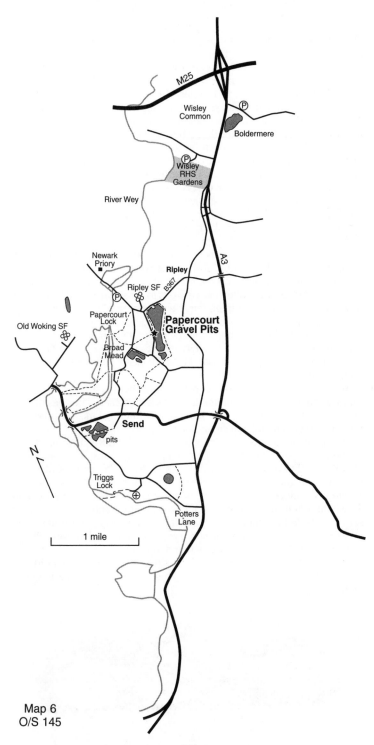

Map 6
O/S 145

Species

Marshes and wet meadows along the river valley are important for wintering thrushes and have breeding Red-legged Partridge (now infrequent), Lapwing, Snipe and Reed Warblers in summer. Grey Wagtail nests at locks and weirs across the area, close to falling water.

Although not large in size, the pits at Papercourt have a good list of breeding birds. Wader passage is interesting and, among other rarities, Spoonbill and Caspian Tern have been seen. The sailing pit has attracted a surprising range of seabirds including Black-throated Diver, Eider, Scaup and Velvet Scoter. Goosander winters, often with Goldeneye and one or two Red-breasted Mergansers. The Goosanders move around the area and are sometimes seen on Boldermere. The small pit near the sailing club is a good place for Goosander and Ruddy Duck. The larger Papercourt Marshes pit is attractive to Gadwall, Teal, Shoveler, waders and other waterbirds. The smaller one may hold a wader or two on the sandy shore. There are intermittent Sand Martin colonies, including one at the north end on the sailing pit.

Mediterranean and Glaucous Gulls have been seen in the large gull flocks that feed at Papercourt and on the wet meadow beside Newark Priory in winter. They roost on the reservoirs at Staines. A flock of several hundred Canada Geese often uses the pits to roost, having fed elsewhere. In winter and early spring there may be a Firecrest or very rarely a Great Grey Shrike in the scrub around the pits.

The wet meadows at Papercourt Lock attract swans, geese, duck and snipe in winter. There are a few Egyptian Geese. Snipe, Little Owl and Short-eared Owl may be on Broad Mead. Flocks of Fieldfares may occur on the rough grass.

Across Polesden Lane from the sailing pit there is a filled pit with a sandy surface suitable for migrants. Fields and nursery land beside this area and outside Ripley Sewage Farm have wintering larks, thrushes and finches, usually including a small flock of Bramblings.

The pits at Send have breeding grebes, Sedge and Reed Warblers.

The more derelict parts of Old Woking Sewage Farm have produced Hen Harrier, Short-eared Owl and Black Redstart. The latter is most frequently seen around the towers on the west side of the site. Lesser Spotted Woodpecker may also occur in this area. Shelduck and Redshank often move between Old Woking and Papercourt. A muddy scrape outside the fence at the east end of the sewage farm has been very good for migrant waders in some years. Records include Grey Plover (rare in Surrey), Black-tailed Godwit and Marsh Sandpiper.

The pit at Potters Lane, Send and the surrounding land may hold partridges, Little Owl, Turtle Dove and Whitethroat, and scarce migrants including Quail.

Teal

The RHS gardens at Wisley have waterfowl and woodland birds, with Kingfishers on the adjacent river. Firecrests have bred. Waxwings have fed on trees near the A3. Wisley Common has Reed Bunting and a few wintering Teal and Snipe in the wetter areas. Crossbills may sometimes be found in the pine woods, where there should be Redstarts in summer. Check Boldermere for Bewick's Swan and Goosander in winter.

Timing

There is not much sailing during the week or in winter, so these are the best times to watch at the sailing pit. The RHS gardens at Wisley are best on quiet mornings.

Access

The A3 runs 1 mile southeast of Send. Approaching from Guildford, leave the A3 at the slip road to Send and turn left at the roundabout. About half-a-mile down on the left, oak trees in Send Hill hold a small rookery. Next, on the left, Sandy Lane leads to the old pits, which are surrounded by mature vegetation. Returning, Send Marsh Road leads to Polesden Lane, where a car can be parked on the grass opposite the entrance to the Guide hut and angling club car park, at TQ 040550. Cross the stile for the footpath around the sailing pit, which also passes the smaller pit near the sailing club. The smaller of the Papercourt Marshes pits is easily viewed from the footpath off Tannery Lane. The other can be seen poorly and with difficulty by climbing a bank in Tannery Lane. Apply to the Surrey Wildlife Trust for a permit to enter the reserve.

If approaching the area from London, leave the A3 at the slip road to Ripley and turn right in Ripley High Street, into Newark Lane (B367), which takes you to the Ripley Sewage Farm end of the site after 0.5 mile (0.8 km). (A permit from Thames Water is required for access to Ripley Sewage Farm, or ask at the gate.) Turn right into Polesden Lane or continue towards Newark Priory. For the meadows at Papercourt Lock, park in the car park at TQ 040575 and take the footpath west off Newark Lane just south of the bridge. This leads to Broad Mead. For Newark Priory continue along Newark Lane across the Wey and the priory marshes are on the right. Pull off the road at a gate to view.

A footpath from Send church takes you half a mile to the water meadows at Triggs Lock. A towpath runs along the River Wey Navigation from Triggs Lock to Newark Lock. Old Woking Sewage Farm can be reached from Carters Lane. There is very limited parking at TQ 029577. Follow footpaths to the west, where views may be obstructed by nettles, or the north.

The RHS gardens and part of Wisley Common are on the north side of the A3, south of the junction with the M25. The gardens are open to the public (small entry fee) most days of the year. RHS members can enter the gardens free. Boldermere is on the east side of the A3. There are car parks on the east side of the A3 in Old Lane, at TQ 079586, and on the west side, in Wisley Lane.

None of the Papercourt or Send sites offers any significant facilities for disabled visitors. Parts of the RHS gardens at Wisley are accessible by wheelchair-users and there is no admission charge for helpers.

Calendar

Resident: Great Crested Grebe, Grey Heron, Mute Swan, Egyptian Goose, Canada Goose, Mandarin, Tufted Duck, Sparrowhawk, Grey Partridge, Lapwing, Snipe, Stock Dove, Little Owl, Kingfisher, woodpeckers, Grey Wagtail.

December–February: Cormorant, chance of Bittern, Bewick's Swan, Wigeon, Shoveler, Pochard, Goldeneye, Goosander, occasional harriers and Merlin, gulls including scarcer species, Short-eared Owl in some years, Black Redstart (irregular), winter thrushes, occasional White-fronted Goose, Firecrest, Brambling, Siskin and Redpoll.

March–May: Wigeon and sawbills leave by early March, but a few Shoveler and Shelduck remain throughout the spring. Grebes and other waterfowl nesting. Waders and terns pass through, especially from mid-April. Avocet has been seen more than once. Sand Martins arrive in March and make burrows in exposed sand cliffs.

June–July: Breeding residents and summer visitors, with occasional late-spring overshoots. Return wader passage commences. Turtle Dove and a chance of Hobby hunting over the pits.

August–November: Cormorant, waders including Green, Common and a few Wood Sandpipers, chance of godwits and Curlew Sandpiper at Old Woking and Papercourt, Lesser Black-backed Gull passage, flocks feeding at Papercourt including dark 'Scandinavian' birds probably of the *fuscus* or *intermedius* races, Yellow-legged Gulls are becoming regular, Sandwich, Common, Little, Black and (very few) Arctic Terns, chats, Yellow Wagtail.

7 THE NORTHWEST SURREY COMMONS   OS Explorer 145/160

Habitat

Northwest Surrey has some of the more rugged western heaths (Map 7). They lie on the sandy Bagshot Beds, which are related to the sands and clays that occur again at Selsey Bill, but are not found elsewhere in the area covered by this book. Cobbett took Bagshot as a benchmark for bad country in *Rural Rides* and used phrases like 'more barren and miserable than Bagshot Heath' to describe places such as Hindhead and parts of the New Forest that he found even worse.

Exploration still has problems despite better roads, because of military activity on MoD lands in the district, where access can be difficult or impracticable. Trespass can be dangerous and there have been accidents in peripheral areas open to public access, so birdwatching, at least

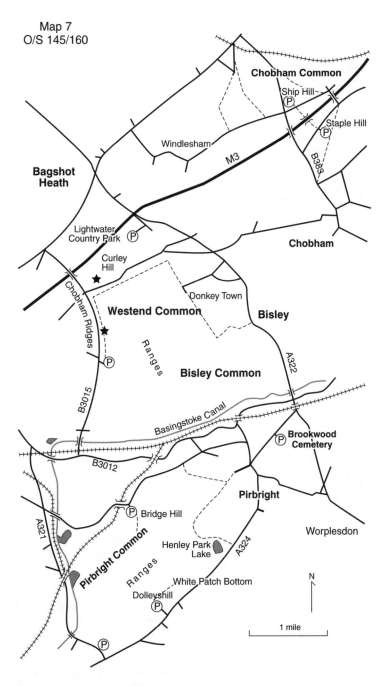

Map 7
O/S 145/160

in the Bisley and Pirbright areas, requires care. That said, the northwest commons have long been highly regarded for the birds that breed and winter there, and the restricted access itself provides a degree of protection.

147

Chobham Common is largely open heath with scattered birch and pine, and stands of bracken among the heather. It has some relatively unusual plants and has NNR status, important for its varied population of spiders. High ground at Staple Hill slopes away to a boggy area at Gracious Pond and there is more wet ground north of the M3, which cuts across the common. The army uses part of the land to the north for testing vehicles. It is also a popular site for model aircraft fliers. Being close to London and the M3, the common attracts many visitors for birdwatching and other recreations. The birdlife has tended to suffer under the combined pressure and, as with other fragile habitats, it should be explored with restraint.

Bisley and Westend Commons are on hilly ground 2.5 miles to the southwest. They have large areas of long grass as well as heather and bracken and cover an area about 3 miles square. The land is used for military training and access to most of it is prevented by an encircling chainlink fence, though good views can be had from high ground on the west side. Bisley rifle range is at the south end. Live artillery rounds are used on ranges to the west and north. Colony Bog, in the middle, is well known to botanists.

Lightwater Country Park, separated from Westend by the M3, is an extension of Bagshot Heath on higher ground to the north. It is managed by the Surrey Heath Borough Council. The pine woods, ponds, rough grassy common and heath are also worth a visit. Nature trails are laid out and there is an information centre. Pipistrelle Bats live in hollow trees and buildings. Adders and Grass Snakes can be found. There are views to Bisley from Curley Hill.

Pirbright Common is an undulating heath, wet in parts, also used by the military for weapons training at certain times, but with public access. Fires occasionally break out on the common, as they do elsewhere in southwest Surrey, leaving dead trees and a variable amount of bare, burnt ground. Mature parts of the common have deep heather and gorse. Pirbright is a valuable site for heathland species, which benefit more from the restricted access than they are harmed by army disturbance. As on other lands used by the military, observe the notices and warning signs and do not pick up unfamiliar or potentially dangerous objects. Henley Park Lake, at the southeast end, is sheltered by trees. A path continues past the lake to more open, higher ground, which affords good views over the commons.

Brookwood Cemetery is largely mixed woodland with clearings and open heath. It is more overgrown than its name might suggest. Most of the area has been left to develop naturally, apart from some exotic shrubs, mainly rhododendrons. Being mainly quiet and secluded it offers good birdwatching opportunities.

The Basingstoke Canal runs east–west between Pirbright and Bisley. It fell into disuse with the decline of barge traffic but restoration work is being undertaken, to keep it open it for pleasure craft.

Species

The district as a whole is a fine area for wintering and migrant raptors. Hen Harriers and Merlins occur in the Pirbright/Bisley area, Goshawk sightings have been increasing, and there is a good chance of seeing a Hobby on the commons. Long and Short-eared Owls are occasionally seen in winter, as are shrikes. Tree Pipit is common and, like Lesser Redpoll, often in the birches. Breeding Lesser Redpolls are now very scarce. Siskins breed intermittently in the pines and Crossbills rather more frequently. Ring Ouzels appear on passage.

Nightjars are present in good numbers in the district as a whole, with c.30 territories at Bisley and Westend, and slightly fewer at Chobham. Stonechat is found in small numbers throughout, preferring gorse patches on the heaths and quickly drawing attention by their noisy behaviour.

Merlin

Dartford Warblers have been very common in recent years. Being resident, they are affected by the severity of the winter and suffer badly if there are prolonged periods of snow cover or frozen ground. Numbers vary greatly between years and can top 200 pairs at Pirbright, which is the main site, following a run of mild winters. Pirbright has at times held exceptional numbers of Redstarts, which nest in holes in dead trees. Burnt areas are good for Woodlarks and at Pirbright have attracted rare migrants in Surrey such as Stone Curlew and Tawny Pipit. There is an old Grasshopper Warbler site at Whitepatch Bottom. Although currently abandoned, it may be used again in the future.

Mandarin is now breeding at Chobham, where Woodcock and Cuckoo are strong features. An autumn passage of chats, mainly Wheatears, may well be seen there and to an extent on other heaths. Lightwater Country Park has breeding Canada Goose and other wildfowl on the ponds, as well as its pine wood and heathland species. Feral Egyptian Geese are sometimes seen, as they are in nearby localities. Grey Wagtails and other waterside species occur along the Basingstoke Canal.

Brookwood Cemetery has Wood Warbler, Goldcrest, Jay and many other woodland species, with a chance of a Hobby and some of the heathland birds.

Timing

For the military lands, normal times for range practice are from about 8am to 4pm, and there is sometimes firing at night. Occasionally the weekends are free, especially at Bank Holiday times and there may be a two-week free period over Christmas and the New Year. These times are only a guide: check with site information on the notices displayed and if necessary with the military. Watch for red flags and lights indicating danger. Lightwater Country Park is open all year. It gets crowded at weekends. Evenings are best for Dartford Warblers.

Access

The southern part of Chobham Common can be approached from Staple Hill, where there is car parking. Take the B383 for 1 mile north from the centre of Chobham village and fork right up Staple Hill for three-quarters-of-a-mile. Car parking is on the right. For the northern part of the common, which is on the other side of the M3, continue along the B383 for 1.25 miles beyond the Staple Hill turning to the monument on Ship Hill. Public footpaths run from there across the heath.

Access to most of Westend and Bisley Commons is prohibited at all times. However, high ground at Chobham Ridges on the west side affords views over both, best in the vicinity of Colony Gate, on the B3105 2 miles north of the junction with the B3012 at Deepcut. There are public footpaths along parts of the perimeter. The best of these, running south from Donkey Town, off the A322 at Westend, provides good views in the vicinity of SU 935595.

Lightwater Country Park is open year-round. It can be approached from junction 3 of the M3. Take the A322 towards Guildford and immediately fork right on the minor road into Lightwater. The park is at the end of The Avenue, a turning on the right, signposted, half-a-mile from the turn-off.

Pirbright Common may be entered at several points. Bridge Hill, on the unclassified road from Pirbright to Mytchett, 1 mile east of Mytchett, at SU 905406, is on high ground and has room for off-road parking. For the approach via Henley Park Lake, take the track north from the A324 1.25 miles south of Pirbright, at SU 934538. Another good access point is from Dolleyshill, at SU 918519. A path from here leads to Whitepatch Bottom. The common includes Ash Ranges, which are in frequent use and only safely accessible at certain times. The whole area is MoD property with definite, but restricted, rights of public access. When firing is to take place, red flags are flown in prominent places around the common to indicate danger areas to which entry is then prohibited.

Brookwood Cemetery is private, but normally open to visitors. If in doubt, check at the office just inside the entrance, which is in Cemetery Pales, a road connecting the A324 and A322 at Pirbright. Limited parking is available outside the entrance.

Most of the area described is unsuitable for wheelchairs but limited access is possible at Brookwood Cemetery and Lightwater Country Park.

Calendar

Resident: Canada Goose, Mandarin, Sparrowhawk, Kestrel, Coot, Green, Great Spotted and Lesser Spotted Woodpeckers, Woodlark, Skylark, Meadow Pipit, Grey Wagtail, Dartford Warbler, Lesser Redpoll, Reed Bunting.

December–February: Hen Harrier, Merlin, Short-eared Owl, Great Grey Shrike. Stonechats are usually absent from the heaths.

March–May: Arrival of Hobby, migrant Goshawk, Common Buzzard, possible Honey Buzzard, roding Woodcock, Cuckoo, Nightjar. Return of Stonechat. Nightingale, Redstart and migrant warblers from mid April (Chiffchaff earlier).

June–July: Nightjar song in late evenings. Tree Pipit display flights. Stonechats with young. Look for summering Siskin. Possible Crossbill irruptions from July.

August–November: Return raptor migration. Whinchat and Wheatear passage. Arrival of winter thrushes.

8 FARNHAM AND THE BLACKWATER VALLEY   OS Explorer 145

Habitat

The Blackwater Valley defines the western border of Surrey from just north of Farnham to the Hampshire/Berkshire border at Camberley (Map 8). There are disused sand pits with shallow pools at Wrecclesham, on the outskirts of Farnham. Cliffs suitable for Sand Martins have been left in older parts of the workings. Some of the land is back-filled with refuse. The River Wey runs through Wrecclesham and floods low-lying meadows in winter. Sand deposits on the east side of Farnham, at Runfold and Seale, are being worked and selectively filled. Some are flooded. A landscaped pit at Tongham has grassy and reedy shores. There is a landfill site at Runfold (SU 887475). Farnham Sewage Farm is on the Aldershot side of the town. Surrounding meadows may be interesting in winter.

The river itself rises near Farnham, where is hardly more than a stream, but it runs through gravel deposits which have been extensively worked, leaving pits of different ages and a consequent variety of habitat. The best are in the area from Aldershot to Frimley, which is fairly heavily built-up and crossed by several railway lines. Badshot Lea Gravel Pit is a large, mature water between Aldershot and Farnham. It is surrounded by trees, mainly willow and alder and patches of reeds, and is used for fishing. There are small islands. North Camp Gravel Pits, on the Blackwater at Ash Vale, straddle the county border.

The Basingstoke Canal enters the county at Ash and runs north through the valley to Frimley, where it bends east towards Woking and Weybridge. The canal is used by pleasure craft and has lush waterside vegetation. The section through Ash is elevated and provides a good vantage point from which to view adjacent areas, especially Ash Vale Gravel Pits, which lie either side of it and also straddle the county border. These are mature pits used by anglers and, in the case of the one south of the canal, by windsurfers. There are smaller and more mature waters along the Basingstoke Canal at Mytchett and Deepcut. Mytchett Lake is an extension of the canal and is rather lush, with yellow flag and water lilies. There is a pounding lake with reedbeds, Greatbottom Flash, a little to

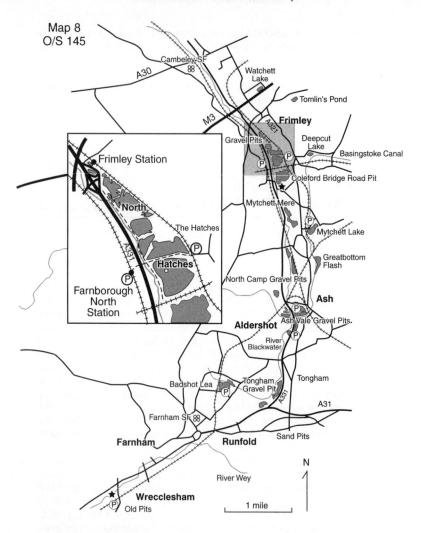

the south. Deepcut (Wharfendon) Lake, to the north, is a smaller water adjacent to the canal.

The gravel pits at Frimley are a mixture of landscaped and overgrown workings in the Blackwater Valley between Frimley and Camberley. The pits are of various sizes, most have islands for breeding waterbirds and other species. The three best are Coleford Bridge Road, The Hatches and North. Mytchett Mere, an old gravel pit south of Coleford Bridge Road, is reedy and surrounded by long grass and scrub.

Tomlin's Pond and Watchett Lake, both in Camberley, are small and lined with trees. The Royal Military Academy at Camberley has two sizeable lakes. Camberley Sewage Farm is on the edge of York Town industrial estate and mainly built over. There is rough grass and scrub and a tip at the back of the site, which drains into the Blackwater River. Adjacent meadows alongside the A331 from the M3 interchange to Blackwater, by the side of the River Blackwater, have proved interesting, especially in winter. Waders and a Shag have appeared there in cold spells.

Species

The most rewarding parts of the area are currently at Wrecclesham, Tongham and Frimley. Overgrown areas in the vicinity the pits hold warblers and resident woodland species. Breeding birds frequent on waters throughout the district include Little and Great Crested Grebes, Canada Goose, Tufted Duck and Coot, all of which, as in other parts of Surrey, have greatly benefited from such man-made habitat. Where conditions are right there may be Little Ringed Plover, although given their preference for the more open conditions in pits that are being actively worked, numbers and locations vary from year to year. The species is most likely to be seen at Frimley. Grey Wagtails are frequent, especially at suitable spots along the canal. Reed Warbler breeds at Ash Vale and Frimley. Sedge Warbler is now mainly seen on passage, although it formerly bred at Frimley.

With the closure of Wrecclesham tip, fewer gulls feed in the area, but a flooded area by the River Wey has proved productive for other species. Waders can be found there in winter and early spring, and there are records of Avocet, Knot, Ruff and Black-tailed Godwit. Badshot Lea is used by wintering wildfowl and has produced some good records over the years.

Tongham Gravel Pits have a good range of duck, including Wigeon, Gadwall and Pochard in winter and the occasional Wood Duck, Ring-necked Duck and Scaup. The many gulls feeding on the Runfold landfill site and loafing at Tongham Gravel Pit are mainly Herring and Lesser Black-backs. Few of these are found in the Frensham roost, so they are probably from the Thames Valley reservoirs. Mediterranean and Yellow-legged Gulls and a Kittiwake have been seen there.

The Frimley gravel pits are perhaps most interesting for wintering wildfowl, with good numbers of the commoner ducks and the chance of a few scarcer species, along with winter grebes. The Hatches has a wintering Wigeon/Gadwall flock with a few Goosander and brief visits from Surrey rarities such as the Brent Goose. Ringing has established that a southern race Cormorant (*P. c. sinensis*) has been present among the wintering Cormorants. Water Rails winter at Frimley and may even breed. Common Terns have begun nesting on an island in Hatches pit. This is probably the only natural site in Surrey, the others all being rafts. Coleford Bridge Road is one of the last pits to freeze, perhaps because of disturbance from water-skiers and is one of the better places to look for scarce grebes and scoter.

Timing

Wrecclesham floods are best on mornings in November–March, avoiding very dry spells. Sand Martins are present at the pit from about mid-April, with a few earlier arrivals in some years. Winter and passage periods are the most interesting at Frimley. For Ash Vale, the south pit will be best early in the day if watched from the canal because of the direction of the light, except on dull days. Windsurfing disturbance is also greater later in the day, especially in summer.

All of the pits can freeze in severe weather, although Ash Vale, which may be deeper than the others, has maintained a small open area even in the most severe of recent winters. Small holes in the ice may be crowded with commoner wildfowl or, as has happened at Ash Vale, might hold something less common such as a Ring-necked Duck.

Access

Wrecclesham floods can be viewed from the A31, on the southbound side half-a-mile beyond the roundabout on the west side of Farnham. Pull off the road onto the grass and watch from inside the car so as not to disturb the gulls. Alternatively turn into River Lane and park there. Continue along River Lane for half-a-mile to a road junction and turn right for the disused sand pit. After a quarter-of-a-mile turn right again to the recreation ground (signposted) where there is car parking. A footpath that passes some rugby pitches leads to the site.

For Tongham gravel pit, take the Tongham turning from the A31 and turn left into Manor Road to park at the end and walk a short distance west to the pits. Alternatively, park off-road on the west side of the round-about at the south end of the A331 and walk northeast to a footpath starting at SU 882488.

Farnham Sewage Farm is in Monkton Lane, off the A324. View from out-side or ask at the gate for permission to enter. Runfold and Seale sand pits can be accessed from minor roads south off the A31 at Runfold. For Badshot Lea approach via Tongham and park in Lower Weybourne Road, preferably off the road itself or in the car park at the entrance, at SU 862489. A footpath runs between the pit and the Farnham/Aldershot railway line and leads to Boxall's Lane. The pit is easily observed from the footpath or the car park. Permission from Farnham Angling Society is needed to walk round — see the notice at the entrance.

Approaching Ash Vale Gravel Pits from the A31, turn north at Tongham and fork right after three-quarters-of-a-mile. On reaching the roundabout by the Greyhound pub continue straight ahead. The pits are 0.5 mile (0.9 km) further, on the left. They can be seen from the Basingstoke Canal, at SU 887514. The canal has towpaths on both sides, readily accessed where the rail and road bridges cross it by the pits. A permit from the angling society is needed for access to the pits north of Basingstoke Canal. The pit south of the canal can be viewed from Culverlands Crescent. Admittance, if needed, should be sought from the windsurfing club. The entrance is on the south side, in Willow Park. North Camp Gravel Pits lie behind North Camp railway station and are most easily accessed from the Hampshire side.

Access to the main part of Frimley Gravel Pits is by well-maintained footpaths from Farnborough North Station, where there is a car park, on the west side, or from The Hatches, where parking is tight, on the east side. A level crossing (take care) and footpath join the two access points and branches north and south of the west side of the pits. The northern path leads to a third access point near Frimley Station and gives good views over North pit, where there is a bench.

Coleford Bridge Road pit, south of the railway, can be accessed from Coleford Bridge Road or by the footpath running south from the footpath between The Hatches and Farnborough North Station.

The Basingstoke Canal towpaths have many points of access. There is car parking at Mytchett Lake (SU 892545), where the whole lake is read-ily viewed. Greatbottom Flash is just to the south, easily seen from the towpath. Mytchett Mere is a private gravel pit and permission will be needed to enter the area. The entrance is on the west side of the A321, at SU 889543, and limited views are available without entering.

Tomlin's Pond (SU 385587) can be approached from Chobham Road and Watchetts Lake (SU 887589) from Watchetts Drive, both in Camberley. The Royal Military Academy (Sandhurst) is on the north side of the A30 in Camberley. The lakes cannot be seen from outside the grounds and permission from the Commandant is needed for entry. At present access is very restricted.

The entrance to Camberley Sewage Farm (Thames Water, Camberley) is in Doman Road, on the industrial estate. View the rough ground at the back from Blackwater Road.

Calendar

Resident: Little and Great Crested Grebes, Canada Goose, Mallard, Tufted Duck, Kingfisher, woodpeckers, Grey Wagtail.

December–February: Duck numbers increase at the pits and Cormorants at The Hatches (Frimley). Occasional wintering Green Sandpiper, gulls (but no roost), less common species including Black-necked Grebe, Shag and Bearded Tit.

March–May: Great Crested Grebe numbers peak at the larger pits in March or April. Wader passage occurs from about mid-March. Little Ringed Plover are often early. Whimbrel in May. Warblers take up territory.

June–July: Reed and Sedge Warblers at the pits. Lapwings begin to flock. Look for Common Tern breeding at Frimley (The Hatches). Mid-July sees the beginning of the return wader passage, with Greenshank, Green and Common Sandpipers.

August–November: Wader passage peaks in August, mainly Green and Common Sandpipers but also Wood Sandpiper, Ruff etc. A few Goldeneye from late October or early November.

9 SOUTHWEST SURREY COMMONS   OS Explorer 133/145

Habitat

The western commons (Map 9) consist mainly of dry, sandy soils with heather, birch and pine the dominant plant cover. Without some management they would mostly revert to pine or birch woodland, but steps are taken to check tree intrusion in a few places. Bogs make an important variation to the habitat. The one at Thursley NNR is carefully managed to maintain a suitable water level on the reserve throughout the year. The dryness of the light sandy soils and the expanses of heather and gorse create a serious fire risk for much of the year and visitors should act with appropriate caution. Raft Spiders are found in the wetter areas. Silver-studded Blue and Grayling are characteristic butterflies of the heather.

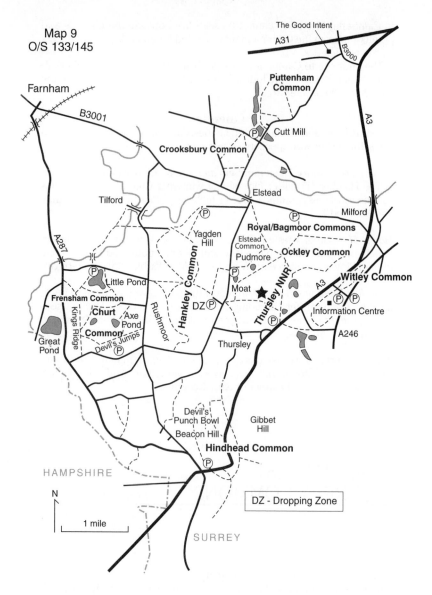

Map 9
O/S 133/145

Species

Fire damage to the habitat of species such as Nightjar, Stonechat and Dartford Warbler can be very great. One species, the Woodlark, sometimes benefits, and quickly moves onto burnt ground. Normally, Woodlarks are best looked for along the edges of the many broad sandy paths and in spring are most easily found by listening for the species' song, which is briefer and more musical than that of Skylark, with a characteristic *tu-lu-lu* phrase. Woodlark numbers vary considerably between years, depending on ground conditions and the severity of the previous winter. Most move away from the commons to nearby farmland in winter.

Dartford Warbler

Winter conditions affect other heathland residents such as Wren. Dartford Warbler, which is on the edge of its range in Surrey, is especially vulnerable and in certain years has been wiped out. The damage may be done by snow alone if the heather is covered for a long period, as in 1961. Prolonged spells of very low temperatures, as in 1985/6, can also be fatal to the species, even if the heather and gorse remain exposed and may be the greater threat, given the effect on food supply. Recolonisation can take a decade. Under favourable conditions, the total Surrey population of the species has exceeded 500 pairs. There is no conclusive evidence as to the origin of the new colonists, but they probably come from more protected populations to the southwest. Stonechat are infrequently seen on the heaths in winter, as most move to sites with a more reliable food supply, in coastal areas or on sewage farms and marshes. Crossbills are irregular breeders on the western heaths, and are more often seen flying over in small parties in irruption years.

Main Birdwatching Zones
The core area is the nature reserve at Thursley. Hankley is adjacent, bleaker and drier. Milford and Witley are dry heaths with scrub and pines. Frensham has two fine ponds. Hindhead has the highest ground and a deep, sheltered valley. The Puttenham area has tree-lined pools.

THURSLEY and OCKLEY (Map 9a, OS Explorer 133/145)

Habitat
Thursley and Ockley Commons make up one of the finest pieces of lowland heath in southern Britain. Much of the area is in the Thursley NNR. The central part of the reserve is a raised peat bog. Once, as old maps show, there was a cart track across it, passing north–south by Pudmore Pond, but this has long since been impassable, the more so since the water level in the bog is now managed by an effective system of dykes and sluices. Stick to the boardwalks in this area, however firm the ground may look.

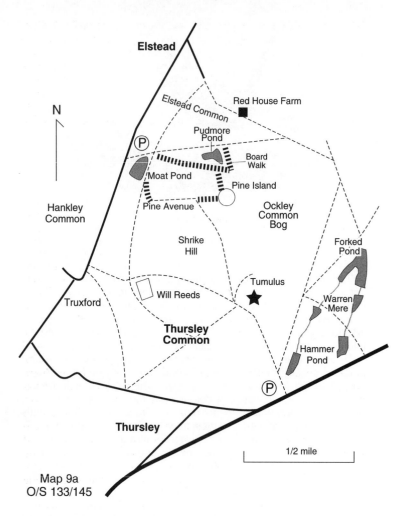

Map 9a
O/S 133/145

A line of low, numbered pylons runs across the bog and there are quite
a few isolated dead trees, some the victims of fires. Local names for features include 'Pine Island' (an isolated group of pines by the boardwalk),
'Pine Avenue' (an avenue of pines which is part of a circular walk around
Pudmore bog) and 'Shrike Hill' (a low, heather-covered hill east of the
avenue of pines).

The commons are rich in dragonflies and 26 species have been
recorded there, believed to be a record for southern England. English
Nature states that up to 10,000 insect species are present, rather dwarfing
the otherwise impressive bird list. There are also many unusual plants, the
most distinctive of which, perhaps, are the insectivorous sundews, on
damp tracks and other places where there has been standing water on
the peaty soil. The round and long-leaved species both occur, the former
being commoner. Cotton grass, scarce in the southeast, is a good marker
of wet ground when it is in flower. Heathland fungi, mosses and lichens
are well represented.

The bog is surrounded by heather moor, which rises steeply at the southern end, and there are scattered copses of pine and birch. Higher ground permits good views across west Surrey. On the east side of the reserve a stream was dammed in earlier times to form a series of pools — the Hammer Pond, Forked Pond and Warrenmere. Drier ground in the southwest corner, at Truxford, was used as a site for army huts during the Second World War. These have long since been cleared and have given way to hawthorn scrub and woodland. In the northeast corner, a similar area exists at Rodborough Common, with access off the west side of the A3. Moat Pond is a small water with some interesting plants and surprisingly good birds.

Species

This is a very fine area for breeding heathland species. Hobbies hunt over the bog area, taking dragonflies and hirundines. Curlews are present in February–July. Nightjars are quite common, with several sharing a feeding ground near Moat Pond. Tree Pipits are found among the birches and there are a few Meadow Pipits. Woodlarks can be heard and seen over Shrike Hill and other places, especially where the heather is short. In good years there can be at least 15 pairs. The best time is March–July. Again, care should be taken to avoid disturbing them. Pine Island and Pine Avenue are good for Redstart. Stonechats are conspicuous in the gorse, where there are also Linnet colonies. Siskin and occasionally Crossbill nest in the pines around Shrike Hill and elsewhere. Dartford Warblers can be seen from the boardwalk and are commonest south of the reserve, where the older age-classes of heather and gorse are established. Care should be taken to keep to paths so as not to disturb them. Reed Bunting is numerous at the margins of the bog. Lesser Redpolls formerly bred, but is now mainly seen on passage.

A tumulus on the south side of the bog at SU 912408 provides a good vantage point for raptors. Thursley Common is a nationally important site for wintering Great Grey Shrike, which is most commonly seen around pylon 39, on Shrike Hill and from the tumulus. Dead trees should be scanned for these and birds of prey. Hen Harrier and Merlin are regular in autumn and winter, Common Buzzard, Kestrel and other falcons in spring

Great Grey Shrike

and summer. Many other birds of prey have been seen here, including Honey Buzzard, Marsh Harrier, Goshawk, Red-footed Falcon and Osprey. There are often a few Teal at Pudmore pools, although not normally in the breeding season. Waders are also sometimes found there. Little Ringed Plover, Redshank, Greenshank and Green Sandpiper are the most frequent but others have included Pectoral and Wood Sandpipers. Waders may also be seen flying over on passage. Passage migration of passerines is not very noticeable, except that of chats, pipits and finches in autumn. Redwings and Fieldfares arrive from October and roost on the bog. Although this is not a major site for rare migrants, a Woodchat Shrike was found in 1999 and over 200 species have been recorded. Maritime species have included a Fulmar and a Leach's Petrel, both rare in Surrey.

Moat Pond has a resident flock of bread-eating Mallards, augmented by a few pairs of Tufted Ducks and in winter by Pochard. The pond is occasionally visited or overflown by rarer species, including Great White Egret, Pintail, Red-crested Pochard, Ring-necked Duck, Scaup, Common Scoter and Osprey. Little Grebe breeds there. Surrounding pines have breeding Redstarts and sometimes Lesser Spotted Woodpeckers, Treecreepers, Siskins and Crossbills.

Hammer Pond may produce Grey Wagtail at the outfall, and an occasional Kingfisher, as well as resident grebes, Mute Swan, Canada Goose, Mallard and Tufted Duck. Wigeon sometimes linger into May. Flocks of up to 100 full-winged Mandarin have been reported from a private lake in the district and reports from Thursley are becoming more frequent. Thorn bushes at Rodborough hold a few Nightingales.

Timing

Raptors are best looked for soon after dawn or from late morning. Hobbies may well be seen at midday, when they are chasing dragonflies. Redstarts begin singing before first light. Dawn and dusk are best for Snipe, Curlew, Cuckoo, Nightjar and Woodcock. Nightjars may not begin churring until 9.30pm. Warm calm days in spring and early summer are best for Dartford Warblers.

Access

The best approach is from Elstead, taking the unclassified road to Thursley that runs between Hankley and Ockley Commons. Park at Moat Pond, on the east side of the road, after 1.5 miles. From here, well-marked paths and a boardwalk lead round the reserve and afford vantage points over the best areas. There are picnic tables by Moat Pond.

Another approach is from Thursley village, where there is a very limited space for parking. Walk north to the commons on a footpath by the cricket pitch. There is also an entrance on the A3 at the southern end of the reserve (look for the brown NNR sign at the gate). This is closer to Hammer Pond but parking space is very restricted.

While in the area, observe the common-sense rules, which are there to protect the fragile ecology of the site against fire, the trampling of the heather, disturbance of scarce breeding species and havoc caused by uncontrolled dogs. Since the area is disused army land, care should be taken not to handle any suspicious objects. It is best to keep to well-worn paths.

Wheelchair access is possible to Moat Pond, but the boardwalks are discontinuous and unsuitable. There are no toilets on site, but there are facilities at the Witley Information Centre, when it is open.

HANKLEY COMMON (Map 9a, OS Explorer 133/145)

Habitat

Hankley Common is predominantly open heath with scattered pines. It has some low, but striking sandy ridges at its southern end, where the steep slopes are covered by deeper heather and gorse. Updrafts along the ridges are sometimes used by model-glider enthusiasts as well as by various raptors. The undulating terrain, with its bleak expanses, has been popular among film-makers. The common has no warning flags or access restrictions but is frequently used for army training exercises including parachuting. Visitors, especially children, should be careful of spent flares, cartridge cases and other military litter that may be on the ground. These should be left where they are. Also keep out of the Dropping Zone (DZ) when it is in use. There are wide paths round the DZ and the rest of the common, and they provide good views.

Species

Hankley is well known for Nightjars, which at the right time can be heard and even seen without leaving the car park. They nest on the ground among the heather, so do not cause disturbance by walking thoughtlessly through it. Nightjars perch in trees, or sometimes on power lines, to churr, moving their heads slowly from side to side, which makes them hard to locate. The males also fly low over the heath, giving a sharp *gooick* call, which makes them easier to find.

Skylarks and Dartford Warblers are usually present. The DZ is a good place to find them, although they may not be easy to see outside the breeding season, when they are not singing. Migrant Wheatears might also be seen there. Many Woodlarks and Stonechats breed but most move away in winter. The common supports large populations of Tree Pipits and Yellowhammers, as well as a few Meadow Pipits. The display flights of Tree Pipits, climbing and then parachuting back to a perch on a low pine or birch, are a frequent sight from April to July.

As on the other western heaths, Hen Harriers and Merlins are among the more frequent winter-visiting birds of prey. Great Grey Shrike is rare. There are a few Snipe at the north end.

Timing

Nightjars are rarely active before it is almost dark. The evening chorus commences as the sun sets. There will be Woodcock then, perhaps at 9.30pm in mid-June, the first churring will be heard. Military training exercises may start at dusk and can be noisy, involving flares, blank ammunition and the blockage of access lanes by vehicles. This is not normally a problem, but at such times try somewhere else.

Access

Approach from Elstead along the Thursley road between Ockley and Hankley Commons (Map 9). About three-quarters-of-a-mile south of Moat Pond there is a zigzag bend from which a lane to the right is signposted to the DZ. Follow this for half-a-mile to a car park on the left. Be aware that this car park may be visited at dusk by police looking for bikers etc and that there may be soldiers on training exercises at any time. The soldiers are used to dog walkers and others walking through the training exercises. There are also footpaths onto the common from Tilford and Elstead, at the north end. From the south take a footpath on the north side of the unclassified road between Thursley and Churt, immediately west of Pitch Place at SU 883391. None of the site is suitable for wheelchairs and there are no seats or benches.

MILFORD AND WITLEY COMMONS
(Map 9, OS Explorer 133/145)

Habitat

Milford and Witley Commons lie south of Milford, between the A246 and A3, opposite the Thursley group of commons. Small areas where chalk has been dumped enrich the flora, which includes aliens such as Turkey Oak, and the curious little New Zealander, Pirri-Pirri Bur, the seeds of which reached Britain clinging to imported wool. Approximately 30 species of butterfly occur, including Green Hairstreak, Purple Emperor and White Admiral. Rabbits are usually conspicuous and there are a few deer. Reptiles include Adder, Grass Snake and Slowworm. At the Milford end the light, rather gravelly soils carry extensive hawthorn scrub, heather and areas of short grass. On Witley Common, pine and deciduous woodland predominates at the north end. The southern part has the best heather, which is grazed by Highland and Shetland cattle to improve it.

The commons are managed by the NT, who run a well-appointed information centre. Nature trails have been laid out and pamphlets are available.

Species

Milford Common is best known for its Nightingales, which mainly breed among the hawthorn scrub and are not always easy to see. There are usually one or two in scrub on the north side of Webb Road. Others are further up the common. Woodlark and Dartford Warbler can be found in good years. A May or June morning visit will find numerous Chiffchaffs, Willow Warblers, Whitethroats, Garden Warblers, Blackcaps and other birds in song among the scrub, with a few Cuckoos and Tree Pipits. The pines at the Witley end are productive for Sparrowhawk and woodpeckers. Other raptors often seen are Common Buzzard and Hobby. Conditions for heathland species are improving.

Timing

Nightingales will be in good voice from about mid-April to late June. They can be heard at most hours of the day and night, but are least active in the afternoon. If you want to hear them perform at midnight, this can be done comfortably from Webb Road.

Access

Approach via the A246 from Milford and turn right into Webb Road, which connects with the A246 after three-quarters-of-a-mile. Park there or at the Witley Information Centre, which is signposted. Be careful not to park on the main roads or to block access points to the common. The Witley Information Centre, on the south side of Webb Road, has a free car park, snacks, toilets and local information. It makes provision for wheelchair entry and has adapted toilets. A Braille guide to the commons is available. The centre is open from late March to early November, Tuesday–Friday 11am–4pm, Saturday, Sunday and Bank Holiday Mondays 11am–5pm. It may close at lunch time. The gate to the car park currently closes at 6pm but check notices. Cycle routes and nature trails are laid out.

FRENSHAM (Map 9, OS Explorer 133/145)

Habitat

Frensham Common lies on undulating ground. Frensham Ponds mark the western edge of the Surrey heaths, and the Great Pond itself is, at one end, partly in Hampshire. Like most Surrey waters, the ponds are artificial, made by damming a stream. This gives them a characteristic shape, shallow and reedy at one end and deeper, with an embankment, at the outfall. The contiguous area of Churt Common has marshy pools including Axe Pond, pine woods and heather moor.

Species

If starting at the Little Pond car park, take the path on the east side of the pond, looking for Great Crested Grebes, Tufted Ducks and other wildfowl on the right, whilst keeping an eye on the heath and sandy fields of Tilhill Nurseries on the left, where there is excellent habitat for Woodlarks and wintering finches. The path round the head of the pond crosses boggy ground on a boardwalk and gives a view of the secluded nature reserve in the southeast corner of the pond, where Garganey and migrant waders might be found. Early in the year there is a chance of Crossbill. They breed intermittently and are also seen in irruption years, then appearing most often in July and August, when their hard *chip-chip-chip* flight call draws immediate attention.

At the south end of the Little Pond some dead birches provide attractive perches for a Great Grey Shrike, if one is wintering on the common. This species has been less regular in recent years but, if not seen at the Little Pond, may be found on the western slope of Kings Ridge, a shoulder of high ground to the west that is the watershed for the catchment area of the two ponds. Great Grey Shrikes may be best found by searching likely looking posts and dead branches. They may also be located when making a quick downward sally for an insect or small bird.

There are substantial reedbeds around both ponds, especially at the south end of the Little Pond. These accommodate one of the county's largest Reed Warbler colonies. Sedge Warbler is annual on passage but a scarce breeder. There are good numbers of Reed Bunting. Water Rails are often seen, mostly in winter, and may be heard squealing in the reeds at the end of the Little Pond in summer. They are known to have bred. The best place and time to look is at the base of the reeds in the southeast corner of the Little Pond when water levels are low. The fortunate observer might then see a dusky, narrow-bodied rail with a long red bill make a quick dash for cover between the reeds.

Following one of the paths up Kings Ridge will get you to the ridge path, which affords excellent views over the commons on either side, out over both ponds. The depth of the heather and development of the gorse varies from year to year. As at other heathland sites, fires cut the heather back, kill the pine and birch saplings and leave clear burnt areas attractive to Woodlarks but damaging to the breeding requirements of Stonechats and Dartford Warblers. In winter there may be little to see on the open heath, apart from a few Wrens and Dunnocks mousing around in the gorse clumps, but as the year advances every bush seems to provide a song post. Stonechat is mostly absent in winter, but some numbers are present at Frensham, as on other Surrey heaths, from March–October. Noisy family parties of young birds are conspicuous in summer. Tree Pipit song flight, with its 'parachuting' descent onto a birch or pine branch is also unlikely to be missed. Meadow Pipit is an uncommon breeding bird in Surrey but a few pairs may be found near the Great Pond car park. Linnet is plentiful and Yellowhammers are conspicuous among the birches.

Continuing over the ridge and down to the Great Pond, the paths cross the A287 and reach a rather eroded area, at the shore of the Great Pond, the subject of some determined reclamation work in parts and attractive to migrant chats. Waders may be found on the sandy shore here during migration. Frensham is one of the two places in Surrey to have provided most of the county's records of Oystercatcher, the other being Barn Elms. Numbers are tiny compared with coastal areas, but they are fine birds to find on a Surrey heath. Whimbrel, Curlew and godwits might also be seen here, feeding or flying over. Both ponds are worth scanning for migrant terns. These are mostly Common but a few individuals of scarcer species occur annually, and flocks of Black Terns may be present for several days. Little Gull may also be seen, and the occasional Kittiwake.

On the south side of the Great Pond, where a small stream marks the border between Hampshire and Surrey (and along which a Spotted Crake once walked, thoughtfully putting a foot in both counties) is an alder copse that is productive for Lesser Spotted Woodpecker, Marsh and Willow Tits and Siskin. In some years, when a Siskin flock collects in March or early April, birds may be heard in full song before they depart. And perhaps not all go, for a few now breed in west Surrey. At the west end of the Great Pond a footpath leads past the small Outlet Pond to the banks of the River Wey, where Grasshopper Warbler used to sing from rough grass on the far bank and may do so again in the future. Other possibilities here include Lesser Spotted Woodpecker, Garden Warbler, Marsh and Willow Tits, Firecrest and even, in spring, an overshooting Golden Oriole.

Frensham has its share of migrant and resident birds of prey. Most spectacular, perhaps, is Osprey, which calls at the ponds annually on its way north or south. Honey and Common Buzzards have also been seen moving through. Common Buzzards seen in summer may be wanderers from more distant Surrey breeding areas. Merlins sometimes appear in winter, although they may be more reliably found on some of the damper commons, such as Chobham or Pirbright. Hen Harriers visit from the other commons from time to time.

Autumn brings more gulls and a winter roost, which in the past peaked at several thousand but is now around 1,000, begins to amass, mostly involving Black-headed Gulls, with the occasional Mediterranean Gull, Little Gull or Kittiwake, most of which are thought to feed on local farmland. This is the only gull roost in the county away from the Thames Valley reservoirs.

Wildfowl wintering at Frensham now include a few Goldeneye and the occasional Ring-necked Duck, Common Scoter, Velvet Scoter and Ruddy Duck among the Mallard, Tufted Duck and Pochard. Many other species have occurred and should certainly be looked for, as should divers and Red-necked, Black-necked and Slavonian Grebes. The divers are sometimes in perplexing plumages and separation of Red- and Black-throated can require care. Wintering Bitterns occur in the reedbeds of both ponds.

They are best seen at dusk, flying between the ponds. A Hoopoe has wintered. Bearded Tits are scarce winter visitors. Cetti's Warbler has wintered on several occasions. It is most easily found by listening for its calls in the Great Pond reedbeds and around the inlet in the southeast corner of the Little Pond.

Churt Common is little watched but Axe Pond has produced a Little Egret and there is a heronry on private land by the west side.

Timing

Local birders find it best to get to the Great Pond very early in the day if possible, because of the area's popularity with dog walkers. Avoid misty mornings because the mist can take a long time to clear. The sandy shoreline attracts migrant waders, especially in May, July and August — usually Sanderling, Ringed or Little Ringed Plovers or sandpipers, but sometimes an Oystercatcher. Note that the Frensham car parks may be locked overnight until 9am, complicating early-morning visits because of roadside parking restrictions.

Access

One way of approaching the area is to take the A287 south from Farnham (Map 9). Note that this does not directly link with the A31 but can be accessed from the traffic lights at Farnham by forking left into Tilford Road and taking the first on the right (Alfred Road). For the Little Pond, after 2 miles on the A287, take Priory Lane, the entrance to which is just south of the Mariner's Hotel, on the left. The lane leads through woodland to a car park at the outfall end of the Little Pond. From here there are footpaths onto the heath, which are unsuitable for wheelchairs.

For the Great Pond, continue on the A287 from Farnham and take the signed turning on the right to a car park and visitor centre on the north side of the Great Pond. Footpaths are mostly sandy but there is a wheelchair loop from below the visitor centre down to the shore. The visitors' centre has toilets. Good views of the pond from various points on the road and a footpath, both of which permit close approach to the water. Kings Ridge can be reached by sandy paths from both ponds.

For the Devil's Jumps and Churt Common follow the A287 south past the Great Pond and after half-a-mile turn left on Jumps Road. There is a car park among the pines on the left, after 1.5 miles. Axe Pond (SU 867402) is most easily reached by walking down a sandy bridle path off Sandy Lane, in Rushmoor.

HINDHEAD (Map 9, OS Explorer 133)

Habitat

Hindhead Common (NT) with wet and dry heath and woodland. It includes the Devil's Punch Bowl, a steep-sided combe running north towards Farnham. There are mature beech woods on the west side, in which there is a great sense of space and quiet at the bottom of the combe. On the east side, cattle grazing has been reintroduced to improve the heather. Nature trails have been established on Gibbet Hill, where there is a viewpoint, and in the Punch Bowl. South of Gibbet Hill there is some damper ground. There are mature pine woods on Beacon Hill.

Species

The woods are more reliable than most for Redstart, Wood Warbler, Firecrest, Marsh Tit, Spotted Flycatcher and Crossbill. Try the bottom of the combe for these. The heather holds the usual resident and summer-visiting heathland species, including Nightjar, Woodlark, Stonechat and Dartford Warbler. Siskin breeds. Various raptors are present.

Timing

Best in spring and early summer, when Stonechats, warblers and Firecrests have established territory. Avoid summer afternoons. The area is less interesting in winter and attracts fewer birds of prey than Thursley or Frensham.

Access

Approaching from Hindhead or Frensham, park at the head of the Punch Bowl, on the north side of the A3. Nature trail leaflets are available from a cafe in the car park. Good paths lead over most parts of the common.

PUTTENHAM, CUTT MILL and CROOKSBURY
(Map 9, OS Explorer 145)

Habitat

Puttenham Common is a mixed habitat of rough grass, bracken and birch with some oak woodland, on sloping ground. A series of tree-lined ponds runs down from the slopes of the Hog's Back to Cutt Mill House, between Puttenham and Crooksbury Commons. The lower pool is private, with a public footpath on two sides. Take care not to walk through the gates of Cutt Mill House. Crooksbury Common lies to the west of the ponds. It is waterlogged in places but the heather and boggy areas are becoming overgrown with birch.

Species

Cutt Mill is an outstanding site for Mandarin with 70 or more there in winter, mainly on the lower pool. Wood Ducks are sometimes seen. Great Crested Grebe and Tufted Duck breed. Listen for Willow Tit in the alders and oaks at the north end. The second pool is used for fishing but also has breeding waterfowl, including grebes. The upper pool, visible only from the dam between it and the second, often has Grey Herons perched in trees on the west side. Wintering species include Goosander and, more occasionally, scarcer wildfowl such as Bewick's Swan, Pintail and Ring-necked Duck. There are numbers of Tree Pipits, Marsh Tits and Yellowhammers and a few Lesser Redpolls on the commons in summer. In good years, at Puttenham there are Stonechats at the northern end and Nightingales near the car park at the south. Crooksbury Common is good for Woodcock, Cuckoo, Tree Pipit and Yellowhammer with, as elsewhere in west Surrey, a chance of finding a Hobby or Nightjar.

Timing

Puttenham Common is a good place for roding Woodcock, which may be seen at dusk from March–July. It gets crowded in the vicinity of the pools at weekends, especially in summer. Crooksbury is less disturbed.

Access

From the A31, take the signposted turning south to Puttenham, along the B3000. Turn right after half-a-mile and then left after another quarter-of-a-mile opposite The Good Intent pub. This reaches the lakes after 1.5 miles. There are good car parks on high ground east of the lakes and under trees on the west side of the middle lake. Crooksbury Common is immediately to the west.

Calendar

Resident: Little and Great Crested Grebes, Grey Heron, Mandarin, Teal, Tufted Duck, Sparrowhawk, Kestrel, Water Rail, Snipe, Woodcock, owls, woodpeckers, Kingfisher, Woodlark, Meadow Pipit, Grey Wagtail, Stonechat, Dartford Warbler, Siskin, Redpoll, Crossbill in some years.

December–February: Divers, Red-necked, Slavonian and Black-necked Grebes, Bittern at Frensham, peak Mandarin counts at Cutt Mill, Goldeneye, sawbills, Ruddy Duck. Gull roost at Frensham Great Pond, Hen Harrier, Merlin, Great Grey Shrike on the commons, Cetti's Warbler at Frensham.

March–May: Crossbills breed very early. Curlew arrive at Thursley in February. Tree Pipits arrive from late March, main warbler arrivals in early April, Nightjar and Nightingale slightly later. Migrant waders pass through Frensham, terns from mid-April. May is outstandingly good for displaying and singing breeders.

June–July: Hobby, Nightjars very active, Nightingale song tails off as the birds raise their young, Stonechat second broods, Reed Warblers and Water Rails at Frensham, noisy family parties of other birds on the heaths and commons, Curlew departs in July.

August–November: Young Hobbies on the wing in August. Autumn passage of duck, terns, raptors, Whinchat, Wheatear. Redwing and Fieldfare arrive early October. Hen Harrier, Merlin, Great Grey Shrike possible from October.

10 ALBURY AND DISTRICT   OS Explorer 145

Habitat

The country round Albury (Map 10) has three ridges of hills. Furthest north are the North Downs, running from Pewley Down east through Newlands Corner to Netley Heath. The chalk is in most places capped by shallow plateau gravels where patches of heath, usually dominated by gorse, bracken and scrub, have developed. The south-facing scarp has turf and a good range of chalkland flora. The Greensand elevations of

Map 10
O/S 145

St Martha's Hill and The Chantries, a ridge of mixed woodland, lie immediately south of the downland. Beyond are some lower sandy heaths at
Blackheath and Albury, rising gradually to the third area of elevated
ground, with peaks at Pitch Hill and Winterfold. You can see the sea from
the top of Pitch Hill, a rare view for Surrey.

Blackheath has open areas of deep heather, mature conifer plantations
and scattered copses, mainly of pine, running east to the bracken and
pine of Farley and Albury Heaths. It is a district of substantial country
properties along the lanes. There are cricket pitches on the edge of the
heath at Blackheath and Albury. Deer abound and are easily seen on
summer evenings, especially towards dusk.

There are several private lakes: Tangley Mere is reedy and can be
glimpsed from the railway at Chilworth. Waterloo and Postford Ponds, at
the foot of St Martha's Hill, are readily seen from public footpaths. The
Tillingbourne is a stream of exceptionally pure water, which has been the
basis of the local watercress industry. Cress beds at Abinger are still in
use, although those elsewhere have been converted to fish farms. The
cress is grown in shallow, gravel-bottomed pans of water enclosed by low
concrete walls, continuously irrigated from the adjacent stream. A spring
in the chalk at Albury rises to form the Silent Pool, a shallow pond of
clear blue water overhung by trees, well known as a Surrey beauty spot.

Species

The stretch of North Downs from Pewley Hill to Newlands Corner and Netley Heath is largely interesting for its breeding birds. Lesser Whitethroats are found in the dense old hedges on Pewley Down and elsewhere. Skylarks, migrant chats and Ring Ouzel can be found, especially if sought early on spring or autumn mornings. Newlands Corner was once famous for its Nightingales, all of which now seem to have gone, and in earlier times this would have been typical habitat for Red-backed Shrikes. In a way, this is a sad place, illustrative of the decline of some traditional southern species. The last Surrey stronghold of the Cirl Bunting was at Pewley. Collared Dove, graceful though it is on garden bird tables, seems poor compensation for the losses.

Other new colonists are noticeable in the district though, including birds of prey and the more regular summer occurrences of Firecrest and Siskin with, perhaps, Serin to follow. Sparrowhawk is now much more common and is very likely to be seen along the Downs or the Greensand hills. A few Woodlarks are reappearing on downland and set-aside sites.

Woods at The Chantries have all the expected deciduous and conifer species. The south slope has open turf and hawthorn scrub and is a place for Nightingales and warblers. Little Owls and sometimes partridges can be seen, with evening appearances by Roe Deer in the fields below. Migrant or wandering Hobbies may be seen, as well as Sparrowhawk and Kestrel. Stands of Scots pine and other conifers should be examined for Crossbill in good years. Firecrests are sometimes found in the district, usually where there is mixed pine and oak, and in spring may be located by their song, which is a distinctive and flattened version of that of the Goldcrest, an abundant bird in most parts of Surrey.

St Martha's Hill has Tree Pipits in summer and sometimes Firecrests. The steep hillside below St Martha's, through the beech woods of Colyers Hanger to Waterloo Pond is excellent for warblers including Wood Warbler, which should be sought among the mixed woodland on the higher slopes.

Waterloo and Postford Ponds have Sedge and Reed Warblers and Reed Buntings, as well as Grey Herons, Kingfishers and other waterbirds. Like a number of well-stocked, tree-lined ponds in Surrey, Waterloo has occasionally attracted a lingering migrant Osprey, sometimes for as long as several weeks.

Little and Great Crested Grebes breed on ponds and lakes, as do Canada Geese and a few Tufted Duck. Mandarin is spreading on the streams. Reedy stretches along the Tillingbourne have sometimes, as at Abinger, held a wintering Bittern. Heronries have been established and lost, as at St Martha's, and are unpopular with fish farming interests, whose managers must protect their stock against the hungry herons.

The Abinger cress beds attract a few waders, most regularly Green Sandpiper, which has sometimes wintered there. Grey Heron and Kingfisher may also be seen, perching on the concrete causeways between the beds to fish.

At Blackheath, the heathland birds are becoming better established among the gorse and heather. Tree Pipits will be active where there is birch and in some years the pines may hold Crossbills. Blackheath is a reliable site for Nightjar. An evening visit to hear them should also produce roding Woodcock. Winter birds are less interesting: the area does not seem particularly attractive to raptors and is little visited by bird-watchers at this season.

Crossbills

Nearby Albury Heath is a good place for roding Woodcock on summer evenings. They can be seen at or below eye-level if watched from the high ground on the west of the road, 1 mile south of Albury Church.

Winterfold has heather, recently enhanced by scrub clearance and conifer woods. Species to look for include Nightjar, Redstart, Dartford Warbler, Wood Warbler, Firecrest and Crossbill. The land rises from Winterfold to the top of Pitch Hill, which is tree-covered and has Redstarts. The farming country south of Pitch Hill, around Ewhurst, is typical of the relict Barn Owl habitat still in the county.

Timing

Most of the places discussed will be more rewarding in spring and summer than at other times of the year. The more heavily walked routes along the downs and hills are best early in the day. Blackheath and Albury are interesting if visited in the late afternoon and evening, when species such as Woodcock, Cuckoo and Nightjar are active.

Access

For Pewley Downs there is roadside parking at the top of Pewley Hill (TQ 006491). From here footpaths lead half-a-mile south to The Chantries, 2 miles east to Newlands Corner and 1 mile (1.6 km) southeast to St Martha's. There is a car park under the trees in Echo Pit Road, at the west end of The Chantries.

You can take a pleasant walk east along The Chantries, either continuing along the ridge to St Martha's or dropping down on the south side to Waterloo Ponds via the old gunpowder works, an enterprise which blew up before the First World War to leave a group of interesting but overgrown ruins by a stream. At the gunpowder works there are ponds, old culverts and other relics which have something to offer industrial historians, anglers and birds alike. A circular route can be made by going via the gunpowder works to Waterloo and Postford Ponds, up the hill to St Martha's and then back via paths on the north side of The Chantries to the car park at the west end.

Newlands Corner and Netley Heath can be approached from the car park at Newlands corner (TQ 041493). Other routes onto Netley Heath are from the car park at Hackhurst Downs, or via the footpath up from the Silent Pool. Car parking for the Silent Pool is on the north side of the A25 opposite the turning to Albury (TQ 059485).

St Martha's has a car park on the west side of Halfpenny Lane (TQ 021484) and another, more convenient for Waterloo Ponds, on the east side of White Lane (TQ 034484).

Blackheath has various bits of roadside parking and a proper car park off Sampleoak Lane at TQ 040463. Look for the sign to The Villagers pub at the crossroads 1 mile south of Chilworth railway station, turn right and drive past it to the car park. Walk east along the broad track from here to Farley Heath. Albury Heath has parking space on the east side of the road at TQ 060469, 1 mile south of Albury Church, down the Farley Heath road. Walk across to the other side for Woodcock.

The Hurt Wood lies 2 miles south of Albury Heath, taking the Winterfold road in Farley Green. The western part of it, Winterfold Heath, has plenty of parking spots, including one looking down across the Weald from the crest of Winterfold Hill, at TQ 062428. Hurt Wood continues over the heights of Pitch Hill and Holmbury Hill and is crossed by other roads running south from Shere and Peaslake. There is a car park below Pitch Hill at TQ 080429, 3 miles south of Shere, for those who wish to start from there. None of the areas described here are very suitable for wheelchairs. Abinger Cress beds are shown on Map 12.

Calendar

Resident: Grebes, Grey Heron, Mandarin, Tufted Duck, Sparrowhawk, Woodcock, Stock Dove, Barn and Little Owls, all three woodpeckers, Grey Wagtail, Firecrest and Crossbill in some years, Redpoll.

December–February: Wildfowl at Waterloo and Postford Ponds, chance of wintering Bittern and Green Sandpiper at Abinger.

March–May: Migrant chats and occasional Ring Ouzel on the downs. Arrival of warblers, best heard in song in May. Marsh Tit at Newlands Corner.

June–July: Woodcock, Nightjars and various heathland species at Albury, Blackheath and Winterfold. Tree Pipits on most of the downs and heaths. Sedge and Reed Warblers at Waterloo Ponds. Crossbill irruptions possible from July.

August–November: Green Sandpiper and perhaps other waders at Abinger. Winter thrushes on the North Downs from early October.

11 CENTRAL SURREY COMMONS

Habitat

A group of commons along the north slopes of the Downs (Map 11) are distinguished by mainly clay or calcareous soils, with some shallow gravels. Those in the Bookham and Epsom districts support mixed but primarily oak woodland, scrub and rough grass with a few boggy areas and pools. Stands of hawthorn are frequent and some of the land has been used for forestry. Higher ground around Epsom Downs is drier, with short turf growing on the chalk. The River Mole meanders northwest across the district. Springs rise at Fetcham to fill old millponds.

Species

Woodland and scrub species predominate, with breeding and wintering waterbirds and occasional rarities at the ponds. The commons are traditional Surrey Nightingale localities, although numbers are rather dependent on the stage of the scrub and plantations. Numbers are currently low except at Bookham. Pochard and Garganey have bred. Mandarin is increasing.

Turtle Dove

Main Birdwatching Zones

Effingham Fish Ponds and the surrounding woods and commons provide habitat for waterbirds, woodland birds and passage migrants. Commons, riversides and ponds from Bookham through to Fetcham support a wide variety of breeding species. Commons and downland at Ashtead and Epsom offer opportunities for observing inland migration and gull movements.

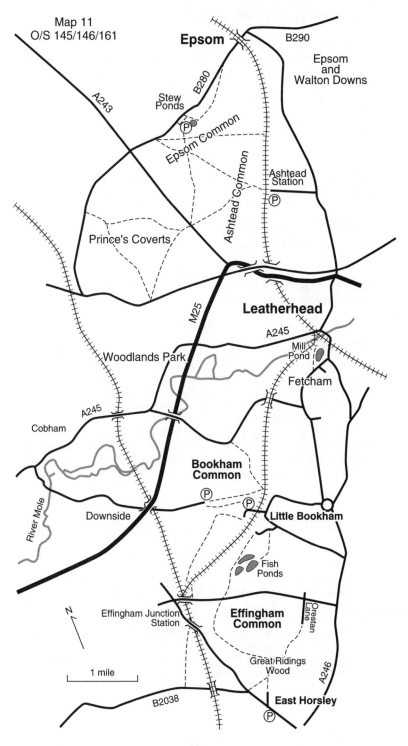

Map 11
O/S 145/146/161

EFFINGHAM and EAST HORSLEY (Map 11, OS Explorer 146)

Habitat

A chain of fishponds on marshy land at Effingham has good cover for wildfowl, with well-covered banks round the pools, and small islands. The surrounding area is bushy, with mature hedgerows. Effingham Common has mixed woodland and scrub with stands of hawthorn. Great Ridings Wood, owned by The Woodland Trust is nearby at East Horsley and includes hornbeam.

Species

Canada Goose and Tufted Duck are resident and other wildfowl winter. Little Grebe and Pochard have bred. Gadwall and Garganey should be looked for in spring and autumn. Lapwings are often seen on an adjacent meadow. This is a good place for passerine migrants, especially hirundines and warblers. Yellow Wagtails of various races have been reported in spring. Scrub on Effingham Common has a few Nightingales. Great Ridings Wood is one of the best Hawfinch localities in Surrey.

Timing

Early morning is best for Hawfinches, which drink from pools in the woods and surrounding properties.

Access

Effingham ponds may be approached on foot from Effingham Common Road, taking a turning half-a-mile southeast of Effingham Junction station that leads to the public footpath crossing the site. Alternatively take the other end of the footpath in Little Bookham. Private parking at the ponds is for anglers with permits. The public footpaths provide good views. Effingham Common runs out to Effingham Common Road, on the south side of Effingham Junction railway station.

Great Ridings Wood may be entered from Orestan Lane in Effingham. Alternatively start at East Horsley, parking at the tennis courts or shops in Ockham Road South (B2039) half-a-mile north of the junction with the A25 at Horsley Towers and take the sign-posted bridle path.

BOOKHAM and FETCHAM (Map 11, OS Explorer 146)

Habitat

Great and Little Bookham Commons are managed by the NT. The clay soils on the higher parts of the commons are covered by deciduous woodland, mainly oak, and the damper low-lying parts have rough grass, hawthorn scrub and small ponds. The commons have a long record of scientific recording under the auspices of the London Natural History Society and there is a large survey literature. Survey work has revealed many interesting plant and insect species. Mammals present include Fox and Roe Deer. The River Mole runs across the commons. There is a millpond by the Mole at Fetcham.

Species

Little Grebe, Kingfisher and Grey Wagtail breed at small pools along the River Mole, which forms the northern boundary of the site. Mandarin breeds in adjacent woodland.

There is a heronry at Bookham. Raptors seen there from time to time include Goshawk, Buzzard and Hobby. Sparrowhawk breeds and is frequently observed. Green, Greater Spotted and Lesser Spotted Woodpeckers are resident on these commons, as are Tawny Owl, Marsh Tit, Nuthatch and Treecreeper. Stock Dove is present in small numbers. Summer visitors include Turtle Dove. With up to ten pairs of Nightingales in the hawthorns, it is currently the best site in Surrey for the species. There are strong populations of the commoner warblers and a few Wood Warblers. Grasshopper Warbler used to be found in the open areas and may return. A Cetti's Warbler once established a territory in thorn scrub along a stream and a Night Heron lingered at one of the ponds. Dense blackthorn stands occasionally hold winter roosts of Short-eared and Long-eared Owls. Winter flocks of Redwing and Fieldfare are regular in scrubby areas. Hawfinches from East Horsley sometimes feed on the common in winter.

Fetcham Mill Pond has small numbers of breeding and wintering waterfowl, including Pochard, and attracts migrants. An Osprey has lingered there.

Access

There are many footpaths and access is unrestricted. One approach is over the footbridge at Bookham railway station to a small car park at TQ 123558. This affords views over the scrub where Nightingale and Hawfinch may be present in season. Footpaths lead over the common. If approaching from the A245 at Cobham, take the minor road to Downside and a car park on the north side of the commons at TQ 120566. Footpaths from Leatherhead run along the bank of the Mole and past Fetcham Mill Pond.

ASHTEAD and EPSOM COMMONS, EPSOM and WALTON DOWNS OS Explorer 146/161

Habitat

Ashtead Common (Map 11) is an area of rough grass, conifer plantation and ancient oak wood land north of Ashtead station. A stream, The Rye, runs through the southern part of the site. Butterflies include Green Hairstreak and Silver-washed Fritillary. It has NNR status on account of its diverse bird life and over 1,000 species of beetle. Prince's Coverts, immediately northwest of Ashtead Common, on the other side of the A243, is mainly plantation woodland.

Epsom Common is adjacent. Woodland and scrub continue to the Stew Ponds, which have been the subject of conservation work. Epsom and Park Downs are on higher ground, partly taken up by Epsom Race Course. The Downs are dry, with turf, rough grass and gorse.

Species

Many woodland and rough grassland species are present. Woodcock, Lesser Spotted Woodpeckers, Redstarts and Marsh Tits should be looked for in Ashtead Woods. Garden Warblers, Blackcaps, Lesser Whitethroats and Whitethroats occur in suitable places across Ashtead and Epsom Commons. Nightingales breed sparingly throughout, but has become scarcer. Until recently the longer grass on Ashtead Common held Grasshopper Warbler. The area is still strong for breeding Linnet and winter flocks of finches and thrushes. There are Grey Wagtails along The Rye.

Mandarin is now breeding on Epsom Common. Hobby is seen occasionally. Little Bittern, Garganey and Osprey have been found at Epsom Stew Ponds. Gull flocks on the Downs reflect migratory patterns, with large numbers of Lesser Black-backs in late summer. The Downs have proved to be good for observing visible passerine migration, mostly Lapwings and gulls, and falls of night migrants such as chats and leaf warblers.

Timing

Visits early in the day are advisable, especially in the Epsom localities, because of heavy public use of downland sites but timing is rarely critical.

Access

A convenient point from which to explore Ashtead Common is the level crossing at Ashtead railway station, from which public footpaths fan out across the common. Park at the station or in the adjacent Woodfield area. Access is also possible from a turning east off the A243, 1 mile north of Leatherhead. Buses run to Ashtead. There is wheelchair access to a small area near the station. The nearest toilets are in Ashtead village.

There is a car park at the Epsom Common Stew Ponds on the B280, three-quarters-of-a-mile west of the junction with the A243. For Epsom and Walton Downs take the B290 for 2 miles south from the centre of Epsom to the racecourse.

Calendar

Resident: Little Grebe, Grey Heron, Mandarin, Tufted Duck, Sparrowhawk, Kestrel, Woodcock, Kingfisher, Green, Great and Lesser Spotted Woodpeckers, Grey Wagtail, Marsh Tit, Redpoll, Hawfinch, Reed Bunting.

December–February: Shoveler, Fieldfare, Redwing, Siskin, Lesser Spotted Woodpecker calling from February, Hawfinches at Bookham Common.

March–May: Redshank, Common Sandpiper, Yellow Wagtail, Nightingale, Grasshopper Warbler, Spotted Flycatcher (may not arrive until the second week of May). Best time for Hawfinch at Great Ridings Wood.

June–July: Lapwing and Lesser Black-backed Gull flocks reappear on the Downs from July. Nightingales sing to about mid-June. Tree Pipit.

August–November: Chance of migrant raptors, Goshawk, Common Buzzard, Osprey and Hobby, Whinchats and Wheatears in open situations such as Epsom Downs, Pied Flycatcher.

12 DORKING HILLS AND LAKES

Habitat

Dorking lies among the highest of the Surrey hills, at the point where the River Mole cuts through the North Downs and the Lower Greensand Ridge (Map 12). Some of the water runs underground through swallow holes in the stony bed of the river, and in dry weather the water can be very low or disappear altogether. Box Hill and Ranmore Common command the heights of the Downs north of the town. Leith Hill and Holmbury Hill, formed of sands and the harder, flint-like chert, lie to the

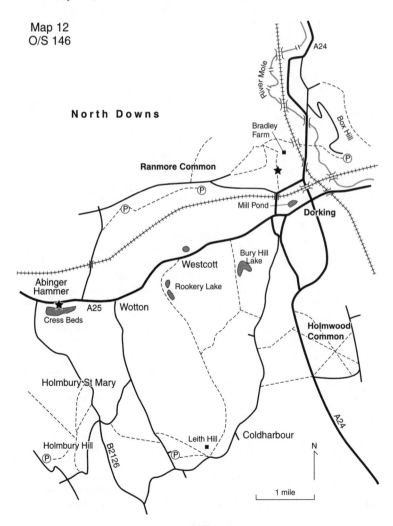

Map 12
O/S 146

177

west. Streams running off the sandy slopes have been dammed in several places to form lakes, of which the largest are at Westcott and Bury Hill. Holmwood Common is an extension of the Greensand on lower ground east of Leith Hill. There is a small millpond at Dorking.

Box Hill (NT) is a pleasant but heavily-used vantage point with some 325 ha of woodland and chalk downland. It is designated a Country Park. Nature walks have been laid out. A cliff on the west side is famous for its cover of Box trees. Other plant specialities include orchids and Stinking Hellebore. There are old chalk quarries in the southern slopes.

Ranmore Common (NT) is on high ground west of Box Hill, on the opposite side of the Mole Valley. It is one of the better places in Surrey for orchids and other chalkland flora, including Green Hellebore. Mixed woodland and bracken-dominated heath on the plateau gravels give way to chalky soils and beech glades on the northern slopes. Rough grass and scrub cover much of the south-facing scarp.

Leith Hill (NT) is the highest elevation in Surrey and the high point in the Weald for the Lower Greensand. A folly tower at the summit takes it to over 300 m and is conspicuous for many miles around. Most of the hill is wooded, with some oak coppice. The dip slopes have been extensively planted, mainly with conifers, and there are a few monkey puzzle trees. Clearance at Dukes Warren (TQ 140440) has created some heather cover. The scarp woodland includes naturally regenerating holly, yew, rowan and beech. Part of the area is an SSSI, designated for its geology, botany (including mosses) and birds. There is a hill fort, Anstiebury Camp, at Coldharbour. Holmwood Common (NT) is a rather overgrown area of sandy heath dominated by bracken, birch and oak.

Holmbury Hill, to the west of Leith Hill is mostly wooded and there are broad rides through the conifer plantations. A large area of Amelanchier scrub, an alien from North America, gives it a place in the botany books. Birds reportedly take the fruit, which appears in midsummer, helping the tree to spread to other parts of the county. There is a hill fort on the summit.

Species

Birds on the tree-covered parts of Box Hill include Sparrowhawk, Kestrel, Woodcock, woodpeckers, Wood Warbler and Nuthatch, and the more open areas have a good variety of scrub and leaf warblers, and finches. Kestrels and Jackdaws nest in the chalk quarries. Mandarin is found along the Mole and migrant Common Sandpipers occur on the stonier stretches.

Open fields at Bradley Farm are a good place to observe visible migration, especially in autumn, the species involved being mainly Skylarks, chats, thrushes and finches. One of the winter gull flight lines from the Thames Valley roosts passes through the Mole gap at this point, fanning out south, east and west at Dorking.

Ranmore Common is similar to Box Hill for birds, though being less visited it is more rewarding to visit. The heath areas have good numbers of Tree Pipits and used to have Nightjars before being overrun by bracken. There were also Wood Warblers and Hawfinches in the woods, but neither has been seen for some time. Woodcocks come to pools for water, and may be seen roding on summer evenings.

The woods on Leith Hill are full of tits, Goldcrest, finches and the commoner warblers in the breeding season. More interestingly, there are also numbers of breeding Redstart and Wood Warbler, Sparrowhawk should be seen and there may be a fleeting glimpse of a Hobby. Woodcock and Tawny Owl are present in the denser parts of the wood. Stonechats have bred at Duke's Warren.

Holmbury Hill is similar but has at times supported extraordinary numbers of Nightjars, feeding over the woodland rides. The viewpoint at the summit is a good place to look for soaring raptors, including Sparrowhawk, Common Buzzard, Kestrel and Hobby. The fairly secluded scattered woodland is worth exploring. Holmwood Common has Tree Pipits and a variety of warblers but few real heathland birds.

Great Tit

The lakes at Westcott have breeding and wintering Tufted Duck. Bury Hill Lake has reedbeds and an island. It is heavily fished from the shore and from boats, but is worth a look, nevertheless, early in the day or as part of a longer excursion towards Leith Hill. Dorking Mill Pond has the usual collection of urban wildfowl and attracts a few passerine and non-passerine migrants.

Timing

Box Hill can be crowded at weekends. Early in the day is best, unless you can visit during the week. Leith Hill and Holmbury Hill are best in spring and summer. Like Box Hill, Ranmore and other places on the higher ground in Surrey tend to be deserted in winter, except for a few tits, thrushes and finches.

Access

Box Hill can be climbed by the footpath starting at the A24 on the north edge of Dorking, at TQ 173513, or by the zigzag minor road behind the Burford Bridge Hotel, 1 mile north of Dorking at TQ 174523. A good path from the north side of Dorking, at TQ 162500, cuts across the fields for half-a-mile, to Bradley Farm where it turns left uphill to Ranmore Common. An unclassified road running northwest from the town leads to car parks on Ranmore, south of the road at TQ 127501 and TQ 140503.

Possible approaches to Leith Hill are by footpath from Dorking, commencing at Milton Street (TQ 149488) and going north past Bury Hill Lake, or by car or bus to Coldharbour. A network of paths leads down the back slopes to Wotton, Westcott and Holmwood Common. Paths over Holmwood Common start at various places along the A24 immediately south of Dorking.

For Holmbury Hill take the B2126 from the A25 at Abinger Hammer and follow it for 2 miles to Holmbury St Mary, then walk south along a track from TQ 108451.

Small lakes at Westcott are reached by public footpaths northeast and southwest from the A25 at TQ 133483. Dorking Mill Pond has good footpaths round it, and is the only part of the area described readily accessible for wheelchairs.

Calendar

Resident: Little and Great Crested Grebes, Mute Swan, Mandarin, Tufted Duck, Sparrowhawk, Kestrel, Woodcock, Stock Dove, Little and Tawny Owls, woodpeckers, Grey Wagtail, Nuthatch, Jackdaw, Redpoll, Reed Bunting.

December–February: Thrush and finch flocks on the lower ground. Ranmore, Leith Hill and other more elevated locations tend to hold fewer birds.

March–May: Woodcock roding, Common Buzzard and other raptors on Holmbury Hill, Redstart, Wood Warblers on Box Hill and Leith Hill, a chance of Firecrest.

June–July: Great Crested Grebe and Tufted Duck with young. Bird song eases off in July.

August–November: Summer visitors depart, starting with Swifts in August. Daily movements of gulls from the Thames Valley to Dorking and beyond begin. Visible migration across lower ground at Dorking, especially Skylark, Fieldfare, Redwing and finches flying east from early October.

13 REIGATE TO GODSTONE   OS Explorer 146

Habitat

Like the Dorking district, the country round Reigate and Redhill straddles the North Downs and the sandy soils further south (Map 13). A narrow belt of Gault clay lies between the two. Deposits of Fuller's Earth occur among the sands and these, together with the sand and chalk, have been worked for many years. There are a number of lakes and water-filled pits. Further east the ridge of sandy hills runs on to Godstone.

Main Birdwatching Zones

The urban area of Reigate and Redhill and its more rural environs holds several small sites of interest. Gatton Park, on Gault clay on the north side of Reigate, has the largest water in the district, Gatton Lake. There are smaller waters at Reigate Priory and Earlswood Common. Agricultural land between Redhill and Godstone, to the east, can offer good birdwatching. An example is around the Sandhills Estate in Bletchingley.

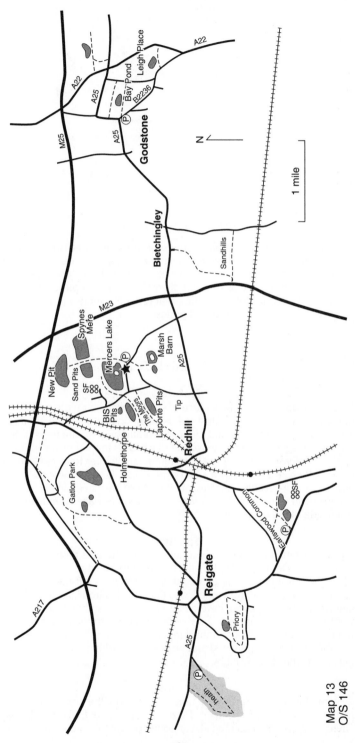

Map 13
O/S 146

Golden Plover and Lapwings

Sand and Fuller's Earth pits to the east of the town at Holmethorpe provide an unstable habitat of waste ground, sand cliffs, pools and stretches of drying silt while being worked. In their later stages they may be landscaped or used as tips and filled. Godstone is a pleasant village of small shops and country eating places where there are more pits, active and exhausted, and several ponds.

REIGATE AND REDHILL

Habitat
Reigate Heath is a small, hilly piece of sandy common on the south side of the A25, west of Reigate. Most of it is a golf course but there are large stands of pine, birch, oak and alder, which attract good numbers of the commoner species. Higher areas, one of which is topped by a windmill, make it a pleasant place to walk, in summer or winter. Reigate Heath is an SSSI. Reigate Priory has a small ornamental lake and woods. There used to be hornbeams but some or all of these have been felled.

Earlswood Common has two lakes. Earlswood Sewage Farm is on the south side of the common.

Species
Black Redstarts have bred in Redhill town centre and there is a large Ring-necked Parakeet roost. Hawfinches used to breed at Reigate Priory when the hornbeams were there but appear to have left the area. As at other sites, patience may be needed to find them. Gatton Lake has a large heronry. Earlswood Lakes have small numbers of summer and winter wildfowl. A Great Northern Diver once stayed on the lakes for several weeks. Breeding birds at Sandhills include Pheasant, Cuckoo, Little Owl and the usual field and woodland edge species, with the chance of seeing Sparrowhawk and Hobby.

Access
Reigate Priory and Earlswood Common are on the west and south margins of the town respectively. There is a car park at Earlswood Lakes. There is no access to Gatton Lake, although public footpaths through the

grounds of the Royal Alexandra and Albert School, from Tower Lane and Gatton Park Road to Rocky Lane, run quite close to it. Limited access, e.g. for wildfowl counts or the heron census, is by arrangement only. In the general interests of birdwatchers, do not trespass. Car parking for Reigate Heath is available on Flanchford Road, on the south side of the A25 immediately west of Reigate. For Sandhills, park in Castle Square, just off the A25 in Bletchingley (TQ 324507). Follow the footpath east along the woodland edge (sign-posted to Nutfield), then south to meet a bridleway. Explore along this south to the motorway, then retrace your steps. A map is advisable. The return distance is 2.5 miles.

HOLMETHORPE SAND PITS

Habitat

Mercer's Lake is a landscaped pit used for sailing. It belongs to British Industrial Sand Ltd (BIS). A picnic area has been provided and there are toilets. A car park, which is open to the public, commands a fine view over the entire water. It is possible to walk round via a footpath. A small part of the lake is a nature reserve and is protected by a line of buoys. Holmethorpe Sewage Farm is on the north side of Mercer's Lake.

Mercer's East, a large worked-out pit northeast of Mercer's Lake has a sand cliff and pools, and is proving to be a useful addition to the area. The Surrey Wildlife Trust has renamed it Spynes Mere and is developing it as a nature reserve.

The BIS Holmethorpe Quarry (also known as Holmethorpe Lagoons) is opposite Mercer's Lake, in Nutfield Road. It contains a number of pits, one of which is flooded, with significant areas of sandy shoreline. Part of the site is still being worked. There are abandoned pits on the west side of Cormongers Lane These are currently difficult of access and unrewarding. A refuse tip further south on the west side of Cormongers Lane attracts huge numbers of gulls in winter. Mercer's Lake, Spynes Mere, the BIS pit and the refuse tip are the places on which to concentrate, though the evolution of other good areas is at hand.

A new pit is being worked north of Mercers Lake (Mercer's West) and an area immediately south of the BIS pit is being redeveloped as The Moors nature reserve by the Surrey Wildlife Trust. It will be a wet meadow site. Two small pits accessible from a footpath running south at the end of Chilmead Lane, off Cormongers Lane, have been landscaped and are currently known as Marsh Barn. Glebe Lake is a small water in the southeast corner of the area.

Species

The pits at Holmethorpe have occasionally produced divers and, more frequently, the scarcer grebes, usually Red-necked or Black-necked. These sometimes appear on other waters in the district. There are large numbers of Canada Geese. A few feral Barnacle and Snow Geese are now regular. Greylags are appearing more frequently following their colonisation of the county from introduced stocks elsewhere and flocks of 50 or more are sometimes on Mercer's Lake and adjacent fields. Fair numbers of wildfowl winter in the district, mostly Teal, Mallard, Pochard and Tufted Duck, but with occasional Wigeon, Scaup, Long-tailed Duck or other wanderer. Tundra Bean Geese have been seen. One or two Shelduck may be seen during the year and have bred, although the habitat is rather marginal. Osprey is sometimes seen on passage, most often in autumn. Hobby appears over the pits in summer. Red-legged Partridge is occasionally seen at the pits. A few Jack Snipe may be found in winter. There is a moderate spring and autumn wader passage, mostly sandpipers and Greenshank, with a Whimbrel or two and godwits. Avocet has occurred. Green Sandpiper is a characteristic bird of the district and might be seen at Mercer's Lake in any month, with up to five in winter. Common Sandpipers are also frequent, but more confined to passage seasons. Little Ringed Plover is a summer visitor to suitable sites.

Many gulls are attracted to the refuse tip. They include Mediterranean, Glaucous and the occasional Iceland. Large flocks of Carrion Crows may be found in winter. Lesser Black-backed Gulls now linger through May and returning immatures are present in good numbers as early as mid-June. Migrant terns are scarce. A Little Owl may be seen near Mercer's Farm. Stubble fields south of Spynes Mere have large Lapwing flocks in winter, sometimes with a few Golden Plovers. There are small Sand Martin colonies. Black Redstarts occur on passage, arriving earlier and leaving later than the common species, often a helpful point when females or immatures are found in unusual places in March, October or November.

Access

Holmethorpe Sand Pits can be reached from Cormongers Lane, a left turn off the A25, half-a-mile east of Redhill. Cormongers Lane has bends and is on a hill. Watch for sand and rubbish lorries. Small roadside parking places afford views over various parts of the area but do park OFF the road because of the lorry traffic, and preferably use the car park above the sailing pit at Mercer's Lake, which is open to the public and is the best place from which to explore the more important parts of the area. The entrance is in Nutfield Marsh Road, off Cormongers Lane. A circular walk can be made from here, beginning along the path round Mercer's Lake to the BIS pits. These and The Moors can be seen from the entrance in South Nutfield Road but the best way of viewing them is to follow the footpath south of the BIS pits to the railway line. Returning to the road, follow it south to Chilmead Farm and then go east along Chilmead Lane to the landscaped pits (also known as Marsh Barn). From here the Mercer's Lake car park can be reached via the cricket ground at the end of the lane.

Spynes Mere can be seen from a bridle path that passes the west end of the lake, behind the windsurfing centre. A National Cycle Route adjoins the site. Glebe Lake can be seen from South Nutfield Road.

View the refuse tip from the entrance on the west side of Cormongers Lane. Do not obstruct it. A public footpath marked as running across the area west of Cormongers Lane is overgrown and not recommended.

There is no provision for wheelchair access.

GODSTONE

Habitat

At Godstone, two old sand pits, which at one time included a small reserve, have now been filled. Other sand pits there are still being worked. Bay Pond, an artificial lake with reedy margins and an alder swamp, is a Surrey Wildlife Trust reserve. Habitat improvements are underway. There are ponds at Rooks Nest Farm and Leigh Place.

Species

Bay Pond has Kingfisher and breeding waterfowl. It is worth scanning for wintering Water Rail. Reedbed improvements might bring in Reed Warblers. Various exotics may be found on the town pond, which is in a corner of the village green. The pond at Rooks Nest Farm is worth a quick inspection in winter. Actively worked sand pits are likely to have Sand Martins.

Access

Godstone is half-a-mile south of the M25, accessed from junction 6. Park by the village green. Bay Pond is behind the White Hart pub and can be well seen from footpaths north and south of the site, running between the High Street and Church Lane. Leigh Place is 1 mile (1.6 km) south-east, on the B2236. Rooks Nest Farm is off the A22 at TQ 362522. View these two from the road only. Viewing may be difficult.

Calendar

Resident: Little and Great Crested Grebes, Grey Heron, Greylag and Canada Geese, Tufted Duck, Red-legged Partridge, Sparrowhawk, Kingfisher, woodpeckers, Grey Wagtail, and possibly Grey Partridge, Tree Sparrow and Hawfinch.

December–February: Occasional divers, Red-necked and Black-necked Grebes, Cormorant, Shelduck, Teal, Pochard, Goldeneye, possibly Wigeon, Gadwall, Scaup, Long-tailed Duck and Smew, Water Rail. Look for Golden Plover among the Lapwings at Holmethorpe. Possible wintering Green Sandpiper. Many gulls at Holmethorpe refuse tip. Redwing, Fieldfare, Brambling. Tree Sparrow (flocks of up to 100 in the past) and Corn Bunting, both at Holmethorpe, appear to have been lost but may reappear. White-fronted Goose movements, other vagrant grey geese in hard weather.

March–May: Sand Martin and Wheatear arrivals from mid-March. Look for Garganey on the pits in April. Godwits, Whimbrel and sandpipers mainly in May. Terns, mostly Common but with a chance of Arctic, from mid-April. Lesser Whitethroat, Whitethroat, Garden Warbler, Blackcap, Chiffchaff and Willow Warbler in hedges and copses around the pits. Rookery on Nutfield Ridge. Breeding birds on the farmland around Sandhills are best seen in May and June. This is also the time when the Gatton heronry is most active.

June–July: Lapwings start to flock. Lesser Black-backed Gulls return to Holmethorpe.

August–November: Autumn wader passage, chance of Spotted Redshank at the pits. Redwing and Fieldfare from early October, Goldeneye from mid-November.

Habitat

The low-lying country north of East Grinstead is drained by closely spaced tributaries of the River Eden (Map 14). Old millponds along the waterways reflect a bygone industrial age. The largest of these are at Hedgecourt and Wire Mill, on the Eden Brook. The district has a number of small woods and copses accessible by footpath. There is some unimproved grassland, best seen at Blindley Heath.

Hedgecourt Pond, a 17-ha stretch of water lying on a bed of Tunbridge Wells Sands, is the most important wildfowl refuge in southeast Surrey. It is relatively secluded and has reeds along the south side and around the west end. The outfall at the east end runs through damp woodland and meadow. The pond is not very deep and freezes in hard weather. It is used intermittently for sailing. The site is an SSSI and 4 ha at the west end are a nature reserve. Botanical specialities include Touch-me-not Balsam and various pond weeds.

Wire Mill, 1 mile to the northeast, is smaller. It has extensive beds of reed and sedge along its edges and woodland on two sides, and is used for watersports and fishing. Blindley Heath is a flat, 26-ha stretch of tall grasses 1.75 miles north of Wire Mill. Drainage is poor and there are several small ponds. Oak and hawthorn scrub has begun to invade. The ponds have interesting sedges and other plants.

Species

Winter Cormorant numbers at Hedgecourt have recently been peaking at over 20 and in January and February there is just a chance of a Bittern in the reeds. Wintering duck include Mandarin, Shoveler and Pochard. Red-throated Diver and Ferruginous Duck have been found. Water Rails are sometimes seen and may stay to breed. Greylag and Canada Geese have bred fairly regularly in recent years. Grey Wagtail may be seen at the outfall, which passes under a narrow roadway along the dam. Kingfisher, which occurs here and along the many streams in the district, will also appear at Hedgecourt. The reedbeds attract Sedge and Reed Warblers, the former scarce in south Surrey, and also a few Reed Buntings. Birches and alders round the lake provide food for Goldfinch, Siskin and Lesser Redpoll in winter. Woodcock is found in copses such as those near

Canada Goose

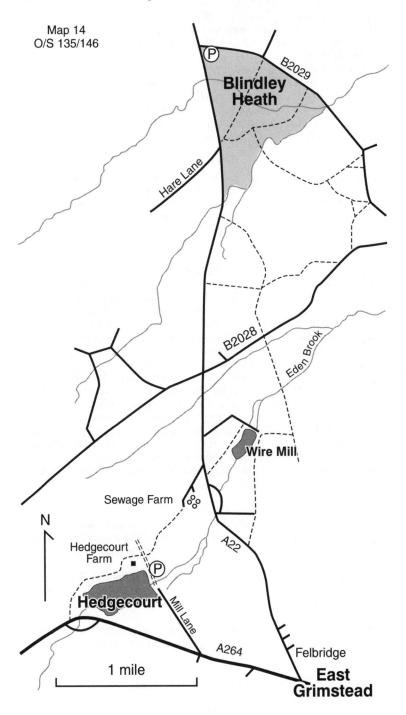

Map 14
O/S 135/146

Blindley
Heath

B2029

Hare Lane

B2028

Eden Brook

Wire Mill

Sewage Farm

N

Hedgecourt
Farm

Hedgecourt

Mill Lane

A22

A264

Felbridge

East
Grimstead

1 mile

Hedgecourt Pond. Tawny Owls and Nightingales occur here and there. As in some other parts of Surrey, Nightingale has become rather scarce in recent years.

Wire Mill has rather fewer waterfowl, but, like Hedgecourt, may have Water Rails in winter and the surrounding reedbeds and scrub hold Sedge and Reed Warblers and Reed Bunting in the breeding season.

Blindley Heath provides a relict habitat for some fairly local species. Snipe winter there. Summer visitors include Turtle Dove, Nightingale and Spotted Flycatcher. Grasshopper Warbler appears to have been lost.

Timing

Hedgecourt is used for sailing, mainly at weekends but on most days during the summer. This drives duck and Coot into shallow bays at the west end. Wire Mill is used for water-skiing and fishing. Early morning is best at both sites, especially when disturbance is expected. Nightingale is easiest to find from late April to early June, their period of most consistent song.

Access

Hedgecourt Pond is at Felbridge, on the western outskirts of East Grinstead. Approach via the A264 (Copthorne Road) and turn off on the north side up Mill Lane. The road passes the east end of the lake, where there is room to park a car and obtain good views of the pond. Alternatively, park in the slip road south of the A264, at the west end of the lake. Cross the road and follow the footpath through Domewood, which will take you round the west and north sides.

Approach Wire Mill via Wire Mill Lane, on the east side of the A22 1.5 miles (2.4 km) north of Felbridge. The lane may be deeply potholed so drive carefully. If walking from Hedgecourt, stay on the Domewood footpath, which continues past a sewage farm to the A22, crosses it and goes on to Wire Mill. The path returns to the A22 through woods on the opposite side of the lake. Blindley Heath lies east of the A22, between Godstone and East Grinstead. There is a small car park north of the heath, at the A22 end of Danemore Lane. Footpaths start from here and from the northeast and southwest corners.

Calendar

Resident: Great Crested Grebe, Mute Swan, Greylag and Canada Geese, Mandarin, Mallard, Sparrowhawk, Water Rail, Woodcock, Tawny Owl, Kingfisher, woodpeckers, Grey Wagtail, Marsh Tit, Reed Bunting.

December–February: Cormorants and chance of Bittern at Hedgecourt. Shoveler, Pochard, Tufted Duck and Goosander (mainly at Hedgecourt), Redwing, Fieldfare, Siskin, Redpoll.

March–May: Mandarin disperse from ponds to streamside breeding sites, Woodcock roding at Hedgecourt, Nightingale, warblers arrive, including Sedge and Reed.

June–July: Wildfowl, warblers and Grey Wagtails with young.

August–November: Terns and Common Sandpiper possible at Hedgecourt, departure of summer visitors.

ADDITIONAL SITES

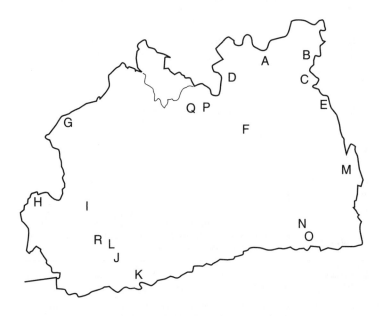

Key & Site	Habitat	Birds of Interest	Peak Season	Nearest Town
A Beddington	Sewage farm	Wader passage, breeding Yellow Wagtail and Tree Sparrow, migrants	May, Aug–Oct	Croydon

OS Explorer 161
TQ 290665

A site with a long history of scarce migrants: Killdeer, Lesser Yellowlegs, Red-rumped Swallow, Bluethroat and Rustic Bunting are among those recorded. Stints in Sep/Oct, Little Ringed Plover, Caspian Gull, strong passage of chats, large Tree Sparrow colony in nest boxes. Being redeveloped. No wheelchair access. Nearby Waddon Ponds (TQ 310650) have Little Grebe and unusual numbers of breeding Coot. Also toilets.

 Access is restricted but views of the lake and other areas are possible from the railway bridge in Mile Road, off the A237 north of Hackbridge railway station and from a connecting footpath between Beddington Park and Mitcham Common that runs along the west side of the site. Car park at the station (parking charge). Roadside parking off the A237. Do not park in Mile Road. Special access arrangements are sometimes made for national rarities, listen for announcements on BirdLine Southeast. Not suitable for wheelchairs or for those with mobility problems.

Key & Site	Habitat	Birds of Interest	Peak Season	Nearest Town
B Dulwich Woods	Deciduous woodland	Woodpeckers, warblers, wintering Firecrest, Nuthatch	Jan–May	Dulwich

OS Explorer 161
TQ 345725

Park in Sydenham Hill Road. Access via Sydenham Hill Nature Reserve. Railway stations at Sydenham Hill and Forest Hill.

Key & Site	Habitat	Birds of Interest	Peak Season	Nearest Town
C Crystal Palace Park	Park with lake	Breeding Shelduck (feral), Spotted Flycatcher, migrants	All year	Penge
OS Explorer 161 TQ 345705	*Park at the National Sports Centre. Weird atmosphere with life-size model dinosaurs in the bushes. Interesting winter visitors including Firecrest.*			
D Berrylands	Sewage works	Passage migrants	Spring	Surbiton
OS Explorer 161 TQ 198681	*Adjacent to Berrylands railway station. View filter beds from Up platform or apply for permit to explore.*			
E South Norwood	Rough grass, wetland, woods	Migrants and winter visitors, waterfowl, falcons	All year	Croydon
OS Explorer 161 TQ 352680	*South Norwood Country Park is the former Elmers End Sewage Farm. Scarce migrants have included Marsh Warbler and Red-backed Shrike, Twite in winter, Tree Sparrow has bred, Corn Bunting possible. Car park near the sports stadium. Rarities (national and local) at nearby South Norwood Lake (TQ 340695) have included Pied-billed Grebe and Sandwich Tern. Beaulieu Heights Wood (entrance in South Norwood Hill at TQ 332696) has wintering Firecrest. Some level tarmac paths at all three sites.*			
F Headley Heath	Acid heath on downland	Woodcock, heathland species	May–Sep	Leatherhead
OS Explorer 146 TQ 205535	*Approach on the B2033. There are car parks on the west side of the road, 2 miles (3km) from Leatherhead. Follow the sandy footpaths.*			
G Olddean Common	Heath and pine woods	Woodlark, Redstart, Stonechat, Wood Warbler, Crossbill, Great Grey Shrike	Dec–Jul	Camberley
OS Explorer 160 SU 893625	*Approach from roads north of the A30 on the London side of Camberley. Area near radio tower is fenced off for bikers, best avoided. Great Grey Shrike site at Wishmoor Bottom, park at the end of Kings Ride, SU875622. Rough paths and no seats.*			
H Bricksbury Hill	Heath and pine woods	Heathland species including Nightjar	May–Jul	Farnham
OS Explorer 145 SU 827492	*Park off the A287 near the radio tower and follow sandy paths northeast. Fine views, and good birds, at Caesar's Camp.*			
I Wanborough	Open corn fields, wire fences	Stock Dove, Skylark, migrant chats, chance of Quail and partridges	Jan–Jun	Guildford
OS Explorer 145 SU 934485	*A good example of old Cirl and Corn Bunting habitat on chalk downland. Flocks of up to 100 Stock Doves in winter.*			
J Hascombe	Mixed woods on sandy hills	Woodcock, Wood Warbler, Crossbill	Apr–Oct	Godalming
OS Explorer 133/134 TQ 002394	*Hascombe Camp is an Iron Age hill fort approached by footpath from Hascombe, on the B2130, 3 miles south of Godalming. Hydons Ball is a small hill to the west at SU9739.*			

Key & Site	Habitat	Birds of Interest	Peak Season	Nearest Town
K Chiddingfold/ Dunsfold	Plantations and farmland	Nightingale and other summer visitors, Firecrest	Apr–Oct	Haslemere
OS Explorer 133 TQ 016353	_Tracts of FC woodland with clearings south of Chiddingfold and Dunsfold. Botany Bay is well known for butterflies (Purple Emperor etc). Limited roadside parking by the entrance, SU977347. Nightingale at Oaken Wood, SU9934. Frillinghurst Wood, between Grayswood and Chiddingfold, is similar. Unmade woodland rides._			
L Winkworth Arboretum	Lake and ornamental woodland	Breeding Water Rail and occasionally Red-crested Pochard, summer and winter migrants	All year	Godalming
OS Explorer 145 SU 996413	_NT. Admission charge. Two miles (3 km) southeast of Godalming, on the east side of the B2130. Bus from Guildford or Cranleigh._			
M Limpsfield Chart	Acid heath on hill	Woodcock, Nightjar, Redstart	Apr–Jul	Oxted
OS Explorer 147 TQ 407519	_Approach on the B269 from Limpsfield. It is 2 miles to the Chart. Car park in Moorhouse Road, TQ427521._			
N Hookwood/ Meath Green	Farm fields, sewage works	Winter finch flocks, migrant waders	All year	Horley
OS Explorer 146 TQ 262430	_Park on roadside grass. Footpath at Hookwood leads over farm fields with winter/spring finch flocks. Meath Green sewage works at TQ268435 consists of three lagoons and can be viewed from an adjacent footpath. Little Grebe, migrant waders._			
O Povey Cross	Airport, wetland, lake	Summer visitors and migrants	All year	Gatwick
OS Explorer 146 TQ 265418	_Access from Povey Cross Road for riverside and views of Gatwick Airport. Little Ringed Plover and Black Redstart have occurred on rough ground near the cargo terminal. Summer migrants by the river and in woods, including Spotted Flycatcher. Breeding Reed Warbler at the Hilton Hotel Lake, approachable by road._			
P Claremont	Landscape garden and lake	Waterfowl, Ring-necked Parakeet, Osprey has occurred	All year	Esher
OS Explorer 161 TQ 128630	_NT property on the east side of the A307, on the south side of Esher. Path round the lake is suitable for wheelchairs._			
Q Esher Commons	Woods, lowland heath and ponds	Woodland and heathland birds, and a few wetland species	All year	Esher
OS Explorer 161 TQ 140625	_Made up of the contiguous Arbrook, Esher, Fairmile and West End Commons, and Oxshott Heath, divided by roads. Black Pond is the best water. Well served by car parks. Esher Commons were made an SSSI because of the variety of habitat and wildlife._			

Key & Site	Habitat	Birds of Interest	Peak Season	Nearest Town
R Milford Farmland	Arable fields	Golden Plover and Lapwing, migrant waders, raptors	Oct–Feb	Godalming

OS Explorer 145
SU 958414

A flock of up to 3,000 Golden Plovers has recently been wintering on arable fields either side of Tuesley Lane, easily seen from gateways. Many Lapwings are usually with them. A few other waders on temporary pools after rain. Red Kite, Merlin and other raptors sometimes present. Park in bays off the road. If the plovers are absent, try Home Farm, from the entrance on the west side of the A3 at SU 944457. Do not enter. Neither site is suitable for wheelchairs, though views may be possible from a car.

SUSSEX

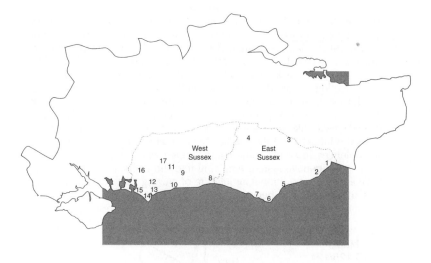

1 Rye Bay
2 Hastings Country Park
3 Bewl Water
4 Ashdown Forest
5 Pevensey Levels
6 Beachy Head
7 Cuckmere Valley and Seaford Head
8 Cissbury and the Adur Valley
9 The Arun Valley
10 Climping Gap
11 Burton and Chingford Ponds
12 Chichester Gravel Pits
13 Pagham Harbour
14 Selsey Bill and Bracklesham Bay
15 Chichester Harbour
16 Kingley Vale
17 Ambersham, Iping and Stedham Commons

Habitat

The area known as Rye Bay occupies the river valleys and coast around the Cinque Port town of Rye and corresponds to the East Sussex part of EN's Romney Marshes Natural Area. Within it lies Rye Harbour LNR, which was established in 1970 by East Sussex County Council and has been recognised as a SSSI, a SPA for birds, and as a candidate Ramsar site, reflecting its importance as a wetland on an international level. This flat, low-lying area comprises a large marine-deposited shingle bank which, close the sea, supports rare plants such as sea pea, as well as more typical species like yellow-horned poppy and sea kale. Over the last 100 years the influence of the sea has been greatly reduced by man-made sea defences. In addition, the naturally high water table has been lowered by a drainage system emptying into the rivers. These two factors have enabled a traditional agriculture of grazing with some arable. The loss of wetland has been partially offset by the extraction of large volumes of shingle, creating wet gravel pits. Within the reserve there are

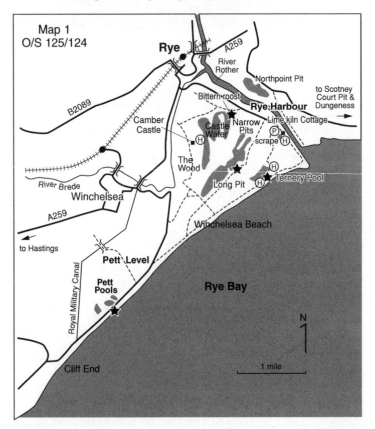

many habitats, which can be broadly described as: intertidal, saltmarsh, reclaimed saltmarsh, drainage ditches, shingle ridges, sand, marsh, pits, scrub and woodland. Further information concerning the reserve can be found on its website (www.naturereserve.ryeharbour.org).

Along the eastern boundary of the Rye Harbour SSSI lies the River Rother which discharges into Rye Bay. Immediately east of the river mouth is Camber Sands, where there are extensive sand flats at low tide and the only sand dune system in East Sussex. Two other sites of ornithological interest lie to the east of the River Rother, Northpoint Pit and Scotney Court Gravel Pit, the latter partly in Kent.

West of Rye Harbour is Pett Level, another SSSI. This area, which is backed by an old sea-cliff, was flooded 60 years ago for wartime defence. However, sea defences were constructed c.50 years ago so it is now mainly a sheep-grazed grassland criss-crossed by narrow dykes. Just behind the seawall near the western end is a series of four reed-fringed pits known as the Colonel Body Memorial Lakes or Pett Pools. Originally dug to provide the clay needed for the construction of the sea wall, they are now a nature reserve in the care of the Sussex Wildlife Trust. The artificial lowering of the water levels every July to attract waders, described in the previous edition of this book, no longer takes place.

Species

This area, being flat and low lying, can feel very exposed in winter. In some severe winters all of the pits freeze over; at such times few birds remain, except for those which feed on the beach. Such conditions are rare and usually there is a wide range of wildfowl, waders, raptors and passerines present. In Rye Bay, a calm day will reveal rafts of Common Scoters with perhaps a few Velvets among them. Up to 2,000 have been recorded in the past but three-figure counts have been the norm in recent years. With them may be large gatherings of Red-throated Divers and Great Crested Grebes, occasionally totalling several hundred. Unfortunately, the English Channel has a chronic oil pollution problem and when strong winds occur, a few disconsolate oiled divers make for the sheltered pits away from the shore. Here they mingle with large numbers of duck. Hundreds of Teal, Mallard, Shoveler, Pochard and Tufted Duck dot these waters, concentrating in the lee of islands or the shoreline when the wind is chilling. Other regular species to look for include Gadwall, which often associate with Coot, Goldeneye and Ruddy Duck. In most winters a few Scaup appear on the pits at Rye Harbour, although a more reliable site for the species is Scotney Court Gravel Pit, where up to 280 individuals have been recorded in severe winters. Rye Bay is undoubtedly the best place in the county to see Smew, especially on Northpoint Pit. In a normal winter a handful of birds are usually present but, if it turns cold, there may be 20 or more scattered around the various gravel pits in the area. A patient search through all of the waterbirds may reveal other unusual species such as Great Northern and Black-throated Divers, Red-necked, Slavonian and Black-necked Grebes, Long-tailed Duck and Goosander. Scotney Court holds the only regular wintering flock of White-fronted Geese (300) in the county. They mingle with feral flocks of Greylag and Barnacle Geese and, in most winters, a few Tundra Bean, Pink-footed and Brent Geese.

The area also holds a variety of waders. On the shore, the more common species such as Oystercatcher, Dunlin and Turnstone are joined by up to 100 Sanderling, 20 Grey Plover and occasionally a few Bar-tailed

Godwits. At Rye Harbour there is a nocturnal roost of up 600 Curlew, most of which feed on Pett Level during the day. Wherever the grassland is short there are flocks of wintering Lapwing and Golden Plover; severe weather often temporarily increases numbers, but if such conditions persist, these are among the first species to depart for warmer latitudes.

Numbers of seed-eating passerines have declined in recent years though flocks of Greenfinches and Linnets and a few Corn Buntings still occur. The area between the Midrips and Winchelsea Beach formerly held a regular wintering flock of up to 100 Snow Buntings, but nowadays just a handful are recorded in some winters. The seawall at Pett has been the most reliable site for the species in recent winters. Grain stores at Rye Harbour attract an unwelcome yet spectacular flock of 300 Collared Doves as well as finches and buntings.

Given the range and numbers of birds present, it is unsurprising that many raptors include this area in their hunting range. Hen and Marsh Harriers, Sparrowhawk, Merlin and Peregrine are regularly seen, in addition to Barn and Short-eared Owls.

No winter visit to Rye Harbour is complete without a late-afternoon stop at Castle Water, where a raised vantage point offers views across a reedbed. As the sun slips below the skyline, Cormorants arrive to roost in the willows in the centre of the pit and are soon followed by 30 or more Little Egrets. The pig-like squeals of Water Rails can be heard from the reeds, but the main attraction is the opportunity to at least catch a glimpse of a Bittern as it flies into roost. Up to ten have been recorded here in recent winters, so there is a very good chance of seeing this elusive species at its only regular wintering site in the county. Barn Owl sometimes hunts over the surrounding fields at dusk.

With the onset of spring, the departure of the winter visitors is accompanied by the appearance of the first summer migrants: a Wheatear standing boldly upright, a Sand Martin feeding low over the pits, or a Black Redstart perched on a groyne. As March progresses, numbers of Sandwich Terns build up at Rye Harbour, sometimes reaching 300 at Ternery Pool by the end of the month. A careful check through the many Black-headed Gulls resting on the shingle islands at this season will almost certainly reveal a number of Mediterranean Gulls, the adults resplendent in their newly acquired summer plumage. Seawatching at Rye Harbour, which lies right at the head of Rye Bay, is not particularly good, but nevertheless southeast winds in April and May can produce a variety of seaduck, waders and terns, and possibly a few Arctic and Great Skuas. In these conditions it is worth checking the pits for both Little Gulls and Black Terns, which may pause to feed for a few hours before moving on. Another feature of Rye Harbour in spring is the nocturnal roost of up to 400 Whimbrel close to Ternery Pool.

Little Terns

By mid-April the arrival of most of the summer migrants is in full swing. On clear days they tend to fly straight over but a shower of rain towards dawn may produce a 'fall'. Species to look for include bright canary-yellow male Yellow Wagtails, Reed and Sedge Warblers singing from the ditches and large gatherings of hirundines over the pits. A walk around the wood at Rye Harbour should produce other warblers such as Cetti's, Blackcap, Whitethroat and Chiffchaff, and possibly Turtle Dove and Cuckoo.

During summer the islands of Ternery Pool are alive with the activities of nesting Black-headed Gulls (400 pairs), Common Terns (80 pairs) and, in some years, Sandwich Terns (250 pairs). The rare Little Tern (25 pairs) also nests on the surrounding shingle, as do up to 50 pairs of Ringed Plovers, 20 pairs of Oystercatchers and several pairs of Wheatears. Great efforts have been made to protect the vulnerable tern colonies; several miles of electric fences have been erected and long hours of wardening put in by volunteers and professionals alike but despite this numbers of all the tern species fluctuate widely from year to year. Ternery Pool is also one of the best sites in the county for Roseate Tern. Although they do not nest at Rye Harbour, a handful of birds are recorded annually, often resting on the shingle islands with other terns close to the Crittall Hide.

Rye Harbour also supports a number of other important breeding species including the county's largest breeding colony of Cormorants (120 pairs) at Castle Water. These include pairs of the continental race *sinensis*. A good selection of other waterbirds includes Great Crested and Little Grebes, Shelduck, Tufted Duck and, in some years, Garganey and Shoveler. Both Lapwing (15 pairs) and Redshank (15 pairs) benefit from the protection afforded by the use of electric fencing to deter marauding Red Foxes and Badgers. Breeding passerines include Yellow Wagtail, Reed and Sedge Warblers, Linnet and Reed Bunting.

By July the breeding season will be drawing to a close for the majority of species. Most adult Cuckoos have left by mid-month and tern chicks will be fledging if the season has been successful. The return passage of waders gathers momentum with a variety of species including Dunlin, Little Ringed Plover, Greenshank, and Common, Green and Wood Sandpipers appearing wherever feeding conditions are favourable. A few adult Curlew Sandpipers and Little Stints often occur, particularly after easterly winds. Wildfowl also increase in number. These include Wigeon, Teal, Shoveler and usually a few Garganey, although once they are in moult (eclipse plumage) they can be quite difficult to identify.

August is a good month for birds of prey; in settled weather with north-east winds scarce species such as Marsh Harrier, Osprey and Honey Buzzard may pass through. In the fields Yellow Wagtail and Wheatear numbers start to increase, whilst the scrub supports increasing numbers of warblers such as Whitethroat and Willow Warbler. By the end of the month and into September come a scattering of Redstarts, Whinchats and Spotted Flycatchers, and many other species including Grey Wagtail and Tree Pipit on the move overhead. Flocks of hirundines reach several thousand and often roost in the reedbeds. They attract passing Hobbies and the resident Sparrowhawks.

Some waders, such as Little Ringed Plover and Whimbrel, will already have passed their peak by early September, but numbers of Curlew Sandpipers and Little Stints often increase as the passage of adults gives way to juveniles. By the end of the month a change is on the way as the first winter birds appear. Flocks of Brent Geese pass west at sea and with good fortune you may see a Merlin or Short-eared Owl. Most of the warblers have gone by early October and, when easterly winds set in, rarer species may appear. Firecrest, Black Redstart and Ring Ouzel are not unusual, and a careful search through the Goldcrests may reveal a Yellow-browed Warbler. October is also often the best month to look for Bearded Tits in the reedbeds at Castle Water and Pett Pools.

As autumn becomes winter, numbers of duck especially Wigeon, Teal and Shoveler start to increase. Offshore, there may be Red-throated Divers, Great Crested Grebes and Guillemots resting on the sea together with rafts of Common Scoter. With luck, a Little Auk might pass by out to sea, for November is the best month for seeing this tiny seabird in Sussex. By December the Bitterns will again be roosting at Castle Water, whilst other species to look for there include Water Rail, Cetti's Warbler and Bearded Tit and perhaps a wintering Firecrest. Flocks of small birds, such as Greenfinches, Linnets and Goldfinches attract raptors and you might see a Hen Harrier, Merlin or Peregrine, as well as the more usual Kestrel and Sparrowhawk. In cold weather watch for Smew on the pits and flocks of White-fronted Geese at Pett Level and, more especially, Scotney Court.

Rye Bay has an enviable list of rarities to its name. A full list of these would take up a large amount of space so mention must be made only of a few. Rye Harbour is obviously well known for its colonies of terns but over the years it has also attracted an impressive list of vagrant terns including Gull-billed, Caspian, Lesser Crested, Bridled, Sooty, Whiskered and White-winged Black, a collection unmatched by any other site in Britain! Waders have included Black-winged Stilt, Collared Pratincole, Sociable Plover, Semipalmated, Least and Baird's Sandpipers, Marsh Sandpiper, Lesser Yellowlegs, Wilson's Phalarope and the county's first Pacific Golden Plover, at Rye Harbour in April 2003.

Timing

The area is well worth visiting at any time of the year, although Camber Sands is definitely to be avoided during summer, when the beach is packed with holidaymakers. The migration periods of April and May and again in autumn bring the greatest variety of species, especially if the wind is from an easterly quarter. Winter also provides excellent birdwatching, as does summer, when activity in the ternery is at its peak. Early-morning visits are best, before too many people are about and when the birds are most active. In winter, activity extends throughout the day. Because Rye Bay is very exposed, a strong wind or heavy rain will make birdwatching uncomfortable and usually unproductive. Pett Level can be viewed from the road. In midwinter a climb onto the seawall here may reveal large numbers of divers, Great Crested Grebes and scoter on the sea. These are best looked for in calm conditions on a rising tide.

Access

Rye Harbour LNR is best reached by taking the A259 west from Rye. Before leaving the town, take an unclassified road to the left, signposted Rye Harbour. Follow this for a mile-and-a-half to the end, where there is a free car park and toilets. From here, walk along the concrete road beside the river past Lime Kiln Cottage (the reserve's information centre) and the Colin Green hide (wheelchair accessible) which overlooks a series of wader pools. On reaching the river mouth, turn right and continue to Ternery Pool where there are two further hides. To return to the car park take the footpath that runs past the Parkes hide at the east end of Ternery Pool. Alternatively, to see more of the area continue along the concrete road to a footpath which runs north through the 'Wood' to Castle Water where there is another birdwatching hide. From here continue across the fields to Camber Castle and then walk north along a farm track, towards Rye. Skirt the top end of Castle Water and, near the green warehouses, cross a ditch to reach the old railway line. To return to Rye Harbour turn right and, on reaching a grassy field, turn half left and walk to the opposite corner of the field to reach Harbour Road. At the road, turn right and walk along the verge back to the car park. To view the Bittern roost at Castle Water, stand on the raised vantage point overlooking the reedbed in the southwest corner of the grassy field.

Northpoint Pit is reached by taking the A259 east out of Rye. After 1 mile turn right onto the B2076 at East Guldeford, continue for a further three-quarters-of-a-mile and the pit is on the right-hand side of the road. From here continue to Camber, where there is access to Camber Sands, and then to Scotney Court Gravel Pit on the border of East Sussex and Kent. These very large pits and some smaller ones are easily viewed from the roadside or from the cycle path from Rye that passes all of them.

Pett Level and Pools are easily viewed from an unclassified road running from Winchelsea Beach to Cliff End, immediately behind the seawall. To reach the site, follow the A259 from Rye towards Winchelsea and turn left to Winchelsea Beach. Continue through Winchelsea Beach and the pools are close to the western end of Pett Level. Park at the side of the road and climb onto the seawall to view the levels, beach and sea. Note that there is no access to the land surrounding the pools, except for anglers with a licence from the EA.

Calendar

Resident: Little and Great Crested Grebes, Little Egret, Grey Heron, Greylag Goose, Shelduck, Gadwall, Tufted Duck, Sparrowhawk, Grey Partridge, Oystercatcher, Ringed Plover, Lapwing, Redshank, Stock Dove, Barn and Little Owls, Green Woodpecker, Meadow Pipit, Tree Sparrow, Goldfinch, Linnet, Reed and Corn Buntings.

December–February: Divers, Red-necked, Slavonian and Black-necked Grebes, Bittern, White-fronted and other grey geese, Wigeon, Teal, Shoveler, Scaup, Eider, Long-tailed Duck, Common and Velvet Scoters, Goldeneye, Smew, Goosander, Marsh and Hen Harriers, Merlin, Peregrine, Water Rail, Golden and Grey Plovers, Sanderling, Little Stint, Dunlin, Jack Snipe, Snipe, Guillemot, Short-eared Owl, Rock Pipit, Stonechat, Firecrest, Bearded Tit, Snow Bunting.

March–May: Gannet, Brent Goose, Garganey, Common and Velvet Scoters, Hobby, Avocet, Grey Plover, Bar-tailed Godwit, Whimbrel, Common Sandpiper, Arctic and Great Skuas, Mediterranean and Little Gulls, Sandwich and Black Terns, Turtle Dove, Cuckoo, Swift, Yellow Wagtail, Black Redstart, Wheatear, Sedge and Reed Warblers, Whitethroat, Willow Warbler, Firecrest, rarities.

June–July: Sandwich, Roseate, Common and Little Terns, Turtle Dove, Cuckoo, Yellow Wagtail, Wheatear, rarities.

August–November: Garganey, Marsh Harrier, Hobby, Peregrine, Little Ringed Plover, Knot, Little and Temminck's Stints, Pectoral and Curlew Sandpipers, Ruff, Black-tailed Godwit, Spotted Redshank, Greenshank, Green and Wood Sandpipers, Grey Phalarope, rarer waders, Arctic Skua, Little Gull, Black Tern, Turtle Dove, Woodlark, Yellow and Grey Wagtails, Black Redstart, Redstart, Whinchat, Stonechat, Wheatear, Ring Ouzel, warblers, Firecrest, Spotted and Pied Flycatchers, Bearded Tit, finches, rarities.

2 HASTINGS COUNTRY PARK

OS Explorer 124

Habitat

Situated close to the busy seaside town of Hastings, it is surprising that this 219-ha country park (which was designated in 1974) does not receive more attention from birdwatchers. For anyone living in the Hastings area, it would make an ideal local patch though the amount of habitat may at first glance seem daunting. The geology of the park comprises outcrops of sandstone plus sandstone seams mixed with bands of clay. The cliffs are therefore very unstable and large cliff-falls occur annually. Where they are more stable, large ledges are found. Old landslips are vegetated with an intriguing mix of stunted willow, birch and oak, punc-

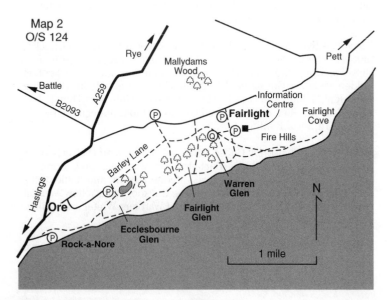

tuated by streams and ponds. There are three narrow glens each covered by woodland or scrub alongside a gill stream. Admixed along the clifftop are areas of bracken, bramble, gorse and open fields. The foreshore is a mix of sand and mud with some rocky outcrops. Much of the park, which is managed by Hastings Borough Council, has been designated as a SSSI.

Species

In winter the sheltered glens support a typical woodland bird community including Green and Great Spotted Woodpeckers, Goldcrest, Treecreeper and Long-tailed Tit, the latter perhaps accompanied by a wintering Chiffchaff or Firecrest. In the more open areas look for Stonechats perched atop gorse bushes; Dartford Warblers have wintered here but is more likely to be observed in late autumn. The cliffs provide resting and roosting places for the Cormorants that feed offshore, and Fulmars begin to prospect for breeding ledges in December. Small flocks of Eider and scoter are often found offshore, but generally few other birds are regular on the sea though Purple Sandpipers may be picked out on the wave-washed rocks below.

The first signs of spring migration are in late February and early March when divers and Brent Geese pass east out at sea. Black Redstart, Wheatear and Chiffchaff are the first migrants to arrive on the land; scarcer species to look for in March include Firecrest, especially in areas of blackthorn, and the occasional Ring Ouzel. A wider variety of species can be expected in April, when some rain before dawn may produce a fall of Willow Warblers together with a scattering of other species. With luck these may include a Redstart, Whinchat or Pied Flycatcher, or even a Hoopoe. Keep an eye overhead for a passing Red Kite, Marsh Harrier or Hobby. Spring rarities have included Black Kite, Sardinian Warbler, Serin and the famous Wallcreeper in April 1977.

The park supports a varied breeding bird community reflecting the diversity of habitats. The wooded glens hold all of the usual woodland birds whilst in the more open scrubby areas there are Meadow Pipits, Whitethroats and Willow Warblers. Other typical scrub- and gorse-loving species such as Stonechat, Linnet and Yellowhammer can be seen singing from their exposed perches. Kestrel, Peregrine and Sparrowhawk also hunt the area in summer, the former using the updraughts created by the cliffs. On the cliffs there are Fulmars (75 pairs), Cormorants (28 pairs in 1992 but only two pairs in 1999), Herring Gulls (30 pairs), Stock Doves and Jackdaws and the occasional pair of Black Redstarts and perhaps still Rock Pipits.

Autumn is a fascinating time with many common migrants passing through in some numbers. If there is a touch of east in the wind, especially between late August and early October, a wide range of scarcer species may be expected including Tree Pipit, Redstart, Pied and Spotted Flycatchers, and with luck a Wryneck. Later, the harsh chuckle of a Ring Ouzel, the sharp call of a Firecrest mixed with the thin notes of Goldcrests or a quivering Black Redstart on a clifftop fence may provide a most rewarding walk. Rarities, perhaps surprisingly, have been conspicuous by their absence, although single Pallas's Warblers were recorded in October and November 1996. As in spring, it pays to keep an eye on the sky overhead for passing raptors; Honey Buzzard, Red Kite, Hen and Marsh Harriers, Common Buzzard, Osprey, Merlin, Hobby and Peregrine have all been recorded in recent years. Hobbies patrol the cliff face, hoping to way-lay migrating passerines.

Early mornings from late September to early November can bring substantial movements of passerines including Skylarks, Meadow Pipits, Grey, Pied and Yellow Wagtails, Chaffinches, Goldfinches, Linnets, Lesser Redpolls, Siskins, Reed Buntings and even a few Great Spotted Woodpeckers. Woodlark, Brambling and Crossbill are recorded almost annually whilst scarcer species have included Stone Curlew, Bearded Tit, Hawfinch and Lapland Bunting. Strong southeast to southwest winds can bring passing seabirds well inshore; divers, Gannets, Arctic Skuas, Kittiwakes and auks can pass by, especially in late the autumn. These are best seen from Rock-a-Nore.

Timing

The best birdwatching is undoubtedly to be had during the migration periods of April–early June and again in August–early November. Light winds from south through to northeast bring the widest range of migrants, but it is essential to be out early in the morning. The Country Park attracts hordes of visitors, especially on fine weekends, so all open areas may be heavily disturbed by mid-morning. A good site for migrants is the overgrown quarry (Q on the map) a short walk southwest of the car parks at Fairlight.

Access

The Country Park lies east of Hastings. Pedestrians can reach it via the East Hill Cliff Railway in the Old Town. Alternatively, the park may be accessed from Barley Lane or adjacent Fairlight Road.

Motorists can reach the park via Fairlight Road from Ore. About 1.5 miles from Hastings seafront, in the centre of Ore, an unclassified road leaves the A259 to the right; it is signed to Hastings Country Park. Two good car parks are available on this road, one just over half-a-mile from the A259, near the Wireless Tower, and the other three-quarters-of-a-mile further on near Fairlight Church. The latter car park is situated adjacent to the visitor centre (phone the Countryside Ranger Service on 01424 813225 for more details). From here it is a short walk to an overgrown quarry (marked Q on the map) that is often good for migrants. For Ecclesbourne Glen, there is a car park along Barley Lane, 1 mile northeast of the seafront; follow the signs for Shear Barn Caravan Park. From here, footpaths south take the walker to the maze of coastal paths, some of which pass through the wooded glens. A complete round walk, including all the glens and the clifftop path, totals about 5 miles and is strenuous walking. As some of the paths are very steep, they can be slippery after rain and are not suitable for those with disabilities. Under these conditions good boots are essential. The beach is remarkable geologically and for its sense of remoteness, but must be walked with caution, on a falling tide. The cliffs are unstable and must not be approached closely. Access is from Rock-a-Nore, Fairlight Glen (a naturist beach so use binoculars with discretion!) and Cliff End.

Calendar

Resident: Cormorant, Sparrowhawk, Kestrel, Peregrine, Green and Great Spotted Woodpeckers, Stonechat, Nuthatch, Treecreeper, Yellowhammer, Long-tailed and Marsh Tits.

December–February: Fulmar, Eider, Oystercatcher, Turnstone, auks, Fieldfare, Redwing, Chiffchaff, Rock Pipit.

March–May: Gannet, Brent Goose, Marsh Harrier, Hobby, Cuckoo, Hoopoe, Black Redstart, Redstart, Whinchat, Stonechat, Wheatear, *Sylvia* and *Phylloscopus* warblers, Firecrest, Linnet.

June–July: Fulmar, Cormorant, Herring Gull.

August–November: Marsh Harrier, Merlin, Hobby, Woodlark, Skylark, Tree and Meadow Pipits, Grey, Pied and Yellow Wagtails, Black Redstart, Redstart, Whinchat, Stonechat, Ring Ouzel, Redwing, warblers including Dartford, Goldcrest, Firecrest, Spotted and Pied Flycatchers, Brambling, Goldfinch, Siskin, Linnet, Lesser Redpoll.

3 BEWL WATER OS Explorer 136

Habitat

Set in an area of outstanding natural beauty in the heart of the High Weald, Bewl Water, which covers 312 ha, is the largest expanse of freshwater in southeast England. It is not, however, a natural feature but a reservoir (holding 6,900 million gallons of water when full) constructed to

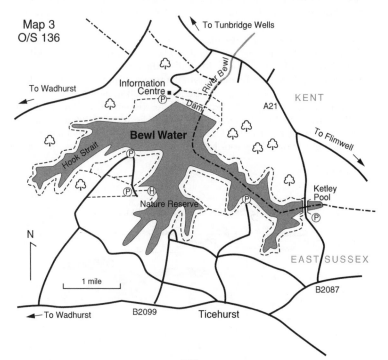

provide sustainable water supplies for Kent and Susses. Completed in 1975, it caters for a wide variety of interests, such as watersports and fishing, although part of it is closed to these activities as a nature reserve, owned by Southern Water and managed by the Sussex Wildlife Trust. A picturesque walk around the perimeter provides views of the reservoir as well as permitting access to a variety of other habitats including farmland, scrub and woodland. Water levels drop slightly in summer and autumn, exposing gravelly or muddy margins. With such a wide range of habitats, it is perhaps unsurprising that over 200 species of birds have been recorded to date.

Species

Wildfowl are the main attraction in winter. Up to 1,000 Canada Geese, 500 Mallard and 1,000 Coot are present, with a good variety of other species. Among the dabbling duck, Wigeon are prominent, often grazing on the short grass of the banks of the reservoir. In a normal winter, some 300–400 birds are usual, but numbers can easily double in cold spells. Gadwall have been increasing in numbers throughout southern England in recent years and over 200 have been seen here, often associating with feeding Coot from which they steal pond-weed. Small groups of Teal feed in the sheltered bays, but only a few Shoveler and Pintail are usually present. As the reservoir is relatively deep (up to 30 m), diving duck such as Tufted Duck and Pochard, which are bottom feeders, are relatively few in number, totalling fewer than 200 of each. A few Goldeneye, mainly females, and Ruddy Ducks may join them. In harsh weather a Long-tailed Duck or a small flock of Smew or Goosander may be present, providing a very wintry sight. Rarer grebes (especially Red-necked) and divers may also occur in such conditions. However, if very cold weather persists, the reservoir can virtually freeze over and most waterfowl are forced to leave.

In general, other species are relatively unobtrusive. A few hundred Lapwings may visit the water's edge to bathe whilst flocks of Fieldfares and Redwings frequent the fields and hedgerows adjacent to the reservoir, perhaps attracting the attention of a passing Sparrowhawk. Flocks of Siskins and Lesser Redpolls may be found feeding in alders.

Spring's approach is evidenced by the departure of the wintering ducks, whilst in the sheltered bays Great Crested Grebes and Mallard commence display. By mid-March, the first Chiffchaffs are singing from the woodland or calling loudly from the shoreline willows. Soon Willow

Osprey

Warblers join them, singing their liquid cascade of notes from the top of bushes. In more open areas Yellowhammers and Reed Buntings utter their high-pitched songs, and by late April Whitethroats, with their dancing song flights, join in. The woodlands support a very different bird community. All of the species typical of the High Weald are present including Stock Dove, Tawny Owl, Green and Great Spotted Woodpeckers, Marsh Tit, Nuthatch and Treecreeper. Both Blackcap and Garden Warbler sing their confusing songs from similar areas, although the latter prefers dense scrub with a thick ground cover for nesting. Mid-May sees the first Spotted Flycatchers and Turtle Doves completing the arrival of the summer visitors. On the water, migrants are also obvious. First, in April, hirundines pass through and if cold, windy weather persists, thousands may be held up, feeding low over the reservoir. As at all large inland waters there is often a passage of Common and Arctic Terns in late April and May; a few Little Gulls and Black Terns may also appear given favourable weather conditions. Sometimes, particularly in a northeast wind, Whimbrel, Curlew or other passage waders, which normally pass along the coast, may fly over or pause for a few hours. Breeding waterbirds include Great Crested and Little Grebes, Canada Geese and a few pairs of Tufted Duck and Kingfishers.

By late July and August, large flocks of Canada and increasing numbers of Greylag Geese gather to moult. At this time the ducks are entering eclipse plumage making them difficult to identify. An occasional Garganey may be present. The muddy margins of the reservoir attract passage waders such as Little Ringed Plover, Greenshank and Green and Common Sandpipers and also Pied, Yellow and, later, Grey Wagtails. Insects attract Swifts and hirundines, as well as a few Black and Common Terns most autumns. Bewl Water is one of the best places to see Osprey in the region. Three or four pass through each autumn, mainly between early August and mid-September; sometimes they remain for a week or more. Hobby, too, is quite likely to be seen. A flock of 11 Little Egrets in August 1996 was perhaps not surprising, given the dramatic national increase since the late 1980s. By late October, finch flocks are noticeable, particularly Goldfinches and Chaffinches, but there may also be early-morning movements of Siskins, Lesser Redpolls and Linnets.

November can bring some unexpected movements especially of Brent Geese. Small flocks are recorded almost annually; occasionally large numbers may occur, as in 1982, when over 1,000 flew south in a ten-day period in early November, including 775 on one day alone. Ducks, too, may appear. Red-breasted Mergansers and Velvet and Common Scoters have been seen in recent years. It is also well worth looking for storm-driven birds following an autumn gale: Shag, Leach's Petrel, Grey Phalarope, Great Skua and Kittiwake have all been recorded.

Bewl Water does not have a long list of rarities to its name, perhaps because it is rather under-watched. Mention must however be made of one of the most unlikely rarities to be recorded in the county — a Blackpoll Warbler from North America, which stayed for 12 days in December 1994! A male Black-eared Wheatear on the dam in May 1988 was only the second county record.

Timing

With such a large area and a diversity of habitats, Bewl Water is worth a visit at any season. However, birds can be difficult to find at times, especially in strong winds. Using the long-distance footpath around the reservoir, it is usually possible to leave behind the many visitors (especially in winter) and just encounter the odd fisherman (the fishing season starts on 21 March and finishes on 21 November). Early morning is best at migration times. Severe winter weather may bring unusual waterbirds, but the reservoir can freeze over.

Access

The main access to the reservoir is from the A21, 3 miles north of Flimwell and 1.25 miles south of Lamberhurst. Here, there is car park (weekdays £4.00 and weekends and bank holidays £5.00, in 2003), toilets and a visitor's centre operated by Southern Water (tel: 01892 890661 for full details). A 13-mile footpath leads from the car park around the perimeter of reservoir. The route is also open to cyclists; bicycles can be hired during the summer months from the car park. There are, however, very few other access points to the reservoir by car. It is possible to stop at the causeway over Ketley Pool, but the best alternative is to take Wards Lane off the B2099, 2 miles west of Ticehurst and then turn first left and second right into Claphatch Lane. At the end of the lane is a small car park from which a short walk leads to a public hide, accessed by a wooden staircase, overlooking the Sussex Wildlife Trust's nature reserve.

Calendar

Resident: Little and Great Crested Grebes, Cormorant, Canada Goose, Pochard, Tufted Duck, Sparrowhawk, Kestrel, Stock Dove, Tawny Owl, Kingfisher, Green and Great Spotted Woodpeckers, Mistle Thrush, Goldcrest, Long-tailed, Marsh and Coal Tits, Nuthatch, Treecreeper, Bullfinch, Yellowhammer, Reed Bunting.

December–February: Scarce divers and grebes, Shag, Wigeon, Gadwall, Teal, Shoveler, Goldeneye, Long-tailed Duck, Smew, Goosander, Ruddy Duck, Lapwing, Fieldfare, Redwing, Siskin, Lesser Redpoll.

March–May: Osprey, Little Ringed Plover, Whimbrel, Little Gull, Common, Arctic and Black Terns, hirundines, Wheatear, *Sylvia* warblers, Chiffchaff, Willow Warbler.

June–July: Turtle Dove, Cuckoo, Swift, Spotted Flycatcher.

August–November: Greylag and Brent Geese, Garganey, scarce seaducks, Osprey, Hobby, Little Ringed Plover, Dunlin, Greenshank, Green and Common Sandpipers, Common and Black Terns, Yellow and Grey Wagtails, Whinchat, Stonechat, Wheatear, Fieldfare, Redwing, passage warblers, finches including Goldfinch, Siskin, Linnet and Lesser Redpoll.

Habitat

Ashdown Forest, a SSSI and a SPA, is the remains of the Lancaster Great Park deer-hunting forest, originally enclosed in 1296. Covering 2,590 ha of the High Weald it contains a fascinating assemblage of wildlife-rich habitats. It is the largest heathland in southeast England with some large patches of heather-dominated heath still extant. However, extensive areas have been invaded by bracken, gorse, birch and pine, whilst the wetter sections are dominated by moor and cotton grass. Some substantial oak and beech woodlands occur, but elsewhere conifer plantations blanket the ground. One important habitat is the gill woodland. Many streams run off the high sandstone block, which rises to 218 m, cutting deep valleys through the soft substrate. In places, bare sandstone is exposed and the steep slopes have become clothed in woodland; here high humidity provides ideal conditions for many plants that are more typical of western Britain, particularly ferns and mosses. The conflicting uses of the Ashdown Forest common land are reconciled by a Board of Conservators, who appoints a Clerk and rangers to undertake its day-to-day management.

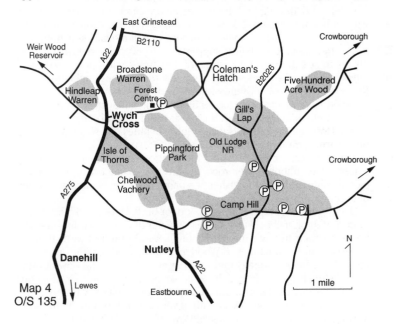

Species

Open heathland is inhospitable in winter and in severe weather it is often almost birdless. A scurrying Wren under the shelter of a gorse bush or a small party of Meadow Pipits is often all that is seen, although an occasional Hen Harrier quarters the heath. A visit on a fine day in

February onwards may be rewarded by the evocative song of the Woodlark, a species that has recently re-colonised the forest after an absence of many years. During winter most of the birds withdraw to the woodland, where large parties of tits including a few Marsh can be found along with flocks of Chaffinches and the occasional Brambling, the latter searching the leaf litter in the beech woodlands. All three woodpeckers are present, although Great Spotted and Green are much more obvious. Other typical woodland species such as Treecreeper and Nuthatch are common, as are Coal Tit and Goldcrest in the conifers. The warning rattle of Mistle Thrushes or the loud scolding of Blackbirds may reveal a Tawny Owl roosting in an ivy-covered tree. Streamside alders often hold flocks of Siskins and Lesser Redpolls, and it is here that Lesser Spotted Woodpeckers are most often seen.

Many of the resident passerines start to sing by mid-March when they are joined by the first returning Chiffchaffs. By late April the whole area is transformed into activity. On the heaths the scattered clumps of gorse hold Linnets and Yellowhammers. Stonechat numbers vary, with perhaps as many as 50 pairs after a series of mild winters. That real heathland specialist, Dartford Warbler also occurs here; up to 90 territories have been found in recent years, but like Stonechat, this species is particularly vulnerable to hard winters, and numbers can crash dramatically. The open heather supports just Meadow Pipits and Skylarks while the heathland edge where pine, birch and bracken have encroached has many Willow Warblers and Tree Pipits. Where over-mature birch, pine, beech or oak with holes are present it is worth listening for the short song of the Redstart. The spectacular males, with shivering flame tails, sing from high in the trees. Ashdown Forest supports up to 80 pairs; one of the best places to see them is the Sussex Wildlife Trust's Old Lodge reserve. At times the sky seems criss-crossed by the trilling song flights of Lesser Redpolls, but it is often impossible to decide just how many males are involved. Keep an eye open too for Siskins, which may now breed in very small numbers in the forest. A dusk visit in June may be rewarded by a pair of Hobbies circling an isolated clump of pines or a Nightjar churring on a warm summer's evening.

Along the streams it is worth looking for Grey Wagtails, especially where water bubbles over rock, but also keep an eye open for the electric-blue flash of a Kingfisher or a pair of whirring Mandarins moving between ponds.

Deciduous woodland is always good for birds. Here, in addition to the many commoner species, the occasional pair of Wood Warblers may still be found, their trilling song penetrating several hundred yards through the woodland. Sometimes a Woodcock is flushed, jinking away low through the trees; normally they are only seen at dusk and dawn during their distinctive roding flight. In some years the coniferous plantations are of interest, for after irruption years a few Crossbills stay to breed.

In late summer the woods are full of young warblers and tits, but soon the migrants slip away. A few passage Whinchats and Wheatears are seen, with perhaps a Hobby stopping off, either to chase the local House Martins or hunt dragonflies over the heath. By mid-October finches are on the move; especially noticeable are Chaffinches and Siskins. Providing the weather remains mild, the heaths continue to hold Stonechats and Dartford Warblers throughout the winter. Early winter is a good time to spot a Great Grey Shrike perched motionless on a dead birch, although they range widely and might be seen anywhere across the forest.

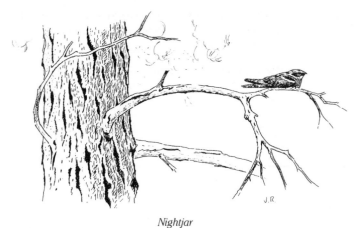

Nightjar

Timing

There is always something of interest in Ashdown Forest, but spring and early summer is undoubtedly the best time to visit. A warm, still spring day is ideal, for then the birds are likely to be at their most active and easier to see. On summer weekends the forest attracts hordes of day visitors, but by walking some distance from the car parks it should be possible to spend many hours without too much disturbance. An evening visit in summer is best for Nightjar and Woodcock. Should it be a very dry summer, the forest becomes tinder dry and is at great risk from fires; almost every year serious heath fires occur. Great care should be taken under such conditions.

Access

Ashdown Forest is crossed by many roads including the A22, A275 and B2026. Perhaps the best place to start a visit, unless arriving early in the morning, is at the Ashdown Forest visitor's centre run by the Conservators. This provides a wealth of background information on the Forest and lies half-a-mile along the unclassified road running east from Wych Cross to Coleman's Hatch. There are over 50 car parks within the forest, many with picnic tables, from which walkers can explore. Free public access on foot exists over most of the area but there are several large private estates that are not common land, as well as a military training area near Pippingford Park to which there is no public access.

To visit the Sussex Wildlife Trust's reserve at Old Lodge it is best to park in the small car park (TQ 469305) beside the B2026 between Maresfield and Hartfield. From here a well-marked nature trail leads around most of the reserve.

Calendar

Resident: Mandarin, Sparrowhawk, Common Buzzard, Kestrel, Woodcock, Stock Dove, Tawny Owl, woodpeckers, Woodlark, Skylark, Meadow Pipit, Grey Wagtail, Marsh Tit, Nuthatch, Treecreeper, Lesser Redpoll, Crossbill, Reed Bunting.

October–March: Hen Harrier, Fieldfare, Redwing, Great Grey Shrike, Brambling, Siskin.

April–July: Hobby, Cuckoo, Tree Pipit, Redstart, Stonechat, Dartford and other *Sylvia* warblers, Wood and Willow Warblers, Chiffchaff, Spotted Flycatcher, Linnet, Yellowhammer.

August–September: Hobby, Whinchat, Wheatear, passage warblers.

5 PEVENSEY LEVELS   OS Explorer 124

Habitat

One thousand years ago the entire Pevensey Levels was saltmarsh flooded by the sea at high tide. Today, however, the 4,000-ha levels are a mixture of pasture with many drainage ditches and quite large tracts of

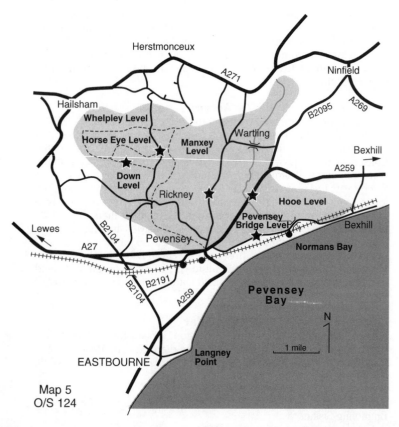

Map 5
O/S 124

210

arable land, much of which has been recently converted by pumped drainage systems. The dyke system still contains many scarce water-plants such as arrowhead, flowering rush and greater spearwort and is very good for invertebrates including Variable Damselfly and the rare Fen Raft Spider. The large channels are conspicuous by their lack of fringing vegetation but the smaller dykes are more interesting ornithologically, remaining well vegetated with fringing reeds, where grazing permits. The southern part of the levels includes a NNR wardened by EN and a Sussex Wildlife Trust reserve (140 ha), neither of which is open to the public accept by permit for scientific purposes.

Species

The levels formerly supported thousands of Lapwing, Snipe and Golden Plover in winter, but recent counts have shown that the wintering popu-lations of these species have fallen dramatically. Numbers may increase in severe weather, but the key determinant is the extent of shallow win-ter flooding, which today is less frequent and extensive than it probably used to be. Lapwing and Golden Plover are widely scattered over plough, winter cereal and grassland fields, but Snipe tends to be concentrated in 'hot spots' where there is a mixture of shallow water and marshy vegeta-tion or leftover stubble. The lucky observer may flush a Jack Snipe from such locations. Occasionally other waders such as Dunlin, Curlew, Redshank and Ruff may take advantage of the wetter areas. Ducks tend to be relatively scarce with small numbers of Teal, Wigeon and Mallard being regular; a few Shelduck, Shoveler, Gadwall and Pintail may join them. The major drainage channel for the eastern part of the levels is Wallers Haven, which discharges to the sea at Norman's Bay; the water level on this is sufficiently high to attract small numbers of Tufted Duck and Pochard, whilst in cold weather it may harbour an occasional Goldeneye, Goosander or Smew. It also acts as a refuge for many of the dabbling duck if they are disturbed.

Cold winter weather can produce exciting birdwatching: Bewick's and Whooper Swans have been recorded, but it is much more likely that the visitor will come across some of the 100 or so Mute Swans that winter here. Geese are more fickle, but White-fronts, Pink-feet and both Taiga and Tundra Bean Geese have been recorded. Severe weather may also drive a flock of wild Barnacle Geese to Pevensey Levels from their Dutch win-tering grounds, a most welcome sight given the many feral birds that now dot our landscape. Geese and wild swans are mostly seen on Horse Eye, Manxey and Pevensey Bridge Levels.

A sudden mass or panic flight of birds may alert the observer to the presence of a raptor. In winter, occasional Hen Harriers, Merlins and Peregrines hunt the area whilst in good years Short-eared Owls may be seen quartering areas of rough grassland. A Little Owl may be flushed from the hedgerows and a dusk visit could reveal a Barn Owl, especially along the minor road to Rickney. Areas of rough grassland attract Skylarks and Reed Buntings, whilst a careful search of such areas, partic-ularly near Middle Bridge, might reveal a Lapland Bunting. Near to the beach a few Stonechats and perhaps an occasional Snow Bunting find food and shelter. A scan of the sea from Norman's Bay may produce addi-tional species such as Red-throated Diver, Eider, Common Scoter, Red-breasted Merganser and auks.

As spring approaches, the wildfowl and waders start to leave. The Grey Herons in the three heronries on the levels can be observed displaying and repairing their nests, whilst Lapwings still twist and turn in display over a few areas. From April, the occasional Blue-headed Wagtail may accompany small flocks of Yellow Wagtails, and Garganey is annual but elusive, frequenting the reed-fringed pool on the road to Norman's Bay or the more open pool on Horse Eye Level. A recent feature has been the occurrence of feeding parties of Hobbies, with up to six recorded over Hooe and Pevensey Bridge Level. In a northeast wind waders, particularly Whimbrel and Bar-tailed Godwit, will fly inland over the levels and small feeding flocks might be encountered anywhere on the wetter grasslands. EN has raised water levels on part of Pevensey Bridge Level and flooded a small area viewable from the minor road to Norman's Bay. When water levels are optimal, this area can attract migrants though conditions have been less favourable for waders in recent years due to the prolific growth of rushes. Several Temminck's Stints and Pectoral and Broad-billed Sandpiper have been noted in the past.

Garganey

Breeding communities of particular interest are associated with the wet grassland, reedy dykes and dense hawthorn hedgerows. As the area of grassland has decreased so numbers of breeding Snipe, Redshank, Lapwing and Yellow Wagtails have declined dramatically, and now occur only in very small numbers. In June, the reedbeds resound with the songs of Sedge and Reed Warblers and to the thin jumble of notes from Reed Buntings, while from the hedges comes the rattle of Lesser Whitethroats.

By mid-June, gathering flocks of Lapwings herald the autumn, as do the first returning Green Sandpipers, which frequent any muddy pools that have not already dried out. From late July, Wheatears, Whinchats, Whitethroats and other common migrants can be seen; Yellow Wagtails gather in flocks feeding among the feet of grazing cattle, every now and again circling round, uttering their distinctive *seeip* calls. Thousands of Swallows may gather to feed over the levels during late August and September, and seek out a reedbed in which to roost, but not before marauding attacks from a Hobby or a Sparrowhawk.

As mid-October is reached so the summer visitors have nearly all left and the westward movement of Meadow Pipits, Chaffinches, Goldfinches, Linnets and sometimes Siskins, provides notice of winter's approach. This is soon confirmed by the appearance of Short-eared Owls in their regular haunts and the thin calls of Redwings as they seek out the ripening haws.

Although not especially noted for rarities, the area boasts an impressive list of scarce birds. Those not mentioned above include Great White Egret, Purple Heron, White Stork, Glossy Ibis, Black Kite, Montagu's

Harrier, Common Crane, Black-winged Stilt, Sociable Plover, Marsh Sandpiper and, exceptionally, Britain's fourth Oriental Pratincole, found on a small muddy pool near Middle Bridge, in August 1993.

Timing

This large area is generally under-watched and can provide fascinating birdwatching at any time of the year, but requires some time to get the best results. The various footpaths that run across the levels are usually deserted, so the area should appeal to the birdwatcher wanting to avoid the crowds. In winter the area is at its best during or just after a severe spell of cold weather, when there is a greater chance of grey geese, wild swans and raptors being present. Throughout migration periods and the breeding season it is best to arrive as early as possible when passerines are most active, but passage raptors tend to appear when the day has warmed up a little.

Access

The A259 connects Eastbourne and Bexhill/Hastings and runs across the centre of Pevensey Levels. However, this is a fast and dangerous road, so the area is best explored from the minor roads that radiate from the roundabout just east of the traffic lights in Pevensey village. The southern section is reached by the narrow road to Norman's Bay, which runs for 2.5 miles past good, often wet, grass fields and reedy dykes. There are two access points over the railway line to the sea. Rather than proceeding to Bexhill, it is best to return to the A27 and take one of the minor roads north. The road to Wartling provides good views over Manxey Level South. However, the narrow winding road which leads via Rickney and then north across Down and Horse Eye Levels to Magham Down accesses the best range of habitats. For those wanting to explore the levels on foot, an OS map is recommended. Good starting points include the Star Inn at Norman's Bay and White Dyke Farm, near Hailsham, the latter providing access to the pool on Horse Eye Level. The 11.5-miles 'Wealden Walk' that starts and finishes at the car park in Peeling Lane, Westham, provides an excellent opportunity to view the levels north of the A27. Remember, however, that the levels are almost wholly a wetland area and can be very muddy or even flooded following wet weather.

Calendar

Resident: Grey Heron, Mute Swan, Canada Goose, Sparrowhawk, Lapwing, Snipe, Redshank, Little Owl, Skylark, Meadow Pipit, Reed Bunting.

December–February: Red-throated Diver (on the sea), Cormorant, Bewick's Swan, White-fronted and other grey geese, Shelduck, Wigeon, Teal, Shoveler, Tufted Duck, Eider, Common Scoter and Red-breasted Merganser (on the sea), Hen Harrier, Merlin, Peregrine, Golden Plover, Snipe, Jack Snipe, Stock Dove, Barn and Short-eared Owls, Kingfisher, Stonechat, Fieldfare, Redwing.

March–May: Garganey, Marsh Harrier, Hobby, Little Ringed Plover, Temminck's Stint, Spotted Redshank, Wood Sandpiper, Black-tailed and Bar-tailed Godwits, Whimbrel, Cuckoo, Water Pipit, Yellow Wagtail, Whinchat, possible rarities.

June–July: Green Sandpiper, Sedge and Reed Warblers, Lesser Whitethroat.

August–November: Marsh Harrier, Hobby, Little Ringed Plover, Greenshank, Green, Wood and Common Sandpipers, Short-eared Owl, Yellow and Grey Wagtails, Whinchat, Wheatear, migrant warblers.

6 BEACHY HEAD   OS Explorer 123

Habitat

The famous chalk cliff of Beachy Head, which on a clear day offers panoramic views as far as Dungeness to the east and the Isle of Wight to the west, is one of the best-known beauty spots in southern England. Rising to 163 m and protruding several miles into the English Channel, it is the highest chalk sea-cliff in Britain. These features undoubtedly contribute to the impressive range of birds seen adjacent to, and from, the cliffs. As they are still actively eroding, the number of safe breeding ledges for seabirds is limited. At their base is a ridged platform of chalk 250 m in width, which is exposed at low water. Originally the entire land surface was chalk downland and chalk heath of outstanding quality, but this has mostly disappeared under the plough. Some, however, remains, and with the demise of intensive rabbit and sheep grazing, other areas have seen an invasion of scrub and, more recently, ash and sycamore. The grassland still supports a wide variety of orchids and other scarce calcicole plants. Eastbourne Borough Council has restored sheep grazing to the downland, and this has had a greatly beneficial effect on the chalk plants. Butterflies include Chalkhill and Adonis Blues, Dark Green Fritillary and Marbled White. In some years large numbers of Clouded

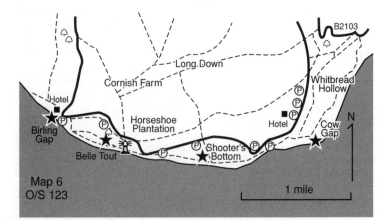

Yellows and Painted Ladies may occur, but in others they are almost entirely absent.

The scrub varies in density; in some areas such as Whitbread Hollow, it is very dense indeed. Horseshoe Plantation at Belle Tout, a small plantation of sycamore, ash, beech and elm, is the only woodland near the clifftop between Beachy Head lighthouse and Birling Gap. Though badly damaged by the October 1987 storm, it has now regenerated and attracts many passerines including annual scarce migrants. The downland east of Belle Tout is managed by Eastbourne Borough Council and the area to the west by the NT.

Species

Cold winter winds sweep across the open, rolling downland and birds are at a premium. An occasional Sparrowhawk, Merlin or Peregrine flashes by, putting to flight the local Jackdaws, while Fulmars are present on their breeding ledges from late November. In severe weather, substantial movements of divers, duck or auks may occur offshore. Ravens have recently returned to Sussex after an absence of 50 years and, although they roam widely, a pair may sometimes be seen patrolling the cliffs in early spring, perhaps attracting the attention of a local Peregrine.

Raven

Spring is generally slow to arrive; the first signs include easterly movements of Red-throated Divers and Brent Geese in early March, and the arrival of the first Wheatears and Chiffchaffs. Firecrests and Black Redstarts, the latter occasionally reaching double figures, may join these. Most days in April and May bring a new batch of migrants, although numbers vary considerably from day to day. A light northerly wind will often produce a fall of Willow Warblers, with perhaps a Redstart accompanying them. Ring Ouzel and Pied Flycatcher are recorded annually whilst the sight of a Hoopoe probing the short downland turf will undoubtedly make for a memorable day.

Rarities are by definition few indeed, but Beachy Head always attracts its share. A Serin may pause briefly to sing in one of the gardens at Birling Gap; other continental overshoots such as Black Kite, Alpine Swift, Bee-eater, Red-rumped Swallow, Subalpine Warbler and Golden Oriole have also been recorded in spring. Marsh Harrier and Osprey are annual whilst Montagu's Harrier and Honey Buzzard occur less frequently. Most raptors pass straight through, undoubtedly attracted by the chalk cliffs visible from a great distance over the Channel.

If a southeast wind is blowing, eyes inevitably turn to the sea. In such conditions large numbers of migrants are pushed towards the south coast of England, becoming more concentrated the further east one progresses. The species involved change as the season advances. The first good seawatching day of the spring, often in mid-April, is characterised by a steady stream of Sandwich Terns and lines of dark, fast-flying Common Scoters skimming the water. Up to 12,000 have been noted in a day in the past but numbers have fallen markedly in recent years; movements in excess of 1,000 are now rare. A few Velvet Scoters may join these flocks. Both Great and Arctic Skuas pass during the last two weeks of April, usually in small numbers, but up to 20 and 50 a day respectively can occur. Late in the month there is often a large but short-lived movement of Bar-tailed Godwits. Numbers vary considerably between years, though in a good season several thousand may be recorded. Many of the flocks are well out to sea, but in those closer inshore, the difference between the smaller, brick red males and the pale, long-billed females can be clearly seen. From then, and through the first two weeks of May, the passage is at its greatest intensity and diversity. Black-throated Divers in resplendent summer plumage are noted most days. Thousands of 'Commic' Terns pass, as do small flocks of Black Terns and Little Gulls. However, most eyes are seeking for less usual species, in particular Pomarine Skua or Roseate Tern. Up to 100 of the former are seen annually, usually in small groups of 2–4, but sometimes 20 or more. Such a flock has a very distinct appearance — heavy birds, many with solid tails, strongly beating their way east, the flock slowly changing shape from a line back to an irregular lump as they pass. Given a strong onshore breeze, Manx Shearwaters may occur, tilting effortlessly through the wave troughs.

Sea passage trickles to an end by the second week of June. Fulmar, Herring Gull and Jackdaw breed on the cliffs, together with the occasional pair of Rock Pipits. From the low scrub the scolding of breeding Stonechats and Whitethroats can be heard, whilst from the dense scrub emerges the rattle of a Lesser Whitethroat. In the rougher grassland Meadow Pipits and a few Skylarks persist, and Green Woodpeckers hunt for ants. A careful search of the trees in Horseshoe Plantation may reveal a roosting Little or Tawny Owl. Midsummer is not generally regarded as a good time of the year for rarities but Common Rosefinch has been recorded on several occasions and Britain's second Crag Martin appeared in July 1988 and a Rose-coloured Starling and Black-headed Bunting in June 1994.

Autumn comes early to Beachy Head. Ringing in Whitbread Hollow has shown that it is the most important departure point for Blackcaps (and probably other *Sylvia* warblers too) in Britain. Counts of 500 or more in a day are made, the birds gathering to feed on the prolific elderberries and blackberries. However, the first to show are Willow Warblers from late July — day counts of up to 1,000 have been made in the past though numbers in recent years have been significantly lower. Subsequently, Lesser Whitethroat and Whitethroat predominate, followed by Blackcap and Chiffchaff in September–October. Scarce species such as Barred and Melodious Warblers occur almost annually, but the sheer number of birds and amount of cover can make finding them hard work. September is a particularly good time, for then Yellow Wagtails, Redstarts, Whinchats, Wheatears and Spotted Flycatchers are usually prominent. A few Pied Flycatchers are noted annually, Grasshopper Warblers may be flushed from areas of long grass, and scarce migrants such as Wryneck and Red-backed Shrike can also occur. Raptors move out from Beachy Head in autumn; a few Marsh Harriers, Ospreys, Common Buzzards and Hobbies are seen annually while Honey Buzzard has become increasingly regular in recent years. Beachy Head proved to be the top site in the country for the latter during the unprecedented influx in autumn 2000. A total of 153 different birds was recorded over an 11-day period, including an amazing 63 (and 12 Marsh Harriers) on 30 September! Sea passage is generally poor, although shearwaters and skuas pass during strong, onshore winds.

October is a month of anticipation, as it is at many coastal headlands. Many of the common species have departed by then but an impressive list of rarities has been noted, including Olive-backed and Red-throated Pipits, Radde's, Dusky and Black-and-white Warblers, and Rustic Bunting. Horseshoe Plantation is often alive with Goldcrests and a careful search may well reveal a Firecrest, its sharp, positive call penetrating above the weaker notes of the numerous Goldcrests. Yellow-browed Warbler and Red-breasted Flycatcher are regular, if not annual, whilst sightings of Pallas's Warbler have increased in recent years, so much so that it is now more regular than Yellow-browed Warbler. Late October and the first half of November is the best time to look for this diminutive Siberian gem. October is also the month to see Ring Ouzels. Numbers vary greatly between years, but when a 'fall' has occurred, areas of hawthorn scrub, especially in Shooter's Bottom and Whitbread Hollow, may attract this scarce species. Black Redstarts and Stonechats perch in more open areas, the latter sometimes accompanied by a Dartford Warbler. Overhead, Tree Pipits and Yellow and Grey Wagtails have given way to finches; substantial numbers of Bramblings, Siskins and Lesser Redpolls mix with the commoner finches and Meadow Pipit. Small parties of Woodlarks may also pass overhead. Sightings of Merlin are regular and the occasional Short-eared Owl may arrive from the sea.

Impressive movements of Woodpigeons are a feature of late autumn. One such movement occurred on 7 November 1999 when an incredible 100,000 birds flew west in just two hours! The fortunate observer may flush a Woodcock or stumble across a roosting Long-eared Owl in early November bur by mid-month the leaves have been blown away and migrants have wisely left, leaving the few winter birds to eke out a living.

Timing

The area amply repays a visit in spring and autumn though the number of birds recorded from day to day varies considerably. Early morning is best when birds are most active and few sightseers are around. Seawatching is also most productive during the first few hours of daylight; by mid-morning it can be very quiet. However, skuas (especially Pomarine) can, and do, fly past at any time of day. When large tern movements take place there can be an upsurge of activity in the evening. To see the greatest range of species, seawatching is best between mid-April and mid-May, particularly the last week of April and the first two weeks of May.

The autumn passage of passerines is much more substantial than it is in spring. Apart from pipits, wagtails and chats, which can be seen for much of the day, most other migrants seem to disappear into the undergrowth by mid-morning. The strong movement of overflying pipits, wagtails and finches ceases even earlier, only being evident for 2–3 hours after sunrise. Raptors move through at any time of day, but many are seen from late morning to mid-afternoon during the warmest part of the day. It is weather conditions that dictate the number and species of birds present. Southeast winds with full cloud cover are best but a wind between southwest and north is rarely productive, particularly for the more unusual species.

Access

Being a well-known beauty spot, access is very straightforward. A loop road runs around Beachy Head from the A259, leaving it at East Dean and returning via the B2103 to the west of Eastbourne. Buses run from Eastbourne seafront to the start of the South Downs Way and the Beachy Head Hotel. Extensive car parks with toilets are situated both at the hotel and at the Birling Gap Hotel, whilst other smaller car parks are dotted along the road from Eastbourne to Birling Gap. The South Downs Way runs the entire length of the cliffs while a network of grassy rides accesses the clifftop scrub. In such a good area for birds, any well-vegetated area could produce something of interest though most birdwatchers concentrate on the known 'hot spots'. One of the best is a small valley known as Shooter's Bottom or 'Chat Vale' east of Hodcombe Farm and which extends from the coast road to the cliff edge. Other areas worth checking include the mature gardens just west of Birling Gap, the gully on the cliff edge west of Belle Tout lighthouse, and the long hedge behind the Beachy Head Hotel.

Access to the farmland is more limited, although there is now open access to the grassland managed by Eastbourne Borough Council. For seawatching in spring it is best to sit on the lower cliffs either side of Birling Gap, as the birds arrive from the southwest, whilst in autumn Cow Gap is better sited to observe birds coming from the east.

It must be emphasised that the cliff edge is extremely dangerous. Do not approach too closely. Also it is easy to get cut off by the tide if walking below the cliff face. The only access points to the beach between Eastbourne and the River Cuckmere are at Birling Gap and Cow Gap, although the access steps are periodically destroyed as the cliff erodes.

Calendar

Resident: Sparrowhawk, Peregrine, Herring Gull, Stock Dove, Little Owl, Green Woodpecker, Rock Pipit, Stonechat, Jackdaw.

December–February: Fulmar, Merlin, Peregrine, Raven.

March–May: At sea, Red-throated and Black-throated Divers, Fulmar, Brent Goose, Common and Velvet Scoters, Red-breasted Merganser, Grey Plover, Knot, Bar-tailed Godwit, Whimbrel, Pomarine, Arctic and Great Skuas, Mediterranean and Little Gulls, terns and auks. On shore, Marsh Harrier, Osprey, Hobby, Hoopoe, Yellow and White Wagtails, Nightingale, Black Redstart, Redstart, Whinchat, Wheatear, Ring Ouzel, warblers, Firecrest, Spotted and Pied Flycatchers, Serin, rarities.

June–July: Lesser Whitethroat, Whitethroat, Linnet.

August–November: Honey Buzzard, Marsh Harrier, Osprey, Common Buzzard, Merlin, Hobby, Woodcock, Arctic Skua, Short-eared Owl, Wryneck, Woodlark, Tree Pipit, Yellow and Grey Wagtails, Black Redstart, Redstart, Whinchat, Wheatear, Ring Ouzel, Redwing, Grasshopper,

Melodious, Dartford, Barred, Pallas's and Yellow-browed Warblers, commoner warblers including Reed and Sedge, Firecrest, Spotted, Red-breasted and Pied Flycatchers, Red-backed and Great Grey Shrikes, Brambling, Siskin, Lesser Redpoll, rarities.

7 CUCKMERE AND
SEAFORD HEAD
OS Explorer 123

Habitat

The Cuckmere Valley is of considerable national importance: it is a SSSI, an Area of Outstanding Natural Beauty and a Heritage Coast. The white cliffs of the Seven Sisters and the old meanders of the Cuckmere River, which fall within the Seven Sisters Country Park, are one of Britain's most familiar landscapes attracting one million visitors a year.

The lower reaches of all rivers in Sussex have been canalised and the Cuckmere is no exception. Unusually, a new channel was constructed thus cutting off the old meanders, which, fortunately, have been retained. Grazing meadows surround the brackish meanders and the river, whilst on the eastern side of the valley adjacent to the shore a scrape of shallow brackish water has been excavated. The beach at the mouth of the Cuckmere supports a range of shingle plants such as sea kale and yellow-horned poppy. To the east lie the chalk cliffs of the Seven Sisters, which stretch to Beachy Head whilst to the west there is the chalk block of Seaford Head, rising to 86 m.

The chalk grassland has a rich flora including a range of orchids, red star thistle and a rare umbellifer, the moon carrot. Patches of scrub have

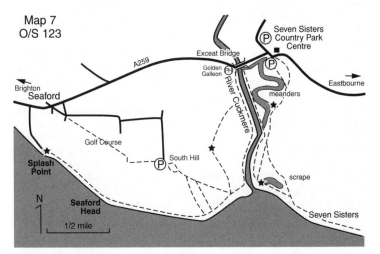

Map 7
O/S 123

developed over this area, particularly on the eastern slope, but sheep grazing has been recently introduced to help maintain the grassland and prevent further scrub encroachment. Inland of the cliff path over Seaford Head is a golf course, and further east blocks of arable fields. The area west of the river mouth and much of Seaford Head is owned by the NT and is a LNR managed by Lewes District Council. The land to the east of the meanders is in the Seven Sisters Country Park, managed by the East Sussex County Council.

Few people realise that this low-lying river valley is under threat from rising sea levels. With this in mind, the many different groups and organisations responsible for maintaining and protecting the Cuckmere have joined together in an exciting long-term project to bring maximum benefits to the wildlife and landscape. Called the 'Cuckmere Estuary Restoration Project' its main objectives are to 1) reinstate flow through the meanders, 2) restore the surrounding floodplain thus recreating intertidal habitats like saltmarsh and mudflats, 3) increase the flow of water through the river mouth, 4) remove the training walls from the mouth of the river, and 5) fill in the straight that currently isolates the meanders. The first phase, planned for autumn 2003 though likely to be delayed, will involve the removal of sections of the flood bank on the western side of the river thus allowing the adjacent grassland to flood. Bird hides will be constructed to enable visitors to observe the newly created habitat.

Species

Most of the interest in winter is concentrated on the Cuckmere Valley, with its wetland and grazing habitats being the main attraction. Under normal conditions it attracts reasonable numbers of commoner wildfowl. Most of the wildfowl are found on the meanders, where up to 30 Little Grebes dive for small fish and a few Cormorants, Little Egrets and Grey Herons search for larger prey. In colder weather much larger numbers of wildfowl are present. The resident herd of Canada Geese may be joined by a small party of White-fronted or Brent Geese whilst numbers of Wigeon may swell to over 1,000.

Small numbers of Ringed Plover, Dunlin and Redshank forage on mud exposed by the falling tide. The fields on the west side of the valley often hold a large flock of Lapwing and sometimes a few Golden Plover. A wintering Common Sandpiper may be present on the river north of the Golden Galleon pub.

The wildfowl and waders are often disturbed by a passing Sparrowhawk; Peregrine too is a regular sight in any month of the year. Listen for the distinctive *krrop* of a Raven. A pair is now resident in the area though they range widely between Seaford and Eastbourne.

The few passerines that are present in winter include a handful of Rock Pipits, which may be flushed from the saltmarsh near the mouth of the river, and a pair or two of Stonechats. Kingfishers are regular at this season and may be seen anywhere in the valley though a good spot is the meander adjacent to the A259. In some years they may stay to breed.

The first signs of spring are noted in early March, with divers and Brent Geese moving east at sea and Wheatears and Chiffchaffs on the land. A few Black Redstarts and Firecrests are usually seen this month, the latter often in the bushes on the western side of the valley. The Cuckmere forms a narrow but distinct valley through the Downs and forms a good migration route. Most springs a variety of waders pause at the scrape, whilst

Spoonbills have stopped there on a few occasions. The small pool just south of Exceat Bridge has held Temminck's Stint several times in early May; up to seven birds were there in 1993. The flooded fields north of the bridge, viewable from the minor road to Litlington, have also proved attractive to this species in recent springs, and to a variety of other waders including Wood Sandpiper and Greenshank. Other species to search for in this area include Garganey, Shoveler and Hobby.

Seawatching is best from Splash Point, at the east end of the promenade at Seaford. Because this site is only slightly above beach level and birds come close inshore, it can be particularly good for observing terns and skuas, as well as scarce grebes resting on the sea in Seaford Bay. During the second half of April and the first half of May an impressive stream of divers, ducks, waders, skuas, gulls and terns pass by. Pomarine Skuas are annual in varying numbers and, if your luck is in, there is always the possibility of a Long-tailed Skua in early to mid-May! Sometimes terns will pause to feed off the end of the breakwater at Splash Point, permitting a better chance of separating Arctic from Common Terns than is possible at most seawatching locations. Even so, it is not easy to certainly distinguish an Arctic Tern by the partially translucent underside of the wing and the sharply defined narrow black tips to the trailing edge of the primaries. The cliffs immediately east of Splash Point hold a colony of 800 pairs of Kittiwakes, which is often disturbed by a passing Peregrine.

Peregrine Falcons

Small numbers of migrants still trickle through during the first ten days of June. By then the breeding season is well under way. On Seaford Head, Stonechats, Whitethroats and Linnets sing from prominent song posts on bramble and gorse bushes. From the cliff below can be heard the low chuckle of Fulmars, some ten pairs of which find crevices on the crumbling cliff face in which to nest. On the shingle beach 1–2 pairs of Ringed Plovers attempt to breed, but are subjected to intense disturbance on an early-summer's weekend, whilst the fields on the western side of the valley hold the occasional pair of Shelduck and Oystercatcher.

Little Egret has now become a regular feature of the valley. Although present throughout the year, the largest numbers are recorded in early autumn, the peak count being 33 in October 2002.

Autumn migration can be very interesting: the muddy margins of the meanders attract a few waders such as Dunlin, Greenshanks and Green Sandpipers, and other waders, especially Common Sandpiper, should be looked for along the river edge. At low tide this can be a good spot for Little Stint and Curlew Sandpiper in late August and early to mid-September; at high tide they fly to the meanders or the scrape to roost. As in spring, raptors move through the valley, and Marsh Harrier, Osprey and Hobby are seen most years.

Hobby

Seaford Head attracts a similar range of passerines to Beachy Head though numbers are smaller. In August, Whitethroats and Willow Warblers predominate, followed by Blackcaps and Chiffchaffs in September. Other expected species include Wheatears, which frequent the short turf near the clifftop, Whinchats and Yellow Wagtails, the latter gathering around the grazing animals to feed on the insects disturbed or attracted by them. A few days of easterly winds may produce a scattering of Redstarts and possibly a Wryneck or Pied Flycatcher. On some days in September there are very large movements of House Martins and Swallows, but perhaps the most exciting period is from the end of the month when movements of Skylarks, Meadow Pipits, Pied Wagtails and finches predominate. The latter include variable numbers of Siskins and Lesser Redpolls, and sometimes a few Bramblings. The last week of September often produces the first significant numbers of Goldcrests. A few Firecrests often accompany these whilst other scarce species, which might be encountered over the next few weeks, include Woodlark, Black Redstart, Ring Ouzel and Dartford Warbler.

Autumn gales bring small numbers of Arctic Skuas and terns inshore with the possibility of storm-driven rarities such as a Grey Phalarope or Sabine's Gull. This is a good time of year to check any areas of exposed mud for rare waders; Pectoral Sandpiper and Lesser Yellowlegs have been recorded in recent years.

Although not generally regarded as a rarity hot spot, the Cuckmere Valley has attracted its fair share of unusual birds over the years. Additional species to those listed above are Night and Purple Herons, Great White Egret, White Stork, Green-winged Teal, Black Kite, Red-footed Falcon, Little Crake, Wilson's Phalarope, White-winged Black Tern, Red-throated Pipit, Woodchat Shrike and Little Bunting.

Timing

The Cuckmere Valley can be productive at any season. Be warned, however, that it can be very crowded, especially at weekends, so it is best to visit early in the morning. An early-morning start is even more important on Seaford Head before the dog-walkers are about; by mid-morning few birds remain in the open. There is little point in searching Seaford Head in winds between north and west, but it can be alive with migrants in light winds with a south or east component. Seawatching usually requires an onshore wind. Between late March and early May a southeast brings the best results, whilst in autumn a south or southwest gale can force seabirds inshore. Severe winter weather usually brings an influx of wildfowl at least during the first week or two of a hard spell, before the frozen conditions eventually push the birds further west.

Access

There are four good car parks in this area. For access to Cuckmere Haven it is best to use the pay-and-display car park at Exceat on the east side of the valley or buses 712, 713 and 714 from Brighton/Eastbourne that stop at the car park entrance. This large car park is locked overnight but it is opened fairly early in the morning. From here there is a tarmac road (suitable for wheelchair users) that leads to the scrape and beach. Alternatively, it is possible to walk the east bank of the river from Exceat Bridge to the beach. Tempting though it may seem, it is inadvisable to wade the Cuckmere at its mouth. To explore the west side of the valley, walk along the A259, cross the river at Exceat Bridge and then walk through the car park of the Golden Galleon, where there is a well-marked footpath that soon forks. The left-hand branch follows the river to the beach (though this path is likely to be lost in the fairly near future) whilst the more popular route runs to the west of the grazing meadows. This path takes one closest to the patches of scrub on the hillside and can produce better overall birdwatching, but as it is often muddy it is not suitable for wheelchairs. From here, too, it is possible to climb to Seaford Head.

On the opposite side of the road from the car park at Exceat is a visitor's centre (tel: 01323 870280) situated in an 18th-century barn that provides useful information on the Seven Sisters Country Park with displays and exhibitions. There is also a shop with leaflets, maps and souvenirs on sale, a restaurant with a walled garden, and toilets.

The easier route to Seaford Head is to drive to the car park at South Hill Barn. This is approached from Seaford via Chyngton Road and Chyngton Way, which flank the golf course on the east side of the town.

For seawatching at Splash Point it is best to use the car park at the east end of Seaford seafront. This car park also provides access to Seaford Head. A steep climb past the ruined fort, with the golf course on your left, leads to the clifftop path that continues to Hope Gap and Cuckmere Haven. Much of Seaford Head can be explored at will though it is important to keep to the paths that run across the golf course. The chalk cliffs here are very crumbly and under no circumstances should one approach the cliff edge.

Calendar

Resident: Little Egret, Mute Swan, Shelduck, Sparrowhawk, Kestrel, Peregrine, Oystercatcher, Ringed Plover, Kingfisher, Green Woodpecker, Meadow Pipit, Stonechat, Raven.

December–February: Red-throated Diver, Little Grebe, Cormorant, Grey Heron, White-fronted and Canada Geese, Barnacle Goose (feral), Dark-bellied Brent Goose, Shelduck, Wigeon, Teal, Peregrine, Dunlin, Curlew, Rock Pipit.

March–May: Divers, Red-necked, Slavonian and Black-necked Grebes, Fulmar, Manx Shearwater, Gannet, Shag, Garganey, Shoveler, Eider, Common and Velvet Scoters, Red-breasted Merganser, Marsh Harrier, Osprey, Hobby, Avocet, Grey Plover, Knot, Sanderling, Temminck's Stint, Dunlin, Bar-tailed Godwit, Whimbrel, Greenshank, Wood and Common Sandpipers, Turnstone, Pomarine, Arctic and Great Skuas, Mediterranean and Little Gulls, terns including Roseate and Black, Yellow Wagtail, Black Redstart, Redstart, Whinchat, Wheatear, warblers, Goldcrest, Firecrest, Goldfinch, Linnet.

June–July: Fulmar, Kittiwake, Lesser Whitethroat, Whitethroat, Linnet.

August–November: Osprey, Hobby, Knot, Little Stint, Curlew Sandpiper, Greenshank, Green and Common Sandpipers, Arctic Skua, Kittiwake, Swift, Sand and House Martins, Swallow, Tree Pipit, Yellow and Grey Wagtails, Black Redstart, Redstart, Whinchat, Wheatear, Ring Ouzel, warblers, Goldcrest, Firecrest, Spotted Flycatcher, Brambling, Siskin, Linnet, Goldfinch, Lesser Redpoll.

8 CISSBURY AND
THE ADUR VALLEY   OS Explorer 121/122

Habitat

A look at a map of Sussex shows that the South Downs are bisected by four rivers flowing into the English Channel. One of these is the River Adur, which is tidal for the 10 miles to Henfield. Between here and Shoreham, where the Adur reaches the sea, there is a variety of habitats. South of Henfield, as far as Bramber, are the Adur Levels, an area of grazing that floods in the winter. Between Bramber and the A27 the wet grassland has been destroyed and winter cereals predominate. South of the A27 is the Adur Estuary, an area of mudflats and saltmarsh dominated by sea purslane. Part of the estuary between the footbridge and the Norfolk Bridge is a small (10-ha) RSPB reserve. West of the river at this point lies a large open expanse of grass at Shoreham Airport whilst south of the railway there are reedy ditches and fields of permanent pasture at New Salt's Farm. Between Shoreham and the harbour mouth the river is fringed with housing and wharves. At the harbour mouth, protected on each side by substantial concrete breakwaters, are some further areas of intertidal mudflats. To the east, just behind the beach, is a gas-fired power station. This lies adjacent to Southwick Canal, a deep basin accessible to

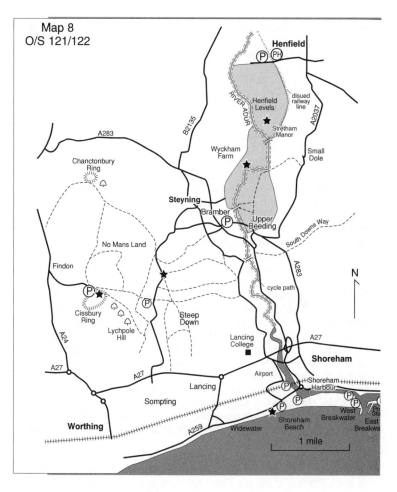

large shipping through a series of lock gates. Widewater, a LNR, is a land-locked brackish lagoon behind the shingle beach at South Lancing.

The South Downs rise steeply from both sides of the valley between Upper Beeding and Shoreham. The 3,400-ha downland block to the west, extending nearly to the A24, still contains some floristically rich chalk grassland and extensive downland scrub, particularly along Lychpole Hill and at Cissbury Ring. The latter site, a well-known Iron Age hill fort, is managed by the NT.

Species

The best winter birdwatching to be had is probably on the Adur Levels and on the tidal section of the river around Shoreham from the A27 to the harbour mouth. The former area usually holds a small herd of Bewick's Swans whilst flocks of feral Greylag and Canada Geese are sometimes joined by a few White-fronted Geese, especially in very cold weather. Under these circumstances it is worth checking the river for Smew and Goosander; a remarkable gathering of 47 Smew was recorded on an unfrozen stretch of the Adur at Henfield in January 1985! Other species typical of the river valleys include Lapwing (1,000) and flocks of Fieldfares and Redwings that may total several hundred. A Little Egret, Green Sandpiper or Kingfisher might be flushed from one of the ditches that cross the area. Further south, between King's Barn and Wyckham Farm, there is a nocturnal Cormorant roost on electricity pylons holding up to 200 birds on occasion. Sightings of Sparrowhawk are regular whilst the occasional Peregrine may also be encountered.

The mudflats of the Adur Estuary support a selection of waders including Ringed Plover (100), Dunlin (350) and Redshank (150). A large flock of Lapwing (750) commutes between the estuary and the airfield whilst the concrete breakwaters at the mouth of the harbour usually host a small flock of up to five Purple Sandpipers and c.20 Turnstones. The occasional Common Sandpiper winters along the Adur between Bramber and the A27. Wildfowl are generally thin on the ground, except in hard weather, when there may be an influx of Wigeon to the fields near New Salts Farm, the brief appearance of a flock of Brent Geese on the airfield, or a Scaup with the Pochard on Widewater. A scan of the sea from Widewater or the harbour mouth might produce a small flock of Eider or Common Scoter; occasionally an Eider ventures into the harbour itself. Southwick Canal can also be productive, especially in cold weather. Little Grebes and Red-breasted Merganser are regular, Red-throated and Great Northern Divers less so. A spell of windy weather will often result in a Shag or an oiled Kittiwake, Guillemot or Razorbill appearing in the harbour mouth. Large numbers of gulls frequent the estuary at low tide and roost in the fenced compounds along the road to the power station. A careful search through these will often produce one or more Mediterranean Gulls. There have also been several records of Iceland and Glaucous Gulls and single sightings of Laughing and Ring-billed Gulls.

Peregrines are now regular and can be seen as they patrol the river. A good spot to see this spectacular falcon is on the power station chimney where one or two roost most evenings.

Typical winter passerines include pairs of Stonechats on the patches of rough grass and scrub around the airfield and at Widewater, a handful of Rock Pipits and often a Black Redstart at the harbour mouth, and a feeding flock of Greenfinches on Shoreham Beach. The occasional Snow Bunting is also recorded.

By mid-March, the first Wheatears and Chiffchaffs have arrived. There are normally several days during the month when sizeable arrivals of Wheatears occur, with birds dotted all the way along the beach between Widewater and the harbour mouth. This is also a good time to find an adult male Black Redstart with its sooty black throat and breast and white wing panel. Watching the spring passage of birds up-Channel can be rewarding here, but it scarcely compares with the major seawatching sites elsewhere along the south coast. Nevertheless, a good selection of ducks, waders and terns can be seen, together with scarcer species such as skuas, Mediterranean and Little Gulls, and Black Tern. As Shoreham Beach is in a bay, it really does require a good southeast wind to bring birds within moderate range. Watching under these conditions has the inevitable bonuses such as a Marsh Harrier, Osprey or Hobby flying in over the sea.

In early summer the downland scrub is full of song. More open areas are occupied by Whitethroats, Linnets and Yellowhammers whilst in the denser scrub Blackcaps, Lesser Whitethroats and Chaffinches take over.

Large areas of downland are used for intensive winter cereal production. Here the diversity of birds is low, although the jangling song of the Corn Bunting can be heard from fence posts and the tops of the bushes. The South Downs are one of the few remaining strongholds for this species in the southeast, but even here numbers are declining rapidly, except where favourable farming practices persist. Other species that may be encountered in areas of arable farming are Grey Partridge and Quail. The latter, although very hard to see, has a repetitive *wet-my-lips* call most frequently heard at dawn and dusk in the Steep Down area. The commonest raptors are Sparrowhawk and Kestrel; other species to watch for are Common Buzzard and Hobby, both of which probably breed in the area. In the river valley, the reed-fringed dykes support quite large numbers of Reed Warblers, whilst those with more scrub are favoured by Sedge Warblers and a few Reed Buntings. Intensive agriculture has reduced the value of many of the ditches, and these species are best seen around the airport or on the levels north of Bramber. The Grey Herons that breed near Henfield are often seen on their feeding flights to or from the surrounding levels. Coastal breeders are few, but Ringed Plover persists at Southwick Beach and Widewater, despite intense human disturbance. An exciting development has been the provision of a Peregrine nest box on the chimney of the new power station. This finally paid dividends in 2002 when a pair successfully reared young.

Corn Bunting

Flocks of post-breeding Lapwings are already in evidence by mid-June, heralding the autumn migration. This is always a time of expectation and Cissbury and Lychpole Hill are particularly good for migrants. Throughout the autumn, passerines feed in the downland scrub. Species recorded are similar to those at Beachy Head with Whitethroat and Willow Warbler predominating in August and Blackcap and Chiffchaff in September. Wheatear and Whinchat are found in more open areas and the calls of Tree Pipit and Yellow and Grey Wagtails are heard overhead. By October most of the warblers have gone and are replaced by Goldcrests and the occasional Firecrest. On some days, when thrushes predominate, the harsh chatter of Ring Ouzels accompanies the first Redwings of autumn. As finch flocks pass overhead, listen for the hard trill of Lesser Redpoll and the wheeze of a Siskin. During August and September raptors move along the Downs, so Marsh Harrier, Common Buzzard, Osprey, Hobby and the occasional Honey Buzzard or Montagu's Harrier might be seen. October is a good month for a Hen Harrier or Merlin, the latter often in hot pursuit of a Skylark or Meadow Pipit.

The best areas for waders are the Adur Estuary and nearby Widewater. A visit in August–September may produce the occasional Knot, Little Stint or Curlew Sandpiper amongst the regular Dunlin and Ringed Plover. It is also worth checking the roosting gulls on the estuary for this is one of only two regular sites for Yellow-legged Gull in Sussex. Up to 60 have been recorded in late summer though counts of up to 20 are more typical. Seawatching is generally less productive than in spring except in strong onshore winds, when shearwaters, skuas and Little Gull may be recorded. A Grey Phalarope could be found in the harbour mouth or on Widewater following an autumn gale; other storm-driven rarities have included Leach's Petrel, Sabine's Gull and Little Auk. As winter approaches, lines of Brent Geese and other wildfowl pass west en route to their wintering grounds. With the shorter days it can be worth stopping to view the airfield at dusk. Both Barn and Short-eared Owls can sometimes be seen hunting over the rough grass adjacent to the runway.

The Adur Valley and surrounding downland have attracted a number of rarities additional to those mentioned above. Few will forget the Great Spotted Cuckoo that stayed for almost a month in April 1990 or the Sociable Plover in late-autumn 1986. Others have included Little Bittern, Cattle Egret, Black Stork, Glossy Ibis, Black Kite, Crane, Kentish Plover, Dotterel, Baird's and Pectoral Sandpipers, Red-necked Phalarope, Alpine Swift and Savi's Warbler.

Timing

The Adur Valley and surrounding downland is worth visiting at any time of year. Spring and autumn bring the greatest range of species, but winter can provide excellent birdwatching, especially in cold or rough weather. The coastal plain between Brighton and Worthing is heavily populated, so it is sensible to visit early to avoid the inevitable disturbance from cyclists, dog walkers, joggers and the like.

Seawatching in spring is usually most productive when a stiff southeast breeze is blowing. Passage usually dies down by mid-morning but may increase again in the evening. Looking out to sea during the afternoon can be difficult as the sun shines into one's eyes and passing birds are silhouetted.

Gulls and waders on the estuary are usually easiest to see up to an hour before high water when they are disturbed by the flooding tide and move elsewhere.

Access

The valley is well served by roads. The A283 from Shoreham to Steyning and the A2037 from Upper Beeding to Henfield run alongside it, while the A27 and A259 cross it near the coast. Additional unclassified roads complete the network.

Access to Henfield Levels is not straightforward and whichever route is chosen will involve a longish walk. Perhaps the easiest to follow is the cycle path that runs along the old railway from Henfield to Steyning (and onto Shoreham). Near Stretham Manor, where the railway crosses the Adur, there are extensive views from the raised railway embankment across the floodplain. The southern part of the levels is best accessed from Steyning, via Kings Barn Lane, or from Bramber by continuing to the end of Pound Lane and taking either of the footpaths that leads to the river. The area between Bramber and the A27 is best explored by following either bank of the river southwards or by picking up the cycle route again at Bramber Castle. To view the estuary south of the A27 it is best to follow the west bank of the river; this narrow path also offers views across Shoreham airport. To visit the beach and harbour mouth, turn south at the round-about on the A259 by New Salts Farm and, from here, follow the road east to the car park at the disused coastguard station west of the harbour mouth. Widewater is reached by turning right near the roundabout and following the signs to the beach car park. From here follow the path (suit-able for wheelchairs) that runs west along the top of the shingle beach towards Worthing. To reach the east side of the harbour mouth involves a lengthy detour. Return to the A259 at New Salts Farm and continue east through Shoreham, Southwick and Portslade to Hove Lagoon. Turn right at the traffic lights and follow the minor road along the beach and past the power station to a car park, from where one can follow the seawall to the harbour mouth. Being flat and concreted it is suitable for wheelchair users though a small flight of steps must be negotiated. Southwick Canal is most easily viewed from the busy A259 between Southwick and Portslade.

To explore the downland, it is best to take the unclassified road run-ning from the A27 at Sompting to Steyning. Although much of this road is narrow, there are several parking areas from where a number of public footpaths, including the South Downs Way, run west towards Cissbury and Chanctonbury Rings and Lychpole Hill, and east to Steep Down. Alternatively, one can follow the A24 north out of Worthing and turn right at the roundabout with the junction of the A280 into Findon. Follow Nepcote Lane onto the Downs and park in the small car park on the north side of Cissbury Ring.

Calendar

Resident: Cormorant, Grey Heron, Mute Swan, Sparrowhawk, Common Buzzard, Peregrine, Red-legged and Grey Partridges, Ringed Plover, Barn and Little Owls, Skylark, Yellowhammer, Corn Bunting.

December–February: Red-throated and Great Northern Divers, Little Grebe, Shag, Little Egret, Bewick's Swan, White-fronted, Greylag and Canada Geese, Wigeon, Pochard, Scaup, Goldeneye, Common Scoter, Eider, Red-breasted Merganser, Lapwing, Purple and Green Sandpipers, Turnstone, Mediterranean Gull, Kittiwake, Guillemot, Razorbill, Kingfisher, Rock Pipit, Black Redstart, Stonechat, Fieldfare, Redwing.

March–May: At sea, divers, Fulmar, Gannet, Brent Goose, Common and Velvet Scoters, Red-breasted Merganser, Avocet, Grey Plover, Knot, Sanderling, Bar-tailed Godwit, Whimbrel, Arctic, Great and Pomarine Skuas, Mediterranean and Little Gulls, Sandwich, Common, Little and Black Terns, Razorbill. On land, Marsh Harrier, Osprey, Hobby, Black Redstart, Wheatear.

June–July: Hobby, Quail, breeding warblers, Linnet.

August–November: Brent Goose, Marsh and Hen Harriers, Osprey, Merlin, Hobby, Knot, Little Stint, Curlew Sandpiper, Arctic Skua, Little Gull, Yellow and Grey Wagtails, Tree Pipit, Black Redstart, Redstart, Whinchat, Stonechat, Wheatear, Ring Ouzel, warblers, finches including Siskin and Lesser Redpoll.

Habitat

Sussex is particularly rich in wetlands due to its many river valleys formed by the streams rising in the High Weald and flowing to the coastal plain. Sadly, these rivers have largely been tamed by canalising their waters within embankments and draining the adjoining floodplain. The Arun Valley, which runs north from the A27 at Arundel to the A283 at Pulborough, however does contain some of the county's best remaining wetlands. Here, various conservation initiatives, especially at Pulborough Brooks RSPB reserve, have reversed previous habitat deterioration so that the area again supports a good selection of breeding birds and internationally important numbers of wintering waterfowl. The following text divides the valley into five main birdwatching zones, each of which is treated in detail.

ARUNDEL WILDFOWL AND WETLANDS TRUST

Habitat

Although there is a substantial wildfowl collection housed in a series of lagoons, a large natural area has been maintained. Here, one of the largest reedbeds in West Sussex fringes other shallow, mud-fringed lagoons fed by a supply of spring water that emerges from the chalk downland.

Species

In winter, the ducks in the wildfowl collection attract wild birds to the reserve. The Mute Swans, Canada Geese, Shelduck, Gadwall, Teal, Pochard and Tufted Duck that use the grounds in the day are sometimes joined at dusk by the valley's Bewick's Swans, which come here to roost. In hard weather it can be worth checking the adjacent Arun for diving duck including Goldeneye, Goosander and Smew. The reedbed may hold an occasional Bittern, but much more likely to be seen is a Water Rail. Normally, they remain hidden in vegetation but when it is cold and frosty birds emerge to feed in the open and are frequently seen very well indeed. A Green Sandpiper or Snipe may also be seen along the muddy margins of the lagoons and occasionally a Kingfisher flashes by. The feeding station in the southwest corner of the reserve attracts the usual woodland birds including Great Spotted Woodpecker and Nuthatch. Alders in the reserve may hold feeding flocks of Siskins and Lesser Redpolls whilst other passerines to look for include Cetti's Warblers skulking in the reedbeds, wintering Chiffchaffs and perhaps a Firecrest foraging with tits in the willow scrub, and Reed Buntings gathering to roost in the reedbed at dusk. At this time of the day, parties of Cormorants fly up the valley to roost in trees beside the river at South Stoke. Numbers vary considerably though more than 200 have been recorded on occasions.

The lagoons in the reserve attract passage waders such as Little Ringed Plover, Greenshank, and Common and Green Sandpipers, with others

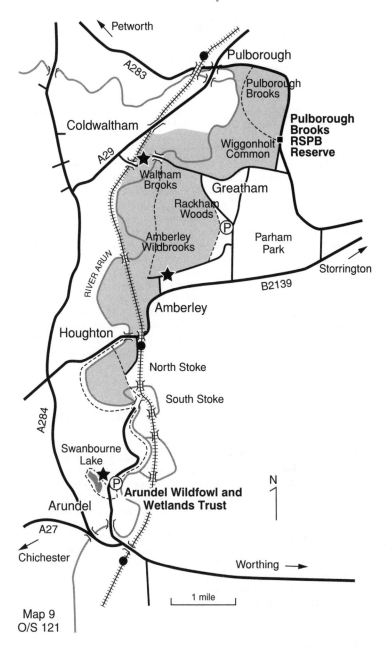

Map 9
O/S 121

such as Whimbrel and Curlew seen or heard passing overhead. The provision of floating rafts within the lagoons has been an outstanding success; in 2001, for example, there were 164 pairs of Black-headed Gulls and three pairs of Common Terns. Other breeding species include Oystercatcher, Lapwing, Redshank and Cetti's, Reed and Sedge Warblers.

SWANBOURNE LAKE

Habitat

This clear, shallow, spring-fed lake is part of the wooded Arundel Park and is adjacent to the WWT reserve. Set in a valley, it is surrounded on one side by mature woodland whilst the other side is more open, with a mosaic of chalk grassland, scrub and woodland. Three small islands in the lake provide resting places for wildfowl.

Species

Swanbourne Lake is a good spot for watching wildfowl at close range. Both Tufted Duck and Pochard come readily to food whilst further out on the lake there are Gadwall, usually in pairs, feeding on the weed brought to the surface by Coot. All breed here and can be seen with their downy young in early summer. Two other species to look for are Mandarin and Ruddy Duck. Originally escapees from the WWT, the former is often seen on, or near to, the middle island, sometimes perched on a tree branch, whilst the latter usually frequents the end of the lake farthest from the road.

A walk round the lake usually produces a good selection of woodland birds such as Green and Great Spotted Woodpeckers, Marsh Tit, Nuthatch and Treecreeper. By late March both Blackcap and Chiffchaff will be singing. Keep an eye skyward, as the yapping of the local Jackdaws may draw attention to a passing Sparrowhawk, Peregrine or Common Buzzard. Grey Wagtails are often seen in winter where the lake drops into the millstream and may remain to breed.

AMBERLEY WILD BROOKS and WALTHAM BROOKS

Habitat

Most of this section of the Valley remains as grazing meadows. The grassland itself is dissected by numerous ditches which support an impressive array of aquatic plants and insects. Sometimes in winter the whole area is flooded, giving the impresssion of a large lake when viewed from the top of the adjacent South Downs. Under these conditions important numbers of wintering wildfowl seek refuge but this is entirely dependent on the extent and timing of winter flooding. Once an almost annual occurrence, this flooding has become less frequent in recent years with the raising of the banks of the Arun and the installation of sluices to drain the water from the surrounding fields. In addition to the open meadows, there are patches of wet woodland consisting of willow and alder carr, and a derelict peat bog with large mounds of tussock sedge. Given the outstanding wildlife value of the Wild Brooks, it is not surprising that it has been designated as a Site of Special Scientific Interest, Special Protection Area and Ramsar site. The Sussex Wildlife Trust has an 82 ha reserve in the western part of the Brooks which is managed in partnership with the RSPB. The RSPB has also recently announced the purchase of 100 ha of land within the Amberley Wild Brooks SSSI with a view to improving the conditions for breeding waders and wintering wildfowl.

Waltham Brooks lie just across the Arun from Amberley Wild Brooks. Here, the riverbanks have been built up as flood defences, but they are still overtopped in winters of very heavy rainfall, thus flooding the whole area. Even in midsummer a large pool in the centre retains some water. As it dries out it exposes muddy margins that attract passing waders such as Green Sandpiper. This too is a reserve (43 ha) managed by the Sussex Wildlife Trust.

Species

Winter wildfowl are entirely dependent on the location and extent of winter flooding, and their distribution can vary from one year to the next. This is especially true of the valley's regular herd of Bewick's Swans, which may be encountered at any one of a number of sites between Pulborough and Offham. When the Wild Brooks are flooded, expect to see many of the same species that occur at Pulborough Brooks including Canada and Greylag Geese, Shelduck, Wigeon, Gadwall, Teal, Pintail and Shoveler. In cold weather a few White-fronted Geese may also be present. Waders include large numbers of Lapwing, a few Dunlin and Ruff, and the occasional Green Sandpiper along the ditches. In late afternoon look for Barn and Short-eared Owls hunting over areas of rough grassland; with luck a Hen Harrier may fly into roost just as the sun sets below the Downs.

When water levels are correct, Waltham Brooks is an excellent site to look for passage birds. Early season brings Sand Martins and the odd Garganey, followed by a variety of waders such as Little Ringed Plover, Common and Green Sandpipers, and Greenshank. Fewer migrants occur on the Wild Brooks, although a small flock of Whimbrel might be found on one of the grazing meadows, or a Whinchat perched on a fence post.

A few pairs of Lapwing and Redshank cling on, but numbers of both have decreased markedly over the past decade. A pair of Oystercatchers that bred on the water meadows north of Greatham Bridge in 2001 was noteworthy in that the species is normally a coastal nester in Sussex. Wildfowl are never numerous but may include the occasional pair of Greylag Geese, Shelduck, Gadwall or Shoveler. The network of ditches supports both Reed and Sedge Warblers and also a few pairs of Reed Buntings. Listen for the reeling song of the Grasshopper Warbler, as the Wild Brooks are one of the few regular sites in Sussex for this scarce species.

Autumn migration is most obvious on Waltham Brooks, where a range of waders similar to the spring can be seen. Hobbies too, are often seen hunting for dragonflies in late August and September.

The sewage works at Coldwaltham is one of the best places in the county for wintering Chiffchaffs. Up to 25 have been recorded including occasional birds showing characteristics of the Siberian race *tristis*.

RACKHAM WOODS

Habitat

This sandstone outcrop right on the edge of Amberley Wild Brooks has been planted with conifers, although old deciduous woodland fringes its western flank, with alder and willow carr extending onto the Wild Brooks.

Species

These provide a sharp contrast to the adjacent grazing meadows. Typical woodland species can be found all year, although they are often most visible in winter and early spring. Green and Great Spotted (and occasionally Lesser Spotted) Woodpeckers, Goldcrest, Long-tailed and Marsh Tits, Nuthatch and Treecreeper are all regular. In winter, flocks of Siskins and Lesser Redpolls feed in the alders in the damper areas. Although Woodcock is present all year, it is not until April, when they start their dusk and dawn roding display flights, that the species is obvious. By then the summer visitors are in, with Blackcap and Chiffchaff being the most common.

Nearby Parham Park has a similar selection of woodland birds, and also Greylag Geese and Mandarins on the pond.

PULBOROUGH BROOKS RSPB RESERVE

Habitat

Despite only being established in 1989, this 170-ha reserve is now one of the most important inland wetland sites in southern England. In a very short time, careful management of water levels and controlled grazing have created an area of wet grassland with an impressive range of breeding birds and internationally important numbers of wintering wildfowl. In addition to the wet grassland, there are also areas of drier grassland with hedgerows and deciduous woodland. An attractive visitor's centre is housed in a converted Sussex barn. Here begins a 2-mile (3-km) circular trail through hedge-lined lanes, which is suitable for pushchairs and manual wheelchairs with a strong helper. A large set-aside field near the visitor centre is managed to attract finches and buntings, and has helped sustain an increasing population of Yellowhammers on the reserve.

Species

The reserve is most important for its wintering wildfowl, the most numerous species being Wigeon (4,000), Teal (2,000), Mallard (500), Pintail (800) and Shoveler (200). Other wildfowl usually present include Greylag and Canada Geese, Shelduck, Mandarin, Gadwall and Tufted Duck. Bewick's Swans are rarely seen on the reserve during the day but may roost here overnight. Up to 2,000 Lapwings are present in the winter months together with 100 or more Snipe and a few Dunlin and Ruff. Unsurprisingly, the concentration of wildfowl and waders attracts birds of prey. Most regularly sighted are Sparrowhawk, Kestrel and Peregrine though Hen Harrier and Merlin also occur. A late-afternoon visit may be rewarded with a ghostly Barn Owl (which has bred in a nest box at the visitor's centre when small mammal populations are high) or a Short-eared Owl hunting over the area.

A similar range of woodland birds to Rackham Woods occurs here. Perhaps the best way to see these is to sit and watch the feeders by the entrance to the visitor's centre. The regular Blue and Great Tits are joined by Great Spotted Woodpecker, Marsh and Coal Tits, and Nuthatch, whilst an occasional Brambling or Siskin may put in an appearance in late winter and, with considerable good fortune, a Lesser Spotted Woodpecker. The area by the car park is one of the best places in the county to see this scarce species though it is possible to visit the reserve many times without seeing one! The set-aside field near the visitor's centre usually holds a few Yellowhammers and sometimes a flock of Linnets. Another declining species to look for is Bullfinch. Although rather secretive, its melancholy *phew* call is often heard along the hedge-lined lanes where there are dense stands of blackthorn.

The creation of the reserve has helped to stem the decline in several species typical of wet grassland. Teal, Garganey, Shoveler, Lapwing, Snipe, Redshank and Yellow Wagtail have all bred in recent years though the latter may no longer do so. The surrounding scrub and hedges support a healthy population of Nightingales; indeed, this is one of the best places in the county to hear this species. The nearby woods and heathland hold both Woodcock and Nightjar though habitat changes may soon result in the loss of the latter. Hobbies regularly hunt over the reserve in summer. A wide range of waders pass through, and numbers of Whimbrel, in particular, can be impressive in spring. Marsh Harriers and Ospreys visit in most years. Notable rarities do occur, and have included Night Heron, Green-winged Teal, Montagu's Harrier, Red-footed Falcon and Hoopoe.

Timing

The Arun Valley can be productive at any seasons but, for the spectacle of sheer numbers of birds, a visit to Pulborough Brooks during winter is recommended. A calm, sunny day in winter can provide very good bird-watching, with a wide range of wildfowl, birds of prey and passerines often present. As Pulborough Brooks is one of the most-visited RSPB reserves, it can be crowded here, especially at weekends, so an early-morning or late-afternoon visit is best. These are also the best times of the day to see raptors. Similarly, Swanbourne Lake is best visited in the morning before it gets too crowded. Those with time on their hands may choose to explore the valley more widely though days with strong winds, heavy rain or poor visibility are best avoided.

Access

Roads surround the valley and most areas are accessible by using footpaths from car parks. There are also railway stations at Arundel, Amberley and Pulborough.

Access to the WWT and Swanbourne Lake is by following the brown duck signs on entering Arundel. Approaching from the east, head into the town from the A27, cross the river and turn immediately right into Mill Road. The lake is on the left after 800 m whilst the entrance to the WWT is further along the road on the right, about 1 mile from the town centre. There is a large car park for visitors. The WWT grounds are well laid out and several large hides affording excellent views overlook the natural area of pools, reed and sallows to the south. There is also a newly constructed boardwalk through the reedbed and excellent facilities for disabled visitors including level access to all areas and free wheelchair loan. Guide dogs are welcome. The reserve is open daily (except Christmas Day) 9.30am–5pm (4.30pm in winter). Admission prices for non-members are adult £5.50, child £3.50, concession £4.50 and family ticket £14.50.

Swanbourne Lake is open all day and a hard but often muddy path runs around the lake and back to the road, where there is limited parking. This area is very popular at weekends and it is usually best to visit early in the day.

For access to the riverbank continue beyond the WWT to the Black Rabbit pub. From here walk south along the west bank of the Arun and then take the narrow and often muddy path along the north bank of the millstream back to the road by Swanbourne Lake. It is also possible to walk north along the west bank of the river from the Black Rabbit to South Stoke and then, by crossing the river at this point, to North Stoke and Houghton Bridge. A possibility here would be to return to Arundel by train from Amberley Station.

Access to Amberley Wild Brooks is restricted to the Wey South Path, which runs north through the middle of the brooks directly from Hog Lane in Amberley village. It is a made-up path, mostly of chalk spoil for the first half-a-mile but can get very sticky in wet weather. Further north it deteriorates and for much of the winter, especially after wet weather, it can be almost impassable — then wellingtons are essential. The area can also be overlooked from the minor road just east of Amberley village and from Rackham Woods. The latter, part of the woodland complex that includes Northpark Wood and Parham Park, can be reached by continuing east along Rackham Street. On reaching the T-junction, turn left and park in the small car park on the left by the old school house.

From here a three-quarter-mile footpath skirts along the western edge of the woodland and returns either along the road or on rides within the wood. To visit Parham Park walk north along the road from the car park. The entrance is on the right just beyond the road junction. Walk through the lodge gates and continue east along the private road (suitable for wheelchair users) past the pond.

Waltham Brooks lie alongside the unclassified road running from Coldwaltham on the A29 to Greatham. Limited parking is available in a small car park adjacent to Greatham Bridge, from where the public footpath that runs alongside the old canal can be joined. Views can be had across most of the reserve from this footpath, which continues over the railway to Watersfield. The water meadows north of Greatham Bridge are also worth checking, especially when flooded. Unexpected species such as Scaup, Long-tailed Duck and Little Gull have been recorded. To visit the sewage works at Coldwaltham, retrace your steps. Just after the road crosses the railway, take the footpath that runs south for about half-a-mile and view from the perimeter fence.

The signed entrance to the Pulborough Brooks RSPB Reserve is located on the left-hand side of the A283, about 2.5 miles north of Storrington village. The reserve is open daily (except Christmas Day) from 9am to 9pm or sunset, if earlier, whilst the visitor centre is open from 10am to 5pm. Admission prices for non-members are adult £3.50, child £1, concession £2.50 and family ticket £7. For those with mobility problems a battery-powered buggy is available for the nature trail and a manual wheelchair for the visitor centre. These need to booked in advance by telephone (01798 875851) or e-mail (pulborough.brooks@rspb.org.uk).

Calendar

Resident: Cormorant, Little Egret, Grey Heron, Mute Swan, Canada and Greylag Geese, Shelduck, Mandarin, Gadwall, Teal, Shoveler, Pochard, Tufted and Ruddy Ducks, Sparrowhawk, Common Buzzard, Kestrel, Lapwing, Woodcock, Stock Dove, Barn, Little and Tawny Owls, woodpeckers, Grey Wagtail, Cetti's Warbler, Marsh Tit, Nuthatch, Treecreeper, Bullfinch, Yellowhammer, Reed Bunting.

December–February: Bittern (rare), Bewick's Swan, White-fronted Goose, Wigeon, Teal, Pintail, Shoveler, Hen Harrier, Peregrine, Merlin, Water Rail, Dunlin, Ruff, Snipe, Green Sandpiper, Short-eared Owl, Redwing, Fieldfare, Chiffchaff, Firecrest, Siskin, Lesser Redpoll.

March–May: Garganey, Hobby, Little Ringed and Ringed Plovers, Dunlin, Ruff, Black-tailed Godwit, Whimbrel, Curlew, Greenshank, Wood and Common Sandpipers, Cuckoo, Nightingale.

June–July: Oystercatcher, Redshank, Black-headed Gull, Common Tern, Grasshopper, Sedge and Reed Warblers, Whitethroat, Lesser Whitethroat, Garden Warbler, Blackcap.

August–September: Hobby, Ruff, Black-tailed Godwit, Greenshank, Green, Wood and Common Sandpipers, Redstart, Whinchat, Wheatear, Spotted Flycatcher.

October–November: Wigeon, Teal, Pintail, Shoveler, Hen Harrier, Peregrine, Merlin, Lapwing, Short-eared Owl, Fieldfare, Redwing, Siskin, Lesser Redpoll.

10 CLIMPING GAP   OS Explorer 121

Habitat

Much of the coastline of West Sussex is developed, so the few gaps in the urban sprawl form important areas for wildlife. One such area, known as the Climping Gap, lies between the mouth of the River Arun at Littlehampton and Middleton-on-Sea, some 2.5 miles to the west. Much of the hinterland is under cereals, but the southeast corner is a golf course. This is separated from the sea by a line of small sand dunes and a vegetated sand and shingle beach, but the rest is shingle with a narrow, artificial bank protecting the farmland. The beach is quite wide at low water and has a patchy mixture of sand, shingle and stony ground. At the east end of the beach is a pier guarding the river mouth. Behind the seawall there are patches of rough ground, blackthorn and hawthorn scrub, and small linear woodlands accessible by public footpaths.

Species

Waders form a prominent feature of the winter bird community though numbers have fallen in recent years, probably as a result of human disturbance. Despite this, the diverse nature of the foreshore provides many habitats, so a wide variety of species can be expected, including up to 100 each of Grey Plover and Sanderling. The latter feed in small groups at the tide edge but can be very mobile, sometimes moving to the many miles of contiguous beaches. Small numbers of Purple Sandpipers used

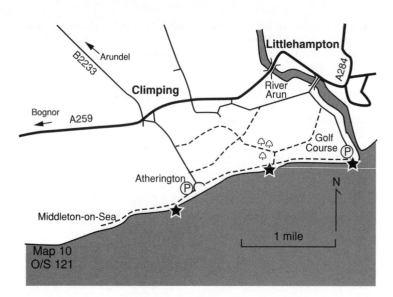

Map 10
O/S 121

to frequent the wooden pier by the mouth of the Arun, but now only occasional singles occur in winter.

The sea here sometimes attracts a few waterbirds. In normal winters a handful of Great Crested Grebes, Cormorants, and Red-breasted Mergansers feed offshore although, because of the low vantage point, they can be difficult to pick out. Severe weather will result in an increase of duck on the sea, with Wigeon and Teal resting on it during the day, and the odd auk or Red-throated Diver being pushed inshore. A flock of up to 100 Mute Swans feeds in the River Arun at Littlehampton. It is well worth checking the gulls on the beach or on the pier, for Mediterranean, Glaucous and Iceland have been seen among the common species.

The agricultural land still attracts small coveys of Grey Partridges. Kestrels and Sparrowhawks are seen regularly and a Short-eared Owl or Merlin may put in an appearance. Seeds from the plants growing on the shingle beach provide food for small groups of Greenfinches, which are sometimes joined by a Snow Bunting. Small numbers of Rock Pipits and Stonechats also occur on the beach, feeding mainly on the emerging seaweed flies that emerge throughout the winter months. The dykes north of the golf course may attract a Little Egret or Kingfisher, particularly in winter.

In March, lines of Brent Geese pass, having just left their important wintering grounds in the harbours to the west. Wheatears can be found here from the first week of March, sometimes accompanied by a Black Redstart. By mid-month, raucous Sandwich Terns can be seen offshore, migrant Chiffchaffs are common and a Firecrest might be found in the bushes by the golf course. Later in spring look for a wide variety of warblers, with the possibility of an added bonus such as a Redstart, Pied Flycatcher or Whinchat. Seawatching in April–May can be worthwhile; small numbers of the typical species such as Common Scoter, Whimbrel, Bar-tailed Godwit, Arctic Skua and 'Commic' and Little Terns pass east, although passage is much more concentrated off Selsey Bill or Worthing.

A few warblers, principally Blackcaps and Whitethroats, breed in the patches of woodland and scrub. The dykes hold a few pairs of Reed and

Sedge Warblers whilst Skylarks and Meadow Pipits can be found in the grassy areas around the golf course.

Passage in autumn can be very good with a wide range of commoner migrants seen annually. August brings mostly warblers, but in September there is a much greater variety including Pied Flycatcher in most years. Rarer species including Icterine, Barred and Aquatic Warblers, Wryneck and Red-backed Shrike have been recorded. The golf course is particularly attractive to Wheatears and Whinchats. A few raptors move through, principally Hobbies, although there have been several records of Ospreys flying out to sea. Later in autumn, the morning coastal movement of Meadow Pipits, Goldfinches, Siskins and Linnets is prominent, and sometimes includes scarcer species such as a few Bramblings or a Woodlark. A Rustic Bunting spent three days in the dunes in October/November 1991. Dartford, Yellow-browed and Pallas's Warblers have all been observed in late autumn in recent years; a good spot to look for the latter (and Firecrest) is the wood behind the car park at Atherington.

Timing

During spring and autumn migration it is important to be out early in the morning. At this time of day birds feed more actively and any visible migration will be at its heaviest. There are also relatively few people around, so there is much less disturbance. The beach faces south, thus for much of the middle of the day birds sitting on the sea are silhouetted against the bright, reflected light. It is pointless visiting here in high summer.

In winter a good time to see the waders is about mid-tide, just before the water reaches the steep shingle beach. Wildfowl on the sea are best seen at any stage during the two hours either side of high tide, otherwise they will be distant. A large tide which is full mid-morning provides a good combination. Strong winds with a distinct southerly component are needed to push passing seabirds inshore.

Access

The A259 Littlehampton–Bognor coast road runs north of this site; access to the two car parking areas is off this road. To reach the harbour mouth, leave Littlehampton on the A259, cross the River Arun and take the first left into Ferry Road. At the end of Ferry Road turn right into Rope Walk and continue to the small car park at the end. A cafe and toilets are located here. Take the boardwalk that runs through the dunes and continue walking west along the beach towards Atherington. To reach the car park at Atherington, return to the A259 and continue west towards Bognor. Take the second left into Climping Street and follow it to the end, where there is a car park behind the seawall. Walk east along the beach towards Littlehampton and then take the footpath that skirts along the northern edge of the golf course. To complete a circular walk, turn right for the harbour mouth on reaching Rope Walk and then walk back to Atherington along the beach.

Calendar

Resident: Mute Swan, Sparrowhawk, Kestrel, Grey Partridge, Skylark, Meadow Pipit.

December–February: Great Crested Grebe, Cormorant, Little Egret, Red-breasted Merganser, Water Rail, Lapwing, Ringed and Grey Plovers, Sanderling, Dunlin, Turnstone, Short-eared Owl, Kingfisher, Rock Pipit, Stonechat, Greenfinch, possibly Snow Bunting.

March–May: Divers on passage, Gannet, Brent Goose, Marsh Harrier, Osprey, Hobby, Bar-tailed Godwit, Whimbrel, Arctic Skua, Sandwich, Common and Little Terns, Black Redstart, Redstart, Whinchat, Wheatear, most warblers, Firecrest.

June–July: Whitethroat, Blackcap.

August–November: Until late September, good for all of the commoner summer migrants, including Redstart, Whinchat, Wheatear and Spotted Flycatcher. During October and November, winter birds appear including Red-breasted Merganser, Sanderling, Rock Pipit and Stonechat, while passage migrants include Black Redstart, Firecrest and possibly Dartford, Yellow-browed and Pallas's Warblers.

11 BURTON AND CHINGFORD PONDS

OS Explorer 121

Habitat

Burton and Chingford Ponds is a LNR and a SSSI, and is jointly managed by the Sussex Wildlife Trust and the Sussex Downs Conservation Board. A mosaic of different habitats makes this a very rewarding area to explore, with the likelihood of seeing a good variety of birds on a relatively short walk. The best way to see this 56-ha reserve is to follow the nature trail, which starts at the mill overlooking Burton Mill Pond, a reed-fringed hammer pond dating from the 16th century. Initially, the nature trail winds through Newpiece, an area of drier woodland where oak, birch and rowan indicate the acidic nature of the underlying sandy soils. From here, the trail passes some huge ancient sweet chestnuts and then Snipe Bog, where the wet meadow is filled with southern marsh orchids in early summer. The outfall of Chingford Pond is reached soon after passing a small housing development. This much shallower lake, surrounded by trees, has extensive muddy margins. Just beyond the outfall, the trail splits. The right-hand fork continues past Crouch Farm to the Warren, a developing oak woodland, whilst the left-hand fork skirts the edge of the wet alder carr fringing Burton Pond. One of the highlights of the walk is the Black Hole, an acid peat bog where the Sussex Wildlife Trust has constructed a boardwalk, as well as removing much of the invading alder, birch and willow. This is a good spot to watch dragonflies including Golden-ringed, Scarce Chaser and Downy Emerald. From here

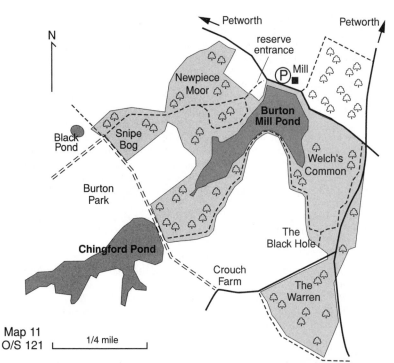

Map 11
O/S 121   1/4 mile

the trail passes through drier acid grassland before reaching the road, from where it is a short walk back to the car park.

Species

Both Burton and Chingford Ponds attract small numbers of wildfowl in winter. The former, being deeper, holds a few Tufted Duck and Pochard, while the latter is more attractive to dabbling duck including Gadwall, Teal and Shoveler. A few Shelduck are usually present. The fascinating display of the Great Crested Grebe can be seen on Burton Pond in spring, whilst other breeding waterbirds include Canada Geese, Mute Swan, Gadwall and Tufted Duck. The reed-fringed edges of Burton Pond hold chattering Reed Warblers from late April and with luck a Kingfisher might be glimpsed flying straight and low across the water, its back flashing turquoise-blue. Look also for Grey Wagtails, which are often seen at the outfalls of both ponds.

The surrounding woodlands hold a typical bird community. A walk in winter is likely to produce mixed flocks of tits, including Marsh, and also parties of Siskins and Lesser Redpolls feeding in the alders. Flocks of Fieldfares and Redwings are found on the adjacent farmland, and also a few Meadow Pipits. As winter turns to spring the woodland birds start to establish their territories. The loud ringing calls of the Nuthatch and the distinctive *tchick* of the Great Spotted Woodpecker are often heard in March, but the main attraction is Lesser Spotted Woodpecker, a species that appears to have declined markedly in Sussex in recent years. Seeing this diminutive bird is never easy, but the area between Burton and Chingford Ponds has been one of its most reliable sites in the county in recent years. A visit in early spring, when the birds are likely to be drumming or calling, is best but do not expect instance success for they can be very hard to find. Even if you do not see a Lesser Spotted Woodpecker there will be plenty of other woodland birds to enjoy, with the added bonus of several species of warblers from mid-April. March is also good for birds of prey. Sparrowhawks display on fine mornings during the month, whilst Common Buzzards breed on the nearby South Downs and can sometimes be seen soaring distantly over the wooded escarpments. Red Kite has been seen at least once and the occasional Osprey may pause to fish in both spring and autumn.

By midsummer the woods are much quieter. This is, however, a good time for a dusk visit, with the possibility of a roding Woodcock or a Little Owl perched prominently on one of the large trees in Burton Park. Look also for Common and Green Sandpipers, which start their return migration in late June and may be seen feeding along the muddy margins of Chingford Pond. Late summer is a good time to find Hobbies hawking for dragonflies.

Cold weather at either end of the year may bring surprises such as a Goldeneye or Goosander, or a Bittern flying across Burton Pond at dusk.

Timing

This is a pleasant spot to visit at any time of the year though it is probably best in late winter and spring when the birds are establishing territories and are in full song. For Lesser Spotted Woodpecker a visit on a warm spring day in March is recommended, when the birds are likely to be calling and drumming, and thus easier to locate.

Access

Burton Mill Pond lies about 3 miles south of Petworth. From Petworth take the A285 south towards Chichester. After crossing the River Rother at Coultershaw Bridge, take the first left. Limited parking is available by the mill on the opposite side of the road from Burton Pond.

Calendar

Resident: Grey Heron, Mute Swan, Shelduck, Gadwall, Tufted Duck, Sparrowhawk, Kestrel, Woodcock, Stock Dove, Tawny and Little Owls, woodpeckers, Grey Wagtail, Goldcrest, Long-tailed, Marsh and Coal Tits, Nuthatch, Treecreeper.

December–February: Teal, Shoveler, Pochard, Goldeneye, Goosander, Water Rail, Meadow Pipit, Redwing, Fieldfare, Siskin, Lesser Redpoll.

April–May: Great Crested Grebe, Osprey, Common Sandpiper, Sand Martin, Reed and Garden Warblers, Blackcap, Chiffchaff, Willow Warbler.

July–September: Osprey, Hobby, Green and Common Sandpipers.

12 CHICHESTER
GRAVEL PITS

Habitat

To the south and east of Chichester lie a series of 20 or so privately owned water-filled gravel pits of varying ages and maturity. Most of these are fringed with willows, sallows and brambles. Typically, there is little marginal reed growth except at Ivy Lake, where there are quite extensive areas of reeds adjacent to the Lakeside Holiday Village. Although subject to considerable disturbance from fishing, water-skiing and windsurfing, the pits attract good numbers of duck in winter, and passage migrants in spring and autumn.

Species

The deeper pits hold up to 500 of both Tufted Duck and Pochard in winter; other diving duck include a few Goldeneye and an occasional Scaup or Long-tailed Duck. Very small numbers of Smew have been recorded in recent winters; check New Pit and Runcton Lake for this attractive species, particularly in hard weather. Dabbling duck do not find the relatively deep water to their liking, but up to 300 Shoveler with their huge spatulate, sieving bills, are able to glean food from the surface layers. Although it is a dabbling duck, by stealing pond-weed from feeding Coots, Gadwall are able to feed in the deep waters of the pits as well as in the shallows. The presence of exceptional numbers of this species (up to 450) in recent winters is probably a consequence of the continuing growth in numbers of continental breeding birds, which are believed to form the majority of the UK's wintering population. A noticeable feature of Ivy Lake is a tree roost of up to 85 Cormorants on the island in the centre of the pit. Careful scrutiny of the margins of the pits during hard weather may bring the reward of a skulking Water Rail, or if very lucky, a Bittern hiding in the reeds.

In early March the first returning Chiffchaffs can be heard and Sand Martins congregate to feed over the pits, especially when they are held up on their migration by rain or cold northerly winds. As spring progresses, the Sand Martins are joined by House Martins and Swallows, and Chiffchaffs by other migrants such as Blackcaps and Willow and Sedge Warblers. By late April, the elegant Common Terns, which breed on rafts put out by the Sussex Ornithological Society, have returned and are sometimes joined by passing summer-plumaged Black Terns or rosy-flushed Little Gulls, especially when the wind is from an easterly quarter. Common Sandpiper frequents the margins of the pits when water levels are low and a few Whimbrel or Bar-tailed Godwits may pass overhead on migration. Osprey is recorded almost annually in spring and autumn though they rarely linger long.

A number of different species of waterbirds breed, of which Great Crested Grebe, Mute Swan, Greylag and Canada Goose are the most conspicuous. Little Grebe, Pochard and Ruddy Duck also breed, at least in some years, although their secretive nature means that they are often overlooked.

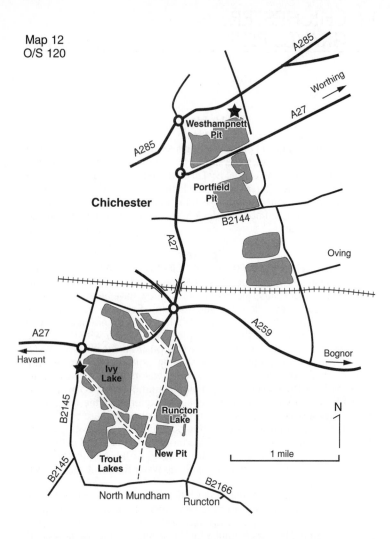

Map 12
O/S 120

Portfield and Drayton Pits attract returning waders such as Little Ringed Plover and Green Sandpiper from late June, although there is no public access to these sites. Large concentrations of Swifts may be seen until early August, with hirundines building up later in the month and perhaps attracting a passing Hobby. Over the water, Black and Common Terns twist and turn, sometimes accompanied by a few Arctic Terns and on several occasions in past years by a juvenile White-winged Black Tern.

Timing

Although large numbers of duck are present throughout the winter, unusual species such as Smew and Goosander are more likely to occur in hard weather. The occurrence of Black Terns and Little Gulls in spring usually coincides with days of heavy tern passage at coastal sites when the wind is from the east or southeast. They rarely remain long and are more likely to be seen in autumn, when birds may linger for several days.

Great Crested Grebe

Access

Two of the northern pits, Westhampnett Lake East and Westhampnett North Lake, lie adjacent to the A27 though only the former can be viewed safely from the road. To do this, approach Chichester from the east and park in the lay-by on the left-hand side of the A27. To view Westhampnett North Lake, continue west along the A27 to the first roundabout by the McDonalds. Turn right here and right again at the next roundabout. In Westhampnett, turn right into Coach Road and view the pit from its northeast corner at the start of the access road to the amenity tip. The other northern pits (Portfield Lake and Drayton Pit) lie behind thick impenetrable hedges and are not readily viewable from the roads that skirt them.

The more accessible southern group of pits is best viewed from one of two footpaths that run alongside them. To view Ivy Lake and the Trout Lakes, turn off the A27 onto the B2145 and park almost immediately on the left-hand side of the road. From here take the footpath that runs along the southwest bank of Ivy Lake past Trout Lakes. On reaching Peckhams Copse Lane turn left and continue walking north through the scrap yard as far as the entrance to the Lakeside Holiday Village. New Pit, Runcton Lake and Vinnetrow Lake can be viewed from this path, the latter through a gap in the hedge almost opposite the end of the footpath past the Trout Lakes, where it joins Peckhams Copse Lane.

Calendar

Resident: Great Crested and Little Grebes, Mute Swan, Greylag and Canada Geese, Pochard, Tufted and Ruddy Ducks, Sparrowhawk, Moorhen, Coot, Green Woodpecker.

December–February: Cormorant, Bittern, Gadwall, Shoveler, Scaup, Long-tailed Duck, Smew, Goosander, Water Rail, Kingfisher, Grey Wagtail, Chiffchaff, Meadow Pipit and Pied Wagtail on adjacent fields.

March–May: Osprey, Common and Black Terns, hirundines, Swift, Reed and Sedge Warblers, Lesser Whitethroat, Whitethroat, Blackcap, Chiffchaff, Willow Warbler.

June–July: Common Tern, Swift.

August–November: Osprey, Hobby, Common, Arctic and Black Terns, Grey Wagtail, roosting Sand Martins and Swallows, warblers.

Habitat

There can be few birdwatchers in Britain who have not heard of Pagham Harbour. An excellent range of habitats and birds, with well-marked public rights of way that allow for easy exploration make it one of the most popular destinations for birdwatchers in southern England. Although probably best known for birds, it also supports an incredible range of other wildlife, including many rare and scarce species. Mill Pond Marsh at Sidlesham has a fine colony of southern marsh orchids, which can easily be viewed from the field gate by the road (there is no public access to the marsh). The vegetated shingle areas on both sides of the harbour support the largest British colony of Chidling pink, a plant that occurs only in Sussex and Hampshire. These areas also hold the best examples of shingle-growing lichens in Sussex; over 80 species have

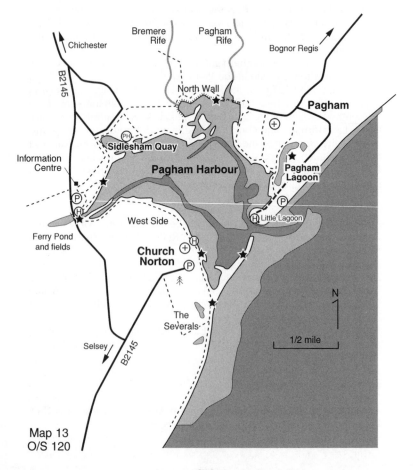

Map 13
O/S 120

been recorded. Part of Church Norton spit has a colony of the Red Data Book snail *Truncatella subcylindrica* and several rare moths are found here, among the total of over 600 species recorded on the reserve. Hairy Dragonflies may be seen around the ditches in May and there is often an influx of migrant Clouded Yellow and Painted Lady butterflies in late summer. In July–August the large female wasp spiders *Argiope bruennichi* can be found sitting in their magnificent webs in the long grasses.

The harbour itself is very muddy, with extensive, but broken, beds of the cord grass (*Spartina*), adjacent to the seawalls. Two deep creeks drain it and between them lies a high *Spartina*-covered bank. The harbour mouth is guarded by two shingle spits, which have been battered by storms and changed shape many times in the past. Coastal defence work has slowed down such changes. A fast flow of water passes through the narrow entrance and over extensive rough gravel deposits on the beach.

Starting on the eastern (Pagham village) side, from the northerly spit at the harbour mouth and moving in an anti-clockwise direction, the first of the main habitats of significance for birds is Pagham Lagoon, a former entrance to the harbour. Between Pagham and Sidlesham, the North Wall gives good views over the Breech Pool and surrounding wet grassy fields. Continuing anti-clockwise, the area around the information centre was once a rubbish tip, but is now restored to rough grassland with some planted trees. West of the B2145, at this point, lies Sidlesham Ferry Pool, a nature reserve owned by the Sussex Wildlife Trust. The footpath along the south shore of the harbour initially runs past some reed-fringed linear pools at the harbour edge. It overlooks set-aside and arable fields inland, and passes through patches of gorse and blackthorn, before reaching a line of stunted oaks. At Church Norton, the churchyard and vegetation around it provides another excellent area, but visitors are requested to respect the consecrated graveyard. The shore is lined here by willows, sallows and blackthorn, and a little farther south by gorse. Two small pools, known as the Severals, lie south along the shingle beach. One has lost most of its open water and is dominated by a dense reedbed. The entire harbour and several adjacent areas are managed and wardened by West Sussex County Council, who has declared it a LNR.

Species

For sheer numbers of birds, winter undoubtedly brings the best bird-watching at Pagham Harbour. Most conspicuous are the Dark-bellied Brent Geese, up to 3,000 of which winter in the area. At low tide they feed in the harbour but at high tide they gather into a single flock on the grassland and winter cereals behind the seawall, where they continue to feed. Careful scanning with a telescope might produce a Pale-bellied Brent Goose or Black Brant, both of which have been almost annual in recent years. Other wildfowl include up to 300 Shelduck, 1,500 Wigeon, 2,000 Teal and 500 Pintail, although numbers may be much higher during harsh weather. Pagham Harbour is also attractive to seaduck. A few Goldeneye and Red-breasted Mergansers are usually present whilst less-regular species include the occasional Scaup or Long-tailed Duck. In most winters a Smew or two can be found on Pagham Lagoon. The open sea off Church Norton is also good for Eider and Red-breasted Merganser, but the main attraction is the concentration of Slavonian Grebes. Over 50 have been recorded on several occasions, representing up to 12.5% of the British wintering population. Great Crested Grebes are also regular, while other species to look for are divers (including Great

Northern), Red-necked Grebe and auks. Severe weather to the east may bring grey geese to the fields adjacent to the harbour. Small flocks of White-fronted Geese are recorded annually, sometimes associating with the Brent flock, but Pink-footed and Bean Geese have also been seen. Very occasionally, a flock of Barnacle Geese may occur, although whether these are wild birds or of feral origin is open to conjecture.

Waders are also a prominent feature of the harbour. Up to 2,000 Dunlin may be present on the mudflats, together with smaller numbers of Oystercatchers (500), Grey Plover (1,000), Knot (200), Curlew (700), Redshank (300) and Turnstone (400). A few Bar-tailed Godwits are found in the sandier areas, while on the flooded fields behind the North Wall there may be hundreds of Lapwing and Golden Plover, together with variable numbers of Black-tailed Godwits. A recent development has been the occurrence of a regular wintering flock of up to 30 Avocets in the harbour, best looked for on a rising tide from the raised bank between Sidlesham Ferry and Church Norton. Other waders to keep an eye open for include Whimbrel, Spotted Redshank and Greenshank, each of which winters in very small numbers.

Avocets

Among the scarcer small birds present in winter is Kingfisher, usually seen flashing along the brackish dykes adjacent to the harbour. A Chiffchaff or Firecrest may winter at Church Norton, while the reedbeds at the Breech Pool and the Severals may very occasionally hold a few Bearded Tits. Listen in these areas for the squeal of a Water Rail and the explosive song of a Cetti's Warbler. The shingle beach often holds a wintering flock of Greenfinches, and occasionally a Snow Bunting takes up residence for several weeks. Severe weather may push small numbers of Woodlarks to the coast, so it is well worth checking through all the apparent Skylarks feeding along the high-tide line. With such a high density of birds, it is unsurprising that raptors regularly hunt over the whole area. Sparrowhawk, Kestrel and Peregrine are the most frequent, while other species to look for are Hen Harrier, Merlin and Short-eared Owl. Gulls are not everyone's cup of tea, but large numbers roost in the harbour each evening. Armed with a telescope and plenty of patience, it should be possible to spot a few Mediterranean Gulls and perhaps the adult Glaucous Gull, present in January 2003 for its sixth successive winter.

The departure of the Brent Geese in early March coincides with the arrival of the first spring migrants. These are usually Wheatear, Black Redstart and Chiffchaff, followed by Sandwich Tern and Willow Warbler later in the month. March is also a good time for Firecrest and there is always a chance of a Ring Ouzel. Soon a steady trickle becomes a flood, and on some days the bushes seem to be alive with Willow Warblers, with perhaps a male Redstart or Pied Flycatcher, or better still a Hoopoe. Raptors pass through in spring; sightings of Marsh Harrier and Hobby are increasingly regular and, with luck, an Osprey might be encountered sitting on a post in the harbour. The Ferry Pool is well worth a look in spring though whether there are any passage waders will depend very much on prevailing water levels. In recent springs they have been kept artificially high so that the surrounding fields are more attractive to breeding Lapwing and Redshank. When muddy areas are exposed, expect to see Little Ringed Plover and Common and Green Sandpipers. Wood Sandpiper is also a possibility, as is Temminck's Stint; in May 1979 there were seven here together! An assortment of ducks may also be present including Teal and Shoveler, both of which probably breed, and with luck a superb male Garganey. Virtually anything can and does turn up; overshooting vagrants recorded in spring include Squacco Heron, Cattle Egret, Black Kite, Black-winged Stilt, Collared Pratincole, Whiskered Tern and Red-rumped Swallow.

Midsummer is relatively quiet. At the mouth of the harbour Sandwich, Common and Little Terns fish in the shallows. Although Little Tern has been lost as a breeder, both Oystercatcher and Ringed Plover benefit from the protection they receive and each year a few pairs breed on the shingle spits. Another important habitat for breeding birds in the reserve is Ferry Pool. Lapwing and Redshank nest here in small numbers, together with a few Shelducks and perhaps a pair of Shoveler. A summering flock of Black-tailed Godwits and the occasional pair of Avocets add further interest. The reserve also supports a few pairs of Little Grebes and there is a small heronry near Halsey's Farm. The reedbeds resound to the jittery song of the Reed Warbler and the more varied and hurried notes of Sedge Warblers. Listen also for the repetitive song of the Reed Bunting and the rattle of a Lesser Whitethroat, the latter in dense hedges. Farmland still supports both species of partridge, albeit in very low numbers, and Little Owls can often be seen in the vicinity of Greenlease Farm.

Spring passage is barely over before the first returning autumn waders appear in late June. By early July return wader passage is well underway and until the end of October a stop at the Ferry Pool is recommended. The summering Black-tailed Godwits are soon joined by a handful of Ruff, while a careful scan of the muddy fringes of the pool may well produce a few Common Sandpipers and a Green Sandpiper or two. By late July a wide range of waders may be present, including Little Ringed Plover, Little Stint, and Curlew and Wood Sandpipers. The largest numbers of Little Stints and Curlew Sandpipers occur from late August into September as the passage of juveniles reaches a peak. A similar selection of species can be seen on the Breech Pool adjacent to the North Wall when water levels are right. Autumn is a good time for vagrant Nearctic waders; Pagham Harbour has an impressive list to its name including American Golden Plover, Least, White-rumped, Baird's, Stilt and Buff-breasted Sandpipers, and Wilson's Phalarope.

Another species to look for in late summer and early autumn is Little Egret. Until recently, it was regarded as a rare vagrant in Sussex, but since 1989 the species has become a regular visitor to the county. At low tide it is not unusual to see 20 or more egrets widely scattered around the harbour, but at high tide they gather to roost near the North Wall, where 40–50 may be present. The largest numbers are recorded in autumn and winter, with numbers tailing off in early spring.

Early autumn is also a good season in which to see birds of prey, especially in settled conditions with light northeast winds. Often a Marsh

Harrier hunts over the cereal fields between Sidlesham Ferry and Selsey, and there is always a chance of a Montagu's Harrier or Honey Buzzard passing through. Ospreys are recorded annually and in some years one may choose to linger in the harbour for several days.

Visible migration is more obvious in autumn than in spring. Swifts and Sand Martins begin to leave in July followed, in early August, by Yellow Wagtails which, as well as flying over, can often be found in small parties associating with cattle. Over the next few weeks a wide variety of passerines pass through the area including Tree Pipit, Redstart, Whinchat, Wheatear, Lesser Whitethroat, Whitethroat, Blackcap, Willow Warbler and Spotted Flycatcher. A few Pied Flycatchers are recorded annually at Church Norton while, with good fortune, a Wryneck may be encountered feeding quietly on the beach next to the Severals. When disturbed, this species flies quickly into cover, where it may remain hidden for long periods, much to the frustration of other would-be observers! By late September the Willow Warblers have been replaced by Chiffchaffs, and numbers of Goldcrests start to increase. Small numbers of Firecrests are recorded in October–November and in some years a Yellow-browed or Pallas's Warbler from Siberia. A few Black Redstarts appear towards the end of October and there is often a Dartford Warbler skulking in the gorse between Sidlesham Ferry and Church Norton. Movements of finches in late autumn may include good numbers of Siskins and a few Bramblings.

With the onset of winter, the teeming waders and wildfowl are often disturbed by a hunting Peregrine or Merlin, while the occasional Hen Harrier or Short-eared Owl may also be recorded.

Mention has already been made of some of the rarities recorded at Pagham Harbour. Over the years an impressive collection of vagrants have been recorded; particularly notable were Britain's first Greater and Lesser Sand Plovers, in 1978 and 1997 respectively, the fourth Trumpeter Finch, in 1984, and 11th Sora Rail, in 1985, and the county's first Collared Flycatcher, in 2002.

Timing

Pagham Harbour is well worth visiting at any season. During migration periods, early morning is by far the best time of day, as there is less disturbance and the birds will be feeding more actively. Ferry Pool is best checked in the morning when the light is behind you. After midday the sun will be in your eyes and many of the birds will be silhouetted, making identification more difficult. In winter, it is the tide which is more important. A high tide around midday is best, enabling you to watch for the 2–3 hours either side of it. This brings the waders closer, flushes dabbling duck from the marshes and brings diving duck and grebes into the harbour. Pagham Lagoon is normally only good during winter, as it is heavily disturbed between spring and autumn.

Access

Pagham Harbour is reached via the B2145, which is signed to Selsey and runs south from a roundabout on the A27 Chichester bypass. The best place to start is at the reserve's information centre (which is open at weekends and during the week, when voluntary help is available). This is sited on the left-hand side of the B2145, about half-a-mile south of Sidlesham village. There is a large car park, a welcome public convenience and, at the centre, the latest information on which birds in the area.

Note, however, that break-ins have occurred at this and all the other car parks in the area. The number 51 bus service from Chichester to Selsey stops at the car park entrance. From here, follow the nature trail south to a hide overlooking Ferry Pool. Provided by the Sussex Ornithological Society, it has provision for wheelchairs and can be reached from the car park on a hard path and level ground. To continue along the nature trail, pass through the gate near the hide and turn left. Follow the old tramway along the edge of the harbour and then turn left before the creek onto a path that returns to the centre. For those with more time, it is also possible to walk from the centre to Church Norton. To do this, pass through the gate by the hide, continue straight ahead over the sluice and then turn left onto the narrow path along the west side of the harbour and past the reed-fringed 'Long Pool'. Eventually the footpath leaves the seawall and drops onto the foreshore for a short distance before skirting along the seaward edge of a field adjacent to Church Norton churchyard. Before reaching the churchyard, there is a set of steps down a steep bank, which returns to the foreshore. Continue towards the sea and there is a large hide set on a raised bank affording excellent views of the harbour. The section of path near the hide is very muddy, but this problem has been solved by the use of strategically placed railway sleepers!

Alternatively, there is a small car park at Church Norton. This is a popular area that can become quite crowded, so careful parking is required. Note that this car park serves the church and may be closed at times. To reach it, follow the Selsey road from the information centre; after about 1.5 miles take a sharp left turn on a right-hand bend, signed to Church Norton, and follow the narrow lane. The car park is tucked around to the left at the end. From here, take the path to the edge of the harbour and turn left following the railway sleepers to the hide that overlooks the harbour. Then retrace your steps and continue to the beach, remembering to check for divers, grebes and seaduck on the open sea. A walk south will provide views over the reed-fringed Severals, while in winter it can be worth walking left to the end of the shingle spit to look for birds in the entrance channel. Note, however, that there is no access to the shingle spit in summer, to prevent disturbance to breeding birds, and birdwatchers are asked to show restraint at high tide, at other times, to avoid disturbing the waders roosting at the end of the spit.

From the information centre it is also possible to walk north to Sidlesham. At the end of the footpath turn right into Mill Lane, continue away from the harbour, past the Crab and Lobster pub, and take the footpath on a sharp left-hand bend to Halsey's Farm. Just before the farm take the first footpath on the right and continue along the edge of a copse and across the fields to the North Wall. There is a well-defined path that continues east along the sea wall to the thatched 'Salthouse' cottage, which in summer serves as a second information centre. Inside the sea wall, just before the 'Salthouse' is the Breech Pool, another wader 'hot spot'. A less well-defined path continues along the east side of the harbour to Pagham Lagoon, but eventually you will have to retrace your steps to the information centre at Sidlesham Ferry.

The easiest way to watch Pagham Lagoon is from the car park at its southern end. To reach this, take the B2166, which leaves the Selsey road near the A27, for 5 miles following signs to Pagham. Here, the road swings to the right, signed to 'The Church', but turn sharp left to 'The Sea'. After 300 m, there is a complex junction where you should turn diagonally right across the 'bus turning area' into Beach Road. Follow this road, observing the signs (the unmade road is potholed and has many ramps) and in just over half-a-mile the car park is reached. Look back at the lagoon, but also walk to the tip of the spit where there is a hide, provided by Kay Optical, offering superb views of the harbour. Sadly, it is only possible to open the hide during the winter because of continued vandalism and misuse in summer.

Visitors to the reserve are reminded that dogs must be kept on a lead at all times.

Calendar

Resident: Little Grebe, Grey Heron, Little Egret, Mute Swan, Shelduck, Shoveler, Sparrowhawk, Peregrine, Red-legged and Grey Partridges, Oystercatcher, Ringed Plover, Lapwing, Redshank, Little Owl, Green Woodpecker, Skylark, Reed Bunting.

December–February: Red-throated and Great Northern Divers, Slavonian, Great Crested and Little Grebes, Cormorant, Little Egret, White-fronted Goose, Dark-bellied and Pale-bellied Brent Geese, Black Brant, Wigeon, Pintail, Teal, Eider, Goldeneye, Red-breasted Merganser, Hen Harrier, Merlin, Peregrine, Water Rail, Avocet, Golden and Grey Plovers, Knot, Dunlin, Bar-tailed and Black-tailed Godwits, Whimbrel, Curlew, Spotted Redshank, Greenshank, Turnstone, Glaucous and Mediterranean Gulls, Short-eared Owl, Rock Pipit, Stonechat, Cetti's Warbler, Chiffchaff, Firecrest.

March–May: Spoonbill, Garganey, Shoveler, Marsh Harrier, Osprey, Hobby, Little Ringed and Grey Plovers, Knot, Temminck's Stint, Dunlin, Bar-tailed Godwit, Whimbrel, Greenshank, Green, Wood and Common Sandpipers, Sandwich, Common and Little Terns, Turtle Dove, Cuckoo, hirundines, Black Redstart, Redstart, Whinchat, Wheatear, Cuckoo, Willow Warbler, Spotted and Pied Flycatchers, Goldfinch, Linnet, rarities.

June–July: Little Egret, Shoveler, Eider, Avocet, Little Ringed Plover, Ruff, Black-tailed Godwit, Green and Common Sandpipers, terns, Reed and Sedge Warblers, Lesser Whitethroat.

August–September: Little Egret, Marsh Harrier, Common Buzzard, Osprey, Hobby, Little Ringed Plover, Knot, Little Stint, Curlew Sandpiper, Ruff, Spotted Redshank, Greenshank, Wood and Common Sandpipers, Arctic Skua, Yellow-legged Gull, terns (including Black), Wryneck, Tree Pipit, Yellow and Grey Wagtails (overhead), Redstart, Whinchat, Wheatear, Reed, Sedge and Willow Warblers, *Sylvia* warblers, Spotted and Pied Flycatchers, rarities.

October–November: Red-necked and Slavonian Grebes, Little Egret, Hen Harrier, Merlin, Peregrine, Short-eared Owl, Meadow Pipit, Black Redstart, Dartford Warbler, Goldcrest, Firecrest, Bearded Tit, finches including Siskin and Brambling, rarities.

14 SELSEY BILL AND BRACKLESHAM BAY

Habitat

The southernmost tip of the Selsey peninsula (known as 'the Bill'), which protrudes nearly 5 miles (8 km) from the main West Sussex coastline, is one of the best places in the county to observe seabird movements in the English Channel. It is also a good spot to observe the visible migration of passerines entering and leaving the country and, although the town of Selsey has developed considerably in recent years, there are still some large vegetated gardens behind the beach and a small playing field that attract grounded migrants. The site of the old Pontins holiday camp, described in the previous edition of this book, is sadly now a large housing estate.

To the west of the town is Selsey West Fields, an area of rough grassland and farmland behind a shingle beach that extends west towards Bracklesham and Earnley, and north towards Sidlesham Sewage Works. The shingle sea defences are under constant threat from rising sea levels and are regularly shored up by the EA.

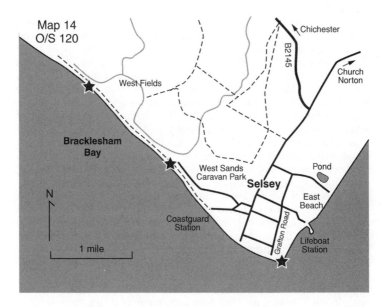

Map 14
O/S 120

Species

In winter it is worth checking the shore from the end of Hillfield Road, past the tip of the Bill to the lifeboat station at East Beach. There is often a wintering Black Redstart to be found in a sheltered spot between the groynes, along with a few Rock Pipits. The wintering Black-headed Gulls are accompanied by increasing numbers of Mediterranean Gulls (up to eight in early 2002), with perhaps a Little Gull after a period of gales. A Glaucous Gull, first seen in 1984, was recorded at East Beach each winter until early 1997. On the sea, especially off the Bill, any of the three divers may be present, with regular sightings of Great Northern in recent winters. Great Crested and Slavonian Grebes, Red-breasted Mergansers and Eider can usually be picked out, although the strong tides mean that birds drift well offshore at times. Large movements of divers and other seabirds may occur in severe weather. A few Oystercatchers and Turnstone are always present.

The West Fields are worth a visit at this season. Flocks of Brent Geese graze the grassland and, if the fields are flooded with winter rain, small numbers of duck may be present. Large flocks of Lapwing and Golden Plover feed on the fields, together with a few Curlews. A wintering Green Sandpiper or a Little Egret may be disturbed from the network of drainage ditches crossing the area. Grey geese are sometimes recorded in severe weather. Wintering raptors include the occasional Hen Harrier, Merlin and, more often, Short-eared Owl though numbers have decreased in recent years with the loss of areas of rough grassland for hunting. Passerines are not very abundant, but a few Skylarks and finches feed among the rank vegetation. Along the field boundaries, small numbers of Reed and Corn Buntings and Yellowhammers might be seen, together with a Stonechat or two. The adjacent West Sands caravan park held a Snow Bunting in late 2002 and is another good spot for a wintering Black Redstart.

Spring migrants are often seen on early dates at Selsey Bill. Most years, Wheatear and Black Redstart occur in the first week of March. These are soon followed by others and, on days in late March, up to 40 or 50 Wheatears can be seen flicking along the beach and perching on the breakwaters. Many Meadow Pipits arrive off the sea during March, with Swallows and House Martins in April and Swifts in May. Despite the encroachment of housing, the area still attracts a few migrants, with perhaps a Redstart, Whinchat or Pied Flycatcher in the Bill House garden or a Yellow Wagtail on the adjacent playing field. On the beach it is worth examining the Pied Wagtails for the much greyer continental race, the White Wagtail. Whilst seawatching, a remarkable range of scarce species has been seen arriving: Marsh Harrier and Hobby are recorded annually, while more unexpected species have included Honey Buzzard, Stone Curlew, Nightjar, Alpine Swift, Kingfisher, Hoopoe, Golden Oriole and Hawfinch! Serins are recorded each spring and sometimes a male will remain to sing in trees and nearby gardens though they rarely stay long; indeed, Selsey Bill is probably the place in Britain to see this small canary-yellow finch from the Mediterranean.

The main feature of spring is the eastbound passage of birds up-Channel. It follows the pattern described earlier for Beachy Head and involves Brent Geese, Common Scoters and Sandwich Terns until mid-April. In the following month, a very wide range of divers, duck, waders, skuas, gulls and terns passes, especially when the wind is from the east or southeast. Selsey Bill does, however, suffer to some extent from the 'sheltering' effect of the Isle of Wight, thus fewer birds are recorded than at more easterly sites. Nevertheless, many birds pass through the narrow waters of the Solent (and thus follow the main coastline), so the views are often excellent. Flocks of Pomarine Skuas are recorded annually and in most years a few Roseate Terns.

The West Fields hold an interesting selection of breeding birds including several pairs of Lapwing and possibly still the occasional pair of Redshank. Waterbirds include up to six pairs of Little Grebes, a pair or two of Shelduck and two pairs of Tufted Ducks. Farmland birds, which have declined significantly in recent years, are well represented by several pairs of Grey Partridges and Corn Buntings. A few Reed and Sedge Warblers and Reed Buntings are found in the wetter ditches, and Stonechats and Whitethroats in patches of bramble and gorse. Seawatching can also be profitable in summer, particularly during and after strong onshore winds. Large feeding flocks of Gannets, totalling several hundred, may be present, whilst other species to look for include Manx and Balearic Shearwaters, Storm Petrel and Arctic Skua. Until recently, Storm Petrel was regarded as a rare visitor to Sussex: in 1996, however, there was an exceptional series of sightings in early July, totalling at least nine birds, enabling many birdwatchers to see this species in the county for the first time. Numbers in subsequent years have fluctuated widely, but 2002 was another good year with possibly as many as 80 birds reported. 2001 will be remembered as the year of the Balearic Shearwater, with over 200 birds recorded in Sussex between mid-July and late September. Selsey Bill received the lion's share of these, with day counts of up to 17 in early August.

Autumn migration commences in late July with a few Wheatears and Willow Warblers but then picks up quickly. August and September bring a very wide range of migrants with numbers rather larger than in spring. Given the loss of habitat at the Bill, warblers and Redstarts are best looked for in the trees and bushes adjacent to the caravan sites at West Fields, while in the more open areas there are Whinchats and Wheatears. Overhead Yellow and Grey Wagtails, Tree Pipits and hirundines move west or south, out to sea. The West Fields attract passage raptors, so it is not a surprise to see a Marsh or Montagu's Harrier, a Common Buzzard or an Osprey drifting through, or a Hobby scything its way out to sea. Easterly winds can bring unusual birds such as a Wryneck or Red-backed Shrike at this time. Seawatching is generally less productive than in spring though a southwest gale can be good, bringing Manx and sometimes a few Sooty Shearwaters, Great and Arctic Skuas, Little Gull and Black Tern.

From late September to early November passage of most summer migrants starts to wind down; Skylarks, hirundines, Meadow Pipits, Pied Wagtails, Goldfinches, Linnets, and, in some years, Siskins and Lesser Redpolls pour south or southwest. With them may be a few Woodlarks or Bramblings. A search of the bushes may reveal a Firecrest among the Goldcrests, while in the more open areas there may be a scattering of Black Redstarts or a Ring Ouzel. By late October, Brent Geese, Wigeon and other wildfowl start their steady build-up, with flocks flying purposefully west to their wintering grounds. Sometimes, too, a Grey Phalarope will drop in after an autumn gale, feeding along the tideline and giving superb views, or a Little Auk might whiz by.

This is also a time when rarities of eastern origin may appear. In recent years these have included Siberian Stonechat, Desert Wheatear, and Pallas's, Yellow-browed and Radde's Warblers.

Timing

Selsey Bill is undoubtedly at its best from early April until mid-May, and again throughout August to mid-November. To seek passerine migrants, either in the bushes, on the ground or flying over, it is best to be out early in the morning. Many strollers, dog-walkers and holidaymakers will be around later, and will invariably scare some birds away. Seawatching is best in spring when there is a light to moderate wind between northeast and south, while in autumn the best winds are gales between southeast and southwest. Like all sites, a light southeast wind is most likely to bring scarcer continental migrants to the area, especially in May and from late August to mid-October. In winter good birdwatching can be had after heavy rain, when the West Fields are flooded, but especially at the onset of a cold spell, when large cold-weather movements of birds may occur.

Access

Selsey Bill is best reached by following the B2145 through the village almost to its end. Just before the sea, turn left into Seal Road and then right at the T-junction into Grafton Road. Park next to the playing field opposite the former coastguard tower known as the Bill House. Most sea-watching is undertaken on the seaward side of the Bill House garden, except in rough weather when the tip of the Bill is more sheltered. Given suitable weather conditions there will inevitably be other seawatchers present, so take a lead from them. Access to Selsey West Fields is through West Sands caravan park, which is at the end of Mill Lane. Drive through the site, keeping the sea on your left until a locked gate and small parking area is reached. From here continue on foot, walking along the top of the beach towards Bracklesham, and view the fields to your right.

Calendar

Resident: Little Grebe, Shelduck, Tufted Duck, Sparrowhawk, Grey Partridge, Lapwing, Redshank, Barn Owl, Yellowhammer, Corn and Reed Buntings.

December–February: Red-throated and Great Northern Divers, Great Crested, Red-necked and Slavonian Grebes, Brent Goose, Shelduck, Eider, Red-breasted Merganser, Hen Harrier, Merlin, Oystercatcher, Golden Plover, Turnstone, Mediterranean and Glaucous Gulls, auks, Short-eared Owl, Rock Pipit, Black Redstart, Stonechat.

March–May: Divers, Manx Shearwater, Fulmar, Gannet, Brent Goose, Eider, Common and Velvet Scoters, Red-breasted Merganser, Marsh Harrier, Osprey, Hobby, Knot, Sanderling, Bar-tailed Godwit, Whimbrel, Common Sandpiper, Pomarine, Arctic and Great Skuas, Mediterranean and Little Gulls, Kittiwake, terns including Roseate and Black, Yellow Wagtail, Redstart, Whinchat, Wheatear, small numbers of warblers, Serin, Gold-finch, Linnet. Look for spring overshoots such as Bee-eater, Alpine Swift or Red-rumped Swallow.

June–July: Manx and Balearic Shearwaters, Storm Petrel, Gannet, Common Scoter, Arctic Skua.

August–November: Sooty and Manx Shearwaters, Brent Goose (mid-September onwards), harriers, Common Buzzard, Merlin, Hobby, Greenshank, Common Sandpiper, Grey Phalarope, skuas, Little Gull, terns, Little Auk (November), Short-eared Owl, Wryneck, Tree Pipit, Yellow, Grey and Pied Wagtails, Black Redstart, Redstart, chats, Wheatear, Ring Ouzel, warblers, Goldcrest, Firecrest, Spotted and Pied Flycatchers, Goldfinch, Linnet.

15 CHICHESTER HARBOUR

Habitat

Chichester Harbour lies southwest of Chichester, with its entrance from the English Channel between Selsey and Hayling Island. The harbour is of national and international importance for landscape and nature conservation, and a number of designations work to ensure its protection. It is an AONB, a Ramsar Wetland of International Importance, a SSSI, a SPA and a candidate Special Area of Conservation. Covering an area of 2,850 ha, part of which is in Hampshire, it comprises four finger-like channels — Emsworth, Thorney, Bosham and Fishbourne — radiating from a southern core area. Most of the intertidal flats are muddy with some eelgrass (*Zostera*) and algae (*Enteromorpha* and *Ulva*) during the warmer months. South of Thorney Island and, to a limited extent, around the harbour mouth, there are areas of sand and shingle. Many of the once-extensive marshes of cord grass (*Spartina*) have suffered dieback, followed by erosion back to a mud base, but this plant remains the dominant species and is especially prominent in the Chichester Harbour Conservancy's Nutbourne Marshes LNR. Small areas of botanically rich marshes are scattered around the harbour; in these, the upright yellow-flowered stems of golden samphire, mauve sea aster and three species of sea lavender push through the dominant sea purslane. At the head of Fishbourne Channel there is a large tidal reedbed.

Most of the land around the harbour is either built-up or intensively farmed. However, a few areas are of special interest, especially as winter roost sites. These are the large sand dune and shingle system at East Head (owned by the NT), a small shingle spit at Ellanore, and inland pools and wet grassland behind Chichester Yacht Basin. However, the most important complex is Thorney Deeps and Thorney Island, virtually all of which is owned by the MoD, but Pilsey Island at the southern tip is an RSPB reserve. The wet grass, scrub and reeds of Thorney Deeps comprise the largest undeveloped area around Chichester Harbour. Two other shingle and saltmarsh islands, North and South Stakes, lie at the southern limit of Nutbourne Marshes LNR. Much of the harbour is used for recreational boating, especially in the summer, while other interests include fishing, walking and wildfowling.

Species

Winter is by far the most important time for birds in the harbour. Then, internationally important numbers of Dark-bellied Brent Geese, Ringed and Grey Plovers, Dunlin, and Bar-tailed and Black-tailed Godwits pour in to feed on the many sheltered mudflats, along with nationally important numbers of Shelduck, Sanderling and Curlew. Most feed inter-tidally but the Brent Geese also feed on grassland and winter cereals, causing problems for coastal farmers. At high tide, spectacular numbers of waders and wildfowl can be seen at close range at the established roost sites, but because of the high levels of disturbance — particularly at weekends — birds do tend to move around. Grey Herons breed nearby and are regular throughout the year, and Little Egrets have become a regular feature in recent years, with nearly 300 recorded at the main roost site in recent

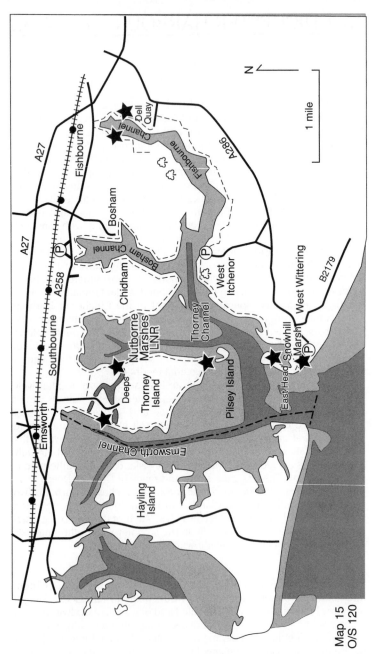

Map 15
O/S 120

autumns. In spring and summer, Common, Sandwich and Little Terns, and Black-headed Gull usually breed and can be seen feeding anywhere in the harbour. Migrant raptors are frequently seen both in spring and autumn, with Marsh Harrier, Common Buzzard, Osprey and Hobby occurring fairly regularly. In winter, sightings of Merlin and Peregrine are regular, the latter hunting the wader roosts.

Little Egret

Main Birdwatching Zones

Many parts of the harbour are accessible by foot, but just two sections are described here to give a flavour of this excellent birdwatching area.

EAST HEAD to WEST ITCHENOR

The sandy areas around East Head harbour a large wader roost during the winter months. Up to 300 Sanderling can be found on the beach on the seaward side of East Head, although they are subject to considerable human disturbance and may move elsewhere. The other species (Ringed and Grey Plovers, Knot, Dunlin, Redshank and up to ten wintering Little Stints) usually concentrate on the sheltered, low saltmarsh area on the inner East Head, but on spring tides they move elsewhere, sometimes as far as Pilsey Island. Winter brings a large flock of over 2,000 Brent Geese. Initially, they feed in the bay inside the spit, but as the season progresses, the grass by the East Head car park is also used, especially at high tide. To be able to sit in the car and watch this vast flock only a short distance away is a fascinating experience. Check carefully for Pale-bellied Brent Goose and Black Brant, both of which have been regular in recent winters. The permanent pastures adjacent to the car park also hold large flocks of Lapwing and Golden Plover in winter, together with a few Ruffs, whilst nearby Snowhill Marsh has a high-tide roost of Snipe and usually a wintering Greenshank or two. The eastern end of the Marsh adjacent to the car park approach road is a good spot for Water Rails, which can often be seen very well. Up to 100 Shelduck can be found among the Brent Geese on the water. A wide range of other wildfowl are here too — Teal and Wigeon among the dabbling duck — while the channel between East Head and Pilsey Island can hold any of the three divers, the five grebes or diving duck. In midwinter Great Crested Grebe, Goldeneye and Red-breasted Merganser are always present, and a careful search of the bobbing shapes may reveal a Slavonian or Red-necked Grebe, a Common or Velvet Scoter or a Guillemot.

Among the many passerines that occur here, it is worth looking for Skylarks, Meadow Pipits, Greenfinches and the occasional Snow Bunting on the tideline, and wintering Stonechats in the dunes. Merlins and Peregrines, which frequent Thorney Island, often make dashing raids over East Head, and sightings of Sparrowhawk are regular.

Migration through the area has been little studied, but the gorse, blackthorn, tamarisks and brambles can hide virtually any of the commoner warblers, while Wheatear and Whinchat perch on the fences around the car park. Although the beach is not ideally sited to observe easterly movements of seabirds and waders in spring, quite substantial numbers of 'Commic', Little and Sandwich Terns, and a few Arctic Skuas and waders, pass sufficiently close to be seen reasonably well.

In summer, small numbers of Ringed Plovers, Shelduck and Redshank breed, but generally there are too many people about to make a visit pleasant.

Autumn migration is not particularly noticeable, although quite substantial numbers of Dunlin and Ringed Plovers can be found roosting at East Head when high water coincides with few dog-walkers. Many passerines, including Pied Flycatchers, Redstarts and Yellow Wagtails, move through the area though numbers are rarely high.

THORNEY ISLAND

Thorney provides perhaps the best birdwatching in Chichester Harbour. It was an island until the saltmarshes between it and the mainland were reclaimed in 1870. These marshes, known as Thorney Deeps, are now brackish grazing marshes with large areas of open saline water, substantial reedbeds and scrub. The island is owned by the MoD and there is no public access, but a footpath around the shore provides excellent views of the harbour. A large, mainly disused airfield towards the southern tip of the island is fringed with small patches of scrub. Mud predominates on the flats to the east and west, but to the south is Pilsey Island, an RSPB reserve to which there is no public access.

Thorney Island is justifiably famous for its wintering birds. The high tide roost at Pilsey Island, which can be seen from the coastal footpath, hosts a spectacular assemblage of waders including up to 15,000 Dunlin, 3,000 Knot, 1,500 Grey Plover, 1,300 Oystercatchers, 800 Bar-tailed Godwits, 600 Ringed Plover and 200 Sanderling. A wintering flock of up to 25 Avocets has become established in recent years. Wildfowl are also much in evidence — small groups of Shelduck, Pintail and Teal forage among the saltmarshes, and very large numbers of Brent Geese commute between the harbour and the mown grass of the airfield. Just off-shore, at the mouth of the Thorney Channel, Great Crested Grebes, Goldeneye and Red-breasted Mergansers can be much in evidence, with up to 30 or more of each. Scarcer species often seen include divers, Slavonian and Red-necked Grebes, Eider, Long-tailed Duck and auks. Wildfowl, too, are a feature of Thorney Deeps. Large numbers of Coot, Wigeon, Gadwall, Teal and Shoveler are joined by an occasional Scaup or Smew, especially in harsh weather. Up to 500 Redshank roost on the Deeps, while wintering waders include up to 20 Greenshanks, a handful of Spotted Redshanks and sometimes a Green or Common Sandpiper.

This assemblage of wildfowl and waders, together with the presence of small wintering flocks of passerines such as Linnets and Greenfinches, attracts many birds of prey. These include regular Merlins and Peregrines, and up to ten Short-eared Owls, which hunt over both the Deeps and the airfield. Barn Owl can sometimes be seen hunting in the same areas. Severe weather may bring flocks of hundreds of Redwings and Fieldfares to the fields, whilst some of the many Water Rails that winter in the Deeps emerge to feed in the open. The sewage works at the junction of Thorney

Road and Thornham Lane has proved attractive to wintering Chiffchaffs in recent years, with up to 26 recorded there. The southern tip of Thorney Island is a good place to look for early migrants, for example, Wheatear and Sandwich Tern, and the reedbeds on the Deeps attract early Sedge and Reed Warblers. Many other passerine migrants filter through during spring. At this time, waders are on the move, often in full breeding plumage. A passage of up to 500 Ringed Plovers during May is notable, and the careful observer may find the odd Kentish Plover with them. Common Sandpipers and parties of Black-tailed Godwits, Whimbrel and Greenshank are among migrant waders to be seen on the Deeps.

There is a diverse breeding bird community here. The Deeps is the most productive area with breeding Little Grebe, Mute Swan, Shelduck, Tufted Duck, Lapwing and Redshank, and a host of passerines. The reedbeds support over 80 pairs of Reed and 60 pairs of Sedge Warblers, three pairs of Cetti's Warblers, five pairs of Bearded Tits and at least ten pairs of Reed Buntings. In the adjacent scrub there are Whitethroats, Linnet and Yellowhammers, and still a few Turtle Doves, while on the farmland there are Grey Partridges and Corn Buntings. A few pairs of Ringed Plovers nest on Pilsey Island, but the terns seen there are mostly from colonies on Nutbourne Marshes LNR. Most of the waders that summer in Chichester Harbour roost on and around Pilsey, including several hundred Oystercatchers and smaller numbers of Bar-tailed Godwits, Grey Plover and Turnstone.

The return passage of waders in late July–August is a major feature. On the Deeps up to 150 Greenshank, 2,000 Redshank and small numbers of Spotted Redshank, Green and Common Sandpipers are a regular feature. By early September, Wigeon, Shoveler and Pintail start to appear, followed a couple of weeks later by the first Brent Geese. The high tide roost on Pilsey Island also increases rapidly, with typical counts of 900 Ringed Plover, up to 2,000 Grey Plover and Dunlin, and 250 Bar-tailed Godwits in late August. On a neap tide they roost on the sands, but if there is disturbance or a high spring tide, they take refuge on the airfield. The wader roost is often disturbed by hunting Peregrines, but keep an eye open too for Osprey, which often occurs here in autumn. 1999 was a particularly good autumn for this species, with a remarkable five recorded at Pilsey on one day in late September! Passerine migration in autumn is good, with the reedbeds at the Deeps providing a roost site for several thousand Swallows and Sand Martins, and smaller numbers of wagtails. The roosts attract dusk raids by Sparrowhawks and Hobbies. The open areas can often, literally, be hopping with Wheatears, Whinchats and, subsequently, Stonechats. Thorney Island is well known for its Little Egret roost on the Deeps. First established in December 1991, it progressively increased in size to a maximum of 281 birds in August 1999. Numbers have been somewhat lower since, with the roost occasionally deserted in favour of Tournerbury Wood on Hayling Island.

Timing

Chichester Harbour is productive all year, although for waders and wildfowl early-morning high tides from August to May are best. By late morning the more popular areas of the harbour are heavily disturbed and the likelihood is that the birds will have dispersed elsewhere. To watch birds to and from their roosts it is necessary to be present about two hours either side of high water. Being south-facing, it can be difficult looking into the sun off the southern tips of Thorney Island or the Chidham peninsula, so slightly overcast conditions are best, as are very light winds. The relatively exposed nature of the harbour and some fairly long walks mean that if there are strong winds and rain, birdwatching can become very uncomfortable. Hard weather can bring in many geese and duck, but it has the opposite effect on other species, such as Black-tailed Godwit and Golden Plover, for they decrease in numbers sharply.

Access

Chichester Harbour is bounded to the north by the A259 Chichester–Havant road, to the east by the A286 Chichester–West Wittering road and to the west by the A3023 on Hayling Island. There are many points of access to the shore, and there is a now a long-distance footpath around most of the 40 miles of shoreline. Car parking is, however, limited. For access to the car park at East Head, take the A286 Chichester to West Wittering road. In West Wittering turn right by the Old House at Home pub and follow the unclassified road towards the beach. Entrance to the car park, which is open 6.30am–8.30pm in summer, and 7am–6pm, in winter, is via a pay barrier. Access to East Head is at the far end of the car park, where it is also possible to walk north along the narrow path beside the harbour to view Snowhill Marsh. There is also a pay-and-display car park in West Itchenor. West Wittering is accessible by bus service 53 from Chichester, but there is no public transport to West Itchenor.

Access to Thorney Island is via Thorney Road, which runs south from the A259 just east of Emsworth. If possible, park by the junction of Thorney Road and Thornham Lane, which lies about a quarter-of-a-mile south of the A259. From here you can gain access to the seawalls on the east and west sides of Thorney Island, the former by following Thornham Lane to its end, the latter by following the footpath west across the fields. On reaching the seawalls, walk south for views of the Deeps and surrounding harbour. For the energetic it is possible to walk around the entire island. This affords fine views of the harbour and makes an excellent viewpoint to watch the many thousands of waders and wildfowl. Access, which is through a MoD security gate, is strictly limited to the public footpath. Allow a whole day to get the most out of this 7 mile walk.

Neither of the areas described above is suitable for wheelchair users. There are, however, paths constructed for wheelchairs at Prinsted and Cobnor, both of which offer views of the harbour. There are also plans to construct a long-distance wheelchair path from Chichester to East Head within the next year or two.

Calendar

Resident: Little Grebe, Cormorant, Little Egret, Grey Heron, Mute Swan, Shelduck, Tufted Duck, Sparrowhawk, Grey Partridge, Oystercatcher, Ringed and Grey Plovers, Black-tailed and Bar-tailed Godwits, Curlew, Redshank, Turnstone, Stock Dove, Little and Barn Owls, Cetti's Warbler, Bearded Tit, Linnet, Yellowhammer, Reed and Corn Buntings.

December–February: Divers, Great Crested and Slavonian Grebes, Dark-bellied and Pale-bellied Brent Goose, Black Brant, Wigeon, Gadwall, Teal, Pintail, Scaup, Eider, Long-tailed Duck, Common and Velvet Scoters, Goldeneye, Red-breasted Merganser, Hen Harrier, Merlin, Peregrine, Avocet, Golden Plover, Knot, Sanderling, Little Stint, Dunlin, Ruff, Jack Snipe, Snipe, Black-tailed and Bar-tailed Godwits, Spotted Redshank,

Greenshank, Guillemot, Short-eared Owl, Skylark, Rock Pipit, Grey Wagtail, Fieldfare, Redwing, Chiffchaff, Greenfinch, Linnet, Snow Bunting.

March–May: Marsh Harrier, Osprey, Hobby, Kentish Plover, Whimbrel, Greenshank, Common Sandpiper, Mediterranean Gull, Sandwich, Common and Little Terns, Cuckoo, Redstart, Whinchat, Whitethroat, Willow Warbler, Yellowhammer.

June–July: Turtle Dove, Sedge and Reed Warblers, Lesser Whitethroat. Wader numbers start to increase from July.

August–November: Wintering wildfowl appear from mid-September, Marsh Harrier, Osprey, Hobby, Little Stint, Curlew Sandpiper, Spotted Redshank, Redshank, Greenshank, Green and Common Sandpipers, Little Gull, Black Tern, Kingfisher, Yellow Wagtail, migrant hirundines, warblers and chats, Spotted Flycatcher, Goldfinch.

16 KINGLEY VALE   OS Explorer 120

Habitat

This outstanding NNR encompasses the largest remaining yew forest in the world, within which is a grove of ancient trees, some over 500 years old, and among the oldest living things in Britain. It is also one of the most important archaeological sites in southern England. Its 14 scheduled ancient monuments include Bronze Age burial mounds at the top of Bow Hill, from which there are superb panoramic views of the surrounding area.

The reserve's woods also contain many other shrub and tree species, the berries and seeds of which provide food for winter flocks of thrushes. On the thin chalk soils of the steep valley slopes there is a rich downland turf with up to 50 species of flowering plants within a square metre, including several species of orchids. The plateau at the top of Bow Hill has a capping of clay overlying the chalk, which produces a very unusual type of vegetation called chalk heath. Here, acid loving plants such as heather and gorse occur alongside more typical chalk plants like thyme and salad burnet. Associated with the herbs and fine grasses is a large number of invertebrates. Of the 58 species of butterfly that breed in England, 39 have been recorded at Kingley Vale, including Chalkhill Blue, Brown Argus, Dark Green Fritillary and Grizzled Skipper in the more open areas, and Purple and Green Hairstreaks and White Admiral in the scrub and deciduous woodland.

Species

Much of the birdlife present in winter months is associated with the wealth of berry-bearing trees and shrubs. In some years an exceptionally

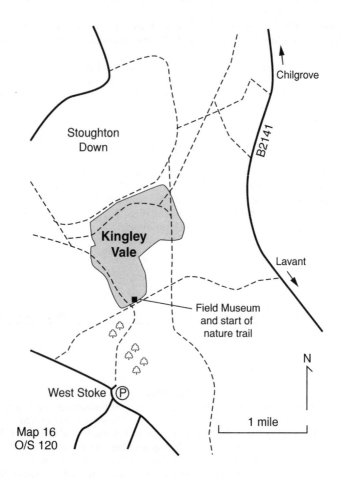

heavy crop, particularly of yew and hawthorn, can attract large numbers of thrushes and finches. In poor crop years much smaller numbers of birds are present.

By late October, the first returning Redwings and Fieldfares are seen. Perhaps their calls will give them away: the Redwing with its thin *sseeip* and the *schack-schack-schack* of the Fieldfare penetrating through the woodland. Both continental and British Song Thrushes and Blackbirds join the feast, whilst the large, noisy and aggressive Mistle Thrushes can be picked out by their larger size, more powerful flight with longer undulations, and white underwings.

Although numbers of finches have decreased in recent years, flocks of Greenfinches and Chaffinches do occur, the latter sometimes accompanied by a handful of white-rumped Bramblings. Hawfinches were recorded in the past though it would be a very fortunate observer who caught a glimpse of this increasingly scarce bird. Tits concentrate in mobile flocks in winter; a careful search through these should reveal Marsh, Long-tailed and Coal as well as the commoner species. The dense scrub holds small numbers of wintering Woodcock, but they are far from easy to locate, unless flushed or seen in flight at dusk.

In recent years, the population of Common Buzzards in Sussex has grown from just a handful of pairs to well over 100. The Downs in the west of the county hold most of these, and it not unusual on a fine day in early spring to hear the plaintive mewing of a pair displaying over the reserve. Other raptors include Kestrel, Sparrowhawk, Hobby (in summer) and Tawny Owl, although the latter is rarely seen and much more likely to be heard hooting, even by day. By mid-March the repetitive *silt salt* of the Chiffchaff heralds the arrival of spring migrants, followed soon after by the descending song of the Willow Warbler. Other sounds to listen for in early spring are the drumming of Great Spotted Woodpeckers and the penetrating *peeu peeu peeu* of a Nuthatch, the latter from the mature trees along the entrance track to the reserve.

Spring merges into summer as Blackcaps, Whitethroats and Lesser Whitethroats, and the occasional Garden Warbler, appear and sing from the scrub. By far the most difficult to separate are the first and last, although with practice the slightly melancholy flute-like notes that close the Blackcap's song are distinctive. Open patches of scrub attract Whitethroat, while the others species prefer denser areas. Nightingales used to breed but no longer do so. The reasons for this are unclear though a possible explanation lies with the loss of nest sites due to Roe and Fallow Deer browsing the understorey. The yew forest is remarkably devoid of birds, but the more diverse areas containing a variety of shrub and tree species hold such attractive birds as Long-tailed Tit and Bullfinch. Yellowhammers sing in the more open areas. Several pairs of Tawny Owls are present, although they are usually only seen when their downy youngsters emerge to sit in the open in midsummer, enduring with equanimity the scolding of a host of passerines, or at dusk. At this time of day, the lucky observer may catch a glimpse of a roding Woodcock or a Little Owl sitting motionless on a boundary fence post.

Kingley Vale was formerly *the* place in Sussex to see the gaudy Golden Pheasant, an introduced species native to the uplands of central China. Sadly, there has been a marked decline in numbers in recent years, so much so that it is probably now extinct on the reserve and very likely in the whole of West Sussex.

For a short period after their songs cease birds can be difficult to see, but then the fledged young emerge and join the autumn migrants. Willow Warblers move through in August followed by *Sylvia* warblers taking advantage of the feast of blackberries and elderberries. A few Redstarts, Whinchats and Spotted Flycatchers may also occur at this time. A Hobby might be spotted overhead, perhaps in fast pursuit of a passing juvenile Swallow or House Martin. By mid-October the haws are ripening, ready to welcome and sustain the thrushes in winter. Thereafter finches are moving and, in some years, Siskins and Lesser Redpolls may pass overhead.

Timing

Kingley Vale is best visited in spring and summer, when the diversity of birds, insects and plants is at its greatest. Given the absence of traffic noise, there are few better places in the county to hear the dawn chorus, though obviously a very early start is essential! Butterflies are best looked for on warm and sunny days; several visits will be needed to see all of the regularly occurring species.

Access

Kingley Vale is situated north of the hamlet of West Stoke, 2 miles west of Mid Lavant through which runs the A286 Chichester–Midhurst road. Access to the reserve is gained by a 15-minute walk along the wide track that runs north from the main car park near West Stoke, at SU 825088. The track is suitable for wheelchairs in the summer but is often muddy in winter. At the reserve's entrance there is a small field centre with permanent displays and more information about the reserve. From here a 2-mile nature trail, covering most of the habitats, is signposted. Other footpaths can be taken to explore the area further. Details are available in a nature trail leaflet produced by EN.

Calendar

Resident: Sparrowhawk, Common Buzzard, Kestrel, Woodcock, Stock Dove, Little and Tawny Owls, Green and Great Spotted Woodpeckers, Stock Dove, Goldcrest, Long-tailed, Marsh and Coal Tits, Nuthatch, Treecreeper, Bullfinch, Yellowhammer.

December–February: Fieldfare, Redwing, Mistle Thrush, Chaffinch, Greenfinch.

April–June: Hobby, Cuckoo, *Sylvia* warblers, Chiffchaff, Willow Warbler.

August–September: Redstart, Wheatear, Whinchat, Spotted Flycatcher.

17 AMBERSHAM, IPING AND STEDHAM COMMONS

OS Explorer 133

Habitat

Ambersham, Iping and Stedham Commons represent some of the best remaining open heathland in West Sussex. They are situated on a band of greensand that extends south and east from the Hampshire/West Sussex border at Liss, to Washington in West Sussex. Though now highly fragmented, studies of the habitats and species have shown that the lowland heathland of Sussex is of national and international significance. Much of the former heathland in this area has been reclaimed for agriculture, planted with conifers or exploited for sand and gravel. Succession on the remaining areas is an ever-present threat, but is currently held at bay by the cooperative efforts of the Sussex Downs Conservation Board, EN, West Sussex County Council, the Sussex Wildlife Trust, the NT and local landowners, coordinated by the West Sussex Heathland Forum. These sites are perhaps the most accessible of the

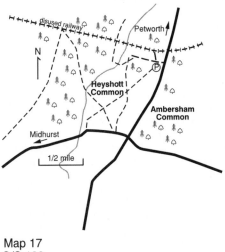

Map 17
O/S 133

Wealden Heaths and provide the visitor with a flavour of what these once-extensive heathlands must have been like.

Species

Taken as a whole, the Wealden Heaths are one the most important sites in Britain for three heathland specialists — Nightjar, Woodlark and Dartford Warbler — and all three can be found at Ambersham, Iping and Stedham.

Although these heaths can seem remarkably birdless in winter, a visit on a fine day in February onwards will almost certainly be rewarded by the evocative song of the Woodlark, as the males re-establish their breeding territories. Early mornings are best, and on some occasions it is possible to find several males in the air together. The lucky birdwatcher may catch a glimpse of a Hen Harrier at dawn or dusk, quartering the heath with its wings held in the classic shallow V, whilst soaring Sparrowhawks and Common Buzzards may be seen from any raised vantage point in early spring.

Woodlark

As the days lengthen, Stonechats become more obvious, calling and singing from the tops of the gorse. Green Woodpeckers frequent the open heath, and the nearby birch and conifer woodland also supports Great Spotted Woodpeckers, and very occasionally Lesser Spotted Woodpecker too. A typical woodland bird community is found here, including Goldcrest, all the tits (except Willow), Nuthatch and Treecreeper. The birches around the heath provide winter feeding for flocks of Lesser Redpolls and Siskins, some of which may remain to breed, whilst stands of conifers should be checked for Crossbills, especially following the periodic irruptions characteristic of this species. Flocks of Chaffinches may hold the occasional Brambling.

March and April brings Chiffchaffs and Willow Warblers, followed soon after by Tree Pipit, whose parachuting song flight is a characteristic feature of the heath in spring and summer. On warm, still days Dartford Warblers sing from the tops of the gorse bushes and heather, while other breeders include Yellowhammer and Linnet, with Reed Bunting in the wetter areas. Garden Warblers frequent the trees adjoining the car park at Iping Common, whilst the occasional pair of Redstarts may breed on Ambersham Common.

By early to mid May the first Nightjars will have arrived, and at dusk their churring song can be heard across the heath. In order to see this crepuscular species, it is best to arrive about half an hour before sunset, and wait for the birds to start calling. Once the churring stops, which usually means the bird has taken flight, listen for the loud slap of the male's wing-clapping display and watch for its white wing patches and tail spots as it flies between song posts. The roding Woodcock's *piss-p* call adds to the special atmosphere of heathland in summer. The patient observer may also be rewarded by views of a Hobby hunting dragonflies over the heath, whilst Tawny Owl can be heard hooting from the adjacent woodland as darkness descends.

In early autumn, family parties of Stonechats and Dartford Warblers can be found scattered across the heath. Look also for Whinchats and Wheatears, which pass through on their return migration to warmer climes. Nightjars continue to churr well into August while Hobbies become more obvious now that they have young to feed. As winter approaches, the heaths are at their quietest. Varying numbers of Stonechats remain in residence, depending on the severity of the weather. Dartford Warblers too remain on the heaths, except in hard weather, often accompanying the Stonechats. The reasons for this association are open to speculation, but it is possible that the warblers may gain advantage from the greater vigilance of the Stonechats. A passing Hen Harrier may disturb a loose flock of Meadow Pipits, and this is *the* season to find a Great Grey Shrike. Although by no means annual, this species has occurred several times in the past and could be encountered on any of the Wealden Heaths.

Timing

Spring and early summer is the best time to visit these sites. To hear Nightjars, a dusk visit on a warm windless evening is recommended; aim to arrive about sunset so you can be in position well before they start calling. For virtually all other species, an early-morning visit on a warm, still day will give by far the best results. Then birds are at their most vocal and active, and there is less disturbance from other visitors.

Access

Ambersham Common is situated 2.5 miles southeast of Midhurst. It is best approached from the minor road that runs north across the common towards South Ambersham. There are a number of small parking areas, from which there is a network of paths, the best of which is the broad firebreak that runs northwest from the minor road towards Little London. The heath on the west side of the road holds Nightjar, Woodlark and Dartford Warbler, while the trees on the east side of the road can be good for Siskin and Crossbill. The disused railway line north of the common gives access to more wooded areas.

Iping and Stedham LNR is 1.5 miles west of Midhurst on the A272. A car park with a height barrier is situated 100 m along the road to Elsted on the right-hand side. Iping Common lies to the west, Stedham to the east. From here a network of paths, some on firebreaks, radiate out, with the main one leading west northwest towards the highest part of the common; this accesses a good range of habitats. For woodland it is best to walk 150 m further down the road to where a track leads east. This track skirts both coniferous and deciduous woodland, and also a deep sand pit where Sand Martins sometimes occur.

At all these sites, it is important that visitors remain on the paths to avoid unnecessary disturbance to breeding birds.

Calendar

Resident: Sparrowhawk, Common Buzzard, Woodcock, Tawny Owl, Green and Great Spotted Woodpeckers, Woodlark, Skylark, Dartford Warbler and Stonechat (both in mild winters), Goldcrest, Long-tailed, Marsh and Coal Tits, Treecreeper, Nuthatch.

November–March: Hen Harrier, Meadow Pipit, Redwing, Fieldfare, Siskin, Lesser Redpoll, Crossbill, possibly Great Grey Shrike.

April–August: Hobby, Cuckoo, Nightjar (May onwards), Tree Pipit, Redstart, Whinchat and Wheatear (on passage), Whitethroat, Garden Warbler, Blackcap, Willow Warbler, Linnet, Yellowhammer, Reed Bunting.

Mandarin

ADDITIONAL SITES

Key & Site	Habitat	Birds of Interest	Peak Season	Nearest Town
A Fore Wood	Deciduous woodland, coppice	Sparrowhawk, woodpeckers, warblers, Marsh Tit, Nuthatch, possibly Hawfinch	Spring/ summer	Crowhurst
OS Explorer 124 TQ 752130	*An RSPB reserve. Park at the village hall opposite Crowhurst church (TQ 765126). Can be very muddy after heavy rain.*			
B Arlington Reservoir	Reservoir, scrub, farmland	Great Crested Grebe, wildfowl including Smew and Goosander in cold weather, Osprey, passage waders, Little Gull, terns (including Black), Cuckoo, Turtle Dove, Nightingale	All year	Polegate
OS Explorer 123 TQ 533075	*South East Water LNR. Pay-and-display car park (closes at dusk) and toilets off B2108. Circular path (1.75 miles/2.8 km) with hide in northeast corner and disabled access to dam. Handy railway station at Berwick. Groups wishing to visit should contact South East Water's Conservation and Recreation Department (tel: 01323 870810).*			
C Lewes Levels	Wet grassland, ditches	Wildfowl, birds of prey, Lapwing and other waders, migrants	Spring/ winter	Lewes
OS Explorer 122 TQ 420080	*Main area is west of the River Ouse. Footpaths along banks of river and from A26 Lewes–Newhaven road. Birds dependent on amount of shallow surface flooding.*			
D Newhaven Tidemills	Tidal creek, shingle beach, fields, harbour	Purple Sandpiper, Kittiwake, Kingfisher, Black Redstart, Wheatear	All year	Newhaven
OS Explorer 122 TQ 458002	*Access from car parks on A259 Newhaven–Seaford road or at west end of Seaford promenade. Wintering Purple Sandpipers best viewed from east arm of harbour at high tide. Autumn flocks of terns can be viewed off Newhaven beach.*			
E Chailey Common	Heathland	Cuckoo, Tree Pipit, Stonechat, warblers (including Dartford)	Spring/ summer	Haywards Heath
OS Explorer 122 TQ 390215	*An East Sussex County Council LNR. Car parks situated off roads crossing the common.*			
F Brighton Marina	Marina, with views out to sea	Divers, Fulmar, Shag, Purple Sandpiper, passage seaduck, waders and seabirds, Kittiwake, auks, Rock Pipit, Black Redstart, storm-driven seabirds in late autumn	Spring/ autumn/ winter	Brighton
OS Explorer 122 TQ 330034	*Car park inside marina. Spring seawatching is best from western arm with a good southeast wind. Eastern arm worth checking for wintering divers, Shags, auks.*			

Key & Site	Habitat	Birds of Interest	Peak Season	Nearest Town
G Weir Wood Reservoir	Reservoir with shallow water, woodland and scrub	Grebes, nesting Grey Heron, wildfowl, Osprey, passage waders, Kingfisher, warblers, woodland birds	All year	East Grinstead
OS Explorer 135 TQ385343	*An unclassified road crosses the western end and another runs to the south, with a car park at the southwest corner and path to hide. The western section is a LNR.*			
H Ardingly Reservoir	Reservoir, woodland	Grebes, wildfowl, Sparrowhawk, warblers		Haywards Heath
OS Explorer 135 TQ 330295	*Owned by South East Water. Car parking is provided near the dam, and two hides are available for public use. Can be viewed from causeway on the minor road between Ardingly and Balcombe, but note parking is restricted.*			
I Wakehurst Place	Woodland, parkland, lakes	Woodland birds, finches (winter)	All year	Balcombe
OS Explorer 135 TQ 340315	*The grounds of this old house are owned by the NT and managed by the Royal Botanic Gardens, Kew. Access is via a large car park off the B2028. Free entry for NT members, charge for non-members. Access to the Loder Valley nature reserve is by permit only from the Wakehurst Place administration.*			
J Buchan Park	Woodland, meadows, ponds, heathland	Sparrowhawk, Woodcock, possibly Lesser Spotted Woodpecker, passerines, Siskin, Lesser Redpoll	All year	Crawley
OS Explorer 134 TQ 245315	*A Country Park managed by West Sussex County Council. The car park is situated just off the A2220 Crawley–Horsham road. The centre has toilets, and refreshments are available at weekends and Bank Holidays.*			
K Ebernoe Common	Pasture, woodland, grassland, ponds, hedgerows	Little Grebe, Mandarin, Woodcock, all three woodpeckers, Nightingale, warblers, Marsh Tit, Nuthatch	Spring	Nutchapel
OS Explorer 133 SU 975278	*The reserve car park is located off the minor road east of the A283 at the grid reference indicated. An information board shows public footpaths through the woodland.*			
L Blackdown	Woodland, scrub, ponds, heathland	Sparrowhawk, Woodcock, Nightjar, woodpeckers, Tree Pipit, Wood Warbler, Crossbill	Spring/ summer	Haslemere
OS Explorer 133 SU 920293	*This forested hill (the highest point in Sussex) is managed by the NT, who is restoring parts of the site to heathland. It provides an excellent vantage point over the surrounding countryside.*			

SYSTEMATIC LIST OF SPECIES

This species list, which closely follows the sequence and scientific nomenclature of *Handbook of the Birds of Europe, the Middle East and North Africa* (Cramp *et al.* 1977–94), includes all species recorded in Kent, Surrey and Sussex during the period 1900–2002 inclusive. A brief description of the status of each species follows, based on the records published in *Birds of Kent* (1981), *Birds in Surrey* (1972), *Birds of Sussex* (1996) and more recent annual county reports. For species that provide a spectacle for birdwatchers, and those with local or restricted distributions, a few sites are identified where these birds may be anticipated.

Red-throated Diver   *Gavia stellata*
Annual winter visitor and coastal passage migrant. Occasional on inland waters.
Sites: Kent — 3, 9. Sussex — 1, 6, 7, 14, F.

Black-throated Diver   *Gavia arctica*
Scarce but annual winter visitor to coastal waters. Occasional inland. Regular passage migrant off the coast.
Sites: Kent — 9. Sussex — 6, 7, 14, F.

Great Northern Diver   *Gavia immer*
Scarce but annual winter visitor to coastal waters. Rare inland. Small but regular spring passage off the coast.
Sites: Sussex — 13, 14.

White-billed Diver   *Gavia adamsii*
Very rare vagrant.

Pied-billed Grebe   *Podilymbus podiceps*
Very rare vagrant.

Little Grebe   *Tachybaptus ruficollis*
Widespread breeding species. Forms large wintering flocks in late autumn.
Sites: Kent — 1b. Surrey — 9. Sussex — 1, 3, 7, 12.

Great Crested Grebe   *Podiceps cristatus*
Widespread breeding species, mainly at inland freshwater sites, passage migrant and winter visitor. Flocks gather around the coast.
Sites: Kent — 3, 9, 11, 12. Surrey — 3, 4, 5, 8. Sussex — 1, 3, 12, 13, B, H.

Red-necked Grebe   *Podiceps grisegena*
Annual winter visitor to coastal waters and inland. Scarce coastal passage migrant.
Sites: Kent — 9, 12. Sussex — 7, 13, 14, 15, F.

Slavonian Grebe *Podiceps auritus*
Annual winter visitor to coastal waters, but rarer inland. Scarce coastal passage migrant.
Sites: Kent — 2, 9. Sussex — 13, 14, 15.

Black-necked Grebe *Podiceps nigricollis*
Annual visitor, less common in winter than the previous two species, but seen more frequently at other times of the year, apart from midsummer. Has bred.
Sites: Kent — 9. Surrey — 4. Sussex — 7, 12, F.

Black-browed Albatross *Diomedea melanophris*
Very rare vagrant.

Fulmar *Fulmarus glacialis*
Passage migrant and breeding species on coastal cliffs. Scarce in late autumn. Very rare inland.
Sites: Kent — 6, 8, H, I. Sussex — 2, 6, 7, 14, F.

Cory's Shearwater *Calonectris diomedea*
Rare vagrant.

Great Shearwater *Puffinus gravis*
Very rare vagrant.

Sooty Shearwater *Puffinus griseus*
Scarce but regular in autumn off coast.
Sites: Sussex — 14.

Manx Shearwater *Puffinus puffinus*
Annual passage migrant, mainly in May–October, off coast. Occasional inland following gales.
Sites: Kent — 3, 6, 9. Sussex — 7, 14, F.

Balearic Shearwater *Puffinus mauretanicus*
Scarce but regular passage migrant in summer and autumn off coast. Has occurred inland.
Sites: Kent — 8, 9. Sussex — 14, F.

Little Shearwater *Puffinus assimilis*
Very rare vagrant.

Storm Petrel *Hydrobates pelagicus*
Rare autumn and winter vagrant, mainly after severe gales. Now seen almost annually in small numbers in midsummer.
Sites: Sussex — 14.

Leach's Petrel *Oceanodroma leucorhoa*
Scarce but regular in late autumn. Rare inland, usually after gales.
Sites: Kent — 1, 3, 6, 9, D.

Gannet *Morus bassanus*
Passage migrant, most numerous in autumn on coast. Rare inland.
Sites: Kent — 3, 6, 7, 9. Sussex — 6, 7.

Cormorant   *Phalacrocorax carbo*
Increasingly widespread, commonly seen on inland waters. Recently established breeding colonies.
Sites: Kent — 5, 9. Surrey — 4. Sussex — 1, 9, 12, 13, 15.

Shag   *Phalacrocorax aristotelis*
Coastal passage migrant and winter visitor, occasional on inland waters.
Sites: Kent — 6, H, I. Surrey — 1. Sussex — 8, 14, F.

Bittern   *Botaurus stellaris*
Scarce but increasing winter visitor, occasionally remaining to late spring. Has bred.
Sites: Kent — 5, 9, 12. Surrey — 2, 9. Sussex — 1, 12.

American Bittern   *Botaurus lentiginosus*
Very rare vagrant.

Little Bittern   *Ixobrychus minutus*
Very rare vagrant.

Night Heron   *Nycticorax nycticorax*
Rare vagrant.

Squacco Heron   *Ardeola ralloides*
Very rare vagrant.

Cattle Egret   *Bubulcus ibis*
Very rare vagrant.

Little Egret   *Egretta garzetta*
Almost resident, mainly around the coast and adjacent marshes. Occasional inland. Large communal roosts in autumn and winter. Increasing as a breeder.
Sites: Kent — 1, 2, 3, 5, 7, 9. Sussex — 1, 7, 9, 13, 15.

Great White Egret   *Egretta alba*
Very rare vagrant.

Grey Heron   *Ardea cinerea*
Widespread resident.
Sites: Kent — 1c. Surrey — 1, 3, 4, 13. Sussex — 5, 9, 15.

Purple Heron   *Ardea purpurea*
Rare, mainly a spring vagrant.

Black Stork   *Ciconia nigra*
Very rare vagrant.

White Stork   *Ciconia ciconia*
Rare vagrant.

Glossy Ibis   *Plegadis falcinellus*
Very rare vagrant.

Spoonbill *Platalea leucorodia*
Almost annual visitor in small numbers, most frequent in spring and autumn. Rarer inland.

Mute Swan *Cygnus olor*
Widespread resident. Large non-breeding flocks form during summer.
Sites: Kent — 3, 5, J. Surrey — 4. Sussex — 5, 8, 9, 10, 15.

Bewick's Swan *Cygnus columbianus*
Regular passage migrant and winter visitor to traditional sites. Occasional elsewhere.
Sites: Kent — 1, 3, 5, 9, H. Sussex — 8, 9.

Whooper Swan *Cygnus cygnus*
Scarce passage migrant and winter visitor.
Sites: Kent — 9.

Taiga Bean Goose *Anser fabalis fabalis*
Rare winter visitor.

Tundra Bean Goose *Anser fabalis rossicus*
Scarce passage migrant and winter visitor.
Sites: Kent — 3. Sussex — 1.

Pink-footed Goose *Anser brachyrhynchus*
Scarce passage migrant and winter visitor.

White-fronted Goose *Anser albifrons*
Regular passage migrant and winter visitor.
Sites: Kent — 1, 3, 9. Sussex — 1, 7, 9.

Lesser White-fronted Goose *Anser erythropus*
Very rare vagrant.

Greylag Goose *Anser anser*
Increasingly widespread resident feral populations. Scarce passage migrant and winter visitor.

Snow Goose *Anser caerulescens*
Very rare vagrant, but status unclear as a result of escapes.

Canada Goose *Branta canadensis*
Increasingly widespread resident feral populations.

Barnacle Goose *Branta leucopsis*
Scarce winter visitor. Occasional cold-weather influxes. An increasing feral resident.

Dark-bellied Brent Goose *Branta bernicla bernicla*
Regular passage migrant and winter visitor. A few oversummer.
Sites: Kent — 1, 2, 3, 9. Sussex — 13, 15.

Pale-bellied Brent Goose *Branta bernicla hrota*
Scarce winter visitor.
Sites: Kent — 3, 7. Sussex — 13, 15.

Black Brant *Branta bernicla nigricans*
Rare but annual winter visitor.
Sites: Kent — 3. Sussex — 13, 15.

Red-breasted Goose *Branta ruficollis*
Very rare vagrant.

Egyptian Goose *Alopochen aegyptiacus*
Scarce but increasing resident. Has bred recently.

Ruddy Shelduck *Tadorna ferruginea*
Rare vagrant, but status unclear as a result of escapes. Feral birds occasionally breed.

Shelduck *Tadorna tadorna*
Common resident, passage migrant and winter visitor to coast. Breeds inland annually.
Sites: Kent — 1, 2, 3, 7. Sussex — 1, 7, 13, 15.

Mandarin *Aix galericulata*
Increasing introduced resident.
Sites: Kent — 11, N. Surrey — 4, 9, 11. Sussex — 4, 9, G, L.

Wigeon *Anas penelope*
Common passage migrant and winter visitor. Has bred.
Sites: Kent — 3, 9. Surrey — 4. Sussex — 3, 7, 9, 13, 15.

American Wigeon *Anas americana*
Very rare vagrant.

Gadwall *Anas strepera*
Scarce but increasing breeding species. Passage migrant and common winter visitor.
Sites: Kent — 1, 5, 12. Surrey — 3. Sussex — 1, 3, 9, 12.

Teal *Anas crecca*
Scarce breeding species. Passage migrant and common winter visitor.

Green-winged Teal *Anas carolinensis*
Rare vagrant.

Mallard *Anas platyrhynchos*
Widespread breeding species, passage migrant and winter visitor.

Black Duck *Anas rubripes*
Very rare vagrant.

Pintail   *Anus acuta*
Regular passage migrant and winter visitor, mainly to coastal areas. Occasionally summers and has bred.
Sites: Kent — 1, 2, 3.   Surrey — 1, 2.   Sussex 9, 13, 15.

Garganey   *Anas querquedula*
Scarce passage migrant and summer visitor. A few pairs breed annually.
Sites: Kent — 1, 3, 5, 9.   Surrey — 4, 9.   Sussex — 1, 5, 9, 13.

Blue-winged Teal   *Anas discors*
Very rare vagrant.

Shoveler   *Anas clypeata*
Widespread but thinly distributed breeding species. Common passage migrant and winter visitor.
Sites: Kent — 1, 2, 3, 9.   Surrey — 1, 4.   Sussex — 1, 9, 12, 15.

Red-crested Pochard   *Netta rufina*
Scarce winter visitor. Status undoubtedly confused by escapes and feral breeding population.

Pochard   *Aythya ferina*
Common passage migrant and winter visitor. Uncommon breeding species.
Sites: Kent — 1, 9, 12.   Surrey — 2, 4.   Sussex — 1, 12.

Canvasback   *Aythya valisineria*
Very rare vagrant.

Ring-necked Duck   *Aythya collaris*
Rare vagrant.

Ferruginous Duck   *Aythya nyroca*
Rare vagrant. True status confused by escapes.

Tufted Duck   *Aythya fuligula*
Widespread breeder and winter visitor. Passage migrant.

Scaup   *Aythya marila*
Passage migrant and winter visitor to coastal waters. Scarce inland.
Sites: Kent — 2, 9.   Sussex — 1.

Eider   *Somateria mollissima*
Winter visitor, passage migrant and non-breeding summer visitor to coast. Very rare inland.
Sites: Kent — 3, 6, 7, 9.   Sussex — 13, 14, 15.

King Eider   *Somateria spectabilis*
Very rare vagrant.

Long-tailed Duck   *Clangula hyemalis*
Uncommon but regular passage migrant and winter visitor, mainly to coastal areas. Occasional on inland waters.
Sites: Kent — 9.   Sussex — 12, 13, 15.

Common Scoter *Melanitta nigra*
Common spring passage migrant and winter visitor, less common non-breeding summer visitor to coast. Scarce inland.
Sites: Kent — 3, 6, 7, 9. Sussex — 1, 6, 7, 14, F.

Surf Scoter *Melanitta perspicillata*
Very rare vagrant.

Velvet Scoter *Melanitta fusca*
Regular passage migrant and winter visitor in small numbers on coast. Has summered. Very rare inland.
Sites: Kent — 9. Sussex — 1, 6, 7, 14, F.

Goldeneye *Bucephala clangula*
Regular passage migrant and winter visitor. Has summered.
Sites: Kent — 1, 2, 9. Surrey — 4, 9. Sussex — 3, 13, 15.

Smew *Mergus albellus*
Scarce but regular winter visitor. Occasional cold-weather influxes.
Sites: Kent — 9, 12. Surrey — 4. Sussex — 1, 12.

Red-breasted Merganser *Mergus serrator*
Regular passage migrant and winter visitor to coast. A few summer annually. Scarce inland.
Sites: Kent — 2, 3, 9. Sussex — 13, 14, 15.

Goosander *Mergus merganser*
Uncommon but regular winter visitor and passage migrant. Occasional cold weather influxes.
Sites: Kent — 9, 11. Surrey — 3, 4, 6. Sussex — 3, B.

Ruddy Duck *Oxyura jamaicensis*
Increasingly common introduced breeding species and winter visitor.
Sites: Kent — 1, 9, 11. Surrey — 4. Sussex — 1, 9, 12.

Honey Buzzard *Pernis apivorus*
Scarce but increasing spring and autumn passage migrant. Now breeds annually.
Sites: Sussex — 6.

Black Kite *Milvus migrans*
Rare mainly spring passage migrant.

Red Kite *Milvus milvus*
Scarce but increasing visitor, mainly in spring and autumn.

White-tailed Eagle *Haliaeetus albicilla*
Very rare winter visitor.

Marsh Harrier *Circus aeruginosus*
Passage migrant showing a marked increase in recent years. Now breeding and wintering regularly.
Sites: Kent — 3, 5, J. Sussex — 1, 6, 13, 15.

278

Hen Harrier   *Circus cyaneus*
Regular winter visitor and passage migrant. Forms roosts in winter months. Has bred.
Sites: Kent — 1, 3, 5, J.   Surrey — 7, 9.   Sussex — 1, 4, 5, 9, 17.

Pallid Harrier   *Circus macrourus*
Very rare vagrant.

Montagu's Harrier   *Circus pygargus*
Scarce but regular passage migrant. Occasionally breeds.

Goshawk   *Accipiter gentilis*
Scarce visitor. A few pairs now breed.

Sparrowhawk   *Accipiter nisus*
Widespread. Increasing breeding species, common passage migrant and winter visitor.

Common Buzzard   *Buteo buteo*
A scarce but increasing breeding resident, passage migrant and winter visitor.
Sites: Sussex — 8, 9, 16, 17.

Rough-legged Buzzard   *Buteo lagopus*
Rare winter visitor and passage migrant.
Sites: Kent — 3.

Osprey   *Pandion haliaetus*
Annual spring and autumn passage migrant. Occasional summer records.
Sites: Kent — 3, 5, 11.   Sussex — 3, 7, 13, 15, B, G.

Lesser Kestrel   *Falco naumanni*
Very rare vagrant.

Kestrel   *Falco tinnunculus*
Widespread breeding species. Passage migrant in small numbers.

Red-footed Falcon   *Falco vespertinus*
Rare vagrant.

Merlin   *Falco columbarius*
Passage migrant and annual winter visitor.
Sites: Kent — 1, 3, 7, 9.   Surrey — 7, 9.   Sussex — 1, 5, 6, 13, 14, 15.

Hobby   *Falco subbuteo*
Increasing breeding summer visitor and passage migrant.
Sites: Kent — 5.   Surrey — 7, 9.   Sussex — 1, 5, 7, 9, 11, 17.

Gyrfalcon   *Falco rusticolus*
Very rare vagrant.

Peregrine   *Falco peregrinus*
Increasing resident, passage migrant and winter visitor. A few pairs now breed.
Sites: Kent — 1, 2, 3, 7, 8, 9, H. Surrey — 1. Sussex — 2, 6, 7, 8, 9, 13, 15.

Black Grouse   *Tetrao tetrix*
Formerly bred. Introductions survived until the 1930s.

Red-legged Partridge   *Alectoris rufa*
Widespread resident, locally common.

Grey Partridge   *Perdix perdix*
Widespread but decreasing resident.

Quail   *Coturnix coturnix*
Scarce summer visitor, recorded in variable numbers from year to year.
Sites: Sussex — 8.

Pheasant   *Phasianus colchicus*
Common and widespread resident. Numbers boosted each year by release of birds for shooting.

Golden Pheasant   *Chrysolophus pictus*
Scarce introduced resident, now close to extirpation in Sussex.

Water Rail   *Rallus aquaticus*
Regular passage migrant and winter visitor. Uncommon breeding species.
Sites: Kent — 5. Surrey — 5, 9. Sussex — 1, 10, 13, 15.

Spotted Crake   *Porzana porzana*
Scarce mainly autumn passage migrant.

Sora Rail   *Porzana carolina*
Very rare vagrant.

Little Crake   *Porzana parva*
Very rare vagrant.

Baillon's Crake   *Porzana pusilla*
Very rare vagrant.

Corncrake   *Crex crex*
Rare passage migrant, very occasionally heard in summer. Formerly bred.

Moorhen   *Gallinula chloropus*
Common and widespread resident.

Coot   *Fulica atra*
Common, widespread resident and winter visitor.

American Coot   *Fulica americana*
Very rare vagrant.

Crane *Grus grus*
Rare passage migrant and winter visitor.

Little Bustard *Tetrax tetrax*
Very rare vagrant.

Great Bustard *Otis tarda*
Very rare vagrant.

Oystercatcher *Haematopus ostralegus*
Regular breeding species, passage migrant and winter visitor to coast.
Scarce inland.
Sites: Kent — 2, 3, 7, 9. Sussex — 1, 13, 15.

Black-winged Stilt *Himantopus himantopus*
Rare mainly spring vagrant.

Avocet *Recurvirostra avosetta*
Increasing passage migrant, winter and breeding summer visitor. Rare
inland.
Sites: Kent — 1, 2, 3, 9. Sussex — 1, 7, 13, 15.

Stone Curlew *Burhinus oedicnemus*
Rare passage migrant. Formerly bred.

Cream-coloured Courser *Cursorius cursor*
Very rare vagrant.

Collared Pratincole *Glareola pratincola*
Rare vagrant.

Oriental Pratincole *Glareola maldivarum*
Very rare vagrant.

Black-winged Pratincole *Glareola nordmanni*
Very rare vagrant.

Little Ringed Plover *Charadrius dubius*
Regular passage migrant, but scarce breeding summer visitor.
Sites: Kent — 9. Surrey — 2, 4. Sussex — 9, 13.

Ringed Plover *Charadrius hiaticula*
Common passage migrant and winter visitor. Local coastal breeder.
Scarce inland, breeding irregularly.
Sites: Kent — 1, 2, 3, 7. Surrey — 4. Sussex — 1, 13, 15, F.

Killdeer *Charadrius vociferus*
Very rare vagrant.

Kentish Plover *Charadrius alexandrinus*
Scarce but regular passage migrant in spring and autumn.
Sites: Kent — 7, 9. Sussex — 15.

Lesser Sand Plover   *Charadrius mongolus*
Very rare vagrant.

Greater Sand Plover   *Charadrius leschenaultii*
Very rare vagrant.

Dotterel   *Charadrius morinellus*
Scarce but regular passage migrant in spring and autumn.

American Golden Plover   *Pluvialis dominica*
Very rare vagrant.

Pacific Golden Plover   *Pluvialis fulva*
Very rare vagrant.

Golden Plover   *Pluvialis apricaria*
Widespread passage migrant and winter visitor. Commonest around coastal areas.
Sites: Kent — 1, 2, 3, 7, J. Surrey — 4, R. Sussex — 5, 13, 14, 15.

Grey Plover   *Pluvialis squatarola*
Common passage migrant and winter visitor to coast. Scarce inland.
Sites: Kent — 1, 2, 3, 7, 9. Sussex — 13, 15.

Sociable Plover   *Chettusia gregaria*
Very rare vagrant.

Lapwing   *Vanellus vanellus*
Widespread but declining breeding species. Common passage migrant and winter visitor.

Knot   *Calidris canutus*
Common passage migrant and winter visitor to coast. Rare inland.
Sites: Kent — 1, 3, 7, 9. Sussex — 13, 15.

Sanderling   *Calidris alba*
Common passage migrant and winter visitor to coast. Scarce inland.
Sites: Kent — 6, 7, 9. Sussex — 1, 10, 15.

Semipalmated Sandpiper   *Calidris pusilla*
Very rare vagrant.

Little Stint   *Calidris minuta*
Regular passage migrant, commoner in autumn.
Sites: Kent — 1, 3, 7, 9. Surrey — A. Sussex — 1, 13, 15.

Temminck's Stint   *Calidris temminckii*
Scarce but regular passage migrant.
Sites: Kent — 1, 3, 7, 9. Sussex — 7, 13.

Least Sandpiper   *Calidris minutilla*
Very rare vagrant.

White-rumped Sandpiper   *Calidris fuscicollis*
Rare vagrant.

Baird's Sandpiper   *Calidris bairdii*
Very rare vagrant.

Pectoral Sandpiper   *Calidris melanotos*
Scarce but regular autumn vagrant.

Sharp-tailed Sandpiper   *Calidris acuminata*
Very rare vagrant.

Curlew Sandpiper   *Calidris ferruginea*
Scarce spring passage migrant, regular in autumn.
Sites: Kent — 1, 3, 7, 9. Sussex — 1, 13.

Purple Sandpiper   *Calidris maritima*
Regular winter visitor to a few coastal sites. Rare inland.
Sites: Kent — 6, I. Sussex — 2, 9, D, F.

Dunlin   *Calidris alpina*
Abundant winter visitor and common passage migrant. Scarce in summer and inland.
Sites: Kent — 1, 2, 3, 7, 9. Sussex — 13, 15.

Broad-billed Sandpiper   *Limicola falcinellus*
Rare mainly spring vagrant.

Stilt Sandpiper   *Micropalama himantopus*
Very rare vagrant.

Buff-breasted Sandpiper   *Tryngites subruficollis*
Very rare vagrant.

Ruff   *Philomachus pugnax*
Regular passage migrant and winter visitor.
Sites: Kent — 1, 3, 5. Surrey — 4, A. Sussex — 9, 13, 15.

Jack Snipe   *Lymnocryptes minimus*
Scarce but regular winter visitor and passage migrant.
Sites: Sussex — 1, 5, 15.

Snipe   *Gallinago gallinago*
Declining local breeding species. Widespread passage migrant and winter visitor.
Sites: Kent — 5. Surrey — 9. Sussex — 5, 9, 15.

Great Snipe   *Gallinago media*
Very rare autumn vagrant.

Long-billed Dowitcher   *Limnodromus scolopaceus*
Very rare vagrant.

Woodcock   *Scolopax rusticola*
Widespread breeding species. Common winter visitor and passage migrant.
Sites: Kent — 4, 10, K, M, P. Surrey — 7, 9, M. Sussex — 4, 17, L, M.

Black-tailed Godwit   *Limosa limosa*
Locally common winter visitor and passage migrant. A few pairs breed.
Sites: Kent — 1, 2, 3. Sussex — 13, 15.

Bar-tailed Godwit   *Limosa lapponica*
Common passage migrant and winter visitor to coast. Scarce inland.
Sites: Kent — 3, 7, 9. Sussex — 6, 7, 15, F.

Whimbrel   *Numenius phaeopus*
Regular passage migrant.
Sites: Kent — 1, 2, 3, 7, 9. Sussex — 1, 5, 6, 7, 9, 13, F.

Curlew   *Numenius arquata*
Common winter visitor and passage migrant. Scarce inland, but breeds annually.
Sites: Kent — 1, 2, 3, 7. Surrey — 9. Sussex — 1, 4, 13, 15.

Upland Sandpiper   *Bartramia longicauda*
Very rare vagrant.

Spotted Redshank   *Tringa erythropus*
Passage migrant, more numerous in autumn than spring. Small numbers overwinter.
Sites: Kent — 3. Sussex — 13, 15.

Redshank   *Tringa totanus*
Widespread but declining breeding species away from the coast. Common passage migrant and winter visitor.

Marsh Sandpiper   *Tringa stagnatilis*
Rare vagrant.

Greenshank   *Tringa nebularia*
Regular passage migrant. Small numbers overwinter.
Sites: Kent — 1, 2, 3, 7. Surrey — 4, A. Sussex — 7, 13, 15.

Greater Yellowlegs   *Tringa melanoleuca*
Very rare vagrant.

Lesser Yellowlegs   *Tringa flavipes*
Very rare vagrant.

Solitary Sandpiper   *Tringa solitaria*
Very rare vagrant.

Green Sandpiper   *Tringa ochropus*
Regular, widespread passage migrant. Small numbers overwinter.

Wood Sandpiper   *Tringa glareola*
Regular passage migrant, commoner in autumn. Scarcer inland.
Sites: Kent — 1, 3, 5, 9. Surrey — 4, 6, A. Sussex — 1, 5, 7, 13.

Terek Sandpiper   *Xenus cinereus*
Very rare vagrant.

Common Sandpiper   *Actitis hypoleucos*
Widespread passage migrant. Small numbers overwinter. Has bred.
Sites: Kent — 1, 7. Surrey — 1, 4, A. Sussex — 7, 9, 15.

Spotted Sandpiper   *Actitis macularia*
Very rare vagrant.

Turnstone   *Arenaria interpres*
Common winter visitor and passage migrant. Scarce inland.
Sites: Kent — 3, 6. Sussex — 1, 8, 13, 15, F.

Wilson's Phalarope   *Phalaropus tricolor*
Very rare vagrant.

Red-necked Phalarope   *Phalaropus lobatus*
Scarce passage migrant, more frequent in autumn.

Grey Phalarope   *Phalaropus fulicarius*
Scarce autumn and winter visitor, usually after gales.

Pomarine Skua   *Stercorarius pomarinus*
Passage migrant, regular in spring along south coast and in autumn more
often on the north coast. Rare in winter and inland.
Sites: Kent — 1, 3, 6, 9, D. Sussex — 6, 7, 14, D, F.

Arctic Skua   *Stercorarius parasiticus*
Common coastal passage migrant in spring and autumn. Scarce in win-
ter and inland.
Sites: Kent — 1, 3, 6, 9, D. Sussex — 6, 7, 14, D, F.

Long-tailed Skua   *Stercorarius longicaudus*
Scarce passage migrant, more regular in autumn. Very rare inland.

Great Skua   *Stercorarius skua*
Regular passage migrant in spring and autumn. Scarce in winter and
inland.
Sites: Kent — 1, 3, 6, 9, D. Sussex — 6, 7, 14, D, F.

Mediterranean Gull   *Larus melanocephalus*
Increasingly regular around the coast and at a few inland sites. Breeding
numbers also increasing.
Sites: Kent — 2, 6, 9, I. Sussex — 1, 7, 8, 13, 14, 15, F.

Laughing Gull   *Larus atricilla*
Very rare vagrant.

Franklin's Gull   *Larus pipixcan*
Very rare vagrant.

Little Gull   *Larus minutus*
Regular spring and autumn passage migrant. Small numbers occur in winter and summer.
Sites: Kent — 3, 9. Surrey — 4. Sussex — 1, 6, 7, 14, B, D, F.

Sabine's Gull   *Larus sabini*
Scarce autumn passage migrant on the coast. Rare inland.

Bonaparte's Gull   *Larus philadelphia*
Very rare vagrant.

Black-headed Gull   *Larus ridibundus*
Common breeder around the coast. Widespread passage migrant and winter visitor.

Slender-billed Gull   *Larus genei*
Very rare vagrant.

Ring-billed Gull   *Larus delawarensis*
Rare vagrant.

Common Gull   *Larus canus*
Common passage migrant and winter visitor. Small local breeding population.
Sites: Kent — 9.

Lesser Black-backed Gull   *Larus fuscus graellsii*
Widespread passage migrant and winter visitor. An increasing number of pairs breed on rooftops mainly in coastal towns.

   (Scandinavian) Lesser Black-backed Gull   *Larus fuscus intermedius*
   Regular passage migrant and winter visitor.

Herring Gull   *Larus argentatus argenteus*
Common breeding resident, passage migrant and winter visitor.

   Yellow-legged Gull   *Larus argentatus michahellis*
   Regular visitor, most frequent in late summer and autumn.
   Sites: Kent – 1, 9, A. Surrey — 4. Sussex — 8, 13.

   Caspian Gull   *Larus argentatus cachinnans*
   Rare, mainly coastal visitor.
   Sites: Kent — 9. Surrey — 4.

Iceland Gull   *Larus glaucoides*
Scarce winter visitor and passage migrant.

Glaucous Gull   *Larus hyperboreus*
Scarce winter visitor and passage migrant.
Sites: Kent — 6, 7, 9. Sussex — 13.

Great Black-backed Gull *Larus marinus*
Common winter visitor and passage migrant. A few pairs breed.
Sites: Sussex — D, F

Kittiwake *Rissa tridactyla*
Common passage migrant and winter visitor. Large local breeding populations. Scarce inland.
Sites: Kent — 8. Sussex — 7.

Ivory Gull *Pagophila eburnea*
Very rare vagrant.

Gull-billed Tern *Gelochelidon nilotica*
Very rare vagrant.

Caspian Tern *Sterna caspia*
Rare vagrant.

Royal Tern *Sterna maxima*
Very rare vagrant.

Lesser Crested Tern *Sterna bengalensis*
Very rare vagrant.

Sandwich Tern *Sterna sandvicensis*
Common passage migrant and summer visitor, scarcer inland. Breeds at a few coastal sites. Occasionally overwinters.
Sites: Kent — 3, 7, 9. Sussex — 1.

Roseate Tern *Sterna dougallii*
Scarce summer visitor and passage migrant.
Sites: Kent — 7, 9. Sussex — 1, 14.

Common Tern *Sterna hirundo*
Common passage migrant and summer visitor. A few pairs breed inland; larger colonies present around the coast.
Sites: Kent — 1, 2, 5, 7, 9. Surrey — 4, 6. Sussex — 1, 9, 12, 15.

Arctic Tern *Sterna paradisaea*
Regular passage migrant in spring and autumn.
Sites: Kent — 3, 9. Surrey — 4. Sussex — 7, 12, F.

Forster's Tern *Sterna forsteri*
Very rare vagrant.

Bridled Tern *Sterna anaethetus*
Very rare vagrant.

Sooty Tern *Sterna fuscata*
Very rare vagrant.

Little Tern   *Sterna albifrons*
Passage migrant and summer visitor. Small numbers breed locally around the coast. Scarce inland.
Sites: Kent — 1, 3, 5, 7, 9. Sussex — 1, 13, 14, 15.

Whiskered Tern   *Chlidonias hybridus*
Very rare vagrant.

Black Tern   *Chlidonias niger*
Passage migrant, regularly seen along the coast and on inland waters.
Sites: Kent — 3, 5, 9. Surrey — 4, 9. Sussex — 1, 6, 7, 12, 14, D, F.

White-winged Black Tern   *Chlidonias leucopterus*
Rare vagrant, more often in autumn around the coast.

Guillemot   *Uria aalge*
Common passage migrant and winter visitor to coast. Formerly bred. Rare inland.
Sites: Kent — 1, 3, 6, 9. Sussex — 1, 9, 14, F.

Razorbill   *Alca torda*
Passage migrant and winter visitor to coast, less common than Guillemot. Formerly bred. Rare inland.
Sites: Kent — 3, 6, 9. Sussex — 9, F.

Black Guillemot   *Cepphus grylle*
Rare vagrant.

Little Auk   *Alle alle*
Scarce but regular late-autumn passage migrant.
Sites: Kent: 3, 6, 7, 9, D. Sussex — 14, F.

Puffin   *Fratercula arctica*
Scarce passage migrant.

Pallas's Sandgrouse   *Syrrhaptes paradoxus*
Very rare vagrant.

Feral Rock Dove   *Columba livia*
Widespread resident, particularly in association with human habitation.

Stock Dove   *Columba oenas*
Widespread resident.

Woodpigeon   *Columba palumbus*
Abundant resident and winter visitor.

Collared Dove   *Streptopelia decaocto*
Widespread resident.

Turtle Dove   *Streptopelia turtur*
Passage migrant and widespread, but decreasing, summer visitor.

Ring-necked Parakeet *Psittacula krameri*
Locally common introduced resident, but absent from Sussex.
Sites: Kent — 6. Surrey — 3, 4, P.

Great Spotted Cuckoo *Clamator glandarius*
Very rare vagrant.

Cuckoo *Cuculus canorus*
Widespread but decreasing summer visitor and passage migrant.

Yellow-billed Cuckoo *Coccyzus americanus*
Very rare vagrant.

Barn Owl *Tyto alba*
Thinly but widely distributed resident.
Sites: Kent — 1, 3, J. Sussex — 1, 5, 9, 15.

Scops Owl *Otus scops*
Very rare vagrant.

Snowy Owl *Nyctea scandiaca*
Very rare vagrant. Status confused by escapes.

Little Owl *Athene noctua*
Widespread resident.

Tawny Owl *Strix aluco*
Widespread resident.

Long-eared Owl *Asio otus*
Thinly distributed breeding species, passage migrant and winter visitor.
Sites: Kent — 1, 3.

Short-eared Owl *Asio flammeus*
Scarce breeding species. Passage migrant and winter visitor mainly to coastal areas.
Sites: Kent — 1, 3, 7. Surrey — 4. Sussex — 1, 5, 9, 13, 14, 15.

Nightjar *Caprimulgus europaeus*
Locally common summer visitor, rarely seen on passage.
Sites: Kent — 4, 10, M, P.S. Surrey — 7, 9, H, M. Sussex — 4, 17.

Common Nighthawk *Chordeiles minor*
Very rare vagrant.

White-throated Needletail *Hirundapus caudacutus*
Very rare vagrant.

Swift *Apus apus*
Widespread summer visitor and passage migrant.

Pallid Swift *Apus pallidus*
Very rare vagrant.

Alpine Swift *Apus melba*
Scarce but almost annual vagrant.

Kingfisher *Alcedo atthis*
Widespread resident.

Blue-cheeked Bee-eater *Merops persicus*
Very rare vagrant.

Bee-eater *Merops apiaster*
Scarce but almost annual vagrant. Has bred.

Roller *Coracias garrulus*
Very rare vagrant.

Hoopoe *Upupa epops*
Scarce but regular passage migrant. Occasional winter records. Has bred.

Wryneck *Jynx torquilla*
Scarce but regular passage migrant, more frequent in autumn. Formerly bred.

Green Woodpecker *Picus viridis*
Widespread resident.

Great Spotted Woodpecker *Dendrocopos major*
Widespread resident. Autumn passage migrant on coast.

Lesser Spotted Woodpecker *Dendrocopos minor*
Thinly distributed, decreasing resident.
Sites: Sussex — 6, 13.

Short-toed Lark *Calandrella brachydactyla*
Very rare vagrant

Crested Lark *Galerida cristata*
Very rare vagrant.

Woodlark *Lullula arborea*
Locally common and increasing breeding species. Passage migrant mainly on coast in autumn.
Sites: Kent — 8, 9. Surrey — 7, 9, G. Sussex — 4, 17.

Skylark *Alauda arvensis*
Widespread but declining resident. Common passage migrant and winter visitor.

Shore Lark *Eremophila alpestris*
Scarce winter visitor and passage migrant.

Sand Martin *Riparia riparia*
Common passage migrant and local breeding summer visitor.

Crag Martin   *Ptyonoprogne rupestris*
Very rare vagrant.

Swallow   *Hirundo rustica*
Widespread summer visitor and passage migrant.

Red-rumped Swallow   *Hirundo daurica*
Rare spring and autumn vagrant.

House Martin   *Delichon urbica*
Widespread summer visitor and passage migrant.

Richard's Pipit   *Anthus novaeseelandiae*
Rare but regular autumn vagrant, very rare in spring.

Blyth's Pipit   *Anthus godlewskii*
Very rare vagrant.

Tawny Pipit   *Anthus campestris*
Scarce passage migrant in both spring and autumn.

Olive-backed Pipit   *Anthus hodgsoni*
Very rare vagrant.

Tree Pipit   *Anthus trivialis*
Local breeding summer visitor and passage migrant.
Sites: Kent — 4, 10, G, R. Surrey — 7, 9, 10, 12. Sussex — 4, 17, E, M.

Meadow Pipit   *Anthus pratensis*
Widespread breeding species, particularly around the coast. Common passage migrant and winter visitor.

Red-throated Pipit   *Anthus cervinus*
Very rare vagrant.

Rock Pipit   *Anthus petrosus*
Scarce local breeding species, passage migrant and winter visitor. Rare away from coast.
Sites: Kent — 1, 2, 3, 6, 7, 8, H, I. Sussex — 6, 7, 8, 14, F.

Scandinavian Rock Pipit   *Anthus petrosus littoralis*
Scarce annual winter visitor, most obvious on spring migration.

Water Pipit   *Anthus spinoletta*
Scarce winter visitor and passage migrant.
Sites: Kent — 3, 5, 7. Surrey — 5. Sussex — 15.

Yellow Wagtail   *Motacilla flava flavissima*
Widespread but local summer visitor and passage migrant.
Sites: Kent — 1, 3, 5, F, J. Surrey — A. Sussex — 1, 5, 6, 7, 13, 14.

Blue-headed Wagtail   *Motacilla flava flava*
Local summer visitor and passage migrant.
Sites: Kent — 3, 7. Sussex — 5.

Citrine Wagtail   *Motacilla citreola*
Very rare vagrant.

Grey Wagtail   *Motacilla cinerea*
Widespread resident and passage migrant, particularly in autumn.
Sites: Kent — 12, N, O. Surrey — 5. Sussex — 4, 9, 11.

Pied Wagtail   *Motacilla alba yarrellii*
Widespread resident and passage migrant.

  White Wagtail   *Motacilla alba alba*
  Passage migrant.

Waxwing   *Bombycilla garrulus*
Scarce winter visitor. Occasional eruption years.

Dipper   *Cinclus cinclus*
Rare winter vagrant.

Wren   *Troglodytes troglodytes*
Abundant resident.

Dunnock   *Prunella modularis*
Widespread resident.

Alpine Accentor   *Prunella collaris*
Very rare vagrant.

Rufous Bush Robin   *Cercotrichas galactotes*
Very rare vagrant.

Robin   *Erithacus rubecula*
Abundant resident and winter visitor.

Thrush Nightingale   *Luscinia luscinia*
Very rare vagrant.

Nightingale   *Luscinia megarhynchos*
Locally common summer visitor. Infrequently seen passage migrant.
Sites: Kent — 1, 4, 12, K, L. Surrey — 9, 11, K. Sussex — 9, B.

Bluethroat   *Luscinia svecica*
Scarce passage migrant.

Red-flanked Bluetail   *Tarsiger cyanurus*
Very rare vagrant.

Black Redstart   *Phoenicurus ochruros*
Scarce breeder. Regular passage migrant and winter visitor.
Sites: Kent — 6, 7, 8, 9, H. Surrey — 1, 4, 6. Sussex — 6, 7, 8, 14, F.

Redstart   *Phoenicurus phoenicurus*
Local breeding summer visitor and passage migrant.
Sites: Kent — R. Surrey — 7, 9, 12, G. Sussex — 4, 17.

Whinchat *Saxicola rubetra*
Widespread passage migrant, particularly in autumn. Has bred.

Stonechat *Saxicola torquata*
Local breeding species, partial migrant and winter visitor.
Sites: Kent — 1, 3, 7, 9, 10, A, R. Surrey — 7, 9, G. Sussex — 4, 6, 7, 8, 17, E.

Siberian Stonechat *Saxicola torquata maura*
Rare passage migrant

Isabelline Wheatear *Oenanthe isabellina*
Very rare vagrant.

Wheatear *Oenanthe oenanthe*
Very local breeding summer visitor and common passage migrant.
Sites: Kent — 9. Sussex — 1, D.

Pied Wheatear *Oenanthe pleschanka*
Very rare vagrant.

Black-eared Wheatear *Oenanthe hispanica*
Very rare vagrant.

Desert Wheatear *Oenanthe deserti*
Very rare vagrant.

Rock Thrush *Monticola saxatilis*
Very rare vagrant.

Swainson's Thrush *Catharus ustulatus*
Very rare vagrant.

Ring Ouzel *Turdus torquata*
Regular passage migrant, more common in autumn.
Sites: Kent — 7, 8, 9. Sussex — 2, 6, 7, 8, 13.

Blackbird *Turdus merula*
Abundant resident, passage migrant and winter visitor.

Black-throated Thrush *Turdus ruficollis*
Very rare vagrant.

Fieldfare *Turdus pilaris*
Common passage migrant and winter visitor.

Song Thrush *Turdus philomelos*
Widespread resident, passage migrant and winter visitor.

Redwing *Turdus iliacus*
Common passage migrant and winter visitor. Has bred.

Mistle Thrush *Turdus viscivorus*
Widespread resident and partial migrant.

American Robin *Turdus migratorius*
Very rare vagrant.

Cetti's Warbler *Cettia cetti*
Scarce breeding resident and occasional passage migrant.
Sites: Kent — 5, 12. Sussex — 1, 9, 13, 15.

Grasshopper Warbler *Locustella naevia*
Scarce and declining summer visitor and passage migrant.
Sites: Sussex — 6, 9.

Savi's Warbler *Locustella luscinioides*
Rare passage migrant. Has bred.

Aquatic Warbler *Acrocephalus paludicola*
Scarce autumn passage migrant.

Sedge Warbler *Acrocephalus schoenobaenus*
Locally common summer visitor and passage migrant.
Sites: Kent — 5. Surrey — 5. Sussex — 1, 5, 9, 15.

Paddyfield Warbler *Acrocephalus agricola*
Very rare vagrant.

Blyth's Reed Warbler *Acrocephalus dumetorum*
Very rare vagrant.

Marsh Warbler *Acrocephalus palustris*
Scarce but regular breeding summer visitor and passage migrant.

Reed Warbler *Acrocephalus scirpaceus*
Locally common summer visitor and passage migrant.
Sites: Kent — 5. Surrey — 2, 9. Sussex — 1, 5, 9, 15.

Great Reed Warbler *Acrocephalus arundinaceus*
Rare vagrant.

Booted Warbler *Hippolais caligata*
Very rare vagrant.

Icterine Warbler *Hippolais icterina*
Scarce passage migrant.

Melodious Warbler *Hippolais polyglotta*
Scarce passage migrant.

Dartford Warbler *Sylvia undata*
Locally common resident, partial autumn migrant and winter visitor.
Sites: Kent — 9. Surrey — 7, 9. Sussex — 2, 4, 6, 13, 15, 17.

Subalpine Warbler *Sylvia cantillans*
Rare vagrant.

Sardinian Warbler *Sylvia melanocephala*
Very rare vagrant.

Desert Warbler *Sylvia nana*
Very rare vagrant.

Barred Warbler *Sylvia nisoria*
Scarce autumn passage migrant.

Lesser Whitethroat *Sylvia curruca*
Common summer visitor and passage migrant.

Whitethroat *Sylvia communis*
Widespread summer visitor and passage migrant.

Garden Warbler *Sylvia borin*
Widespread summer visitor and passage migrant.

Blackcap *Sylvia atricapilla*
Widespread summer visitor and passage migrant. A few winter.

Greenish Warbler *Phylloscopus trochiloides*
Rare vagrant.

Arctic Warbler *Phylloscopus borealis*
Very rare vagrant.

Pallas's Warbler *Phylloscopus proregulus*
Scarce but increasingly regular late-autumn vagrant.
Sites: Kent — 6, 7, 8, 9. Sussex — 6.

Yellow-browed Warbler *Phylloscopus inornatus*
Scarce but regular vagrant, mainly in autumn.
Sites: Kent — 3, 6, 7, 8, 9. Sussex — 6, 10.

Hume's Warbler *Phylloscopus humei*
Very rare autumn vagrant.

Radde's Warbler *Phylloscopus schwarzi*
Very rare autumn vagrant.

Dusky Warbler *Phylloscopus fuscatus*
Very rare autumn vagrant.

Western Bonelli's Warbler *Phylloscopus bonelli*
Very rare vagrant.

Wood Warbler *Phylloscopus sibilatrix*
Passage migrant and local breeding summer visitor but declining.
Sites: Sussex — 4. Surrey — 9.

Chiffchaff *Phylloscopus collybita*
Widespread summer visitor and passage migrant. Small numbers winter.

Siberian Chiffchaff *Phylloscopus collybita tristis*
Scarce late-autumn migrant and winter visitor.
Sites: Kent — 6, 7, 9. Sussex — 9.

Iberian Chiffchaff *Phylloscopus ibericus*
Very rare vagrant.

Willow Warbler *Phylloscopus trochilus*
Widespread summer visitor and passage migrant.

Goldcrest *Regulus regulus*
Widespread breeding species and passage migrant.

Firecrest *Regulus ignicapillus*
Rare breeding species and scarce but regular passage migrant. A few
overwinter.
Sites: Kent — 6, 7, 8, 9, 10, G. Surrey — 9, E. Sussex — 1, 2, 6, 7, 9, 10, 13.

Spotted Flycatcher *Muscicapa striata*
Widespread, but declining summer visitor and passage migrant.

Red-breasted Flycatcher *Ficedula parva*
Rare spring vagrant, scarce but regular in autumn.

Collared Flycatcher *Ficedula albicollis*
Very rare vagrant.

Pied Flycatcher *Ficedula hypoleuca*
Scarce spring and regular autumn passage migrant. Has bred.
Sites: Kent — 3, 6, 7, 8, 9. Sussex — 6, 13.

Bearded Tit *Panurus biarmicus*
Local breeding species, passage migrant and winter visitor.
Sites: Kent — 5. Sussex — 1, 15.

Long-tailed Tit *Aegithalos caudatus*
Widespread resident.

Marsh Tit *Parus palustris*
Widespread, possibly declining resident.
Sites: Kent — 4, 10, G, L, P, S, T. Surrey — 9, 10, 11. Sussex — 4, 9, 11, 16, 17.

Willow Tit *Parus montanus*
A scarce resident following rapid decline.
Sites: Sussex — G.

Crested Tit *Parus cristatus*
Very rare vagrant.

Coal Tit *Parus ater*
Widespread resident.

Blue Tit *Parus caeruleus*
Abundant resident.

Great Tit *Parus major*
Abundant resident.

Nuthatch *Sitta europaea*
Widespread resident, declining in some areas.

Wallcreeper *Tichodroma muraria*
Very rare vagrant.

Treecreeper *Certhia familiaris*
Widespread resident.

Short-toed Treecreeper *Certhia brachydactyla*
Very rare vagrant.

Penduline Tit *Remiz pendulinus*
Rare vagrant.

Golden Oriole *Oriolus oriolus*
Scarce but regular spring migrant. Has bred. Rare in autumn.

Isabelline Shrike *Lanius isabellinus*
Very rare vagrant.

Red-backed Shrike *Lanius collurio*
Scarce passage migrant. Formerly bred.

Lesser Grey Shrike *Lanius minor*
Very rare vagrant.

Great Grey Shrike *Lanius excubitor*
Scarce winter visitor and passage migrant.
Sites: Surrey — 9, G. Sussex — 4.

Woodchat Shrike *Lanius senator*
Rare vagrant.

Jay *Garrulus glandarius*
Widespread resident. Passage migrant in varying numbers. Occasionally irruptive.

Magpie *Pica pica*
Widespread resident.

Nutcracker *Nucifraga caryocatactes*
Very rare vagrant.

Chough *Pyrrhocorax pyrrhocorax*
Very rare vagrant or escape. Formerly bred.

Jackdaw *Corvus monedula*
Widespread resident.

Rook   *Corvus frugilegus*
Locally common resident.

Carrion Crow   *Corvus corone*
Widespread resident.

Hooded Crow   *Corvus cornix*
Rare winter visitor.

Raven   *Corvus corax*
Status unknown due to incidence of escapes or released birds, but now breeding annually in Sussex.
Sites: Sussex — 6, 7, 8.

Starling   *Sturnus vulgaris*
Common resident, passage migrant and winter visitor.

Rose-coloured Starling   *Sturnus roseus*
Rare vagrant.

House Sparrow   *Passer domesticus*
Common resident, but declining in some areas.

Tree Sparrow   *Passer montanus*
Declining breeding species, now scarce. Passage migrant and winter visitor.
Sites: Surrey — A.

Red-eyed Vireo   *Vireo olivaceus*
Very rare vagrant.

Chaffinch   *Fringilla coelebs*
Common resident, passage migrant and winter visitor.

Brambling   *Fringilla montifringilla*
Passage migrant and winter visitor. Occasionally in large numbers.
Sites: Kent — 4, 10. Surrey — 4, 6, 9. Sussex — 2, 4, 6, 17.

Serin   *Serinus serinus*
Scarce but annual passage migrant.
Sites: Kent — 6, 7, 8, 9. Sussex — 6, 14.

Greenfinch   *Carduelis chloris*
Widespread resident, passage migrant and winter visitor.

Goldfinch   *Carduelis carduelis*
Widespread breeding species and partial migrant. Smaller numbers winter.

Siskin   *Carduelis spinus*
Widespread winter visitor and passage migrant. Small numbers now breed annually.
Sites: Kent — 5, 10, Q. Surrey — 4, 5, 9, 10. Sussex — 2, 4, 6, 9, 11, 17.

Linnet *Carduelis cannabina*
Widespread resident and partial migrant. Wintering flocks favour coast.

Twite *Carduelis flavirostris*
Scarce and decreasing winter visitor and passage migrant.
Sites: Kent — 7.

Mealy Redpoll *Carduelis flammea*
Scarce passage migrant and winter visitor.

Lesser Redpoll *Carduelis cabaret*
Declining breeding species, passage migrant and winter visitor.
Sites: Sussex — 4, 6, 11, 17.

Arctic Redpoll *Carduelis hornemanni*
Very rare vagrant.

Two-barred Crossbill *Loxia leucoptera*
Very rare vagrant.

Crossbill *Loxia curvirostra*
Scarce passage migrant and winter visitor, occurring in large numbers in
irruptive years. A few pairs breed.
Sites: Kent — 4, 10, G, M. Surrey — 7, 9, 10, G. Sussex — 4, 17.

Parrot Crossbill *Loxia pytyopsittacus*
Very rare vagrant.

Trumpeter Finch *Bucanetes githagineus*
Very rare vagrant.

Common Rosefinch *Carpodacus erythrinus*
Rare vagrant.

Pine Grosbeak *Pinicola enucleator*
Very rare vagrant.

Bullfinch *Pyrrhula pyrrhula*
Widespread but decreasing resident.

Hawfinch *Coccothraustes coccothraustes*
Thinly distributed, declining resident.
Sites: Kent — 4, 10, K, T. Surrey — 11. Sussex — A.

Black-and-white Warbler *Mniotilta varia*
Very rare vagrant.

Golden-winged Warbler *Vermivora chrysoptera*
Very rare vagrant.

Blackpoll Warbler *Dendroica striata*
Very rare vagrant.

Common Yellowthroat *Geothlypis trichas*
Very rare vagrant.

Dark-eyed Junco *Junco hyemalis*
Very rare vagrant.

White-throated Sparrow *Zonotrichia albicollis*
Very rare vagrant.

Lapland Bunting *Calcarius lapponicus*
Regular passage migrant, declining winter visitor. Rare inland.
Sites: Kent — 7.

Snow Bunting *Plectrophenax nivalis*
Scarce passage migrant but regular winter visitor.
Sites: Kent — 1, 3, 7, C, D. Surrey — 4. Sussex — 1, 13, 15.

Pine Bunting *Emberiza leucocephalos*
Very rare vagrant.

Yellowhammer *Emberiza citrinella*
Widespread but declining resident.

Cirl Bunting *Emberiza cirlus*
Formerly a scarce breeding species; now a very rare vagrant.

Rock Bunting *Emberiza cia*
Very rare vagrant.

Ortolan Bunting *Emberiza hortulana*
Scarce passage migrant.

Rustic Bunting *Emberiza rustica*
Very rare vagrant.

Little Bunting *Emberiza pusilla*
Very rare vagrant.

Reed Bunting *Emberiza schoeniclus*
Locally common resident, passage migrant and winter visitor.

Pallas's Reed Bunting *Emberiza pallasi*
Very rare vagrant.

Black-headed Bunting *Emberiza melanocephala*
Very rare vagrant.

Corn Bunting *Miliaria calandra*
Locally common but declining resident.
Sites: Kent – 1, 3, 7, 9, J. Sussex – 6, 8, 9, 14.

Northern Oriole *Icterus galbula*
Very rare vagrant.

GLOSSARY OF TERMS

A number of initials, words and expressions, used in the text, may not be familiar to the reader: most are commonly used by birdwatchers and have a precise, usually ornithological meaning.

AONB — Area of Outstanding Natural Beauty

Auk — A seabird of the Razorbill/Guillemot family.

Aythya hybrids — Hybrids between ducks of the genus *Aythya*, normally involving a Tufted Duck or Pochard, which can have a confusing resemblance to scarcer members of the genus, such as Lesser Scaup and Ferruginous Duck.

Backing — An anticlockwise change of wind direction.

BOU — British Ornithologists' Union.

Bund — An artificial embankment to retain water.

Coasting — Flying along the line of the coast, usually involving birds on migration, often into a headwind.

Common woodland passerines — Those small birds resident in most English woods and parks, e.g. Wren, Dunnock, Robin, thrushes, tits, Nuthatch, Treecreeper and Chaffinch.

Crèche — An assembly of still-dependent young of several families. Crèches of young Canada Geese and Shelduck form in June and July.

Dabbling duck — Surface feeders such as Mallard and Shoveler.

Diving duck — Species that feed by swimming underwater, such as Tufted Duck and Pochard.

Drumming — This word describes two different activities: a) a rapid bill-tapping sound made by both sexes of Great and Lesser Spotted Woodpeckers, essentially to attract mates; and b) the flight display of the Snipe, a sound produced by the vibration of the outer tail feathers.

Eclipse plumage — The dull, camouflaged plumage obtained by male ducks during their post-breeding moult.

EN — English Nature

EU — European Union

Fall	Mass arrival of passerine night migrants, usually along the coast.
Feral	Introduced by man and now living in a wild state, e.g. Canada Goose, Ruddy Duck.
FC	Forestry Commission
Gravel or sand pit	A pit worked for gravel or sand. Exhausted pits normally fill with water if no longer pumped and are then sometimes turned into nature reserves, or used for sailing or fishing.
Heligoland trap	A large, funnel-like trap of wire mesh, in which birds are caught for ringing — an important tool in the study of bird migration.
Hirundine	A bird of the swallow or martin family.
Irruption	An arrival of certain specialised feeders from the continent, e.g. Waxwing or Crossbill, when their population is high and food runs short in their native areas. Irruptions vary greatly in size and are more marked in eastern Britain.
KWT	Kent Wildlife Trust
LNR	Local Nature Reserve.
Migrant	A bird that summers in one part of the globe and winters in another.
Mist-netting	Another means of catching birds for the purpose of ringing — a fine, black net is strung between poles.
MoD	Ministry of Defence
NNR	National Nature Reserve.
NT	National Trust
Passerine	A small perching bird; used to describe all small land-birds.
Race	A subspecies: Britain's Pied Wagtail *Motacilla alba yarrellii* and the Continental White Wagtail *Motacilla alba alba* are races of the species *Motacilla alba*.
Ramsar	A Convention signed in Ramsar, Iran, in 1971, which is used to designate Wetlands of International Importance.
Raptor	A diurnal bird of prey such as the Kestrel or Buzzard; excludes owls.

Reservoir	In the Thames Valley these are large, embanked (bunded) structures built for the storage of pumped water. Elsewhere, they may be created by damming river valleys.
Roding	The display flight of the Woodcock, usually seen at dawn or dusk.
RSPB	Royal Society for the Protection of Birds.
Sawbill	A duck with a serrated bill edge to grasp fish — Red-breasted Merganser, Goosander and Smew.
SBBO Census Area	The Sandwich Bay Bird Observatory recording area, for which daily counts of species present are made.
Seabird	One of the mainly pelagic or coastal species, not normally seen inland, such as Manx Shearwater, Gannet, Common Scoter or Arctic Skua.
Seawatching	Scanning the sea to observe passing seabirds.
Shorebird	A wading bird usually associated with the coast, such as Dunlin or Sanderling, but usually used (like 'wader') to describe all such species.
SNCI	Site of Nature Conservation Importance.
SPA	Special Protection Area.
SSSI	A site notified by English Nature as being a Site of Special Scientific Interest. Not necessarily notified for its birds.
SWT	Surrey or Sussex Wildlife Trust
Thermalling	The use of rising, warm air currents to gain height. Most often associated with raptors, but not exclusively so — gulls often thermal.
Trip	A collective term for a group of Dotterel.
Veering	A clockwise change of wind direction.
Wader	A bird that feeds on mud, water or marsh, e.g. Dunlin, Curlew, and including some plovers and Woodcock, which have adapted to drier ground, but excluding herons, etc.
Acrocephalus warbler	Those warbler species normally associated with reeds, like Sedge and Reed Warbler, of the genus *Acrocephalus*.
Phylloscopus warbler	A 'leaf warbler', e.g. Willow and Wood Warblers, Chiffchaff and scarce related species of the genus *Phylloscopus*.

Sylvia warbler	One of the scrub-haunting warblers, e.g. Blackcap, Whitethroat of the genus *Sylvia*.
Waterbird	A collective term for birds normally found on or near inland water.
Waterfowl	A collective term, more particularly applied to ornamental collections of swans, geese and duck.
Wildfowl	A collective term usually applied to duck, geese and swans.
Winter thrushes	Those that visit Britain from northern Europe in winter, chiefly Fieldfare and Redwing flocks, but Blackbirds and Song Thrushes also arrive to join local birds.

FURTHER READING

Clark, JM (1984) *Birds of the Hants/Surrey Border.* Hobby Books.

Cramp, S *et al.* (1977–94) *Handbook of the Birds of Europe, the Middle East and North Africa* Vols. 1–9. Oxford University Press.

Cromack, D (ed.) (2004) *The Birdwatcher's Yearbook and Diary.* Buckingham Press.
This is an annual fact-filled publication, which no birdwatcher can afford to be without. Names & addresses of organisations, tide tables, book reviews, Schedule I species, articles, etc.

Drewett, J (1987) *The Nature of Surrey.* Barracuda Books.

Dymond, JN, Fraser, PA & Gantlett, SJM (1989) *Rare Birds in Britain and Ireland.* T & AD Poyser.

Gibbons, DW, Reid, JB & Chapman, RA (1993) *The New Atlas of Breeding Birds in Britain and Ireland.* T & AD Poyser.

Gillham, EH & Homes, RC (1950) *The Birds of the North Kent Marshes.* Collins.

Harrison, JG & Grant, PJ (1976) *The Thames Transformed.* Andre Deutsch.

Hewlett, J (ed.) (2002) *The Breeding Birds of the London Area.* The London Natural History Society.

James, P (ed.) (1996) *Birds of Sussex.* Sussex Ornithological Society.

Lack, P (1986) *The Atlas of Wintering Birds in Britain and Ireland.* T & AD Poyser.

Oliver, PJ (1991) *Birdwatching on the North Kent Marshes.* Privately published.

Parr, D (ed.) (1972) *Birds in Surrey.* Batsford.

Stride, R (2000) *Birds of the Isles of Surrey.* Dayfive Publications.

Taylor, DW, Davenport, DL & Flegg, J (1981) *The Birds of Kent.* Kent Ornithological Society.

Taylor, DW (1996) *Birding in Kent.* Pica Press.

Wernham, CV *et al* (2002) *The Migration Atlas: Movements of the Birds of Britain and Ireland.* T & AD Poyser.

Wheatley, JJ (in press) *Birds of Surrey.* Surrey Bird Club.

USEFUL ADDRESSES

Bird Observatories

Dungeness Bird Observatory (DBO)
The Warden, Dungeness Bird Observatory, Romney Marsh, Kent TN29 9NA
(tel: 01797 321309).

Sandwich Bay Bird Observatory Trust (SBBOT)
The Manager, Sandwich Bay Bird Observatory, Guilford Road, Sandwich,
Kent CT13 9PF (tel: 01304 617341).

Reserves

Blean Woods NNR
The Warden, 11 Garden Close, Rough Common, Canterbury, Kent CT2 9BP
(tel: 01227 462491).

Dungeness RSPB
The Warden, Boulderwall Farm, Dungeness Road, Lydd, Romney Marsh,
Kent TN29 9PN (tel: 01797 320588).

Elmley Marshes RSPB
The Warden, Kingshill Farm, Elmley, Sheerness, Isle of Sheppey, Kent ME12
3RW (tel: 01795 665969).

Northward Hill & Cliffe Pools
The Wardens, RSPB Office, Northward Hill Reserve, Bromhey Farm,
Eastborough, Cooling, Kent ME3 8DS (tel: 01634 222480).

Oare Marshes LNR
Kent Wildlife Trust, Tyland Barn, Sandling, Maidstone, Kent ME14 3BD (tel:
01622 662012).

Pagham Harbour LNR
The Warden, Visitor Centre Selsey Road, Sidlesham, West Sussex (tel:
01243 641058).

Pulborough Brooks
The Warden, Uppertons Barn Visitor Centre, Wiggonholt, Pulborough, West
Sussex RH20 2EL (tel: 01798 875851).

Riverside Country Park
The Warden, Riverside Country Park, Lower Rainham Road, Gillingham,
Kent ME7 2XH (tel: 01634 378987).

Rye Harbour LNR
The Warden, 2 Watch Cottages, Nook Beach, Winchelsea, East Sussex
TN36 4LU (tel: 01797 223862).

Sevenoaks Wildfowl Reserve
John Tyler, Tadorna, Bradbourne Vale Road, Sevenoaks, Kent TN13 3DH
(tel: 01732 456407).

Stodmarsh NNR
English Nature Kent Team, Countryside Management Centre, Coldharbour Farm, Wye, Ashford, Kent TN25 5DB (tel: 01233 812525).

The Swale NNR
English Nature Kent Team, Countryside Management Centre, Coldharbour Farm, Wye, Ashford, Kent TN25 5DB (tel: 01233 812525).

Thursley NNR
The Warden, Uplands Stud, Brook, Godalming, Surrey GU8 5LA.

Tudeley Woods
The Warden, 12 The Grove, Crowborough, East Sussex TN6 1NY.

Bird and Wildlife Organisations

Hants and Surrey Border Bird Report
John Clark, 4 Cygnet Court, Old Cove Road, Fleet, Hants GU13 8RL.

Haslemere Natural History Society
Haslemere Educational Museum, High Street, Haslemere, Surrey GU27 2LA.

Kent Ornithological Society (KOS)
Secretary: Annie Abrams, 4 Laxton Way, Faversham, Kent ME13 8LJ (tel: 01795 533453).

Kent County Recorder
Don Taylor, 1 Rose Cottages, Old Loose Hill, Loose, Maidstone, Kent ME15 0BN (tel: 01622 745641). Annual *Kent Bird Report* from Membership Secretary, Dave Sutton, 61 Alpha Road, Birchington, Kent CT7 9ED (tel: 01843 842541).

Kent Wildlife Trust (KWT)
Tyland Barn, Sandling, Maidstone, Kent ME14 3BD (tel: 01622 662012).

London Natural History Society
Ornithological Section Secretary, Ms N Duckworth, 9 Abbey Court, Cerne Abbas, Dorchester, Dorset DT2 7JH.

English Nature (Kent)
South East Regional Countryside Management Centre, Coldharbour Farm, Wye, Ashford, Kent TN25 5DB (tel: 01233 812525).

English Nature (Surrey and Sussex)
Howard House, 31 High Street, Lewes, East Sussex BN7 2LU (tel: 01273 476595).

Royal Society for the Protection of Birds (RSPB)
South East Regional Office, Second Floor, Frederick House, 42 Frederick Place, Brighton BN1 4EA (tel: 01273 775333).

Surrey Bird Club
Secretary, Mrs G. M. Cook, 'Moorings', Vale Wood Drive, Lower Bourne, Farnham, Surrey GU10 3HW. Annual *Surrey Bird Report* available from J. Gates, 90 The Street, Wrecclesham, Farnham, Surrey GU10 4QR.

Surrey Wildlife Trust
School Lane, Pirbright, Woking, Surrey GU24 0JN (tel: 01483 488055).

Sussex Ornithological Society
Secretary: Richard Cowser, Beavers Brook, The Thatchway, Angmering, West Sussex BN16 4HJ (tel: 01903 770259) email: secretary @susos.org.uk Annual *Sussex Bird Report* available from J. E. Trowell, Lorrimer, Main Road, Icklesham, Winchelsea, East Sussex TN36 4BS.

Sussex Wildlife Trust
Woods Mill, Henfield, West Sussex BN5 9SD (tel: 01273 492630).

Other useful addresses

Kingsnorth Power Station
Station Manager, Nature Study Centre, Kingsnorth Power Station, Hoo, Rochester, Kent ME3 9NQ. This is the address to write to regarding organised visits to the Nature Study Centre at Kingsnorth Power Station.

Ministry of Defence Ranges
Ash Range Office (tel: 01252 325233).

National Trust (Kent and East Sussex)
The Estate Office, Scotney Castle, Lamberhurst, Tunbridge Wells, Kent TN3 8JN.

National Trust (Surrey and West Sussex)
Southern Region, Polesden Lacey, Dorking, Surrey RH5 6BD.

National Rivers Authority (Southern Region)
Recreation and Conservation Officer, Guildbourne House, Chatsworth Road, Worthing, West Sussex BN11 1LD.

National Rivers Authority (Thames Region)
Kings Meadow House, Kings Meadow Road, Reading, Berks RG1 8DQ.

Thames Water Utilities Ltd
The Wardens Office, Thames Water Utilities, Cumnor Road, Farmoor, Oxford OX2 9NS. This is the address to write to for a one-year birdwatching permit which gives admittance to the Queen Mary and Walton Reserves (cost £8).

The Witley Centre
Witley, Godalming, Surrey GU8 5QA.

Websites

Beddington Sewage Farm
http://myweb.tiscali.co.uk/johnnyallan/index.html
Dungeness Bird Observatory http://www.dungenessbirdobs.org.uk
Kent Ornithological Society http://www.kentos.org.uk
Pagham harbour http://www.sussexnatureweb.btinternet.co.uk
RSPB http://rspb.org.uk
Rye Harbour LNR http://www.naturereserve.rhyharbour.org
Sandwich Bay Bird Observatory Trust http://www.sbbo.co.uk
Surrey Bird Club http://www.sbclub.ukonline.co.uk
Sussex Ornithological Society http://www.susos.org.uk
Sussex Wildlife Trust http://sussexwt.org.uk
Wildfowl and Wetlands Trust http://www.wwt.org.uk

CODE OF CONDUCT
FOR BIRDWATCHERS

Today's birdwatchers are a powerful force for nature conservation. The number of those of us interested in birds rises continually and it is vital that we take seriously our responsibility to avoid any harm to birds. We must also present a responsible image to non-birdwatchers who may be affected by our activities and particularly those on whose sympathy and support the future of birds may rest.

There are 10 points to bear in mind:
1. The welfare of birds must come first.
2. Habitat must be protected.
3. Keep disturbance to birds and their habitat to a minimum.
4. When you find a rare bird think carefully about whom you should tell.
5. Do not harass rare migrants.
6. Abide by the bird protection laws at all times.
7. Respect the rights of landowners.
8. Respect the rights of other people in the countryside.
9. Make your records available to the local bird recorder.
10. Behave abroad as you would when birdwatching at home.

Welfare of birds must come first
Whether your particular interest is photography, ringing, sound recording, scientific study or just birdwatching, remember that the welfare of the bird must always come first.

Habitat protection
Habitat is vital to a bird and therefore we must ensure that our activities do not cause damage.

Keep disturbance to a minimum
Birds' tolerance of disturbance varies between species and season. Therefore, it is safer to keep all disturbance to a minimum. No birds should be disturbed from the nest in case opportunities for predators to take eggs or young are increased. In very cold weather disturbance to birds may cause them to use vital energy at a time when food is difficult to find. Wildfowlers already impose bans during cold weather: birdwatchers should exercise similar discretion.

Rare breeding birds
If you discover a rare bird breeding and feel that protection is necessary, inform the appropriate RSPB Regional Office or the Species Protection Department at The Lodge. Otherwise it is best in almost all circumstances to keep the record strictly secret in order to avoid disturbance by other birdwatchers and the attentions of egg collectors. Never visit known sites of rare breeding birds unless they are adequately protected. Even your presence may give away the site to others and cause so many other visitors that the birds may fail to breed successfully. Disturbance at or near the nest of species listed on the First Schedule of the Wildlife and

Countryside Act 1981 is a criminal offence. Copies of Wild Birds and the Law are obtainable from the RSPB, The Lodge, Sandy, Bedfordshire SG19 2DL (enclose two second-class stamps).

Rare migrants

Rare migrants or vagrants must not be harassed. If you discover one, consider the circumstances carefully before telling anyone. Will an influx of birdwatchers disturb the bird or others in the area? Will the habitat be damaged? Will problems be caused with the landowner?

The Law

The bird protection laws (now embodied in the Wildlife and Countryside Act 1981) are the result of hard campaigning by previous generations of birdwatchers. As birdwatchers we must abide by them at all times and not allow them to fall into disrepute.

Respect the rights of landowners

The wishes of landowners and occupiers of land must be respected. Do not enter land without permission. Comply with permit schemes. If you are leading a group, do give advance notice of the visit, even if a formal permit scheme is not in operation. Always obey the Country Code.

Respect the rights of other people

Have proper consideration for other birdwatchers. Try not to disrupt their activities or scare the birds they are watching. There are many other people who also use the countryside. Do not interfere with their activities and, if it seems that what they are doing is causing unnecessary disturbance to birds, do try to take a balanced view. Flushing gulls when walking a dog on a beach may do little harm, while the same dog might be a serious disturbance at a tern colony. When pointing this out to a non-birdwatcher be courteous, but firm. The non-birdwatchers' goodwill towards birds must not be destroyed by the attitudes of birdwatchers.

Keeping records

Much of today's knowledge about birds is the result of meticulous record keeping by our predecessors. Make sure you help to add to tomorrow's knowledge by sending records to your county bird recorder.

Birdwatching abroad

Behave abroad as you would at home. This code should be firmly adhered to when abroad (whatever the local laws). Well-behaved birdwatchers can be important ambassadors for bird protection.

This code has been drafted after consultation between The British Ornithologists' Union, the British Trust for Ornithology, the Royal Society for the Protection of Birds, the Scottish Ornithologists' Club, the Wildfowl Trust and the editors of *British Birds*.

Further copies may be obtained from The Royal Society for the Protection of Birds, The Lodge, Sandy, Beds. SG19 2DL.

INDEX OF SPECIES BY SITE NUMBER

This index is not all-inclusive. However, it does contain all those species in the Systematic List that are without a county site reference, along with a majority that have specific references, but omits certain species that are widespread and commonly seen. K refers to Kent, SY to Surrey and SX to Sussex.

INDEX OF SITES AND PLACE NAMES

Page references are given for all sites and place names included in the text.